Chinese Migrant Networks and Cultural Change

CHINESE MIGRANT NETWORKS

AND CULTURAL CHANGE

PERU, CHICAGO, HAWAII, 1900–1936

A DAM M c K EOWN

T HE U NIVERSITY OF C HICAGO P RESS
C HICAGO AND L ONDON

Adam McKeown is assistant professor of history at Northeastern University.

The University of Chicago Press, Chicago 60637
The University of Chicago Press, Ltd., London
© 2001 by The University of Chicago
All rights reserved. Published 2001
Printed in the United States of America
10 09 08 07 06 05 04 03 02 01   5 4 3 2 1

ISBN (cloth): 0-226-56024-4
ISBN (paper): 0-226-56025-2

Library of Congress Cataloging-in-Publication Data

McKeown, Adam.
    Chinese migrant networks and cultural change Peru, Chicago,
Hawaii, 1900–1936 / Adam McKeown.
        p.   cm.
    Includes bibliographical references and index.
    ISBN 0-226-56024-4 (alk.)—ISBN 0-226-56025-2 (alk. pbk.)
    1. Chinese—Foreign countries.   I. Title.
DS732 .M39   2001
304.8′0951′09041—dc21

                                                                00-011903

CONTENTS

FIGURES

TABLES

As I complete the last revision of this manuscript, I still encounter phrases and ideas which have lingered from its first manifestation as a research paper for a seminar in American Immigration History at the University of Chicago in 1992. Much of the credit for the genesis of this work belongs to Douglas Knox, who first introduced me to the Chinese immigration documents at the Chicago branch of the National Archives and the field notes of Paul Siu at the University of Chicago.

Clara Chu and Michael Gonzales kindly provided me with initial contacts that paved the way for my visit to Peru. A year of research in Peru from 1994 to 1995 was supported by a grant from the American Council of Learned Societies/Chiang Ching-kuo Foundation Fellowship Selection Committee, with funds provided by the Chiang Ching-kuo Foundation. While in Peru, I was affiliated with the Pontificia Universidad Católica del Perú. Humberto Rodríguez Pastor generously opened his home and collection of material on the Chinese to me. Of the many other people who helped make my stay in Lima happy and productive, Liliana Com, Joseph Cruz, Iván Hinojosa, and Walter Huamaní deserve special mention.

Two grants from the Center for East Asian Studies at the University of Chicago and one from Swarthmore College helped fund writing and research in Chicago, California, and Hawaii. I am grateful to my mother for helping make my stay in California comfortable and focused. Scott Forsythe at the National Archives in Chicago, Daniel Nealand at the National Archives in San Bruno, California, and the staffs at the National Archives and the archives of the Ministry of Foreign Relations in Lima, the Grau Regional Archives in Trujillo, the East Asian Library at the University of California in Los Angeles, and the Chicago Historical Society were all very accommodating in the facilitation of my research.

My dissertation advisor, Guy Alitto, has supported and encouraged all that I have undertaken. I would not have survived the feudal environment of a large research university without his protection and attention. Prasenjit Duara consistently stimulated and challenged my thinking. Gerald Suttles offered detailed and insightful comments on early drafts of this manuscript, offering a level of attention that was hard to come by in my graduate education. Lauren Benton, Philip Kuhn, Erika Lee, Lillian Li, Pat Manning, Sucheta Mazumdar, Vasant Kaiwar, and anonymous reviewers have also provided support and valuable comments on portions of this work. Doug Mitchell and his assistant Robert Devens have been the most encouraging of editors, making the transition from dissertation into published book a relatively pleasant process.

  This book is inseparable from my own experience living in China, falling in love with my wife, Cecily, accompanying her transition to the United States, and becoming part of a transnational Chinese family. By and large, I like the isolation of research and writing, but I could not have endured it so easily without Cecily. Of course, I alone am responsible for any mistakes or confused thinking to be found in this book.

The different dialects among Chinese migrants, the unavailability of Chinese characters for some names I have encountered, and changing transliterations at different times and places have made it difficult to follow any consistently satisfactory scheme of romanization. Most Chinese words have been transliterated into pinyin, except in the following cases, where I used the most common local transliteration: (1) personal names, except for Chinese diplomats and well-known personalities; (2) names of businesses; (3) names of migrant associations whose unique local role I want to emphasize, such as the Six Companies and the On Leong Tong.

The glossary lists Chinese characters (when known) for local people, institutions, and Chinese vocabulary. Well-known Chinese people and places are not included.

CHAPTER 1

Chinese Migration in Global Perspective

"Lee K. K.," a Chinese laundryman interviewed by sociologist Paul Siu in the 1930s, said, "We overseas people can find no place in China. We can only spend money when we get back to China. No matter how much money we bring home, but as soon as the money is spent, we must come back here."[1] Yet, in *The Chinese Laundryman*, his University of Chicago Ph.D. dissertation based on his interviews, Siu wrote, "No Chinese laundryman . . . has ever seriously attempted to organize his life around the laundry, saying, 'I feel at home in this country and laundry work is my life, my career, and my ambition. I hope to be a prosperous laundryman.'"[2] At first glance, these two statements seem to leave the Chinese migrant in a limbo, neither here nor there. Attempting to define himself in terms of China or the United States, he finds himself at home in neither. Although the experience of Chinese laundrymen in the 1930s as interpreted by Paul Siu is not exemplary for all Chinese migrants, these two quotations still illustrate a basic problem in talking about Chinese (or any) migrants: the difficulty of producing formulations of identity and history that are not centered in nation-states or some other territorially based sociocultural grouping. We have little means by which to describe lives and social organization that straddle those units. Even migrants who, in practice, lived lives and created institutions which spanned those boundaries were still reluctant to conceive of themselves beyond one of the territorially based anchors of their networks.[3] Nonetheless, such a global perspective is necessary to understand cultural and organizational aspects of Chinese migration. It helps us to understand how migrants could, indeed, live both here and there. Such a perspective must be carefully articulated with a context of diverse local orientations and encounters, revealing the patterns that link them and how they emerge at particular historical moments in a shifting global order.

NATION-BASED RESEARCH

The disjunctions in migrant experience suggested by the opening quotations are mirrored in much academic work on Chinese migrants. Rather than dropping the migrants into a limbo, however, these works tend to assert one side or another as the proper center from which to understand migrant lives: either as immigrants who settled and helped create a new land, or as sojourners and *huaqiao* (overseas Chinese nationals) oriented toward China. Consider, for example, the following two quotations. The first is from a work of Chinese American history by Sucheng Chan:

> Contemporary observers charged the Chinese with a refusal to assimilate to American ways, and many scholars have stressed how the Chinese have adamantly preserved their culture in the United States. Many Chinese values, practices, and patterns of social organization were indeed transferred to American soil, but the fact remains that Chinese communities that developed in America were by no means replicas of those in China.[4]

The second is from a *huaqiao* history published in Taiwan in 1993 by Huang Jianchun:

> By and large, the social organization and customs of overseas Chinese . . . were all carried abroad from rural life in China. In the long term, the transference and preservation of Chinese culture abroad led to mutual development and an unbreakable bond between overseas Chinese society and the Chinese homeland. Much evidence shows the difficulty of severing the Chinese soul within those living abroad. Precisely because of this, the great majority of overseas Chinese had a great concern for the security of their country. This sentiment did not depend on the existence of the Qing or Republican governments, but mostly emerged from the natural disposition to cherish one's home.[5]

Each of these statements is taken from an exemplary work of primary research. While not entirely exclusive—potential for overlap appears in the ideas of "mutual development" and "transfer" of culture— they each emerge from very different research agendas that result in competing narratives of the history of Chinese migration. Chan's work is part of a larger project in contemporary Asian American studies to incorporate Chinese as important actors in American history. It emphasizes the adaptations of Chinese social organization in the United States, and explains them as necessary and unprecedented responses to unfamiliar challenges. Although Chan pays more attention than many Asian American historians to Chinese nationalism, transnational families, and continued links to China, she does not follow the implications of these descriptions so far as to reformulate her narrative of migration as a monodirectional relocation followed by locally conditioned transformation.[6] In their most strongly America-centered versions, Asian American histories have treated continued links beyond America and the persistence of Chinese culture abroad as little more than by-products of exclusion and racism, and have seen Chinese Americans primarily as exemplars of longstanding American ideals of freedom, democratic principles, and individual struggle.[7]

Huang Jianchun, on the other hand, is firmly embedded in a tradition of Chinese-language scholarship that goes back over ninety years, emphasizing the enduring love, patriotism, connections, and contributions of Chinese to their homeland. Most original research has focused on participation in revolutionary movements, the restrictive and unsupportive policies of the Qing government, remittances, investment in and contributions to China, and economic success and recognition abroad.[8] In its most extreme version, this scholarship may even talk of the patriotic resistance of Chinese emigrants against assimilation.

This disjunction is especially clear in debates over the idea of the Chinese immigrant as a sojourner. Scholars trained in Chinese studies tend to support some version of the sojourner concept as a useful approach to understanding Chinese migration.[9] Asian American scholarship, on the other hand, rejects the sojourner concept, arguing that it is used by anti-Chinese agitators and immigration scholars to "exclude [Chinese] categorically from American immigration history."[10] Attempts to bridge these opposing views of Chinese as either settlers *or* sojourners have ended up as weak compromises. They usually assert that some were settlers, some were sojourners, and others changed their orientation over time.[11] The dichotomy between these two perspectives could be multiplied and complicated by examples from other places and disciplines. Taken together, however, they do not amount to a coherent panorama of the networks and processes of Chinese migration. Rather, the conflicts between competing nation-based claims regarding the histories of Chinese migrants serve to obscure and confuse the transnational activities of those migrants.

Another consequence of nation-based histories of migration can be seen in the way Hawaii has been enveloped by Asian American history at the expense of perspectives centered on the activities of migrant networks. Sucheng Chan treats Hawaii as an example of regional variation. Even pre-annexation Hawaii is teleologically projected as part of American history, as in the 1880s when Hawaii and California "led the nation" in the development of capitalist agriculture, and "neither region was a frontier any longer."[12] This perspective would have fit the agendas of white Americans in Hawaii, but it would have been problematic to Chinese merchants and rice planters, not to mention native Hawaiians. Chinese in Hawaii may have taken advantage of the American market, but they were more directly linked to the Hawaiian royalty and business networks tying them back to China than to California. To be sure, Chan's primary purpose in making the link between nineteenth-century California and Hawaii was to underline the importance of economic transformations in shaping the flows of migrant labor. Nonetheless, a history written from the perspective of Chinese networks and economic expansion would have to cross contemporary political boundaries, by linking California more strongly with Mexico and Canada before the 1920s, rather than with Hawaii. It would create a vision of economic growth as something other than (albeit closely linked to) the political expansion of nations.

When talking about Chinese in Peru, Chicago, and Hawaii, it is certainly desirable to use vocabulary that recognizes their engagement in local sociopolitical relationships. Yet, the very act of putting all three locations in a single book implies the existence of links between these locations. Those links should certainly include China but should not be understood solely in terms of China-based assumptions. Moreover, a recognition of those links should not imply that Chinese experiences in all three locations were essentially the same. How can we recognize the particularities of each migrant community while simultaneously drawing attention to the extra-local connections of those communities, and to the physical movement, networks, and discourses that embed them within a much wider web of relationships that includes China, Hong Kong, and global orders of economic activity and status?

A GLOBAL PERSPECTIVE

A global approach to Chinese migration can help overcome the disjunctions between nation-based approaches. Such an approach might begin by describing the institutions, flows, and sentiments that made up a global circulation of people, goods, and money. To leave it at that, however, would merely add one more perspective to those that already exist. Thus, we must also understand how transnational activities articulated with more locally defined activities and identities. How did concerns particular to villages in South China, to overseas Chinese communities in non-Chinese nations, and to businesses, families, and networks that stretched across oceans come together as a single phenomenon? How were these concerns entangled with economic and ideological shifts on a global scale? [13]

An emphasis on global patterns should not merely assert the primacy of global forces over local. Too often, local and global histories have positioned themselves in opposition to each other, with each side suspicious of what it sees as the other's claim to be the site of all social change and significance. Proponents of local perspectives often criticize global histories as totalizing narratives, offering programmatic schemes and excessively broad generalizations that marginalize the significance of local knowledge and agency. Unfortunately, this criticism is often justified. Even the more nuanced and sophisticated global perspectives tend toward reductionism, such as Immanuel Wallerstein's world-systems theory, which claims that most social phenomena, from national development to family structure, are determined by their position within the capitalist world-system. [14]

Critics have countered this overdeterminism by describing how local societies are more complex than these master narratives can account for and by arguing that the effects of outside influences are mediated by local cultural and social structures. In short, global flows do not determine local social structures, but are appropriated and transformed by them. [15] These localizing arguments are often convincing, but the empirical cases are usually limited to a narrow scope in time and place. Brought together, they offer only a disconnected hodgepodge of local variations. Eric Wolf has criticized this as a "model of the world as a global pool hall in which entities spin off each other like so many hard and rounded billiard balls." [16] This metaphor is graphic, but perhaps somewhat exaggerated. The image of rounded sponges is probably more appropriate for more nuanced depictions of local perspectives, such that fluids and "influences" are transferred and absorbed by the balls. These sponges may be structurally altered or even dissolved by these influences, but in the aggregate they still do little more than bounce off of each other. Thus, they offer little contribution or challenge to the wider generalizations of global narratives, be they highly structured world-systems accounts of global economic polarization or accounts of the more generally appreciated but still poorly understood process of how the world has come to be organized into the nation-state system.

Ideally, a useful global perspective would see the world as a field for historical understanding, in the same way that nations, cities, and ethnic groups have already become arenas for the production and contestation of historical narratives. It would provide a stage from which to understand geographically dispersed activities, such as migration, which thread through and straddle territorially based units. Thus, a global perspective would have to pay careful attention to how different scales and platforms of analysis articulate with each other, yet it would also challenge visions of the world order as a mosaic of discrete sociopolitical entities that are the primary units from which meaning and history are created. It would center attention on "links" and "connections," rather than marginalize them as secondary phenomena that occupy the interstices between nations or civilizations.

This articulation between different platforms of analysis can already be seen in the production of local histories. For example, the history of a village does not merely take the biographies of everybody who ever lived there, place them next to each other, draw out some similarities and differences, and describe a few examples of interaction between them. Villages also have institutions, patterns of land development and economic growth, demographic trends, and other features which are better perceived through generalization, statistical agglomeration, and histories of groups and issues written from perspectives other than those of individual participants. At the same time, none of these other perspectives necessarily obviate the insights provided by biographies. Similarly, the history of a nation-state such as the United States does not just take histories of smaller entities like Boston, Alabama, the Columbia River Basin, Ford Motor Corporation, and the Hopi Indian Reservation, put them next to each other, draw out some similarities and differences, and describe a few examples of interaction between them. Topics like presidential actions, federal legislation, foreign relations, war, and population movements can only be well understood at a national level. Other topics, like industrialization, ethnic relations, and cultural histories depend on local case studies, but such studies are meaningless if not set in relation to each other through an understanding of national (and global) patterns.

The key point is that national histories have become successful arenas for the formulation of historical narratives and issues. The relationships between national histories, local histories, and biography, while sometimes debated (perhaps not as much as they should be), are rarely seen as problematic. Scholars challenge and change national narratives, and even try to undermine the legitimacy of the nation by describing it as an ideological construction, but the politics and identity of nations still remain the arenas that have given shape to these debates. This sense of comfortable articulation is lost, however, when we move up to world history. Modern historical scholarship has its origins in the legitimization of the nation-state, and historians have been slow to move beyond those roots. The quest to delimit and elaborate the particularities and heritages of specific nations and peoples understandably makes many historians mistrustful of approaches that can potentially flatten and engulf the subtle details of local experience under global generalities. At a more practical level, the demands of archival research and commonly accepted standards of professional competence also make claims to expertise at a global level seem dubious.

Despite these reservations, some themes and issues are still not easily contained within national histories, such as the environment, urbanization, and economic relations. Subjects like industrialization, migration, and ethnic relations cannot be adequately addressed until nationally based studies are put in a global context. The establishment of such a context, however, entails more than just extending the net to capture more data. For example, a person writing on Lowell, Massachusetts, is not expected to have a detailed knowledge of every person, ethnic group, factory, and event originating in Lowell. Rather, she is expected to have enough knowledge to be able to draw out patterns that fit the data that she does have. Thus, rather than seeing national and local histories as ends in themselves, a global approach will integrate localized research with knowledge of transnational activities and global patterns.[17]

Siu's Sojourners and a Global Perspective on Migration

Migration is a topic that obviously spans different regional and national histories and appears readily amenable to treatment from a global perspective. In practice, however, the concepts and vocabulary regularly used to describe and analyze migrants are deeply embedded in nation-based perspectives. A global perspective on migration has yet to be well articulated.

Many migration studies establish a polarization between concepts like push and pull, emigration and immigration, sending society and host society, or tradition and adaptation, which privilege the perspectives of nations that frame the two ends of migrant journeys. Metaphors like the "uprooted" and "transplanted" serve to describe migration as a kind of break, characterized by monodirectional movement and relocation in a new land. Ideas like assimilation and integration underline how interest in migration is usually justified by an ultimate interest in the inclusion of migrants into a national identity. Return migration, global patterns, and institutions that facilitate the transnational circulation of goods, money, and people are recognized and even researched by immigration historians, but such topics are rarely incorporated into the stories of particular groups in any meaningful way. The return migrants are people who drop out of the story, and the networks of circulation are of interest primarily as the causes that pushed people into the new nation.[18] Immigrants are seen as either here or there, and no room is left for more complex orientations and circulation.

The conceptual force of nation-based analytical categories is evident in the way they shaped Paul Siu's 1952 article, "The Sojourner." This article was an attempt to fill in the disjunction between the United States and China, to create a transnational space for migrants such as those described in the quotations at the chapter opening. Siu ultimately failed in this task, however, because of his dependence on the conceptual vocabulary of assimilation. He started with a conventional definition of sojourners as people who travel abroad to complete a job as quickly as possible before returning, but went on to describe how this ambition was rarely fulfilled. A sojourner's trip was often more permanent than originally expected, and the sojourner built a life in which he seemed to exist simultaneously in two different lands. When he did manage to return home, his relationships were no longer the same as before he left: "When [the sojourner] gets home he finds it hard to stay and wants to go abroad again."[19] Thus, the sojourner's lack of orientation to his country of residence did not merely imply a more fundamental orientation to his country of origin. Both the new expectations developed abroad and the expectations of the people at home about what a person who had made such a journey was supposed to have become made a return to the past impossible. "As time goes on he becomes, unconsciously perhaps, more of a sharer in the racial colony, developing a mode of living which is characteristic neither of his home nor of the dominant group."[20]

Even trips home gained much of their significance in the context of sojourning fellows: "The return trip is the result of a social expectation of members of his primary group as much as of his individual effort; their sentiments and attitudes make his trip meaningful. The trip shows that he is a person to be admired, to be appreciated, to be proud of, and to be envied."[21] Whether or not a sojourner actually returned to his home country, or whether he even wanted to, was not so significant as the existence of a general discourse that constantly drew attention to the possibility of returning: "The sojourner may make several trips back and forth, he may make only one trip, or he may not make any trip at all. . . . The mere fact that one has never made the return trip is by no means proof that he is not a sojourner."[22]

Siu tried to construct a migrant space as a focus of analysis in its own right, rather than as mere movement from one site to another. He was only partially successful, however, because his work was deeply embedded in the assumptions of assimilation. As an explanation of social change, the idea of assimilation is inextricable from the perspectives and institutions of locally dominant societies. It rests on the binary conception of identity that one either is or is not incorporated into a particular society. Although Siu categorized cosmopolitan people like diplomats, foreign students, foreign correspondents, and anthropologists as sojourners, he perceived their social worlds as narrow and isolated from the mainstream of assimilation and acceptance. He thought that the sojourner was an exception to the rule, rather than a new approach to migration and culture in general, as shown by his frequent use of the word *deviant* to describe sojourners.[23] This is also evident in his off-handed suggestion that the race relations cycle could be modified from "contact, conflict, accommodation, and assimilation," to read "contact, conflict, accommodation, and isolation."[24] On one hand, this formulation was a recognition that assimilation was not inevitable, underlining Siu's insistence on the creation of a new identity. On the other, it takes a step back from a migrant-based transnational perspective and returns to the perspective of territorial national cultures setting the terms by which participation and isolation are understood.

The idea of assimilation is a powerful one because its biases are often cloaked in the garb of universal transformation. In its weakest form, this garb is merely the assertion that the process of dropping one culture in favor of another is natural and predictable. A stronger form is the way that many theorists viewed integration into modern American cities not merely as assimilation into a dominant culture but as emancipation into a modern society organized on rational and individualistic principles. This individualism was set in opposition to "culture"—the "traditional" bonds and customs that shaped life in the lands from which immigrants came. Robert Park, whose ideas informed much of what Siu wrote, spoke of migration as a step toward liberation from the bonds of culture, often using the word *emancipation* where others might say *assimilation*. Writing of life in American cities, Park asserted that "the breaking-up of the isolation of smaller groups has had the effect of emancipating the individual man, giving him room and freedom for the expansion and development of his individual aptitudes."[25] In this way, he projected the individualist rhetoric of the United States into a universalistic statement on human nature. Siu's sojourners were people restricted rather than emancipated by their distance from these norms.

Siu attempted to bridge the gap between the two poles of migrant life, but he was unable to develop a convincing alternative to narratives of migration dominated by the process of relocation and assimilation, partly because assimilation narratives had taken up a cloak of universal truth that was hard to cast off, and partly because he followed the standard sociological practice of the time by describing sojourners in terms of mentalities and personal orientations. He never elaborated the social and institutional bases of sojourning, and was never able to see beyond the personal dissatisfactions of individual migrants. Moreover, this dissatisfaction was often expressed through a vocabulary of national identification which was increasingly prevalent during the early twentieth century.[26] His sojourners appear trapped in perpetual isolation shaped by personal choice and by prejudice from the dominant society. A discussion of the family strategies, business networks, native place associations, remittances, and investments that made migration, in and of itself, a source of profit and site of self-reproducing transnational circulation would provide a much better context from which to understand the orientations of sojourners. As Charles Tilly concluded in an overview of migrant networks, "Once we recognize the network structure of migration, some of the old, standard questions stop making sense. . . . It is not very useful to classify migrants by intentions to stay or return home, because intentions and possibilities are more complex than that—and the migrants themselves often cannot see the possibilities that are shaped by their networks. . . . In short, we ought to think of migration as we think of community structure: not reducible to individual characteristics and intentions."[27]

Diasporic Perspectives

The glory days of assimilation as a central issue in the social sciences are long past. But issues of acceptance and integration still dominate most migration studies, while approaches like Siu's have fallen to the wayside. Of course, nation-based approaches to migration have been enormously fruitful, if the number of manuscripts and extent of debate are any indication. Nonetheless, our understanding of migration—both within and across national histories—can be further developed by a careful look at some of the assumptions that have heretofore shaped our analyses and by more thorough incorporation of extra-local processes and links that have been downplayed. Over the past two decades or so, a revival of the idea of diaspora and the formulation of other concepts such as transnationalism, globalization, and the deterritorialized nation-state have suggested alternatives to the nation-state as perspectives from which to approach issues of migration, global social organization, and identities that cross territorial and cultural boundaries. They all suggest frameworks in which mobility and dispersion can become the starting points of analysis. Many of these approaches, however, present themselves as descriptions of recent shifts in global order and thus present difficulties for historical analysis.

For example, the idea of transnationalism implies the priority of nations as the basic units being crossed. Movement and migration are defined in opposition to states as a recent upswelling that subverts both the concrete mechanisms used to erect and patrol national borders and the ideological constructions of purity that legitimize states. A vocabulary of fluidity and hybridity has grown alongside transnationalism, further suggesting opposition to the kinds of static social categories promoted by state-building.[28] One consequence of situating transnationalism in opposition to states is to deny the way in which closely bounded territorial nation-states have risen coterminously with increased global migration over the past two centuries. The past is left, without critique, to the domain of nation-states and depictions of migration as a monodirectional process. No room is left to understand how the construction of distinct national-cultural units and the intermingling of people were different aspects of the same global historical processes.[29] Depictions of transnationalism as a field of fluidity and hybridity also tend to homogenize migrant groups (or, in what amounts to nearly the same thing, dissolve them into a formless field of infinite diversity) by avoiding analyses of class, hegemony, and the production of cultural distinctions within migrant flows. Thus, the idea of transnationalism provides few tools with which to construct a longer history of global migrant networks.

Recent work on globalization theory provides a promising vocabulary of nodes, flows, networks, and flexibility but also tends to situate itself as a description of phenomena that have emerged only over the past few decades, generally as a consequence of increasing global communication.[30] Moreover, discussions of globalization are largely divided into two poles that have yet to find a common space of interaction. One pole consists of globalization as a primarily economic force, placed in opposition to local cultures and constantly threatening to overwhelm them.[31] This work has identified significant shifts in global economic patterns over the past century—in particular, the transformation from "Fordist" forms of concentrated capital and production to "post-Fordist" forms of flexible accumulation. Yet, despite claims to describe an unprecedented transformation, the basic arguments by both critics and celebrators of economic globalization still amount to rehashes of debates that have existed since before the *Communist Manifesto,* which argued, "The bourgeoisie, by the rapid improvement of all instruments of production, by the immensely facilitated means of communication, draws all, even the most barbarian, nations into civilization. . . . It compels all nations, on pain of extinction, to adopt the bourgeois mode of production; it compels them to introduce what it calls civilization into their midst."[32]

The other side of globalization theory concentrates mostly on cultural flows and the production of identities and social imagination in situations of complex cultural interaction.[33] This work paints a subtle and complex picture of global interactions, but often at the cost of disassociation from concrete social, political, and economic processes.[34] The idea of diaspora has played a prominent role in work on cultural globalization, often as a field for the play of multiplicity, fluidity, hybridity, the dislocations of modernity, or the decentered textures of postmodernity.[35] These diasporas, however, are not depicted in a context of historical time, except to project back to an originary moment of dispersal such as the slave trade. Little attempt is made to trace how diasporic consciousnesses are embedded in shifting global structures. As a result, the very emphasis on diversity and self-determination is not historicized and can appear as a naive expression of contemporary ideals of self and social identity.

Use of the word *diaspora* has not gone uncontested, especially by scholars who recall the close association of the term with the particularities of the Jewish experience. Some scholars have resisted any extended use of the term *diaspora* altogether, while others have used the Jewish experience as a standard by which to define other migrations as diasporas.[36] Some scholars even propose checklists of characteristics to help determine what is and is not a diaspora.[37] Diasporas defined in this manner are quite the opposite of hybridity and multiplicity. Rather, they suggest essential and unchanging cultural identities that persist despite exile and dispersal. This approach is more of a prescription than a description of diasporas, defining them a priori as entities that exist outside of history. It describes diasporas by the very labels, such as Chinese, Indian, or Gypsy, which need to be interrogated when conceptualizing a diaspora. Historical analysis is then the construction of a linear narrative of origins and development for that group, rather than an investigation of the different processes whereby diasporic subjects have been produced at historical moments.[38] This approach to diaspora has much in common with nation-based histories. Even the territorial basis of national histories is preserved in the common assertion that diasporas are characterized by yearnings for the homeland.

These trends and debates can be seen in recent studies of Chinese migration, where a vocabulary of diaspora, multiplicity, mobility, flows, and shifting identities has risen to challenge visions based on tropes of monodirectional immigration and "cultural nationalism."[39] In response, such approaches have been rejected as a dangerous distraction from pressing issues of local politics and acceptance. As Tan Chee Beng put it, in reference to Chinese ethnics in Southeast Asia, "We fear being perceived as scattered communities without a sense of belonging, whatever the good intentions of the term's users." [40] Both sides, however, have tended to see diaspora as a transformation in migration that has occurred over the past thirty years, roughly contemporaneous with the rise of this new vocabulary used to describe it. This debate has rarely extended into perceptions of history. For example, proponents of diaspora in Asian American studies have tended to describe the status of earlier Chinese migrants as primarily shaped by policies of "containment and exclusion." [41] That is to say, they have left interpretations of the past to be shaped by knowledge produced from the perspective of discrete national units, without inquiring into the accuracy of such descriptions and the possibility that diasporic approaches could revise such understandings. Perspectives such as the one that Siu attempted to develop continue to remain in the shadows.

Grounding Migration

Some work on diaspora has tried to stake out a middle ground between hybridity and essentialized identity. It has appropriated diaspora as a way to conceptualize cultural bonds, ties to a homeland, transnational organizations and networks linking people together across geographic boundaries, and dispersion. It usually focuses on the concrete networks and discourses by which links and identities are maintained. [42] The ability to trace processes and links that escape the purview of nation-based histories is indeed the strength of a diasporic perspective. Yet the autonomy of these global processes and identities should not be emphasized at the expense of disassociating them from the many local contexts where they touch ground.

How, then, can we talk about global links and networks without essentializing them, but instead embedding them in innumerable local adaptations and identifications? An answer to this question is closely related to our understanding of culture and its relevance in contexts of migration and change. Criticisms of essentialized diasporas have much in common with critiques of holistic understandings of culture as bounded, static, and totalizing. These criticisms have emphasized how the *idea* of culture is rooted in the ideological legitimation of inequality and domination. In this sense, ideas of diaspora and culture are aspects of the construction of an international world order of discrete groups, and they distract us from the complex structures of interaction. Yet, many critiques target the rather thin conceptualizations of culture that are, unfortunately, common in migration studies. These conceptualizations offer simple understandings of culture as a set of superficial values and characteristics which are lost, gained, and replaced through the process of assimilation into the local society.[43] The social construction of culture may well have an ideological component, but the mere description of that component does not obviate the fact that human action takes place within institutional structures and socialized assumptions about appropriate behavior. These structures and assumptions may shape human action in mutually unintelligible ways, and their transformation is a much more complex process than mere loss and replacement.

Even among critics of the idea of culture, Pierre Bourdieu's concept of the *habitus* is one of the more widely accepted accounts of the creation and relevance of cultural difference. Bourdieu shows how individuals can become cultural actors without their actions being predetermined by culture, thus leaving room for adaptation and change that amount to something other than the mere loss and destruction of culture. The flexibility and potential for diversification within the *habitus* offer a good departure point from which to understand how migrants circulating through global networks could develop their own institutional structure and "culture" that spanned and interacted with a multitude of local contexts.

In Bourdieu's words, the *habitus* is "principles which generate and organize practices and representations that can be objectively adapted to their outcomes without presupposing a conscious aiming at ends or an express mastery of the operations necessary in order to attain them."[44] The theoretical starting point for the *habitus* is that holistic cultural systems constructed from a bird's-eye view by anthropological observers are unable to explain the practice of individuals who have a partial, ground's-eye view of their social relations. Cultural actors do not possess the systemic cultural logic necessary to calculate in any absolute way their own best interests or to act with complete consistency in terms of that logic. Individuals agents interact with their environment through a loose process of metaphor and analogy, deploying and adapting familiar concepts in an unsystematic, ad hoc manner. The field of meanings and relationships in which these relationships are generated—the *habitus*—is "inscribed" onto the mental and physical attributes of individuals from childhood, through interaction with people and the environment. In fact, the *habitus* is inseparable from the social institutions, physical environment, and threads of domination through which it is manifested. This inscription appears as common understandings of body language, words, social obligations, and status distinctions. Within these common understandings, the "symbolic capital" of cultural status markers and deportment is entwined with and imposed by economic and physical power.

Bourdieu also emphasizes the power of history and precedent in generating and regulating perceptions, innovations, expressions, and actions:

> The *habitus*, a product of history, produces individual and collective practices—more history—in accordance with the schemes generated by history. It ensures the active presence of past experiences, which, deposited in each organism in the form of schemes of perception, thought, and action, tend to guarantee the "correctness" of practices and their constancy over time, more reliably than all formal rules and explicit norms. . . . [The *habitus*,] at every moment, structures new experiences in accordance with the structures produced by past experiences, which are modified by the new experiences within the limits defined by their power of selection, [and] brings about a unique integration . . . of the experiences statistically common to members of the same class.[45]

The *habitus* generates and restricts human action, yet every action also reconceptualizes those preconceptions and generates new ones, so that it is constantly changing through a process of innumerable accumulated ad hoc actions. For example, institutions come into being through principles of incorporation embedded in the *habitus,* and, in turn, the growth of these institutions and their momentum toward autonomous self-preservation are instrumental in reshaping the *habitus.*

The *habitus* is useful in that it outlines a cultural field within which distinction and change are part and parcel of the continual reproduction of cultural structures and assumptions. Lauren Benton has also invoked Bourdieu in her attempt to understand patterned interactions on a global scale by "reimagining global structure by bringing into light institutions that are constructed out of practice and do not exist at, or even bridge, separate 'levels,' but themselves constitute elements of global structure."[46] She sees the daily encounters of people and institutions as the very fabric of world history. "Like God and the devil, culture is in the details of patterns and associations, notions of strategy, and collective knowledge, which together both shape and represent those institutions. Thus, global institutions are not to be viewed as structures set against, and constrained by, cultural norms."[47] Similarly, the encounters of migrants around the world need not be seen as a series of cultural collisions, but as a constant process of mutual adjustment.

Nonetheless, the extension of Bourdieu's work to a global scale offers some problems. The *habitus* was an attempt to explain and describe cultural difference. It is dependent on childhood socialization into statistically common experiences and was certainly not meant to be understood on a global scale. Bourdieu's description of how cultural actors improvise their actions without a systematic knowledge of the larger whole is certainly relevant to understanding the improvisations that must take place during intercultural encounters. Yet the improvisations he describes are still formulated in the context of principles and relationships embedded in the local environment and social organization. The limits imposed by this context are necessary to establish an order by which actions can be made meaningful and mutually coherent. The "immigration of ideas" to a different *habitus* always damages those ideas: "Such immigration separates cultural productions from the system of theoretical reference points in relation to which they are consciously or unconsciously defined."[48] When referring to Algerian migrants in Paris, Bourdieu talks only of influences which cause the degeneration of the *habitus.*

Thus, the *habitus* provides few tools for the understanding of cross-cultural interactions. When localized cultural inscription is privileged, it is hard to imagine intercultural relations as anything other than chaos or domination through brute force. Hybrid peoples like Chinese converts to Christianity, who rejected much of what they saw around them as being "Chinese" and "pagan" without ceasing to perform acts of Chinese custom, are lost in the cracks between *habiti,* transitional figures at best. Friendly relations across *habiti,* such as between the Chicago merchant Moy Dong Chew and local ward boss Hinky Dink Kenna or between rice farmer Wong Aloiau and King Kalakaua of Hawaii, are conceivable only on the most instrumental level. Nonetheless, as we shall see, such people and relationships occupied crucial interstices of migrant life. Links with outsiders were central reference points of migrant communities and institutions.[49]

Culture(s) on a Global Scale

How can this notion of the mutually constitutive relationship of individual, institution, and collectivity be salvaged from the *habitus* and applied to situations of geographic dispersion and intercultural interaction to which no single *habitus* can be readily affixed? That is, how can migration be understood on a global scale? Some Chinese migrants had families and residences dispersed across the world, were skilled in the dress, language, and customs of more than one culture, raised different children in accordance with different cultural mores, and yet showed no signs of being "torn" between different cultures. The very idea that their identities should be torn, divided, hybrid, or even fluid gives priority to bounded and territorial perspectives as the norm. Is it possible to talk about such people without resorting to a vocabulary of fragmentation and multiple identities?

David Palumbo-Liu has made a similar critique of Bourdieu: "In short, we have not yet been able to come up with a theoretical model that might predict the outcome of the transposition of cultural objects across an increasingly disjunctive world wherein the particular habitus of social agents is shot through with new information and new objects from around a globe to which we have yet to be habituated." [50] Palumbo-Liu, however, is primarily talking about objects and meaning as they move through and are differentially appropriated within a highly disjunctive global landscape. Migrants and their networks, on the other hand, maintain a certain amount of stability and connection across those disjunctions. How are we to understand networks and individuals that continue to produce their own meanings while simultaneously straddling such diversity and differential appropriation?

Perhaps the question of how to understand migration on a global scale would be better phrased as follows: How can we speak of migration as an intersection of multiple forces and discourses? One result of recent critiques of culture in academic writing has been a decline in the use of the term *culture* as a noun, and the blossoming of its use as an adjective. The precise meaning of a "cultural" analysis is still vague, but it generally implies a focus on discourse, representation, ideology, and description of the ways that meaning, social behavior, and organization are historically produced. That is to say, rather than being discarded, the idea of culture has been transformed into a fruitful analysis of the mechanisms and assumptions by which "culture" shapes our lives. The debates over culture have resulted in a more historically situated understanding of culture. Diasporic perspectives can be approached in the same way. Rather than focusing on the existence of discrete diasporas, we should trace the ways in which transregional structures and movement have shaped human activity and consciousness. Moreover, those structures and networks are not entities in and of themselves, but patterns that are inseparable from their local manifestations.

A Global Field

Two assumptions that go beyond Bourdieu's conception of the *habitus* seem necessary to understand cultural interactions at a global scale. The first is that mutual interaction is not necessarily dependent on socialization into broadly common principles. Bourdieu may still insist that meanings are damaged in translation without concluding that common forms of communication are dependent upon common meaning. Intercultural relations can be understood as the development of common forms of communication and behavior that order participants without necessarily homogenizing their subjectivities.[51] Difference plays an important role in the internal structure of groups. Therefore, the process of encounter and communication is just as likely to create a structure of difference as it is to result in homogeneity. I elaborate on this process in chapter 4, which describes how local communities and the imperial government in China interacted through ritual. Each side had differing interpretations of the ritual, yet through mutual participation a certain ordering was attained. Mediators who bridged those differences facilitated the process of communication, but their own status depended upon the maintenance of the differences. This process of creating a common and functional means of communication can both stabilize and obscure differences.

In the early-twentieth-century world, the formulation of difference took place through categories such as national character, culture and habits, and immigrant and ethnic heritages. Such formulations of difference also created broad similarities—such as the creation of internationally recognized state institutions, internalization of nationalism, and adherence to discourses of race and culture. These made up common languages of interaction by which the world was ordered. They did not necessarily preempt other interests and consciousnesses, but they did provide a forum for interaction.

If this field of interaction was to provide a basis for institutional and individual encounters that gave participants some confidence about what to expect, we must assume it had some structural form. Thus, we must also go beyond Bourdieu in assuming that some kind of cultural field is possible on a translocal scale, patterning the relationships of groups and peoples. Of course, such a structure would be qualitatively different from local *habiti,* and should not be understood as a kind of homogenizing global culture. It would only exist through its manifestation in institutions, local phenomena, and ad hoc encounters, always shifting and looking different from different parts of the world. Nonetheless, it would still occupy a space beyond any individual culture or group and pattern the relationships between them.

Roland Robertson, in his writings about globalization, has attempted to articulate a "global field" as a "sense of a general mode of discourse about the world as a whole *and* its variety." [52] He writes,

> The global "system" is not reducible to a scene consisting merely of
> societies and/or other large-scale actors. Individuals, societies, the sys-

tem of societies, as well as mankind, are to be treated in terms of one coherent analytical framework. . . . As the general process of globaliza- tion proceeds, there is a concomitant constraint upon such entities to "identify" themselves in relation to the global-human circumstance. In addition, globalization also yields new actors and "third cultures"— such as transnational movements and international organizations— that are oriented, negatively or positively, to the global-human cir- cumstance. . . . I will argue that cultural pluralism is itself a constitutive feature of the contemporary global circumstance and that conceptions of the world-system, including symbolic response to and interpreta- tions of globalization, are themselves important factors in determin- ing the trajectories of that very process.[53]

Robertson's global field has four primary reference points by which contemporary people make sense of the world and interact with each other: (1) national societies, (2) the world system of societies, (3) selves, and (4) humanity. These components both complement and contradict each other. For example, we can simultaneously feel ourselves to be mem- bers of a unique society and yet claim to think and act in terms of all hu- manity; or we can assert our own individual uniqueness while simulta- neously believing that unique national and cultural heritages decisively shape people's subjectivity. The idea that societies have enough in com- mon to partake of a world system of societies and the idea that all people have their individuality in common provide bridges between different components. At the same time, these contradictions are integral parts of the structure. For example, the supposedly universal values of humanity provide standards (such as diligence and the capitalist spirit, or human rights) by which inequality among societies can be explained and justi- fied.[54] As Bourdieu would have it, any systematic logic suggested by these reference points is illusory, but they shape human practice nonetheless.

Robertson argues that these reference points are not absolute aspects of human identity, but are particular to the contemporary process of glob- alization. Unfortunately, Robertson's understanding of history as a process of increasing world connectivity that has expanded from early modern Europe is not fruitful. A better historical approach would be to trace shifts in the global field over time while also considering fields that are not nec- essarily global but transregional in scale. A field of Chinese migration in the early twentieth century could be defined by four components: (1) net- works, (2) international status, (3) ethnic identity, and (4) individuals. These are briefly described here and further elaborated in chapter 3 as as- pects of particular historical moments. The actual field of Chinese migration is in reality far more complex than these four components suggest, but to formulate it in this way does, to rephrase Robertson, help conceptualize a general practice of Chinese migration in the early twentieth century as a whole *and* in its variations.

Networks

Networks are almost indistinguishable from institutions: the businesses, families, native place associations, and sworn brotherhoods that fill this book. These institutions were the nodes in interlinked networks that moved people throughout the world. These networks were built on, perpetuated, and produced symbols like initiation rituals, family ideology, communal worship, and common language. Thus, they were the channels by which domination could be exerted and profit accumulated. Networks and institutions were also the sites at which global forces like markets and labor opportunities were channeled into the production of actual human movement.

Far from being homogeneous, the institutional nodes of these networks took on different faces in different situations. Family and lineage came to the forefront in villages in China, while sworn brotherhoods were a common means of networking people beyond individual villages. Native place, surname, sworn brotherhoods, and businesses were most relevant abroad, and even these took particular configurations in local situations. In Chicago, the network of traditional institutions was particularly dense and powerful, with sworn brotherhoods rising to the top. In Peru, businesses were the most appropriate means to take advantage of opportunities for social mobility. In Hawaii, reformulated versions of native place and surname associations, as markers of ethnic heritage, best served the interests of locally born Chinese and their weakening transnational networks.

International Status

The significance of international status is somewhat different than that of national consciousness. It is difficult to gauge the extent to which Chinese migrants had developed a deeply rooted national consciousness before the anti-Japanese war and how this was different from earlier accommodation to the imperial bureaucracy, shared written language, and rituals. Clearly, however, migrants did increasingly link their fates to the international reputation of China. They sought diplomatic representation, looked for recognition from the Chinese state, and helped propagate visions of a modernizing China. They also sought status within local states by portraying themselves as respectable merchants, willing and able to engage in the commercial activities of a modernizing world. The organization and reorganization of Consolidated Benevolent Associations and Chambers of Commerce under the patronage of Chinese officials (which may have helped forge at least a regional consciousness among South Chinese migrants) and expatriate political parties illustrate how this status consciousness interacted with the networks, causing transformations on both sides.

Ethnic Identities

Ethnic identities were formulated in terms of local social structures, although usually with reference to wider discourses of race, nation, and migration. The construction of a unique ethnic heritage in terms that justified inclusion into a larger national whole and the definition of differences as beneficial rather than harmful were common aspects of ethnic identities. The locally born Chinese of Hawaii were most deeply invested in an ethnic identity. They constituted themselves as a group in multiethnic Honolulu that exemplified the kind of pioneering immigrant heritage that made America strong. Pride in the modernization of China was used to underline the suitability of Chinese as American citizens, and links to China and migrant associations were reformulated as ties to an immigrant past that was the basis of a local civic identity.

The self-representations of Chinese in Peru and Chicago developed a more complex interweaving of local and international discourses. The Chinese in Peru drew on their official connections and international trading activities to present themselves as cosmopolitan merchants helping to develop untapped natural resources and link the nation to international markets and modernization. Rather than striving to become objects of integration into Peruvian society (which was still very amorphous and subject to debate, in any case), the Chinese tried to identify with Europeans and North Americans as the standard-bearers of Peruvian nationhood. That is to say, the more they defined themselves in terms specific to the Peruvian situation, the more they identified themselves in terms of Chinese citizenship, transnational networks, and international status.

Chinese in Chicago, on the other hand, were just one of many migrant groups trying to make a living in a rapidly expanding industrial metropolis. In this context, local Chinese elites found it in their best interests to dominate an isolated ethnic enclave. They presented this enclave as a self-reliant business community, specializing in laundry services and mild exotica. Although they were relatively removed from the antagonism and debates that had surrounded the Chinese on the West Coast, the legacy of Western networks still strongly shaped the associations and occupations of Chinese in Chicago. Through tightly controlled associations and connections with local politicians, they even managed to protect gambling and laundry activities from the interference of aggressive racketeers and other outsiders. Chinese nationalism and links to home villages were important themes among Chinese in Chicago, but they were played out in the context of struggles for power between migrants trying to dominate the circumscribed resources of Chinatown.

Individuals

In the case of migrants, the individual was often *homo economicus,* more a reference point for the articulation of self-interest than a self-conscious focus of identity. Economic gain was often the main purpose and justification of migration, and it was the main thing that could be translated into cultural status back home and abroad. Migrants moved through networks and manipulated symbols of status with an eye toward profit and the manipulation of others who could be exploited for profit. Some individuals, such as Aurelio Powsan Chia in Lima and the Moy brothers in Chicago, had a significant effect on how networks took shape locally. In turn, the opportunities created by migrant networks and the expectations of family shaped the direction of individual ambitions. As ethnic identities developed, however, more self-conscious individual identities grew along with them. These identities were often articulated in terms of cultural conflict. Such a formulation was not necessarily the natural result of migration and integration but was closely linked to discourses of group distinction and assimilation that were increasingly popular throughout the world.

Although I have argued for the necessity of a global perspective on Chinese migration, none of these four reference points offer a particularly global vision. Taken individually, they were all rather parochial in their outlook. Taken together, they describe a complex transnational field of migrant activity. This field was, in turn, integrated into larger structures of global economic flows, international relations, and national self-definitions. Chinese migration contributed to the ever-shifting shapes of these structures, whether through the international negotiations of Wu Tingfang in Peru, the participation of Chinese in the definition of Hawaiian identity, the importance of Chinese in shaping the border-guarding machinery of the Bureau of Immigration, their role in extending world markets into Peru and Hawaii, or their contributions to the changing ideals of nationalism through their support of various Chinese political activists on a global stage.

OVERVIEW OF SUBSEQUENT CHAPTERS

Chapter 2 compares immigration laws, demographic statistics, and economic activities of Chinese migrants to Peru, Chicago, and Hawaii, presenting important background material for the second half of the book. It also develops my argument for the necessity of a global perspective by showing that many common explanations of migrant situations based on local or national circumstances are insufficient for understanding the similarities and differences between these locations. In particular, most discussions of the American exclusion laws are unable to account for their very different effects in Hawaii and the United States, and no consistent correlation can be found between local status, economic success, and new immigration.

Chapter 3 outlines a global perspective on Chinese migration from 1842 to 1949, focusing on the three components of networks, nationalism, and ethnicity mentioned above and trying to situate them as historical processes. Chapter 4 looks at associational practices and ritual behavior in South China in order to contextualize Chinese migration as the extension of a cultural and organizational landscape that is also a result of constant adaptation. The discussion of Chinese ritual emphasizes how lines of communication developed that both defined and preserved group solidarity and difference, which helps to illuminate how migrants could integrate into local situations without necessarily losing their links to China. Space for the incorporation of outsiders into migrant worlds existed even before contact, although that space would not necessarily remain the same after prolonged encounters.

Chapters 5–7 focus on Chinese in Peru, Chicago, and Hawaii in the early twentieth century. Local adaptations are depicted as aspects of diasporic networks and as examples of different ways in which the global networks and social organizations could themselves be transformed. Briefly, the Chinese in Peru tried to climb local ethnic structures by casting themselves as transnational cosmopolitans, the Chinese in Chicago forged a relatively secure niche for themselves through isolation and self-commodification as exotica, and the Chinese in Hawaii utilized their associations and networks for the purpose of identification as local ethnics. The conclusion (chapter 8) situates these three cases into a larger narrative of Chinese migration.

My choice of these three locations always arouses curiosity. One important reason is that migrants to all three places were from roughly the same small region of China, and they arrived at roughly the same time, thus providing a basis from which to describe variations. When I first formulated this project, I developed a complex list of overlapping differences and similarities that could be explained, such as the differing effects of American exclusion laws, the effects of plantation labor in Peru and Hawaii, the different numbers of female migrants, the differing reputations for assimilation, the rise of different institutions to prominence, and the relatively high levels of social and economic attainment in Peru and Hawaii as compared to Chicago.[55] Many of these comparisons still shape the argument in chapter 2. The project is no longer comparative, however, in the sense that a comparison usually tries to isolate variables that have caused differences. My primary goal now is to demonstrate the necessity of taking global processes into consideration when understanding migration. Those networks and processes cannot be understood in isolation from their manifestation in particular locations, and each location is treated as a case study to show different aspects of these networks. These three cases do offer a wide range of diversity by which to demonstrate these different aspects, yet that diversity could have been obtained by looking at almost any three locations in the Western hemisphere. All of them are aspects of the same global history and the same history of Chinese migration.

CHAPTER 2

Immigration Laws, Economic Activities, and the Limitations of Local Contexts

Nation-based histories of Chinese immigration often appeal to discriminatory immigration laws and social marginalization to explain a perceived lack of integration and the extremely heavy proportions of men in Chinese immigrant communities. Yet, the imposition of the American exclusion laws in Hawaii in 1898 led to a rapid normalization of gender ratios, unlike in the United States, where an extremely high proportion of males persisted for nearly two generations after the enactment of exclusion in 1882. Moreover, in Peru, where exclusion laws were not systematically enforced until 1930, the proportion of women was lower than in either Hawaii or the United States. Restrictive legislation had some effect on migrant demographics in all these places, but was not a determining variable. Similarly, there is no direct link between social acceptance and immigration. Proportionally more migrants poured into the United States than into Hawaii and Peru during the first half of the twentieth century, despite deeper anti-Chinese prejudice and less chance of economic mobility above the status of laundryman or restaurant worker.

We can better understand these variations when we take global economic relationships and the survival strategies of Chinese transnational families into account. The majority of migrants were unskilled laborers, looking to maximize the advantage to their families. The eastern United States was attractive to new migrants in the early twentieth century because it offered more opportunities for people with little capital and skill to open small, independent businesses. The more clear-cut racial and economic stratification in Peru and Hawaii created middleman occupations that produced many notable migrant success stories, but offered limited opportunities to new migrants after earlier migrants had come to dominate the niches. Yet some aspects of Chinese migrant communities are still best explained from a local perspective. For example, the greater tendency of Chinese women to settle and raise families in Hawaii at the end of the nineteenth century had important consequences for the shape and status of Chinese institutions and community there. This tendency is best explained by a complex array of local factors that, by the 1930s, produced a strong, locally born generation of Chinese. Global and local factors have to be understood in conjunction.

This chapter provides background information on immigration laws, economic activities, and demographics of Chinese migrants in the United States, Hawaii, and Peru. Much of the data was produced by state administrative institutions and has the limitations of nation-based perspectives. Nation-states had an interest in secure borders and internal surveillance that many migrants attempted to avoid. As a result, the census and immigration numbers may be incorrect by as much as 100 percent. They are most useful in the context of a comparative argument that focuses on trends rather than absolute numbers. Comparison shows that causal links that seem to hold in one location do not hold in others, and a simple nation-centered focus on immigration laws or racial structures is usually inadequate to explain various aspects of Chinese integration and demographics.

LOCAL MIGRATION REGULATIONS AND DEMOGRAPHICS

The Exclusion Laws in the United States

Most recent studies of the Chinese in the United States regard the social and emotional impact of the Chinese exclusion laws and prohibitions against the naturalization of Chinese as the main reason for the low proportion of women and for the decreasing population prior to the 1920s. Combined with wider discussions of racism, they are also used to explain Chinese isolation from mainstream society. Most of these studies have concentrated on the continental United States and paid little attention to the impact of exclusion laws in Hawaii. Indeed, a comparison of the impact of the exclusion laws in Hawaii and on the mainland shows that their effects cannot be so easily generalized, and they were probably not as significant in the formation of Chinese migrant demographics as a simple reading of the legal decisions or tales of individual hardship might lead us to believe. Immigration restrictions were always enforced in the context of a particular place and time, and their effects changed accordingly.

The Chinese exclusion laws emerged from the strong anti-Chinese movements in California and other Western states in the second half of the nineteenth century. The Chinese were one of many groups of migrants and settlers originally attracted to California by the gold rush after

1848. As the gold was exhausted in the late 1850s, they found other opportunities in a variety of occupations throughout the Western states: as miners for other minerals, as farmers and agricultural laborers, as cannery workers and cigar makers, as domestic servants, as proprietors of service industries like laundries and restaurants, and, most notably in the 1860s, as railroad construction workers. White workers never extended a particularly warm welcome to the Chinese at the best of times, and by the 1870s the conjunction of an economic downturn in the West and the completion of several railroads that left many Chinese unemployed spurred anti-Chinese agitation to an even greater intensity. The most common justifications for this agitation were that cheap Chinese competition forced out white labor, kept wages low, and contributed to the monopolizing ambitions of wealthy capitalists. Such complaints may have had some validity in localized instances, but they cannot be generalized as an accurate description of the role of Chinese in the development of the West.[1]

However shaky its factual foundation may have been, the anti-Chinese movement was passionate and violent, achieving results that went beyond individual acts of terrorism to having Chinese virtually barred from most industrial jobs (salmon canneries in the Pacific Northwest being a major exception). The promulgation of the Chinese exclusion act of 1882 was its first and major victory at a national scale. This law prohibited the entry of all Chinese laborers into the United States who did not already reside in the country at the time of enactment. The 1888 Scott Act established stricter requirements for returning resident laborers, demanding proof of a family, business interests, or debts amounting to a thousand dollars in the United States in order for a return permit to be granted. The Geary Act of 1892 required the registration of all Chinese laborers resident in the United States.[2]

These pioneering attempts at restrictive immigration law required constant vigilance, investigation, and categorization of individuals. Their implementation was accompanied by confusion, inefficiency, and repeated attempts at clarification, resulting in a maze of amendments and judicial decisions that became encrusted around the original legislation, as both excluders and excludees wrestled through loopholes and unclear points for as much advantage as they could get. A significant source of problems for the government and of opportunities for circumvention by the Chinese was the division of the responsibilities for enforcement and interpretation among the State Department, the Internal Revenue Service, the Federal Courts, and the Collector of Customs. This resulted in a lack of coordination, struggles over jurisdiction, and conflicts among different understandings of proper procedure and the limits of administrative discretion. Perhaps the most significant conflict was between immigration agents, who insisted that the migrant was responsible for proving his right to enter or reside in the United States, and judicial procedure, which assumed innocence until guilt was proven and thus made the Bureau responsible for proving that an applicant did not have the right to enter.

After its formation in 1891, the Bureau of Immigration strove mightily to centralize power over all aspects of immigration in its own hands. An 1895 court decision confirmed the power of the bureau to be final arbiter in all cases reviewed at ports of entry—no more appeal to the courts. The frequent utilization of habeas corpus, by which many Chinese had claimed wrongful imprisonment by the bureau and been released by the courts, was no longer an option unless faulty procedure on the part of the bureau could be proven.[3] A regulation created by the Department of the Treasury in 1898 broadened the scope of exclusion by allowing admission only to a carefully defined class of "exempts," rather than to just any Chinese who was not a laborer. The exempt classes were merchants, teachers, students, ministers, diplomats, and their immediate families.[4]

The most important step toward centralization was taken in 1903 when enforcement work that had been divided between the Internal Revenue Service and Collector of Customs was consolidated within a Bureau of Immigration that was newly reorganized under the Department of Commerce and Labor. This centralization was congruent with a renewed zeal by bureau officials to exclude the Chinese more completely, combat fraud, and to make exclusion in general more efficient, "scientific," and "businesslike." This zeal reflected both the progressive administrative optimism of the times and the appointment of actively anti-Chinese commissioners of immigration. A better coordinated system of cooperation with the State Department and its consuls in Hong Kong and China was established, laws were interpreted more rigorously, and continued efforts were made to block the right of appeal to the courts on citizenship and deportation cases. With the inclusion of the Chinese in the general immigration law of 1924 (which had been formulated in the context of lessons learned in dealing with the Chinese) as aliens not eligible for citizenship, the bureau finally achieved its ambition of being able to handle most Chinese cases under the much better designed provisions of the new laws and avoid the contested complexities of the exclusion laws. Requirements for return certificates as merchants and citizens were made stricter, deportation proceedings were less unwieldy, and the Chinese wives of American citizens were forbidden to enter until a 1928 court decision established the right of entry for all wives married before 1924.[5]

Despite this administrative consolidation and a few successes in halting some of the more audacious schemes of illegal entry, the bureau continued to fall short in its attempts to block fraud and evasion. Before 1915, the annual reports of the commissioner general of immigration were filled with frustration over the difficulty of properly enforcing the exclusion laws. By the early twenties, the bureau seemed to have given up the attempt, consoling itself with the fact that Chinese immigration was not increasing and the total population was decreasing. Whether or not the claims by which Chinese attained admission were truthful was no longer a major point of concern, so long as they were extensively documented and cross-referenced. The report of 1920 declared Chinese immigration to be no longer a problem. It discounted all the previous years of frustration with the phrase, "The annual immigration from China has not changed materially during more than a quarter of a century, and it long ago responded to exclusion."[6] The commissioner admitted that Chinese continued to sneak in across the borders from Mexico and Canada, by small boat across the Gulf of Mexico, or as stowaways on larger, trans-oceanic boats, but he asserted that their lives in America were made more difficult because there were no records of them in the increasingly comprehensive bureau files.

Chinese migration networks adapted to every step in the bureau's consolidation of power. The strength of these diffuse networks was their flexibility in the face of bureau rigidity. The bureau might detect isolated frauds, but could barely make a dent in the entire practice of illegal immigration. One of the more common frauds used by Chinese to obtain documented entry at the ports was the creation of false mercantile companies with many partners.[7] The most far-reaching frauds were the many schemes to obtain entry as a United States citizen. The Chinese were greatly aided in this by the San Francisco earthquake and fire, which destroyed thousands of birth records, and by interpretations of the original exclusion legislation which allowed deportation decisions based on questions of citizenship to be appealed to the federal courts. Whereas the procedure in hearings administered by the bureau assumed that no Chinese was a citizen unless he could prove the conditions of his birth to the satisfaction of the bureau, court procedure assumed that any Chinese who claimed citizenship had the right to remain in the United States unless the bureau could prove beyond any doubt that he was born outside of the United States, something that was impossible to do, given the resources of the bureau. Thousands of migrants took advantage of the opportunity in 1903 and 1904 to walk over the border from Canada to districts in northern New York and Vermont which were under the jurisdiction of judges known to be bribable or sympathetic to the Chinese. After crossing the border, the Chinese would be immediately arrested by the bureau and, after a short hearing, sentenced to deportation. They would appeal this decision to the courts and receive discharge papers. The exact status of the bearers of these papers was never made clear. The papers were not proof of citizenship, but were sufficient to claim that the holder was not in the country illegally. In practice, the bureau found that as far as migration matters were concerned the certificates could not easily be contested unless it was proven that the judge who issued them did so under corrupt circumstances.[8]

The Supreme Court decision on the Sing Tuck case in April 1904 gave the bureau the right to determine citizenship cases without the right of appeal to the courts for any Chinese arrested within a mile of the border. Nonetheless, the ramifications of this episode in the northeast and of similar discharges throughout the country were felt for decades in the continued transnational movement of these discharged migrants and their children.[9] The bureau frequently asserted that if all the Chinese who claimed birth in San Francisco were actually born there, it would mean that 600 to 800 male children had been born to every Chinese woman who had lived in San Francisco before the fire.[10] The most lasting legacy was the openings provided for tens of thousands of Chinese migrants claiming to be foreign-born children of these citizens. American citizens with wives in China would claim the birth of male children on every visit to China. Some of these spaces, known as "slots," were used to bring in their own children, and others were sold to other young migrants who could fit the characteristics of age and dialect of the nonexistent son. Elaborate strategies by the bureau to investigate the truth of these claims through detailed interviews and cross-referencing were frustrated by equally elaborate Chinese creations of fictional kinship networks and coaching papers that anticipated most of the questions the immigration officers would ask.

Exclusion and Women

Despite the continued entry of Chinese, the United States census counts from 1860 to 1940 suggest the exclusion laws did have a noticeable effect on the Chinese population in the United States (see table 1). By 1920, the number of Chinese counted in the United States had decreased to 57.3 percent of the peak population recorded in 1890, which was the result of a burst of immigration immediately before the exclusion laws were enacted in 1882. What the exclusion laws cannot explain, however, was the low proportion of women that never increased significantly until after 1920.

Table 1

Chinese Population in the United States, 1860–1940

Year	Total	Men	Women	Percent Female	Percent Urban
1860	34,933	33,149	1,784	5.1	
1870	63,199	58,633	4,566	7.2	
1880	105,456	100,686	4,779	4.5	
1890	107,488	103,620	3,868	3.6	
1900	89,863	85,341	4,522	5.0	
1910	71,531	66,856	4,675	6.5	75.9
1920	61,639	53,891	7,748	12.6	81.1
1930	74,954	59,802	15,152	20.2	87.7
1940	77,504	57,389	20,115	25.9	91.6

Source: Kung 1962: 33, 41

The provisions of the exclusion laws do not suggest that this should have been the case. Laborers were prohibited from bringing their wives in, but women were still eligible for admission as merchants, teachers, wives of merchants, children of merchants, citizens, derivative citizens, and, until 1924, as wives of citizens. From 1882 to 1924, new immigrants could have potentially included equal numbers of women and men. Moreover, the great majority of the single laborers who stayed in the United States after 1882 would have died by 1920, meaning that most residents should have been eligible to bring their families over.

Chinese women never came anywhere near taking full advantage of their opportunities for immigration. From 1908 to 1924, 4,709 merchants and teachers were admitted for the first time, and 13,610 Chinese entered with the status of returning merchant. Only 2,588 women entered in this period as wives of merchants, amounting to 19 percent of the total number of returning merchants. In contrast, 11,014 Chinese were admitted as the children of these merchants, the vast majority of whom were male. Men were also much more likely to take advantage of opportunities to enter as citizens. Of the 36,259 citizens of Chinese descent admitted from 1909 to 1924, only 1,537, or 4.2 percent, were women. The 2,818 women admitted as wives of citizens from 1907 to 1924 were only enough to provide mates for 7.2 percent of the 38,861 male citizens admitted over that period, not to mention those who never went back to China.[11] Their numbers were certainly not enough to compensate for the anti-miscegenation laws in many states and the fact that many Chinese men were reluctant to marry American-born Chinese women, who they felt made unsuitable wives and mothers.[12] Moreover, in 1936, the San Francisco office of the Bureau of Immigration recorded that the 14,276 citizens of Chinese descent who had entered over the previous eleven years reported having parented 33,611 sons and only 2,813 daughters.[13]

The harsh requirements of admission to the United States, sometimes requiring months of detention, an arduous sea journey, and humiliating investigations, could have deterred many men from even attempting to bring wives and daughters overseas. That is to say, exclusion may have precluded the immigration of women even before they left China. This could have been especially true in the early years of exclusion, when many women were suspected of being prostitutes. By the early twentieth century, however, entry for Chinese women was generally more assured of success than for men. Immigration inspectors admitted that they subjected girls who applied for admission as children of merchants and citizens to less rigorous investigations than boys, believing that they were much more likely to be genuine relatives.[14] From 1907 to 1924, 87 women seeking entry as the wives of merchants were rejected at the port of entry, amounting to 3.1 percent of the 2,806 applicants. In contrast, 2,328 children of merchants were rejected, amounting to 16.5 percent of the 14,078 applicants. Similarly, only 112 wives of citizens were rejected from 1907 to 1924, equaling 3.9 percent of the total applicants. Even less likely to be rejected were women who applied for entry as citizens, of whom the 26 rejections amounted to 1.7 percent of the total applicants from 1909 to 1924. On the other hand, the 2,425 male Chinese rejected when seeking admission as citizens in this period amounted to 6.5 percent of the total applicants.[15] Chinese women were not migrating to the United States in the early twentieth century, but the exclusion laws were not the cause.

Chinese in Hawaii before Annexation

The demographic effects of exclusion were much different in Hawaii than in the continental United States. Exclusion had little immediate effect on the gender balance in the United States and was much less successful in stopping the immigration of single males. In Hawaii, on the other hand, exclusion led to a rising predominance of families and a rapid equalization of the sex ratio. Although adult women were no more numerous in Hawaii than on the mainland in the years immediately preceding the enactment of exclusion, they were much more likely to produce children. Within forty years after the enactment of exclusion laws in Hawaii, the Chinese population had a numerically stable population with a balanced sex ratio, as the mostly male generation resident in Hawaii since before annexation in 1898 died off. In contrast, the Chinese population in the United States declined by nearly half in the forty years after exclusion, and still consisted of less than 20 percent women.

The Chinese presence in Hawaii predated the implementation of the exclusion laws by more years than did the Chinese presence in the United States. Hawaii was an important point in the early trans-Pacific China trade, being a stopover for ships carrying furs from the northwest coast of North America and a source of sandalwood (thus its Chinese name, Sandalwood Mountain), two of the few commodities that were easily marketable in Canton in the early nineteenth century. By the 1820s, luxuries from China, such as silk umbrellas and Chinese beds used as carriages, had already become standard trimmings for the splendor of the Hawaiian royalty. Chinese people were also part of this early exchange, and a Chinese migrant was reported to have established a sugar processing enterprise on the islands in 1802. By 1828, thirty to forty Chinese were resident on the islands. In the 1830s, Caucasian planters recruited Chinese "sugar men," who brought their own sugar processing equipment, and Chinese carpenters to work on the plantations. Chinese continued to grow and process sugar throughout the nineteenth century, but trade generally proved to be more attractive than agriculture, and Chinese commercial houses were among the most important businesses in Honolulu in the middle of the nineteenth century.[16]

This trading population was a significant part of the economic life of Honolulu, but never amounted to more than four hundred Chinese before the middle of the nineteenth century. Larger numbers of Chinese migrants arrived later because sugar plantation owners needed more laborers. Contracted migrant laborers were seen as a particularly suitable solution to labor needs because they were believed to be easier to control and retain than native Hawaiian laborers, who could easily escape to home and were thought to be incorrigibly lazy. The Masters and Servants Act of 1850 provided for the creation of the Hawaiian Board of Immigration and the importation of contracted laborers under government sponsorship. The first shipment of 175 Chinese bound for the plantations arrived in January 1852 from Fujian province. The project did not catch on, however, and only 2,332 Chinese entered Hawaii from 1853 to 1875. More than a quarter of these arrived in 1865, recruited directly by the government to take advantage of the favorable sugar market in the United States at the end of the Civil War. It was not until the ratification of the Reciprocity Treaty between the Hawaiian Kingdom and the United States in 1876, abolishing tariffs on sugar and rice exports to the United States, that the labor trade was rejuvenated. The governor of Hong Kong banned con-tract emigration to Hawaii in 1878, after having heard through Chinese sources that emigrants were bound into virtual slavery on the Islands (la-bor conditions on Hawaiian plantations were usually better than in most other locations, and such information is most likely linked to competi-tion between different Chinese labor recruiters), but emigration quickly shifted further up the Pearl River Delta to the port of Whampoa. At least 24,126 Chinese entered Hawaii between 1878 and 1885, an average of about 3,000 a year, most of whom were recruited on behalf of the sugar planters by Chinese companies.[17]

The rise in Chinese immigration was simultaneous with the growth of anti-Chinese movements and government plans to reduce or halt Chi-nese immigration. White journalists who were sympathetic with white la-bor parties in California had the highest public profile in promoting anti-Chinese sentiments, but their arguments that the growing dominance of Chinese in artisanal and merchant enterprises throughout the islands was pushing the Hawaiians out of a livelihood also found strong support among native Hawaiian residents and congressmen. Anti-Chinese senti-ments were easily conflated with sentiments against the powerful white planters who imported them and with the belief that increased immigra-tion in general threatened to overwhelm the declining native population. Missionaries also contributed to anti-Chinese rhetoric by asserting that the "abnormal" proportion of Chinese males was a corrupting influence on the Hawaiian female population and led to immorality and the spread of opium among the natives.

Anti-Chinese bills aimed at restricting occupational activities and the sale of land to Chinese had been passing in the Hawaiian Assembly since 1874. More than twenty anti-Chinese petitions were presented to the legislature between 1878 and 1884. The first laws to be enacted stipu-lated standards of health that would be required of all immigrants who came in search of work as laborers. In 1883, a quota of 2,400 new Chinese admissions a year was established. Returning residents who had obtained passports before leaving Hawaii, women, and the children of residents were allowed to enter in unlimited quantities. In 1884, the quota of new Chinese admissions was reduced to 25 per ship. In 1885, laborers were prohibited from obtaining return passports. In 1888, all Chinese without passports were prohibited from entering, except for those who had been especially invited by the minister of foreign affairs.[18]

Planters made up for much of the slack by importing Japanese and Portuguese laborers, but they still pushed through a new law in 1890 per-mitting the entry of 5,000 Chinese laborers a year. These laborers had to

be requested by particular plantations, and had to sign five-year contracts, after which they would return to China. A month before the overthrow of the Hawaiian monarchy and the establishment of a Caucasian-
dominated Republic in January of 1893, this law was expanded to allow
Chinese to enter Hawaii as merchants and teachers, and to permit children under ten and women to join relatives already resident in Hawaii.
This new legislation was in part a response to a perception that the Japanese were becoming too numerous in the islands, a fear that emerged
more clearly in 1896 legislation requiring plantation owners to request
twice as many Chinese as Japanese. A supplementary amendment of 1894
stipulated that a portion of the laborers' earnings would be paid into a
government-supervised fund for their repatriation to China after their
contracts were fulfilled. These laws led to another burst in immigration,
with at least 17,000 more Chinese arriving from 1894 until annexation in
1898, an average of nearly 3,500 a year. Even then, supply exceeded demand, and many migrants paid Chinese recruiters as much as a month's
wages in order to be selected for immigration.[19]

Exclusion in Hawaii and the Mainland

Hawaii was annexed by the United States in 1898. The demographic response to the formal implementation of the exclusion laws in that year
was much different in Hawaii than in the United States. In Hawaii, the
Chinese population decreased immediately by about 15 percent in the
twelve years directly after exclusion (see table 2), partly because the funds
for repatriation that had been deducted from the pay of Chinese laborers
who had immigrated over the previous five years continued to be administered for the purchase of return passages. More than 6,270 Chinese left
the islands in the five years between 1900 and 1905, continuing the trend
of about 1,300 departing per year in the 1890s.[20] After 1910, the Chinese
population in Hawaii began a trend of gradual increase characterized by
a numerically stable male population and an increasing female population. On the mainland, the Chinese population had remained steady for
about a decade after the implementation of exclusion, and then the male
population decreased by about 40 percent over the next thirty years as
the female population remained steady (see table 1). At this point, around
1920, the male population began to remain steady, and the proportion of
women began to increase, accounting for much of the total increase in
the Chinese population on the mainland. In both locations, this rise in
the proportion of females corresponded to an increase of locally born
Chinese in proportion to the predominantly male sojourners, rather than

Table 2

Chinese Population in Hawaii, 1853–1940

Year	Total	Men	Women	Percent Female
1853	364			
1860	816			
1866	1,306	1,196	110	8.4
1872	2,038	1,937	107	5.2
1878	6,045	5,814	231	3.8
1884	18,254	17,383	871	4.8
1890	17,457	16,367	1,090	6.2
1896	21,626	19,167	2,459	11.3
1900	25,767	22,301	3,466	13.4
1910	21,764	17,239	4,526	20.8
1920	23,507	16,197	7,310	31.1
1930	27,179	16,568	10,611	39.0
1940	28,774	17,136	11,638	40.4

Source: Glick 1938: 176; Nordyke and Lee 1989: 209–10.
Note: Numbers for 1853–1884 include foreign-born only.

to an increase in female immigration, a shift which occurred around 1900 in Hawaii and 1920 on the mainland.

Patterns of male migrant circulation were different in Hawaii and the United States. Locally born Chinese played a much more important role in maintaining the male population on Hawaii, whereas the population of Chinese men on the mainland was constantly depleted and replenished by migrants traveling back and forth from China. A total of 11,400 Chinese (including citizens) were admitted into Hawaii from 1907 to 1924, about half of the average Chinese population of those years. The 105,309 admissions to the mainland in this period was a number about two-thirds higher than the average population. Even though these figures suggest that exclusion was more efficient in keeping new immigrants out of Hawaii (the isolation of the islands in the middle of the ocean helped make illegal immigration less common), legal admission was actually a less risky proposition than in the United States. From 1907 to 1924, only 459 Chinese applicants were barred from entering Hawaii, amounting to 3.9 percent of the 11,659 applicants. In the United States, on the other hand, the 7,663 rejections during this period amounted to 6.8 percent of the 112,972 applicants.[21] Even if we were to date exclusion in Hawaii

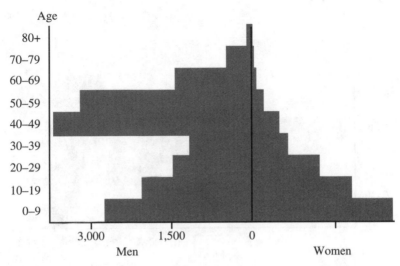

Figure 1 Age Distribution of Chinese Residents in Hawaii, 1920.
(Source: Nordyke and Lee 1989: 209–10)

back to the first anti-Chinese immigration laws in the 1880s, the gender and age of the Chinese population in Hawaii began to normalize in a way that suggested the importance of locally born Chinese in relation to immigrants at least fifteen years sooner than in the United States.

This difference in demographic trends can be perceived more vividly in a graphic comparison of the distribution of age groups in each location at a particular length of time after exclusion. Figure 1 shows the age distribution of Chinese in Hawaii in 1920, and figure 2 shows it for the United States in 1900, each approximately twenty years after the implementation of exclusion. In Hawaii there is a nearly normal sex distribution for all Chinese born in the previous forty years since 1880. If we assume that eighteen to thirty was a likely age range for migration, it seems that the predominantly male immigration which would have created an unbalanced sex ratio stopped with exclusion in 1898 and that the more natural sex distribution of locally born Chinese began to take over.

In the United States, on the other hand, there is a normal sex distribution only in the small population of Chinese under ten years old. Among Chinese aged eleven to forty, the sex distribution was still extremely biased toward males, suggesting the persistence of migration as a determining factor in the demographic makeup of the Chinese population there. Even in 1930, fifty years after exclusion, the beginnings of an equal gender distribution in the United States can only be seen in the

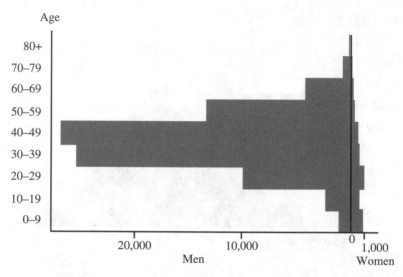

Figure 2 Age Distribution of Chinese Residents in the United States, 1900. (Source: United States Census, 1900)

generations born after 1910 (figure 3). Of that small generation of children that showed a normal sex distribution in 1900, the total number of women had slightly more than doubled by 1930, whereas twelve times as many men could be counted. If the population trees for the United States were further broken down into regions, we would see that the gender imbalance was even greater for the eastern United States and that the bulk of the men were even younger, reflecting both the shorter history of settlement and the fact that it was the preferred region for much new migration in the twentieth century.

The roots of these different reactions to exclusion can be better pinpointed by graphing the changes in the proportion of women in Hawaii and the mainland over time. Figure 4 takes the enactment of exclusion as a baseline, and shows the relative proportion of Chinese women over time before and after exclusion. In Hawaii, the proportion of women began to increase in the ten years before exclusion, and continued that increase until parity was achieved in the 1950s, with only a slight leveling off during the depression. On the mainland, the proportion of Chinese women decreased over the ten years before exclusion, and remained low for thirty years, after which it increased at a rate comparable to that in Hawaii. Exclusion does not seem to have significantly affected trends in either location.

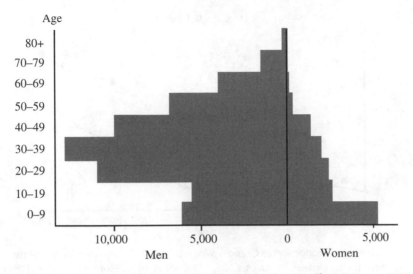

Figure 3 Age Distribution of Chinese Residents in the United States, 1930. (Source: United States Census, 1930)

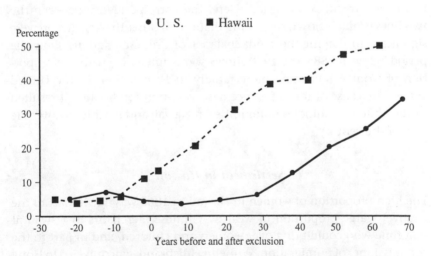

Figure 4 Proportion of Chinese Women in the Continental United States and Hawaii in Relation to the Enactment of Exclusion. (Sources: Glick 1938, Kung 1962, Nordyke and Lee 1989)

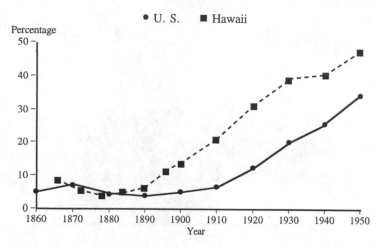

Figure 5 Proportion of Chinese Women in the Continental United States and Hawaii by Year. (Sources: Glick 1938, Kung 1962, Nordyke and Lee 1989)

Figure 5 plots these changes in terms of year rather than proximity to the enactment of exclusion. Here, the correspondence between the two lines is much closer, suggesting that forces other than exclusion were significant in shaping the gender balance of Chinese migrants. Only the period between 1885 and 1910 shows some difference, with the proportion of women increasing more rapidly in Hawaii than in the United States. The cause of this difference deserves attention because it resulted in very different Chinese communities in Hawaii and in Chicago after the turn of the century.

Settlement in Hawaii

The high proportion of women in Hawaii in 1866 was due in part to the relatively large proportion of wealthy Chinese merchants in Hawaii at that time who could bring over women and children, and in part to the commissioner of immigration, Wilhelm Hillebrand, who traveled to Hong Kong in 1865 to recruit Chinese laborers for work on sugar plantations. He fell short of his intention to bring back at least 20 percent women, but the fifty-two he brought back still made up 10 percent of the total recruits, and were enough to boost the sex ratio on the islands.[22] The debates surrounding the desirability of bringing Chinese labor to Hawaii in the 1860s and 1870s were accompanied by numerous assertions that the Chinese would be more desirable if they brought their women with them, because as single men they exerted an undesirable influence on the morality of the native Hawaiians. By the time Chinese migration reached significant numbers in the 1880s, the encouragement of women was no longer a major concern, although the advance payment of thirty-five dollars offered to female immigrants destined for plantation work was higher than the twenty-five dollars offered to men. Also, much of the restrictive immigration legislation enacted in the 1880s did not extend to the admission of women and children.[23] Nonetheless, these measures had few results, and the proportion of women actually decreased and remained lower than in the United States through the middle of the 1880s.[24] By the 1890s all attempts to encourage the immigration of Chinese women had been dropped, and the 409 women who arrived from 1893 to 1899 amounted to only 2.1 percent of 19,010 Chinese immigrants, similar to the proportion entering the United States.[25]

The key to the burst in the proportion of Chinese women in Hawaii in the 1890s is found not in immigration but in the greater tendency of Chinese women to raise children in Hawaii. In 1896, two years before exclusion, 1,132 of the Chinese women in Hawaii were under the age of fifteen, amounting to 46 percent of the total female population, compared to only 33.9 percent on the mainland in 1900. Of those girls, 982 were born in Hawaii, 73 percent of whom had been born in the previous six years.[26] Like men, immigrant women continued to make up a larger proportion of the Chinese women on the mainland in the early years of the twentieth century. The 1,791 Chinese women who entered Hawaii from 1909 to 1924 made up less than a third of the average female population in that period. The 6,949 women who migrated to the mainland over this period were slightly more than the average female population of that period.[27]

In Hawaii, there were 2.6 children for each married woman at the time of exclusion. This rose by 1910 to a steady average of more than 3 children each until the Second World War (table 3). The proportion of children to married women on the mainland was a much lower 1.5 children each in 1900, after which it rose to a maximum of 2.7 in 1930 (see table 4). The proportion of unmarried Chinese women older than fifteen on the mainland averaged slightly less than 20 percent of the total during the three decades from 1900 to 1930, while in Hawaii this proportion gradually rose from 8.5 percent in 1896 to 23.2 percent in 1930. Adult Chinese women in Hawaii before the turn of the century were more likely to be married and produce children than in the United States, but by 1930 patterns of marriage and birth had become quite similar.

Several causes may explain the proportionally higher settlement of childbearing Chinese women in Hawaii in the 1880s and 1890s. Few

Chinese worked as prostitutes in Hawaii compared to the United States. This can account for the higher proportion of unmarried adult women and lower fertility (married women could also have been prostitutes) in the United States. Other causes must still be invoked to explain why the lower number of prostitutes was compensated for by an increase in fam-

Table 3

Chinese Women and Children in Hawaii, 1878–1940

Year	Total Women	Percent Under 15	Married Women	Percent Married	Total Children Under 15	Children per Married Woman
1878	231					
1884	871					
1890	1,090		559	51.3		
1896	2,459	46.0	1,119	45.5	2,854	2.5
1900	3,466	48.1	1,409	40.6	3,667	2.6
1910	4,526	53.5	1,555	34.4	5,136	3.3
1920	7,310	49.1	2,416	33.1	7,375	3.1
1930	10,611	46.5	3,212	30.3	10,044	3.1
1940	11,638	35.9			8,527	

Source: Glick 1938: 176, and 1980: 165; Nordyke and Lee 1989: 209–10; General Superintendent of the Census 1897, tables 8 and 9.

Table 4

Chinese Women and Children in the United States, 1880–1940

Year	Total Women	Percent Under 15	Married Women	Percent Married	Total Children Under 15	Children per Married Woman
1880	4,779					
1890	3,868		1,951	50.4		
1900	4,522	33.9	2,157	47.7	3,026	1.4
1910	4,675	39.5	2,016	43.1	4,504	2.2
1920	7,748	43.1	3,046	39.3	7,434	2.4
1930	15,152	46.1	5,574	36.8	15,266	2.7
1940	20,115	38.0	7,155	35.6	16,424	2.3

Source: Kung 1962: 33–36; United States Census, 1900 and 1930.

ily women. The encouragement of Chinese women to come to Hawaii in the 1860s and 1870s may have accounted for a few of these women, as may the long mercantile history of Chinese in Hawaii, which produced a relatively high proportion of wealthy Chinese with the financial means to bring over family members. Perhaps even more significant were the Chinese who grew wealthy and influential in remote rural areas, where they often became highly respected village elites. The prestige and wealth of such men were usually more invested in local business and village status than in international trade, and they often established local families with a dozen children or more. Many of these families resulted from alliances with Hawaiian women, but not all of those children would have identified as Chinese.[28] Also, the many Chinese Christians (most of whom were Hakkas) who migrated to Hawaii in the nineteenth century through missionary networks were more likely to think of migration in terms of the transplantation of nuclear families. Finally, the excellent, missionary-run secondary education system in Honolulu, which included students of all races, appealed to a handful of parents, resulting in fewer children being sent back to China for their education. No one of these causes is sufficient explanation on its own, but taken together they can account for that extra few hundred women whose descendants would become so significant in the following years.

Neither Hawaii's reputation of being more racially tolerant, nor the superior economic position of the Chinese on the Islands, nor even the relative ease of admission seems to have encouraged increased migration there in the early twentieth century. Opportunities for the newcomer— other than the plantation—were much less abundant in Hawaii, whereas the United States provided many opportunities to work in small laundries and restaurants. Although Hawaii was less attractive for the support of transnational families, it did provide slightly better attractions for the settler. The exclusion laws made it nearly impossible for plantation laborers to immigrate and find work, but they left opportunities for individuals to come and work in small businesses among networks of relatives and fellow villagers. Thus, while exclusion led to a sharp decline in immigration and the predominance of families in Hawaii, it had little notable effect in the United States other than to reduce the flow of male immigrants.

Chinese Restriction in Peru

A look at immigration legislation in relation to Chinese migration to Peru supports the point that the demographic effects of immigration restrictions must be considered in a social and temporal context. Peru is particu-

larly good for comparison with Hawaii because in both locations migrants from Zhongshan (many from the same villages and families) were
in the majority, both were sites of Chinese plantation labor, and in both
places Chinese had reputations for successful integration and assimilation into complex, multiracial societies. Despite these apparent similarities, a smaller proportion of women and children migrated to Peru than
to the United States or Hawaii, even though women were explicitly exempted from many restrictive immigration laws.

A Chinese presence in Peru can be traced even further back than in
Hawaii. As early as 1613, thirty-eight Chinese, probably from the Philippines, were recorded as living in Lima.[29] The roots of the modern Chinese
migrant community go back only to the importation of plantation laborers in the middle of the nineteenth century. The importation of African
slaves had been abolished in 1836, and the slaves themselves were emancipated in 1854. The cotton and sugar planters on the Peruvian coast
turned to Chinese as the most likely source to replenish their dwindling
corps of laborers. In 1849 the so-called Chinese Law was passed in congress to provide for the importation of indentured Chinese workers. As in
Hawaii, this labor migration proceeded in fits and starts over the first
twenty years, but by 1874 nearly one hundred thousand Chinese had arrived in Peru, over half of them in the four years from 1870 to 1874. Most
of them were shipped out of Macao because reports of the kidnapping
and deception of recruits and of heavy death tolls during the ocean passage
had led the Hong Kong government to ban the departure of contracted
Chinese to Peru in 1862. This bad treatment was notorious throughout
the world, and continued once the migrants landed in Peru. The contracts
were generally for a period of eight years—compared to five in Hawaii—
and low pay, brutal punishments, and owners who often ignored contracts led to a situation sometimes characterized as "semi-slavery." Laborers who survived their initial eight years usually found themselves in debt
for opium and other goods bought in plantation stores and had to recontract themselves for periods of one year at a time. International pressures,
exerted mostly by the British, brought this labor trade to an end in 1874.[30]

The end of the contract labor trade was marked by the signing of the
Treaty of Friendship, Commerce and Navigation between China and Peru,
guaranteeing free migration and trade between the two countries. Some
planters hoped that migration to the plantations would continue under
these conditions, and even made an unsuccessful attempt to establish a
steamship route between Hong Kong and the Peruvian port of Callao via
Hawaii in 1874.[31] Few Chinese (or Peruvians for that matter) took advantage of the opportunity to migrate over the next thirty years. The slow

and expensive passage, made either by sailing ship or by steamer via San Francisco, as well as the bad reputation of Peru discouraged further migration and left the Chinese already there in relative isolation. By the turn of the century, Chinese migration had increased to a couple of hundred per year, but not until the establishment of a direct steamship line between Hong Kong and Callao in 1904 did Peru again became a significant destination for Chinese migrants.

The years from 1905 until May 1909 were the golden years of free migration to Peru, with as many as three thousand Chinese a year arriving in Callao. But, in what is already a familiar pattern, the growth in Chinese migration was accompanied by a corresponding rise in local anti-Chinese activities. These activities reached a peak in Lima on 25 May 1909 when a rally of the Worker's Party expanded into a general anti-Chinese riot that spread throughout the city. Rioters looted more than twenty Chinese shops and injured several Chinese. The president of Peru was quick to sacrifice Chinese interests in his attempt to smooth over relations with the laboring classes, issuing a decree four days later that no Chinese would be allowed to land in Callao unless he could show cash resources equal to five hundred pounds sterling in his possession.[32]

This crisis led to the first visit in twenty-three years by a Chinese ambassador to Peru.[33] Wu Tingfang, the Chinese ambassador to Cuba, Peru, and the United States, arrived in Lima on 7 July 1909. Over the next two months he negotiated a migration agreement with the Peruvian government known as the Porras-Wu Protocol. Wu drafted the protocol based on the Gentleman's Agreement of 1907 between Japan and the United States, in which Japan had assumed responsibility for restricting emigration to the United States.[34] The protocol stipulated that all immigration to Peru would be "voluntarily" halted by China. "Immigrants" were defined as all men coming to Peru in search of employment, and a system was outlined whereby names of prospective "non-immigrants" would be investigated by the local Chamber of Commerce in China and then forwarded to the governor of the province, who would supply them with a passport. Passport holders would then proceed to the Peruvian consul in Hong Kong to receive a visa before boarding the ship. That is to say, the objectives of the protocol were essentially the same as the American exclusion laws, except that the Chinese rather than the Peruvian government had the responsibility of enforcing them.

In practice, the stipulations of the protocol were almost entirely ignored. The first boat to arrive in Callao from China in 1910 after the protocol was signed carried nearly eight hundred Chinese, which was no reduction in the numbers that had landed in previous years. The Peruvian government accused the Chinese of issuing passports to "immigrants" in contradiction to the stipulations of the protocol. The Chinese government promised to work with the Peruvians in investigating this problem, but any serious attention they might have given it was diverted by the revolution of 1911.

Peruvian officials took the control of migration into their own hands with little regard for the terms of the protocol. By 1914 the Peruvian Ministry of Foreign Relations explicitly articulated the two rules that had been effectively shaping Chinese migration to Peru since 1911 and would continue to shape it over the next sixteen years. Only two categories of Chinese were allowed entry: (1) those with papers of special permission to replace departed employees in Chinese commercial houses that had been investigated and issued by the Chinese legation in Lima and visaed by the Ministry of Foreign Relations, and (2) returned residents who had reentry papers stamped by the ministry. Women and children were not explicitly accounted for in these orders, but the large number of children arriving in Callao, nearly equal to that of adult men in 1915, impelled the ministry to restrict them as well. The final form of this restriction was formulated in February 1916, when the ministry ordered the consul in Hong Kong to allow only five children to migrate per boat and then only with rigorous proof of relationship to a father or uncle traveling with him (although, in practice, most boats carried from eight to twenty-three children).[35] Accompanying this order was another requiring similar proof for women accompanying their husbands to Peru. It was a requirement formulated primarily in anticipation of a problem, as the low numbers had yet to make the migration of women an issue, and it proved to be somewhat unnecessary. Many consuls over the next few years seemed unaware of the requirements of proof of marriage for women, or admitted to not enforcing them as strictly as the rules against men and children, yet the numbers of female migrants did not increase significantly. Of the 11,489 migrants leaving Hong Kong for Peru between 1911 and 1930, only 551, or 4.9 percent, were women, a much smaller proportion than migrated to the United States or Hawaii.[36]

But even these ministerial rules are an inadequate guideline from which to accurately depict a flow of migration characterized by extensive corruption and subject to sudden and arbitrary manipulation resulting from factional struggles in the Peruvian government. In the years from 1911 to 1930, Chinese migration to Peru was increasingly unpredictable, swinging between periods of complete suspension and ever larger numbers of new arrivals (see chapter 5). In the aggregate, however, immigration never reached pre-1909 levels. Peruvian consuls in Hong Kong counted at least 9,597 Chinese departing to Peru from 1904 to 1909, compared to only 12,263 who left in the twenty years from 1910 to 1930. Legitimate admission at Callao was also augmented by illegal entry, mostly from northern Chile. The coup of August 1930 brought a populist government to Peru. One of its first acts was to implement a more clear-cut immigration status for the Chinese: *all* Chinese immigration was banned. After a year and a half, this prohibition was loosened to allow entry to a strictly controlled quota of twenty returning residents per month, along with their immediate families.[37]

The number of Chinese migrants to Peru from 1909 to 1930 was slightly larger than the number of migrants to Hawaii from 1908 to 1924, for a total Chinese population that was 20 percent to 50 percent smaller. The difference in immigration regulations, however, leaves us no firm basis from which to compare the attractiveness of the two countries for migrants. We are also left to wonder why so few women migrated to Peru. The low proportion of female migrants is reflected in Chinese the population statistics for that country shown in table 5. The proportion of women among the Chinese in Peru was even lower than in the United States, ranging from a low of 1.1 percent in the Department of Lima in 1908 (and probably even lower in the nineteenth century) to a high of 5 percent for the entire country in 1940.

Varying standards of data collection have contributed to some of the severe fluctuations in the numbers in table 5, but they are still sufficient to show that the new waves of immigration in the twentieth century never brought the Chinese back up to more than a third of their population in the nineteenth century. As we will see below, many Chinese migrants in Peru were as financially and socially successful as the migrant elite of Hawaii, yet few brought wives over. Poor educational resources and the lack of missionary networks connecting Peru to China may have contributed to the lack of families in Peru. In addition, I believe that wealthy Chinese in Peru were different from those in Hawaii in that they frequently identified as foreign nationals and as cosmopolitan, international merchants, whereas many merchants in Hawaii were deeply rooted in local rural life. This may have facilitated the maintenance of families that were equally transnational. Although I cannot account completely for the relative lack of female migrants to Peru, the important point is that migration legislation is not sufficient to explain a lack of women. After 1930, new male immigration was banned, and Chinese were cut off from their transnational families much more effectively in Peru than in

Table 5

Chinese Population of Peru, 1876–1940

Year	Peru	Department of Lima	Province of Lima	Percentage of Population	City of Lima
1876	49,956	24,298	11,958	10.9	5,642
1891					4,676
1903					3,258[a]
1908			6,996 (76)	4.0	5,123
1920			3,821	1.7	
1921–4	[16,000]	8,085 (183)			
1931			5,128 (220)	1.4	3,920 (182)
1931–2		7,232			
1936	8,270	4,840			
1940	10,915 (550)	6,871 (315)			

Source: Censuses of Peru for 1876, 1908, 1920, 1931, and 1940; Census of Foreigners, 1936; Millones Santagadea 1973: 80, for 1891; Census of 1908, p. 89, for 1903; Registros de Extranjería, National Archives, Peru, for 1921–24 and 1931–32; Mayer de Zulen 1924: 109 for the 1921–24 national estimate.

Notes: Figures in parentheses are for women and have already been calculated into the total figure. The figure in brackets is an estimate made by the Chinese legation. The City of Lima refers to the central districts of the city. The province extends to the surrounding suburbs and rural districts of the Rimac Valley, and the department includes several coastal valleys to the north and south of Lima, extending about fifty miles inland.

[a]Includes a few Japanese.

either Chicago or Hawaii. The increasing difficulty of international movement led a handful of residents to relocate their families in Peru, and a significant locally born generation (distinct from the half-Chinese children of nineteenth-century migrants) finally began to emerge in the 1950s.

LOCAL MIGRANT ECONOMIES

The Chinese populations in Chicago, Peru, and Hawaii in the early twentieth century were either highly urbanized or rapidly urbanizing. Migrants worked mostly in small, independent, yet interlinked businesses providing services or engaging in trade. They rarely worked for non-Chinese except as domestic servants, although that job was decreasingly common after the turn of the century. We could easily argue that racism in all three locations had excluded them from employment in non-Chinese businesses, but we must remember that Chinese in Hawaii and Peru also avoided the large agricultural interests that actively sought their labor. That is to say, job opportunities were increasingly shaped by the networks that brought Chinese abroad in the first place.

The demographic growth of any one of these migrant populations was inversely proportionate to the local social and economic status of the Chinese. In Chicago, the Chinese population more than doubled from 1900 to 1930, although there was little to attract the new migrant other than manual labor. The success of the wealthiest migrants was easily overshadowed by the industrial and economic glory of Chicago. The Chinese population of Peru remained fairly stable after the 1909 protocol was signed, even decreasing in the 1930s, but most migrants there could look forward to a small corner store of their own. The more educated could hope for a position as manager or administrator in one of several large and influential Chinese commercial and agricultural enterprises. In Hawaii the Chinese population also remained stable during the first half of the twentieth century, perhaps even decreasing for China-born migrants, but Chinese there had achieved relatively high economic and social recognition. As in Peru, the migrant elites were wealthy and respected, but in contrast to either of the other locations, Chinese in Hawaii were engaged in a very diverse range of occupations, with many attaining middle-class status. This situation had much to do with the prominence of a locally born population. A new migrant was more attracted by the immediate availability of profitable, unskilled work and a favorable exchange rate than by the possibility of eventually becoming a respected member of local society or by the egalitarian promises of national rhetoric. The most direct influence on migration choices were usually kinsmen who could get a man past immigration barriers and set him up with a job.

Chicago

No Chinese are recorded as having resided in Chicago until 1880, when 209 were counted by the United States census. The growth of the Chinese population in Chicago in the late nineteenth century was part of a general trend of new and established Chinese migrants forsaking the western United States for other parts of the country. Many Chinese are said to have been attracted to Chicago by the demand for clean clothes created by the many visitors to the Colombian World Exposition of 1893. Whatever the causes, this diffusion eastward was not so much a gradually en-

Table 6

Chinese Population in Illinois and Chicago, 1870–1940

| | ILLINOIS | | | | | |
Year	Total	Men	Women	Percentage Female	Chicago	Percent in Chicago
1870	1	1	0	0	0	0
1880	209	206	3	1.4	172	82.3
1890	740	725	15	2.0	567	76.6
1900	1,503	1,472	31	2.1	1,209	80.4
1910	2,103	2,030	73	3.5	1,778	84.5
1920	2,776	2,523	253	9.1	2,353	84.8
1930	3,192	2,796	396	12.4	2,757	86.4
1940	2,456	1,955	501	20.4	2,013	82.0

Source: United States Census, 1870–1940.

croaching wave as an aggregation of trips back and forth in many directions between population centers in the United States and a few villages in Taishan county. At least 15 percent of Chinese men in Chicago in the early twentieth century were of the Moy surname, from the district of Duanfen.

The Chinese population in the Midwest was highly urbanized from its inception (see table 6). But Chicago was important not only as a place where many Chinese lived but also as a social and economic center for Chinese throughout the Midwest. Businesses and associations in Chicago channeled goods and communication to smaller Chinese communities in Minneapolis, Duluth, Indianapolis, Milwaukee, and St. Louis, from which businessmen traveled on circuits to laundries and tea stores in smaller towns throughout the region.

Other calculations suggest that the census numbers undercount the Chinese population by 50 percent to 100 percent. A count made in 1926 by University of Chicago graduate student Ting-chiu Fan of all the Chinese registered in the most important Chinese associations resulted in a list of 4,019 individuals, not including women and children. Additional interviews with prominent Chinese led him to suggest 4,500 as an estimate of the total Chinese population in Chicago that year, and 3,500 as a likely figure for 1920. Other estimates include the 5,000 to 6,000 suggested to a *Tribune* reporter by a prominent Chinese in 1931, 5,500 estimated by another Chinese graduate student in 1932, and 1,739 estimated by two white University of Chicago researchers in 1934.[38]

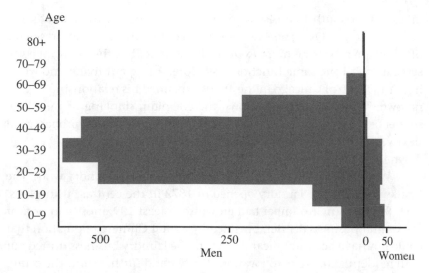

Figure 6 Age Distribution of Chinese Migrants in Chicago, 1910. This graph represents 1,778 Chinese and 345 (16%) "others," which probably included Japanese, Indians (Asian and North American), and Middle Eastern peoples. (Source: United States Census, 1910)

The increase of the Chinese population in Chicago from 1890 until 1920 shown in table 6 contrasts with a decrease in the Chinese population in the United States as a whole. Chicago was an important destination for new Chinese migration to the United States in the early twentieth century. The effects of this could also be seen in that the proportion of women in Chicago was somewhat smaller, and the average age of the migrants was ten to twenty years younger than in the United States as a whole (figure 6).

By the 1880s, a small cluster of Chinese businesses had already gathered on South Clark Street at the southern edge of the central business district, forming the nucleus of the first Chinatown, which was in the heart of one of the largest and most famous vice districts in the Midwest. The Chinese were just some of the many men using this area as a temporary bachelor residential center. Most of the early Chinese residents of Chicago lived in their laundries and restaurants spread throughout the city, coming to Chinatown once a week or less to socialize, gamble, and get a good meal, staying more permanently only when unemployed.

The vice district was gradually relocated and then harassed out of existence after the turn of the century by reformers, city officials, and redevelopers. Chinatown followed this flight, relocating in 1912 about two miles farther south to an isolated location surrounded by railroads and industrial zones. Over the next thirty years, the businesses and residents of Chinatown became more exclusively Chinese, but they continued to serve many of the same functions as before. A migrant living and working in a suburb of Chicago in the 1930s explained his relationship to Chinatown: "One gets degraded down there. Opium smoking or gambling, sooner or later you'll fall for it. If you don't this year, you'll probably fall next year. I see no bright ideas in going down there very often. Yes, I go down there every week." [39]

Work for the Chinese in Chicago usually meant laundry work. The first known Chinese laundry opened in 1872 in the central business district. By 1883, their number had grown to at least 199, mostly in or near the central business district, operated by a total Chinese population that could not have been significantly larger. The laundry business drifted out with residential districts to locations further and further from the center of the city, completely evacuating the central business district by 1913. [40] Aside from laundry work, Chinese in Chicago worked primarily as restaurant owners and workers, as household servants, and in retail trade. The proportion of laundrymen gradually decreased over time in favor of restaurant work and, to a lesser extent, commercial occupations. Chinese had operated restaurants serving American food in Chicago since at least the Colombian Exposition. By the turn of the century they had also started serving Chinese food, although most sales continued be of Western dishes. [41] A handful of these restaurants were quite upscale, offering live music, dancing, and elaborate decor. The Depression led to the closing down of many larger Chinese restaurants in the 1930s and their replacement by small, take-out chop suey places. The surviving large restaurants concentrated in Chinatown, which was redone to attract larger numbers of white clientele. [42]

Gambling was another important industry that provided a livelihood not accounted for in the above surveys. [43] It was also the main foundation of power and wealth among the migrants in Chicago. Very few migrants made much more than a living wage from laundries, or even restaurants and import-export businesses. Gambling and the protection of gambling were the most common sources of wealth and status among Chinese migrants in Chicago. The migrant elite were invested in the maintenance of a segregated Chinese economy, where migrants earned a steady income and channeled it toward Chinese-dominated entertainments that eventually led to their pockets. They also had an interest in the semilegal status of gambling, which required their mediation with police and local officials. Low prospects for outside mobility and the social isolation of Chinese underwrote the dominance of a local migrant elite that controlled violence within the migrant community and the majority of connections outside that community.

Peru

Chinese laborers brought to Peru in the nineteenth century worked mostly on the coastal cotton and sugar plantations, but they also dug guano on offshore islands for fertilizer, worked as domestic servants, and built railroads into the mountains (a project in which they had limited success because of altitude sickness). Many laborers continued hiring themselves out to the plantations on a yearly or daily basis after their eight-year contracts had expired, some even ending up as foremen, mechanics, craftsmen, and small renters. The largest fortunes among the ex-laborers were made by the men who organized and occasionally kidnapped their free countrymen in Peru into labor gangs that were then contracted to the plantations. Much of the money these contractors earned came from concessions to operate stores on the plantations. Such contracted Chinese labor gangs were common until the late 1890s, when many of them were getting too old for the hard work.[44]

Other ex-laborers moved into the coastal towns, where they worked mainly as artisans, manual laborers, and peddlers. Chinese in Lima congregated near the central market, on Capón street. As with the early residents of Chinatowns in Chicago and Honolulu, Chinese were just one of many ethnic groups. Some Chinese in Lima barely managed to subsist, selling boiled water, collecting excrement, and peddling sweets, peanuts, sesame paste, and porridge. The more successful could find a permanent location from which to sell their wares, although it often amounted to little more than a literal hole in a wall. Occupations providing more substantial incomes included the sale of charcoal, laundry work, growing and selling vegetables, raising and selling pork, shoemaking, baking, and operating simple restaurants serving Peruvian food.[45] Many Chinese were not able to save enough to provide for themselves in their old age, and large numbers of old, indigent Chinese men lived in the streets of Lima by the early twentieth century. The Chinese Benevolent Society of Lima sponsored the repatriation of 165 of these old men to China between 1909 and 1924, where many died in a home for the elderly maintained for them in Canton.[46]

Some of the early Chinese entrepreneurs moved to more distant towns higher up on the western slopes of the Andes. They worked in artisanal occupations or sought the patronage of local landowners and gained access to land as renters or sharecroppers. They were also involved in transportation and the distribution of goods. Travelers' memoirs noted how inconvenient, and at times nearly impossible, overland travel would have been through many parts of the country without Chinese mule drivers, guides, and inns. By the 1920s, many remote villages whose previous economic contact with the outside world had been almost exclusively through barter at seasonal fairs and labor migration to the plantations were now served by a stream of Chinese traders and peddlers constantly transporting goods back and forth, and readily offering advances and credit. Chinese pioneering activities extended to the Amazon, where they joined the many other adventurers attracted by the rubber boom at the turn of the century. The Chinese found their opportunity, however, not in the direct exploitation of rubber but in provisioning rubber camps. They grew rice and vegetables on land they cleared themselves and utilized their extensive networks across the Andes, as well as their generally amiable relations with the native population, to develop a dense commercial distribution system.[47]

Much of the vision and capital that underwrote the more pioneering economic penetration was brought by Chinese who came to Peru as merchants rather than laborers. Early indentured laborers to Peru appear to have come from all over the Pearl River Delta, as well as from Fujian province and Zhaoluo prefecture in western Guangdong. The new waves of migration were dominated by men from Zhongshan county, who made up about 50 percent of the Chinese population by the 1920s. The economic elite consisted mostly of Zhongshan Hakkas. Many of the more important merchants had come to Peru looking to establish branches of commercial houses already established in Hong Kong and San Francisco. They imported luxuries to sell to Peruvians and foodstuffs and medicines to sell to other Chinese, as well as becoming involved in the sale and distribution of Peruvian products throughout the country. Like the Italian migrants who had arrived earlier, they challenged the old landed elite with wealth gained through independent commercial networks. As early as the 1890s, several of the larger Chinese companies started renting agricultural land and managing their own plantations, using local rather than Chinese labor. Many of these agricultural investments were pioneering attempts to develop the profitability of agriculture for its own sake, rather than just using agricultural earnings to finance other endeavors. With the boom in the world demand for cotton brought by the First World War, these companies became flourishing agricultural export concerns. By 1924, Chinese operated at least twenty-four plantations, as well as an insurance company and a shipping company that ran boats across the Pacific from Callao to Hong Kong.[48]

The general demographic trend for Chinese in the 1920s was a retreat from far-flung inland residences to the coastal cities, especially Lima. Wealthy Chinese used Lima as a node of commercial networks that were increasingly global in their reach and increasingly integrated with non-Chinese transportation and markets. Even the poorer Chinese who arrived after 1904 did not want to work in crafts and carry goods across the mountains. Instead, they worked in small food stores, butcher shops, and bars in the cities and towns, linked to the larger firms through ties of credit. They gradually supplanted the Italians in their dominance of these businesses, and the "Chinese on the corner" became a fixture throughout Lima. Restaurants serving Chinese food to Peruvians, known as *chifas*, were increasingly popular in the 1930s. Chinese in Peru in the early twentieth century were climbing the social hierarchy of residence, respectability, and occupation. By the 1940s and 1950s, Chinese and their children had begun to diversify into a wider spectrum of urban occupations, most notably the sale of shoes, the manufacture of furniture, and a few professional occupations.

Hawaii

Contract laborers and independent migrants had made up two distinct waves of immigrants to Peru, but in Hawaii they were contemporaneous and interrelated. Merchants had established themselves in Hawaii prior to the large-scale arrival of laborers and played an important role in the organization of labor migration, bringing in laborers to work on white-owned sugar plantations as well as on their own rice and sugar plantations. The shorter time periods and more generous pay of Hawaiian contracts, as well as the strong Chinese commercial infrastructure already in place throughout the islands, made it easier for individuals to move on to some other activity after the expiration of a contract. Distinguishing between indentured laborers and free migrants was difficult in Hawaii because many migrants had their contracts arranged by uncles and cousins who continued to assist them after their contracts ran out. The Chinese companies that recruited migrants sometimes even paid white sugar planters to release laborers from their contracts early. In 1882, despite nearly 14,000 Chinese having entered in the previous five years, only 5,037 were working on the sugar plantations. In 1897, the year of highest Chinese employment on the sugar plantations, only 8,114 Chinese could

be found on them. Yet 13,300 Chinese had been reported as rural laborers a year earlier, many of them working on Chinese rice plantations.[49]

Chinese began growing rice in the 1860s, taking over fields previously used to grow taro, the staple food of the declining native Hawaiian
population. By the turn of the century, rice exports made up a significant
portion of the Hawaiian export economy, and Chinese had been pains-
takingly reclaiming swamp land to extend their rice crops. Large rice
plantations hired many wage laborers, but after the exclusion laws made
it difficult to import laborers, partnership schemes and smaller operations
became more common. Two kinds of partnership scheme predominated:
the *he ban,* in which a group of Chinese invested in land and tools, and divided the labor equally amongst themselves; and the *fen gong,* in which the
workers shared in the proceeds of the crop unequally with a wealthy individual or company that provided the tools and land but no labor. A few
small plots continued to be cultivated by independent farmers. Many rural areas given over to rice planting centered around a village or a store, and
the inhabitants often had little contact with non-Chinese other than temporary Hawaiian laborers and the occasional visit of a landlord or tax collector. Even plows, water buffaloes, and fruit trees were imported from
China. Large Chinese companies acted as marketers and brokers between
landlords, laborers, and millers. Often these companies made more money
from the right to provide groceries and other supplies to planters than
from the financing of cultivation or the profits made from the crop.

The rice industry declined after 1910. The many causes contributing to this downturn included the falling price of rice; the growing importance of sugar cane on the islands, which diverted much water from
paddy lands; competition from mechanized farms in California and Texas
that were growing new breeds of rice; land exhaustion; and the paucity
of new migrants willing to work in the fields as a result of exclusion.
Many planters and partnerships turned to vegetable and taro cultivation,
and Chinese continued to dominate the manufacture of poi (made from
taro) in the early twentieth century. A few Chinese ventured into the cultivation of pineapples, bananas, and coffee, not to mention well drilling,
whaling, and shark fishing, generally using non-Chinese labor. Chinese
involvement in these industries was never very significant, and they were
largely left to other migrants by the 1930s.[50]

The decline of the rice industry at the turn of the century coincided
with the gradual concentration of the Chinese population in Honolulu,
although they maintained an important presence in rural areas through
their commercial activities. Many Chinese who had grown wealthy from
rice and ranching continued to maintain local stores as these other invest-

ments grew less profitable. These stores were the financial nodes of many small villages and their main channel of contact with the outside world. They brought in manufactured goods from Honolulu and sent native products back, dealing with local Hawaiians in terms of barter, credit, trust, and a toleration of a margin of loss for the sake of good business relations. The shopowners also tended to be the first residents to introduce innovations like cars, electric generators, and refrigerators, occasionally holding local offices like postmaster and even having local streets named after them. By the late 1920s, even these rural stores began to disappear as more and more Chinese relocated in Honolulu.

The Honolulu Chinatown had been known as the "native quarter" before Chinese began to concentrate there. In the 1880s nearly three-quarters of the Chinese in Honolulu lived there with their businesses, mixing with other ethnic groups. After the Chinatown fire of 1900, businesses and residences became more dispersed throughout the city.[51] In Chicago, by contrast, businesses and newly emerging Chinese families had increasingly concentrated in Chinatown in the 1920s and 1930s, slowly changing it from a bachelor enclave into a more purely Chinese district. Chinese artisans had also been an important presence in Honolulu before the twentieth century, particularly as tailors and shoemakers. By the turn of the century, Chinese concentrated more and more in commercial activities and dominated fish and vegetable peddling. By the early twentieth century, peddlers were replaced by permanent shops with diversified merchandise, and Chinese dominated the wholesale distribution of canned goods and several types of Hawaiian produce throughout the Islands and abroad. Less successful Chinese and their locally born children were engaged in domestic service, laundry work, and vegetable growing. When not working in their family businesses, locally born Chinese also held a large variety of professional, skilled, and semiskilled positions.[52]

As in Peru in the early twentieth century, slightly over half of the Chinese in Hawaii were from Zhongshan county. Unlike the situation in Peru, no single group dominated the migrant economy in Hawaii. Chinese in Hawaii also engaged in a much wider range of lucrative commercial activities than the Chinese in Chicago or Peru, although the opportunities for a poorly capitalized migrant were much fewer. There was cutthroat competition among Chinese in the trading of goods that were part of their "niche." At the same time, the Honolulu Chinese were quite conscious of their relatively strong position in the local economy. They often noted that they did not have the large, heavily capitalized enterprises of the whites, but were ubiquitous in mid-level retail trade and generally more successful than other ethnic groups. They consciously networked among themselves to maintain this niche. The flip side of this strength was the difficulty of venturing into businesses that were outside of familiar networks, and locally born Chinese who desired professional occupations were often frustrated by limited opportunities before the 1950s.[53]

LOCAL CONTEXTS AND THEIR LIMITATIONS

Table 7 offers a brief comparison of some aspects of Chinese migration to each of the three locations examined in this book. In short, social and occupational status was best in Hawaii and worst in the Midwest. Nonetheless, the population grew most rapidly in Illinois and remained most stag-

Table 7

General Comparison of Peru, Chicago, and Hawaii, 1900–1940

	Peru	Chicago	Hawaii
1900 population (% women)	[10,000]	1,209 (2.1%)[a]	25,767 (13.4%)
1940 population (% women)	10,915 (5%)	2,013 (20.4%)[a]	28,774 (40.4%)
Change in population, 1900–40	Negligible	+166.5%	+11.7%
Immigration, 1907–1924	12,501	?	11,400
Immigration laws	Variable restrictive regulations after 1909; exclusion after 1930	American exclusion laws	American exclusion laws
Occupations (in order of numerical importance)	Shopkeepers Wholesalers Artisans Plantation managers	Laundrymen Restaurant workers Household servants Shopkeepers	Small businessmen Wholesalers Rice growers Professionals
Local status	Objects of violence, marginalized, yet wealthy Chinese were upwardly mobile.	Isolated, marginalized	Relatively wealthy; second to whites in ethnic hierarchy

[a]No data is available for Chinese women in Chicago, so the percentages of women are taken from census figures for Illinois. Over 80 percent of the Chinese in Illinois lived in Chicago.

nant in Hawaii (these figures mask a bulge in Peru in the 1920s), although both were subject to the same immigration laws. The relative proportions of women do not correlate well with any of the other factors, and are probably best understood through a combination of factors, as suggested above.

The occupations of Chinese migrants were shaped by local social structures in all three locations. Racial hierarchies in Peru and Hawaii created a space for mid-level trading and manufacturing activities between the larger enterprises of white elites and the low levels of commercial activity in villages and among the urban poor. As immigrants, Chinese could develop strong economic networks by drawing upon a variety of spatially dispersed connections. This social and economic gap was not so pronounced in the United States (except in the South, where Chinese also acted as small merchants). Relatively large working and middle classes along with competition from other immigrants kept the Chinese from many of these opportunities. On the other hand, the large working population provided a clientele for small service occupations such as laundries and restaurants. The relatively small proportion of Chinese in relation to rest of the local population also meant that these opportunities were more difficult to exhaust than those in Peru and Hawaii.

The precedents of earlier migrants also shaped the activities of later migrants, so that migrants did not always take advantage of any opportunity that might be available. For example, although Chinese in Chicago experienced little of the direct opposition that had caused their predecessors in the Western states to limit themselves to small service occupations, they rarely tested those limits by going beyond those occupations. Migrant elites were invested in perpetuating the local status quo of Chinese migrants. Similarly, the Chinese laborers in nineteenth-century Peru rarely tried to go beyond following Afro-Peruvians and other ex-plantation laborers into life among the coastal poor, leaving the middleman occupations to Italian immigrants. Only with the later arrival of new migrants whose perspectives were shaped by the global networks emanating from the Hong Kong mercantile world did Chinese develop the resources and ambition to exploit the many commercial opportunities in Peru. Finally, the Chinese of Hawaii had become a part of the rising Honolulu middle class by the 1920s, with an economic base in a wide range of mid-level retailing activities. Nonetheless, many of them still believed they could succeed only in a limited range of pursuits that they saw as their ethnic niche, which had been shaped by the global trading and labor-recruiting connections of previous merchants. They generally predicted dire consequences for any Chinese who tried to trade or produce commodities outside of that niche, even though such endeavors would occasionally be quite successful. The Chinese thus helped perpetuate the dominance of white business on the Islands.[54]

Local structures are not sufficient to describe migrant economies and demographics. Chapter 3 describes family strategies in China that aimed at relatively short-term economic gain and encouraged migrants to move where quick profit could be made with relatively low start-up capital. They took advantage of the many Chinese businesses and institutions that were dependent on and perpetuated constant migration. The channels and networks created by these institutions shaped the migrants' adaptation to local economic opportunities, as well as their political and cultural development.

CHAPTER 3

Chinese Diasporas

The period from 1842 to 1949 can loosely be called the era of modern Chinese migration, when movement from South China was shaped by an increasingly lively and industrializing world economy. A global perspective highlights the transnational institutions and diasporic circulation of people, goods, money, and ideas that made up that migration. It is not necessarily a panorama of Chinese migration around the world, but an analysis of the different ways in which the nodes of migrant networks were linked together and how they changed over time.

A history of diasporic Chinese has yet to be written, but a focus on different aspects of diasporic activities—all of which were deeply inter-related with each other and with larger global forces—helps to highlight shifts that came to the forefront at particular historical moments. In rough chronological order, I discuss Chinese migration in terms of labor flows, networks, nationalist flows, and ethnicization. Labor flows from South China expanded rapidly from 1850 to the 1870s, sending workers to newly emergent cash crop economies around the world. These flows were most strongly determined by outside forces, but the Chinese also participated in their creation. The recruitment of laborers also laid the groundwork for networks of business and migration built on the particularistic relationships of family and village. By the turn of the century, most migration moved through these networks, dividing migration into a multitude of distinct grooves that entwined and intersected at key nodes. Nationalist flows describe the politics of defining and mobilizing Chinese identity in terms of modern nation-states, which became increasingly prominent after 1900 and reached a peak in the anti-Japanese war of 1937 to 1945. Ethnicization is the flip side of nationalism, whereby migrants began to interact and identify themselves primarily as part of local non-Chinese societies. This trend has always existed, but became predominant after the Second World War.

THE PEARL RIVER DELTA REGION

The vast majority of Chinese migrants to the Western hemisphere came from one of many villages within a small area of about ten thousand square kilometers on the west side of the Pearl River Delta in Guangdong province. Three or four days of walking, with perhaps a short boat trip or two, could have brought a prospective migrant from one of these villages to embarkation points in Canton, Macao, or Hong Kong (see figure 7). The coastal regions of Fujian province and the Chaozhou and Jiaying areas of eastern Guangdong also supported strong traditions of overseas migration; however, with the exception of a few boatloads of plantation laborers carried to Hawaii and Latin America in the mid-nineteenth century, they have produced few migrants to the Western Hemisphere until recently.

Migrants traveled abroad not merely as Chinese but also as members of a large range of other social identities that sliced the Pearl River Delta landscape. Kinship, village, administrative unit, dialect, and the subethnic distinction between Hakkas and *bendi* were some of the identifications most likely to be evoked by migrants abroad. At home, Pearl River Delta society could be even more complex, with distinctions between residents of hills, flatlands, and reclaimed delta lands; town and village; aboriginal groups and "civilized" Han Chinese; and the "boat people" *(danjia),* who

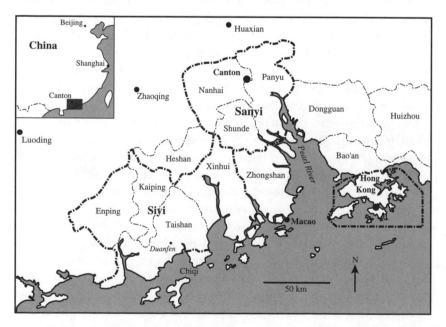

Figure 7   The Pearl River Delta Area

were believed to be an inferior caste and were treated accordingly by both their neighbors and the imperial administration.[1]

Administratively, the core of this region was divided into nine counties: Zhongshan county (known as Xiangshan until 1924) just north of Macao; the counties of Panyu, Shunde, and Nanhai, which surround Canton and are often grouped together as the Sanyi (Three Counties); of Taishan (known as Xinning until the 1930s), Enping, Kaiping, and Xinhui, which are commonly grouped together as the Siyi (Four Counties); and Heshan county, which is sometimes added onto the Siyi, in which case they are known as the Wuyi (Five Counties). Zhongshan includes three nearly unintelligible dialect groups scattered in villages throughout the county: a dialect similar to Chaozhou speech, one more similar to Cantonese, and Hakka. In the middle of the nineteenth century, the Sanyi and the Siyi were somewhat more homogeneous regions in terms of dialect (although still encompassing large variations), and often defined themselves in comparison with each other. The Sanyi was wealthier, with greater proportions of flat and fertile farmlands and higher levels of commercialism and cash cropping. The Siyi was a more impoverished region of hills and small farmers. Accordingly, Sanyi people saw themselves as more cultured and cosmopolitan than the "backwater hicks" of the Siyi. Sanyi speech was often described as a variation of the "standard" Cantonese spoken in Canton city, whereas the varieties of Siyi speech were placed lower on the cultural hierarchy as unintelligible local dialects. This linguistic hierarchy was pervasive enough that many Siyi native place associations abroad held their formal meetings in standard Cantonese rather than in local dialects.[2]

Hakka (*kejia*, literally "guest families") migrants have accounted for at least 15 percent of Chinese migrants to the United States, Hawaii, and Peru. They came mostly from Zhongshan county, but from surrounding areas as well. Hakkas are a dialect group that had emerged in the mountainous Jiaying prefecture of northeast Guangdong by at least the twelfth century. By the sixteenth century they had begun to migrate into enclaves throughout southeast China, mostly in mountainous regions where they opened wasteland and produced forest products for lowland markets. They began to arrive in the prosperous Pearl River Delta area in the late seventeenth and early eighteenth centuries, even moving into the lowlands of Zhongshan county and establishing settlements among the *bendi* (literally "native earth") Differences in language and custom—such as the unbound feet of Hakka women—were reinforced by *bendi* portrayals of themselves as wealthy, civilized lowlanders and of Hakka as untrustworthy, backwards mountain people, and began to harden into antagonistic ethnic boundaries. Official gazetteers often referred to Hakkas as "guest bandits" *(kefei)*, and some *bendi* even claimed they were not Han Chinese at all. Individual families or lineages might occasionally move back and forth between identification as Hakka, *bendi,* or even as an aboriginal group like the Yao, but the categories themselves were drawn with increasing rigidity.[3]

Tensions came to a head in the Siyi during the violent Hakka-*bendi* wars after 1853, which concluded in the 1870s with the resettlement of defeated Hakkas into southwestern Guangdong and the recently created sub-county of Chiqi, carved out of the southern tip of Taishan county (subsequently reintegrated in 1954). The wars also furthered the self-conscious elaboration of a Hakka ethos in Guangdong. Hakka ethnic pride agreed that Hakkas were distinct but described that distinction as a higher level of Chinese cultural orthodoxy, marked by diligence, honesty, origins in north China, and, during the Republic, patriotism and progressiveness. That is to say, they depicted their distinctiveness as a form of ultra-Chineseness, and their marginality was inseparable from the assertion of centralizing standards. Hakka emigrants were especially active in the creation of Hakka institutions and identities that often traced their roots to mythical migrations from North China. The historical emergence of the Hakkas, entwined as it is with migration, economic forces, and ideological struggles, offers a good prelude to similar processes that would take place among the migrants who spread out from the delta in increasing numbers after 1850.

Origins of Modern Chinese Migration

Gradual changes across the South Pacific and Southeast Asia over the nineteenth century shaped the emergence of "modern" Chinese diasporas built around the expansion of capitalism, nationalism, and modernist ideologies. These changes included increased European colonial penetration into Southeast Asia, the expansion of global markets and economic networks throughout the Pacific, and the displacement of the Fujianese junk trade by European sailing vessels (managed by both Europeans and non-Europeans) in the first half of the century, followed by the relatively inexpensive steamship lines that helped increase and channel the flows of Chinese migrants in the second half of the century.[4]

Within these larger trends, the establishment of a British colony at Hong Kong and, to a lesser extent, the creation of treaty ports in Xiamen (Amoy) and Shantou (Swatow) on the South China coast had the most direct effect on the shape and volume of Chinese migration.[5] First occupied by the British in January 1841, the island of Hong Kong was officially ceded in the Treaty of Nanjing in 1842, a result of the Opium War between Britain and China. The significance of the Opium War has often been interpreted as marking the penetration and disruption of a traditional rural economy by Western capitalism. Much local research argues, however, that the depth and effects of this penetration beyond treaty ports varied greatly from place to place, and that these effects were not felt immediately but as a gradual series of adjustments over decades.[6] The most immediate effect of the Opium War on the Pearl River Delta region north of Hong Kong was the shift in foreign trade to newly opened treaty ports further north on the coast, resulting in a short depression (further influenced by a depression in Britain) in an already complex, commercialized, and outward-looking economy.[7] Of more long-term significance was the creation of Hong Kong as an outpost of British imperialism, closely linked to an expanding Pacific economy. Hong Kong and the treaty ports became portals through which local merchants could more easily search out and link up with economic opportunities, and facilitate access to laborers from South China. Before the 1850s, Pearl River Delta merchants had much experience with foreigners but, unlike the merchants of Fujian (who had managed much of the Canton trade through the early eighteenth century), tended to stay at home rather than travel overseas in search of profit. The establishment of Hong Kong marked the beginning of a decisive shift away from the Fujian merchant networks and Hakka miners from western Guangdong as the main axes of Chinese migration and toward Hong Kong as the primary node through which Chinese overseas migration increased to unprecedented volumes.

Migration abroad from South China was just one stream in a larger pattern of movement to cities, frontier areas, and rural areas throughout China, and into northern lands like Mongolia, Siberia, and Manchuria.[8] A Cantonese villager was just as likely to migrate to the local county town, Canton, Shanghai, or some other urban center as to go abroad. Similarly, as villagers from relatively poor counties like Kaiping in Guangdong province migrated abroad in search of profit, so even more impoverished villagers from further inland would migrate to Kaiping to work as wage laborers on the lands left behind.[9] In terms of the institutions and structural forces that shaped migration, the border of the Chinese empire may not be the most useful point at which to make a distinction between different kinds of migration. That is to say, flows of domestic and international migration shifted within the context of the same general forces. Institutions and networks channeled migrants and adapted to new situations whether in Canton or San Francisco, and economic shifts on a global scale over the course of the nineteenth century were responsible for a gradual shift in the main streams of Chinese migration away from rural and frontier areas to port cities in China and throughout the world.

For the purposes of this book, however, we want to understand the increasing orientation of migration from South China to points outside of China after 1850. Explanations that draw attention to the mid-century rebellions and worsening land-man ratios as push factors generally fail to account for the particularities in time and place of this migration.[10] The great increase of the Chinese population over the eighteenth century fails to explain why emigration from South China, and from the Pearl River Delta region in particular, did not take off until the 1850s and continued to grow in the late nineteenth century as political and economic stability returned and the population remained level.[11] Attention to the correlation of regional economic cycles with migration can provide more help in understanding long-term flows of emigration. During the century-long economic downswing of the Pearl River Delta area after the 1830s, Hong Kong was a portal to the increasingly lively economy over much of the Pacific. On the other hand, western Guangdong and Fujian provinces experienced an economic upswing over this same period. Migration also increased from these areas, although not to the extent that it did from the Canton area. Thus, some correlation of emigration with economic cycles seems probable but is not sufficient to understand why Chinese increasingly chose to migrate overseas at this time.

Similarly, although most of China experienced violent turmoil from the 1850s through the 1870s, other regions of China did not produce significant numbers of overseas migrants. The Red Turban rebellion, the Hakka-*bendi* wars of the Pearl River Delta area, and the other lineage and village feuds throughout South China in this period were milder in their destructive force than what was taking place elsewhere.[12] Perhaps only the laborers recruited through deception and kidnapping in the early years of the labor trade can be linked to social unrest. Even then, access to opportunities through Hong Kong and the treaty ports was most responsible for channeling local restlessness and lack of opportunity into concentrated overseas flows. Unrest and scarcity of local opportunities existed in South China, but, as we shall see below, emigration as a family strategy depended more on stability, precedent, and opportunity than on disorder and poverty. That the burst in overseas migration during the second half of the nineteenth century should flow through Hong Kong, Xiamen, and Shantou rather than northern treaty ports like Shanghai or Tianjin was a result of the connections and networks established through a long tradition of migration and exchange in the Pacific that gave people in South

China the experience and means to take advantage of opportunities presented by a changing Pacific economy.

LABOR FLOWS

One of the most immediate effects of the establishment of Hong Kong was the rise in Chinese labor migration over the subsequent four decades. Chinese had for centuries been working throughout Southeast Asia in mines and agricultural enterprises, recruited and organized through a wide variety of debt bondage and profit-sharing schemes.[13] A few attempts had even been made by non-Chinese to import laborers to plantations in Trinidad and Brazil in the first half of the nineteenth century. After the middle of the century, however, this labor migration began to increase. Chinese migration to the British colony of Singapore—which was both a major point of transshipment and a free trade entrepot that had already attracted Chinese living in Southeast Asia—rose quickly in the 1840s. The recruitment of laborers to Cuba after 1847 and to Peru after 1849 would, over the next two decades, result in the first significant flows of indentured Chinese laborers outside of Southeast Asia. In these two cases, the rise of the Chinese labor trade was closely tied to the gradual demise of African slavery and the search by plantation owners for a viable alternative.[14] In a more general sense, this increase in labor migration was tied to the expansion of world markets into the Pacific. Thus, labor could be used with increasing profit in agricultural and mining enterprises even in places that were not compensating for the demise of slavery.[15] This more general development was closely linked to the establishment of Hong Kong as an outpost of British imperialism and a convenient site from which to escape the restrictions of the Chinese government against the recruitment of laborers. Some of the earliest attempts at labor recruitment in the 1850s by planters from Peru, Cuba, and Hawaii had been in Xiamen, but local resistance quickly turned recruitment efforts to the Pearl River Delta as a better base for such activities.[16]

The bulk of this labor migration was controlled by Chinese. In the villages of South China, Chinese "crimps," paid by the head for each laborer they could recruit, used a variety of means to entice potential migrants, including kinship networks, material advances, promises of fortunes for the taking, payment of gambling debts, deceit, the purchase of prisoners taken in feuds, and kidnapping.[17] Peru and Cuba were the only places for which non-Chinese controlled recruitment at every level above the village. In much of Southeast Asia, Chinese controlled the organization of labor all the way to the production and marketing of goods. The rise in Chinese labor migration was linked with the expansion of the world economy, but not only in terms of chattel shipped around in accordance with Western needs. Chinese actively participated in the production of capitalist expansion in the Pacific. At times, Chinese interests could even block Western needs. For example, entrenched Southeast Asian recruiting rings and officials opposed to Western-dominated recruiting forced a British attempt to recruit laborers for South Africa in 1904 to relocate its operations from Guangdong to northern China.[18]

Contracted Chinese labor migration peaked in the 1870s, although it has continued in some form or another to this day. More than any other aspect of Chinese migration, labor movement has already received much attention from a global perspective.[19] Scholarly interest in this migration, however, views it primarily as an aspect of the expansion of Western capitalism, and little attention has been given to Chinese participation in its production or to how this migration led to the creation of further migrant networks. In fact, labor recruitment often led only to the temporary or permanent relocation of people and did not necessarily result in any permanent structures of migration. Extreme examples of labor migration as temporary relocation were the transportation of 62,000 laborers from the northern provinces of Shandong and Zhili to the South African gold mines in the first decade of the twentieth century, and of nearly 140,000 to France to build roads and dig graves and trenches during the First World War. Nearly all of these laborers were returned to China after the completion of their tasks, leaving behind few, if any, lasting structures of migration.[20] An example of permanent relocation appears in nineteenth-century Peru, where Chinese who had finished their indentures were left isolated and impoverished, with few active connections to China. They tended to take Spanish names, intermarry, and gradually integrate into the coastal lower classes, creating no strong transnational links.

The earliest laborers brought to any region tended to be either temporary or unable to maintain transnational connections, but they often laid the basis for more stable diasporic flows. Some would become merchants and craftsmen, and others would provide the connections and clientele to attract new merchants and craftsmen, who would, in turn, create a much wider and self-perpetuating system for the circulation of goods, money, information, and people. As these larger networks became established, migration in order to labor became less an end in itself and more of a first step in the hopes that after the contract was completed, or debts repaid, a real fortune could be made. Through Chinese involvement in managing the labor trade, global networks of migration begin to emerge, rather than just movement and relocation. The profit to be gained by organizing and transporting laborers facilitated the increased power of a diaspora elite that had a direct interest in the continued circulation and relocation of people. The greater the control of non-Chinese interests over migration, the greater the likelihood that labor migration would result only in dispersion rather than the emergence of continued migration and transnational connections.

DIASPORIC NETWORKS

The labor diaspora most clearly overlaps and provides groundwork for the network diaspora in the process of recruitment. Networks are the transnational institutions, organizations, and personal connections that made migration into a viable economic strategy and stable system for the circulation of goods, people, information, and profit. If labor needs drew increasing numbers of Chinese overseas after the middle of the nineteenth century, the networks created by these laborers and recruiters perpetuated migration through the first half of the twentieth century, long after the laboring opportunities had been greatly curtailed by exclusionary laws and the recruitment of workers from other areas. These networks not only facilitated and directed movement, but also depended on the continued generation of movement as a source of profit.[21]

Chinese participation in the gold rushes to California and Australia in the 1850s was even greater than the contemporaneous growth in labor migration and even more dependent on access to world communication channels that flowed through Hong Kong. As many as thirty thousand Chinese migrated to San Francisco in 1852 (*total* emigration from Hong Kong would not reach that level again until the relaxation of emigrant shipping regulations to Singapore in the mid-1870s), and migration continued at several thousand a year to California and Australia in the 1850s.[22] Gold rush migration exemplified the credit-ticket system, in which labor and network migration become indistinguishable. Credit-ticket migrants arrived abroad indebted for the cost of their passage. This debt was transferred from transportation brokers to employers, and various migrant institutions or companies often assisted with the movement and supervision of these human investments.[23] This system was clearly a means of mobilizing labor, but it did not depend on indentures (although contracts for debt repayment were still common) and the extreme methods of physical force that characterized indentured migration. The legacy of the credit-ticket system was also more long-lasting than indentured labor in that even when the institutionalized practice of credit-ticket migration died out in a particular locality, the networks and organizations built on kinship and native place still persisted and helped channel further flows of chain migration.

Transnational Families

Families were one of the most basic institutions making up migrant networks. Migration from South China was rarely a trailblazing endeavor on the part of an individual migrant. He quite likely followed in the footsteps of an uncle, father, grandfather, or even great-grandfather who had made the trip before him. Over generations, individuals from such migrant families may have been born in China and yet lived most of their lives abroad, returning to China only long enough to inseminate their wives and create the next link in the chain. Personal motivations often had a role in the departure of an individual: some boys longed for adventure, some were piqued by the sight of a returned villager flashing his accumulated wealth, some were trying to evade pillaging bandits or possible conscription by local armies, some wanted to escape an unpleasant family situation or a wife they did not like, and others just could not stand the idea of farming.[24] Whatever the personal ambitions of a migrant, his family often allowed him no choice, as migration was just one of a variety of investment strategies designed to keep the family line solvent. A prudent and fertile family might develop a safely diversified portfolio by assigning one son to work the family fields, one to hire out to the neighbors as a wage earner, one to study for an official position, one to take up some business opportunity in a nearby town, and others to seek fortunes in distant lands like Canada or Thailand. One of them was bound to bring success and wealth back to the family, or at least a steady stream of support.[25]

The common depiction of Chinese migrant communities as bachelor communities is only accurate if we insist that families must be geographically unified nuclear units of cohabiting spouses and children. More important for many Chinese families was the maintenance of a patriline through time, from dead ancestors to descendants not yet born. Earning the material resources to maintain and extend this patriline and its physical manifestation as altar and household was often a primary motivation for migration. Many migrants left their villages only weeks after having married, usually just long enough to assure that their brides were carrying children. Many others made special trips back to China after a few years abroad, especially to take a wife and start producing descendants. As long as the migrant and his wife continued to share the same kitchen as his brothers and parents, they continued to be a part of the extended family, no matter how long he had been away and what his family situation overseas was. Because of his income, the distant migrant was often the main decision maker of the family, even if not entitled to such status by seniority. When local violence led to China-based family members relocating in a county seat, Canton, or Hong Kong, remittances sent by migrants often assured that the family did not become permanently scattered. A formal division was the only way to break up the stem family, although a migrant was never excused from the wider responsibilities of the patrilineal descent line.[26] If division had taken place and the migrant moved his wife and children overseas, he would still often maintain a house in his village in case of a possible return. He would even spend money maintaining and improving the house, looking to impress fellow migrants abroad as much as people in the village.[27] Like the family, the village also became a transnational entity.

Migrant households could also be amenable to the establishment of more than one localized nucleus. When allowed by local sentiment and legislation, Chinese would occasionally form alliances with local non-Chinese women. Many of the local women married by Chinese, as well as wives brought in from China, were actually second wives. Polygamy was practiced by Chinese men born outside of China as well. If the migrant's first marriage occurred abroad, relatives at home might not even consider it to be a real marriage and still make plans to acquire a primary bride in the village. The primary wife usually remained in China, maintaining the household and raising children born of any of her husband's alliances. Some of these primary wives even encouraged the marriage of their husbands to local women, because the men were then more likely to feel the weight of their responsibilities and less inclined to gamble, visit prostitutes, or otherwise dissipate their earnings in the recreations common to men without families.[28]

Alliances with non-Chinese women tended to incorporate the women into migrant networks as much as they integrated the grooms into local society, and not all non-Chinese wives realized what they were getting into. Reports of Peruvian women begging in the streets of Hong Kong in order to earn passage back to Peru caused repeated scandals in early-twentieth-century Lima.[29] They all told the same story of marrying a Chinese man in Peru, accompanying him to China, and then being left there as a secondary wife when the husband returned abroad. Most of the women claimed to have been impressed by how diligent and considerate their husbands had been at home. They traveled to China knowing nothing of the other wife, or wives, fully expecting the same favorable treatment to continue, only to find themselves suddenly at the bottom of a spousal pecking order with no sympathy from their husbands. Hawaiian women, coming from a stronger tradition of multiple-partner alliances, seemed to be more open to the Chinese family situations, occasionally becoming close friends with the primary wife after moving to China. The most significant problem in Hawaii, at least according to Hawaiian missionaries, was the abandonment of wives and children in Hawaii by men returning to China.[30]

Migration was not the only contingency that might lead to dispersed families. In silk-producing areas of the Pearl River Delta area south of Canton, the custom of delayed transfer marriage often resulted in wives not moving into their husbands' households for years after marriage. When they had access to the financial resources to support themselves, many wives tried to make this arrangement permanent, usually buying a secondary wife for their husband as compensation. Nonetheless, for the welfare of their souls after death, few women wanted to avoid marriage completely, often moving into their affinal home only when death was imminent in order to assure that the tablet containing their soul would be set on the family altar and properly worshiped. Other strategies to circumvent the necessity of a living husband included marrying the ghosts of dead men, arranging for their natal families to worship their tablet after death, or joining spinster houses that would provide the necessary worship. Some of these unmarried women followed the examples of their brothers by migrating to Canton, Hong Kong, and Singapore to work and send money back to their natal families.[31]

Tempting as it is, no direct connection can be made between these customs and the practice of dispersed migrant families. Delayed transfer marriage was restricted to very localized areas in which silk production provided an independent source of income for women. Moreover, from the perspective of the bride, delayed transfer marriage was the inverse of life as a migrant wife. A delayed transfer bride was determined to live apart from her in-laws, while the bride of a migrant lived with and served her in-laws even while her husband was absent. Nonetheless, the practice of delayed transfer marriage still highlights how integration into a family line was often a more important concern than the cohabitation of geographically localized nuclear families. Ancestor worship, centered on the family altars and graves in the home village, was an important medium through which to fulfill the duties of filial morality and provide for the comfort of the soul after death. Many of the first migrant associations provided for the bones of the dead to be shipped back to families in China or at least to be worshiped with rudimentary sacrifices if they remained interred abroad. Even Catholic Chinese in Peru had their bones sent back when possible, despite the objections of the archbishop of Lima, who had his own fears that the bodies would not be properly cared for in China.[32]

While families often provided the framework for migration, they could also be changed by migration. Many families considered the possibility of access to migration privileges when arranging marriage alliances for their children. Migration to Peru, the United States, and Hawaii after annexation was mostly possible through access to proper documentation that certified close kinship to certain classes of residents. False documents and the fraudulent transfer of valid documentation had a high market value in China. Using such documents was much less risky when the overseas resident sponsoring the migration was also a relative, and they were often provided as dowry or bride-price. Transferring such documents to people linked by marriage bonds meant a higher likelihood that they would provide more opportunities for further migration after the migrant established himself, thus strengthening interaction and bonds between affinal families.

Affinal ties were further strengthened through the provision of employment, assistance, advice, and companionship abroad. Such cooperation with affinal kin was much more common overseas than in China.[33] Women living abroad also took advantage of the absence of cohabiting parents-in-law to redefine their families, often maintaining a remarkable amount of contact with their natal families. Chinese family histories from Hawaii often note how immigrant mothers tended to be the most memorable and prominent figures at home, often keeping business records and educating the family while the fathers concentrated on work. At times they even ran separate household economies by raising and selling pigs, chickens, or eggs, or by pocketing extra profit when they sold something at a higher price than their husbands would have expected. They used the money to provide dowries for their daughters, to support their children's education, to pay for their own visits to China (during which they may have bought jewelry or other goods which could be resold abroad), and to invest in property that provided for them as widows.[34] Similarly, children in China usually had little contact with their maternal relatives, but those born abroad tended to think of family as both the patriline and matriline, perhaps even emphasizing the latter because of the influence of the mother. In 1937, Clarence Glick made a list of relatives (excluding grandparents) counted by thirty-six Hawaii-born Chinese. The list included 358 paternal relatives in Hawaii and 127 in China, compared to 528 maternal relatives in Hawaii and only 87 in China.[35]

Transnational Villages

Migration as an economic strategy could go beyond single families to incorporate entire villages and lineages. In some villages, all the able-bodied men were sent overseas, leaving behind agricultural fields gone wild, and women, children, and elderly people living on remittances. A village two kilometers down the road without any significant advantages or disadvantages in local economic circumstances may have produced no emigrant families at all.[36] Some villages even established schools to train children in knowledge like language, geography, and bookkeeping, subjects that would be useful in their future lives abroad. The remittances might be used to maintain traditional rituals and lifestyle, or to develop a local commercial or political monopoly for a particular lineage. This occupational specialization in migration was similar to that of other villages and regions which became famous for producing furniture, edible delicacies, stonecutters, officials, generals, and prostitutes.[37]

Chinese migrants throughout the world were people frequently on the move, making liberal use of telegraphs, mail, railways, and shipping lines to keep in touch with fellow-migrants and families.[38] Letters, sent both through regular mail services and put in the hands of fellow migrants making a trip home or abroad, were crucial for maintaining migrant networks and for reminding migrants of their responsibilities and the reasons why they had emigrated. Most migrants, however, failed to tell villagers at home how difficult their lives were abroad. Rather, they devoted much time at home to conspicuous consumption, providing entertainment and banquets for friends and villages, renovating their homes, giving gifts, showing off the sewing machines, radios, and cameras they brought for their families, and the gold watches, diamond rings, and suits of fine material they had acquired for themselves. Such behavior was intended as much to impress fellow migrants abroad, who were sure to hear of it through gossip, as to impress villagers in China. They also cultivated a reputation of success and wealth to be found abroad that helped perpetuate the cycle of migration. Most young men considering migration to the United States knew that they would probably work in an *yiguan* (clothes establishment), but very few had any idea that this meant a hard life of washing clothes rather than selling or making them.[39]

Most migrants recreated their villages as networks of mutual supervision and support abroad by preferring to work with kin, buying food and supplies from them, borrowing money from them, and selling their businesses to them. This often limited their horizons, but it also provided for the wide circulation of scarce resources. Not only could migrants apply to kinsmen for loans, but kinsmen were nearly obligated to provide them if possible. Debts could be carried for several years, and a single sum of money often circulated to provide start-up capital for several individuals.[40] These networks could be widely dispersed around the globe. Address books carried by Chinese arrested by immigration officials in Chicago listed individuals and companies located in New York, Montreal, Seattle, California, Vancouver, Alaska, Havana, Mexico, and Hong Kong.[41] Like the family, the village also became a transnational entity.

The mechanisms of trust and supervision that made up these networks could also expand beyond the reinforcement of links with fellow villagers. In 1904, the Chinese managers of a boarding house near a Chicago area race track claimed a "wide acquaintance amongst horsemen, jockeys, book-makers, bettors, and others who follow the races" and told immigration officials how they kept tabs on people who owed them money:

> I have known my customers for years, and know their circumstances.
> When I need money, I know to whom I can go and collect on account,
> at any time, and I do so. . . . I keep track of them in their travels around
> the country, and as they improve their financial conditions from time
> to time, I shall be able to collect on the accounts, as I verily believe,
> for they are people who are likely to make money, and if I am here to
> attend to those matters, I can then induce them to pay me. . . . When
> by chance I meet people who can give me information about those
> above-named who owe me money, I shall make inquiries, and when I
> learn of one who is able to pay all or part of what he owes me, I shall
> manage to collect in some way.[42]

Similarly, a Chinese in Vancouver interviewed in 1924 depicted both the flexibility and the disciplined insularity of these networks when he remarked that "[the Chinese] place no confidence in anything anyone says unless they are Chinese. But if a friend of theirs tells them that you are all right, they accept you entirely. They never question you; they are very friendly. Canadians who wanted to do anything could do it easily if they just went at it right."[43] Villagers and kinsmen may have grown up deeply embedded in these relationships of trust and cooperation, but life was not forever limited to the social arena described by these childhood bonds. People could behave so as to lose that trust, just as outsiders could gain access through appropriate behavior. The networks were not bounded, but gradually melded into the surrounding society.

Such a context makes it somewhat irrelevant to ask what a particular migrant's personal ambition was, whether he intended to settle abroad like an immigrant or to return to his home like a sojourner. A migrant had to mobilize the resources to which he had access, and these resources came hand in hand with social expectations and demands. To gain access to the resources of the migrant community, an individual had to live up to the standards that maintained his honor and the honor of his kinsmen, such as maintaining an active interest in the village, living up to his business deals, and having a wife who behaved virtuously. Not all migrants lived up to these demands, but few did not feel their pull. Even Chinese not born in the village could find themselves enmeshed in these far-flung networks. In 1922, a California-born Chinese accompanied his father back to China for the first time. Before leaving, he had told his American girlfriend that he would definitely return to the United States within six months, still single. After arrival in China he was forced to write otherwise:

> But it was all useless for my refusal, and everyone was a stranger and
> against me, too, on the point of marriage and religion in this village
> away in the inland of China. Had I known the conditions that exist in
> our village, I would not have gone into the tangle. But it was rather
> hard for me to avoid it, for I must accompany my dad to his destina-
> tion. . . . In those few days my life companion was fixed for me by my
> folks before I knew anything about it. . . . I got to do it, for to refuse
> will cause trouble on both sides.[44]

This was a young man who had largely identified himself as an American, yet he was unable to avoid a future that lay far beyond the scope of his intentions and perceptions. These networks were both powerful sources of opportunity and burdensome responsibilities.

Hong Kong

Chinese Hong Kong was a city built largely on an economy of migration. Institutions and businesses in Hong Kong were links in a worldwide chain of services that supported migration and made it into a viable economic strategy. By the end of the nineteenth century, Hong Kong was more important as a hub for these networks than as a center of labor recruitment. Chinese Hong Kong was free from the exactions and corruption of Chinese officialdom, and it was underwritten by a British legal, administrative, and commercial infrastructure designed to promote free trade and access to the world economy. Thousands of business establishments in Hong

Kong, calling themselves letter offices *(xinju)*, banks *(yinhao)*, Golden Mountain Firms *(jinshanzhuang)*, and companies *(gongsi)*, specialized in the movement of goods, people, and money between China and locations around the world. Many of them maintained exclusive connections with stores and banks in China and abroad, sometimes as administratively integrated branches, but usually through less formalized connections involving kinship and village ties. Some of these businesses were financed as small partnerships and others by capital from larger companies, surname associations, and lineages both abroad and in China. Lineages in the villages and migrant associations abroad rarely took direct responsibility for their management, but the overlap in official personnel and funds could be significant.[45]

Perhaps the most competitive and profitable service provided through these businesses was the movement of people. All aspects of migration were commoditized: steamer tickets, false identities, access to consuls and visas, successful medical exams, citizenships, human smuggling opportunities, and witnesses who could claim to be a migrant's mother or to have known him when he was a babe in arms. Migrants in the United States often claimed that anybody with enough money to give judges, lawyers, smugglers, and interpreters could eventually manage to get around the exclusion laws.[46] Many Hong Kong businesses had employees and associates in local consular offices who helped expedite customs and migration formalities.[47] These connections with officials and information about changing immigration procedures and border security were easily translatable into cash or favors and jealously guarded against competitors. For migrants who could not afford the fees, bribes, and surcharges attached to these requirements, the firms in Hong Kong would also provide credit. Larger firms even provided dormitories and waiting rooms. These businesses also served as links to employment opportunities abroad, which both assisted the migrants and helped the lenders to keep an eye on their investments. Thus, a well-integrated, transnational business network could simultaneously stake a claim in the lucrative migrant traffic, block access by competitors, and assure that their affiliated interests overseas would never lack for manpower and goods. Western companies that operated, chartered, and provisioned ships also shared in the profits of continued migration.[48] These services were essential to the maintenance of geographically extensive migrant networks that could persist for decades and over generations. Without the services offered by businesses and associations in Hong Kong and the treaty ports, migration would rarely have been feasible or lucrative as a survival strategy for a household. At the same time, movement itself became a self-perpetuating source of profit, and an interest to be defended, above and beyond any other benefits that might be gained from migration.

Transnational Institutions

In Chinese migrant communities around the world, these networks were institutionalized as sworn brotherhoods, mercantile companies, and surname and native place associations. These associations called upon a variety of symbols, such as ritual oaths and bonds of kinship based on distant or mythical ancestors, to legitimize themselves and create lines of trust and control among their members. In turn, the very institutionalization of these symbols reinforced their significance as concrete concerns shaping the lives and culture of migrants.

In their smallest and least formalized manifestation, overseas organizations were gatherings of men from the same village and lineage in China who came together out of a sense of friendship, familiarity, and mutual responsibility that had been strengthened in the context of shared experiences abroad. These gatherings were often associated with a store or a couple of rented rooms, providing a place to stay during visits and hard times, remittance and letter-writing services, supplies needed by members in their work and daily life, and a chance for gossip and socializing. The members might look out for each other by sending a man to check up on a fellow who had not come to town for several weeks from his distant workplace or to fill in for a migrant who was unable to attend to his work. They also created an atmosphere of peer pressure and ostracism for members who patronized another store or did not live up to their financial or moral responsibilities.[49]

Village, district, and surname associations were more formalized institutions, with officers, a charter, and, if possible, a meeting hall and altar. Many such associations developed out of smaller gatherings, whereas others were incorporated from scratch, often with the support of wealthier migrants whose interests they supported. The functions of these institutions varied but could include the usual mutual aid and mediating services, acting as vehicles of formal representation in the face of the larger migrant and non-migrant communities, coordinating fund-raising for charitable projects like hospitals or passage to China for indigent migrants, providing constituencies for socially ambitious individuals, and creating platforms to facilitate the organization of labor and credit networks. The most powerful institutions could even establish and enforce business regulations. The authority of these institutions often extended back to China, where they could be called upon to mediate and intervene in village affairs.

Although the bonds of kin and native place were appealed to in creating these associations, larger associations extended membership to people who would have been strangers in China. In the end, migrant demographics and local political interests tended to shape the scope of membership more than alleged ties of common sentiment. Many associations even found ways to expand beyond a single surname, such as the Longgang Associations, which have appeared around the world as an alliance of the Guan, Liu, Zhang, and Zhao families, based on the oath of the Peach Garden sworn by four characters of the same names in a popular novel, *The Romance of the Three Kingdoms*. Similarly, the geographic divisions that defined native place associations were extremely flexible. The native place associations (often called *huiguan*) of nineteenth-century San Francisco were notorious for fighting, dividing, and fusing due to struggles between families, cliques, and classes. In 1862, the Deng and Hu families of Kaiping and Enping counties seceded from the Siyi *huiguan* to form the Hehe *huiguan*. Later, the numerically preponderant residents of Taishan county also broke off from the Siyi *huiguan* to form the Ningyang *huiguan*, except for the Yu family from Taishan, which joined the Hehe. By 1905 almost all the members of the Hehe *huiguan* were either Yus from Taishan or Wangs from Kaiping.[50]

Smaller village and surname associations often incorporated themselves as subdivisions of larger associations, which then became excellent sites for the mediation of disputes between members of different smaller organizations.[51] Many migrant communities produced a representative umbrella organization, often called a *zhonghua huiguan*, or Consolidated Chinese Benevolent Association (CCBA). Sometimes they were organized under the influence of Chinese diplomatic officials and performed many of the functions of a consulate. In situations where local government objected to the political organization of local Chinese, such associations were formed under the auspices of a hospital, school, or other charitable organization, such as the Tung Wah Hospital in Hong Kong. After 1906, the Chinese government encouraged the creation of Chambers of Commerce, some of which competed or collaborated with CCBAs to become central nodes of migrant communities. In all cases, these organizations presented themselves as forums for the resolution of major conflicts and as institutions which could represent the entire migrant community in the face of non-Chinese society. Membership usually had some pretensions to encompassing a cross section of the local migrant community, either through a formal system of representation by native place and other powerful organizations or through inclusion on an individual basis of men widely recognized to be at the nodes of important social networks.

Migrant organizations have also been created around a large variety of other pretexts, including sworn brotherhoods, political parties, chambers of commerce, cemetery societies, religious groups, civic organizations, labor organizations, guilds, and literary clubs, some of which are discussed in more detail in chapter 4. Taken as a whole, they were the fabric within which migrant social life took place. In Paul Siu's work, the man without an association was the most isolated of men, and men who belonged to small associations were men without access to power.

These associations have often been depicted from nation-based perspectives either as mutual aid organizations that eased the transition into a new society, or as conservative associations concerned with the maintenance of traditional ways. In practice, these associations played both of these roles and more. They were also the means by which migration became a transnational field of activity.[52] Locally, they made up the structure through which migrants could make business connections, have business deals guaranteed, give and receive favors, and build prestige. In China, they were institutions through which migrants could protect their families, contribute to their villages, and build their status within the village. They were also the vehicles through which funds could be raised to move families to Canton or Hong Kong when bandits threatened, to establish schools, build walls around villages, raise militia, establish village industries and commercial monopolies, rebuild ancestral halls, and re-edit genealogies. At the county level, they could work with or put pressure on local home-county governments; their activities ranged from getting local authorities to help chase down and prosecute embezzling business partners who had fled back to China to sponsoring candidates for election to local assemblies. Beyond the county, they were the infrastructure by which funds were solicited for reformist and revolutionary parties, disaster relief in China and abroad, the war against Japan, public works projects, rural reconstruction projects, and charities.[53]

Hsiao Teh-seng's Correspondence

The correspondence of Hsiao Teh-seng is an excellent illustration of how networks could shape the life of an individual migrant. Hsiao arrived in Chicago in the summer of 1921, leaving a wife, two daughters, and a son in China. His younger brother, Teh-him, was already in Minneapolis, and many other relatives resided in the Midwest, Mexico, and Cuba.[54] Most of

Hsiao Teh-seng's written correspondence, however, was with his elder brother, Hsiao Teh-sin, who had lived in America previously and returned to China. Within weeks after Teh-seng's arrival in America, Teh-sin was already asking him to take care of some financial matters he had left unresolved there, including the collection of an unpaid debt from one cousin, with which he would repay money owed to another. Teh-sin also had opinions about how Teh-seng should take care of his own affairs. Referring to information provided by Teh-him about laundries for sale by clansmen who were returning to China, Teh-sin wrote, "You wanted to buy Uncle Sai-kai's business. I heard this business is pretty good; it consists of all kinds of machines. In Teh-gun's place, there is only one washing tub. You have to do it by hand with the rest. Upon reading this letter, please buy Sai-kai's business instead." [55] In the same letter, Teh-sin also asked that Teh-seng urge their kin in Chicago to buy stocks in the local newspaper in China, promising to list contributors' names prominently in its pages. His letters also referred frequently to money needed to edit the clan genealogy and have it printed up "Western-fashion."

Teh-sin did not expect only handouts and donations. By November he was urging Teh-seng to invest in a scheme he had worked up to manufacture hosiery out of imported material and to send some cloth samples. When soliciting investments, he appealed not only to pecuniary interests but also to honor and intelligence, writing of an aunt who had invested some of her remittance money that "she is a he-man-woman. To compare her with those foolish 'Golden Mountain Men' who only buy land in the village, she has far more brains indeed." [56] He said the factory would be an excellent occupation for village women who were then engaged in the rather unprofitable activity of making uniforms for a local army in Canton.

The variety of needs for money in China seemed endless. In late November, Teh-sin's concubine had been kidnapped by bandits, and he needed $20,000 for ransom. [57] In December he wrote about the need for money to purchase a clan house in Canton, as the young clan members studying there had no place to stay during their vacations. "We are indeed losing face. . . . Please do not regard this as an unimportant thing." [58] Cousin Tah-wo wanted to purchase a son, and Teh-sin said it could easily be arranged if Teh-seng sent two hundred dollars. He also complained that money sent back to the family had all been taken by "Wu's mother," and he hoped that next time Teh-seng could send the money directly to him. In the summer of 1922, bandits attacked the village, and most of the families moved to Hong Kong. Teh-sin urged Teh-seng to round up contributions from the other kinsmen in Chicago, Minneapolis, and Duluth to build a wall around the village. "The village's life and death is depending on you. Take note of this." [59] In August, he pressured Teh-seng to get the kinsmen to invest in a cement factory in which he had an interest.

Teh-seng and the other relatives in America had a hard time keeping up with the demands. By the end of 1922, Teh-sin wondered when the money would arrive: "I wrote to you, but you seem to pay little attention to me." [60] Although Teh-seng was an official in the Hsiao surname association in Chicago, he found it difficult to milk contributions from the members, particularly those from other villages. They delayed in the contributions to the Canton clan house by demanding that the contribution books be sent to Chicago to make sure that their donations were recorded properly. The clansmen in Duluth justified their delays in contributing by accusing the Chicago kinsmen of delaying even more. Teh-seng blamed this situation of mistrust and evasion on "some of the low-down, undisciplined individuals in our clan." [61] By 1924, clan members in China, the United States, and Australia were making direct accusations of inappropriate use of village funds which had been sent back. They blamed Teh-sin for not making sufficient monetary efforts to get cousin Ying Sheung out of jail, saying he had spent the money collected for this purpose on his own household. In Chicago, the blame fell on Teh-seng's head, because, in addition to being Teh-sin's brother, he had also been responsible for soliciting and transmitting the money.

At the same time, relatives in China were asking Teh-seng to extend his moral influence over their family members in Chicago; one man asked Teh-seng to convince his older brother not to waste all of his money on aviation school. Other family members down on their luck in the Midwest asked for assistance in paying back their debts. Teh-seng's youngest daughter had no trust in the self-control of her new husband, who had emigrated to Chicago but had not written back for four years. She asked Teh-seng to watch over him, writing, "Please do not have the idea that he is only your half son and so you do not have to bother about him. Please tell me something about what he is doing." [62] Teh-seng's nephew asked for help in his plan to migrate to America to learn English, writing that, "I am sorry to say that I, your nephew, am one who has no special ability, and cannot be expected to accomplish anything great, . . . but my ambition is still big." He thought that America would offer not only a chance to realize his ambitions but also to wash away the "humiliation of an embezzling uncle." [63] On his part, the embezzling uncle Teh-sin was also looking to Teh-seng to help relieve his humiliation, requesting that one thousand dollars be sent to cover the equivalent that cousin Teh-him (not their younger brother) had entrusted him to transmit to another cousin, but which he had used for his own purposes instead. Teh-sin was quite indignant at being criticized for his treatment of Teh-him, writing that "it was I who looked after his brother and siblings [while he was in America]. I bought a nephew for him. . . . I now cut off my brotherly sentiment with that son of a bitch forever." [64]

Teh-seng's wife and children were of little help in easing the pressure. They sent frequent requests for money to help with household expenses and provide gifts for relatives getting married. His older daughter wanted a gold watch, complaining that "big uncle's daughters have gold watches, but we do not. . . . My venerable one [her father] can use his own judgment whether jade should be inlaid or not." [65] His wife was particularly unsympathetic to Teh-seng's predicaments and had her own opinions about what he should be doing with his money: "Month after month, I was longing for your money, but all you sent were plain letters." [66] She also complained that his contribution of five hundred dollars to the Canton clan house was much larger than the two hundred dollars contributed by "one wealthy man" in the village: "I am so poor now, I have to pawn things in order to have money to buy food, while you go donating money, trying to wear your high hat." [67]

She was even more critical of Teh-sin and his influence over the family, writing, "I do not want to take care of your home any more. Even though you are a slave to them, none of your brothers love you. Why should you have pity on your brothers? . . . Do not listen to his business propositions unless I have words agreeable to it. . . . You think I am happy here, but I am not. No matter how hard I please you, you do not seem to pay any attention to what I say." [68] Teh-seng replied in defense of his brother, and his wife claimed it caused her to fall ill for a month. She later wrote, "You said your brother and sister are dear to you. When I got sick, who ever gave me sympathy? Who ever showed their kindness by bringing me water and tea? When water is clean, the stones underneath are shown: In the course of time a person's heart reveals its kindness or evil. But you do not heed me. You just write and say this and that and make a crazy woman out of me." [69] The brothers were concerned that the frequent quarrels between their wives were losing face for the family.

The correspondence saved by Teh-seng declines between 1924 and 1930. When the Depression began to affect his earning ability, many letters from home berated him for not sending enough money, for not writing enough, and for avoiding responsibility. One cousin accused him of being devious and irresponsible: "You should be able to come home, but why do you have a new address instead?" As that tactic did not result in remittances coming his way, he later turned to pathos: "I have no right to kill myself until I pay my debts. Life is tough."[70] The bandit problems in the village had died down, and many relatives were asking for money to move back and make up taxes they had left unpaid. Other relatives wanted money to open a rice store in Hong Kong. In Chicago, the local Chinese Consolidated Benevolent Association had moved to a new address, and the Hsiao surname association had to scrape up money to present it with a suitable gift. Teh-seng's own house in the village was infested with termites, and his wife demanded he send money to take care of that. Her dissatisfaction ran far deeper, though: "There is a Lou-fal monastery near Canton; let me go there and become a nun, and let your brothers take care of the children. I am not your lifelong partner. Please think it over; when you are old in the future, are you going to depend on your children or depend on your brothers? I pray you send me two hundred dollars so that I can have money to spend in the monastery. Now, I do not care how hard you work in America; I have no more pity on you."[71] Teh-seng's own needs turned out to be irrelevant in the long run, as he died within a year after receiving this letter.

Teh-seng's correspondence gives a sense of the extent to which his day-to-day concerns were still framed by the bonds and social pressures of relatives at home, throughout the Midwest, and even as far away as Australia. In essence, the village had extended beyond its territorial boundaries to people scattered around the world. Teh-seng was expected to be active in providing for the security and prestige of his family and village—in the form of money for walls, genealogies, taxes, ransoms, clan houses, luxuries, business investments, and education—as well as to provide advice and pressure to kinsmen in Chicago. His own movement abroad was integral to supporting smaller migrations of kinsmen to Canton and Hong Kong. Native place and family associations gave social form to peer pressure, obligations, struggles for status, and his own feelings of shame and personal ambition. These pressures could be resisted and negotiated, but were inescapable as part of the fabric of migrant life. Yet Teh-seng's place in this fabric was not the same as if he had remained at home. The quality of his bonds and the level of respect he earned were increasingly dependent solely upon his ability to accumulate and judiciously distribute money. He continued to be linked to his village despite migration, but migration had also changed the nature of those links.

Migrant Grooves

From a global perspective, we can imagine these migrant networks as a collection of rays emanating from hubs in Hong Kong and other South

China treaty ports, spreading out in one direction to South China villages and in the other to different locations around the world, further branching out from secondary nodes like San Francisco and Singapore. For most migrants, these rays were isolated grooves, stretching from their villages, past the various nodes, and on to migrant communities where they worked. They were the institutionalization of the precedents and assistance of relatives and fellow villagers who had migrated before them and made further migration possible. They shaped the view from emigrant villages in such a way that social distance was not congruent with geographic distance. In the eyes of a villager, distant Jamaica may have seemed easier to travel to and more familiar than the local county town. Nearly all of the Chinese in Jamaica before the 1980s came from five villages located at the border of three counties between Hong Kong and Canton, an area that has produced few migrants to any other location in the world. The original 640 migrants had been recruited as contract laborers to Jamaica in 1884, setting in motion a chain of migration that has continued to this day. Moreover, for years after the opening of the Panama Canal, migrants to Jamaica still followed an exhausting and costly route by boat to Vancouver, by train to Nova Scotia (on which they had to pay high Canadian passage taxes), and finally by boat to Jamaica.[72] This underlines the extent to which networks could crystallize into inflexible, self-reproducing grooves. The economic choices open to a migrant were limited by the precedents of previous migrants, the skills and connections they could transmit to him, and the boundaries of occupations conceded as "suitable" for Chinese by the non-Chinese society in which they lived.

Only a few elites were able to travel freely across these grooves. These elites also dominated the interaction between networks, channeling them through the dense institutional complexes that were the fabric of Chinese communities in migrant nodes such as Hong Kong and Chinatowns throughout the world. Credit, along with the institutions and symbols mobilized to protect and distribute credit, was crucial as a medium binding networks internally and necessitating cooperation between networks. Credit and debt were the bonds by which Chinese could mobilize and exploit labor, and provided the opportunities for individuals to obtain the capital to migrate and to establish small stores, distribution networks, and middleman occupations. The ability to guarantee and protect such exchanges lay in the cohesiveness of particular networks, which was facilitated by the formation of associations that could institutionalize the maintenance of trust and solidarity. Successful institutions were, in turn, made stronger by elites with access to connections and resources outside the network that could be mobilized to help guarantee internal transactions. In turn, power and wealth became focused on the individuals and institutions who could dominate and control such access. The frequent incidents of conflict and competition within and between migrant associations emphasize the extent to which they were locked together in the pursuit of common goals.[73]

These networks were often subversive to nation-states. They undermined immigration laws and other barriers against mobility designed to preserve territorial and cultural integrity. They introduced residents who might have no interest in loyalty and integration into the locale. Yet diasporic networks were also shaped by and even dependent upon nation-states. The small concentrations of Chinese in border regions like El Paso, Texas, and the desert of northern Chile on the Peruvian border draw attention both to these borders and to the profits that could be made by carrying people across them. The knowledge, connections, and ability required to transport goods and people past immigration and customs proceedings, both legally and illegally, were an immense source of power. The elites who could dominate these crossings had privileged access to goods and labor. They thus had an interest both in promoting the continued transgression of these boundaries and in confining interaction with non-Chinese to channels that they dominated.

These grooves were a transnationalism made possible through parochialism: local specialization in international movement. The meaning of "local" changed, however, as territory was replaced by transnational social bonds and institutions as the bases of parochialism.[74] At the same time, these grooves were inseparable from the expanding global economy and channels of trade, communication, and transportation established by non-Chinese. The picture that emerges is not a monodirectional one of global forces shaping local history, but of the most particular and localized bonds of family and village making up the very fabric of global movement.

DIASPORIC NATIONALISM

By the turn of the century, many of the Chinese who crossed national borders had also begun to reconceptualize their understandings of home, culture, loyalty, and self within the terms set by those nations and borders. The global politics that privileged members of strong and territorially sovereign states were increasingly obvious to many Chinese over the first half of the twentieth century. Home was no longer just a village where the family altar was located, a central node in a chain of relationships. It was part of a much larger entity, a motherland, which included strangers who spoke unintelligible dialects and yet, if nationalist propaganda were to be believed, were inalienably linked to each other by virtue of race, culture, history, and affection. Moreover, they increasingly understood their own status as tightly linked to the status of China as a strong and territorially sovereign state. These transformations in personal and communal self-perceptions were not necessarily the direct result of encounters between Chinese migrants and the people among whom they lived; they arose as well from engagement with ideas and sentiments carried abroad by intellectuals and officials from China who were sensitive to wider global power relations and conceptions of peoplehood.

Officials, Reformers, and Revolutionaries

By the 1870s, representatives of the Qing empire were less likely to condemn emigrants as "traitors" and more likely to move across diasporic networks to establish links between migrants and the imperial government. Their early motivation (often prompted by international attention to the plight of contract laborers) was to bolster the prestige of the empire by establishing diplomatic representation and extending official protection to the migrants, and they were actively involved in the organization of *zhonghua huiguan* throughout the world in the 1880s. By the late 1890s, they increasingly saw overseas Chinese as a fruitful source of financial contributions and loyalty, obtainable in return for a few symbols of official recognition and opportunities to invest in modernizing projects in China. At the turn of the century, reformer and revolutionary nationalist organizers, many of whom had been exiled from China, joined these activities in a more concentrated and aggressive manner. They were both more diligent in searching for wide bases of contributions and support and more generous in their distribution and promises of recognition.[75]

The first nationalist movement from China to gain a widespread following among migrants was the Emperor Protection Association. It was founded on 20 July 1899 in Victoria, Canada, by the exiled Cantonese scholars Kang Youwei and Liang Qichao.[76] It preached the establishment of a constitutional monarchy built on the symbols of empire and Chinese culture (its name derived from a belief that the emperor supported reform but was prohibited from acting on his convictions by the Empress Dowager and other court officials). The refined scholarly demeanor of Kang along with the engaging speeches and journalism of Liang appealed strongly to many migrants. Through the use and distribution of the symbols of empire, such as official clothes and medals, in return for generous contributions, the reformers appealed to the merchant-gentry aspirations of the migrant elite while orienting them toward visions of a modernized and internationally respected homeland.

The interests of reformers and migrants converged in many respects. Joining the association was a chance for migrants to simultaneously promote their own prestige as politically active individuals and the prestige of China as an internationally respected nation. On their side, the reformers hoped to harness previously established migrant networks and the entrepreneurial skills of the migrants to their own fund-raising and organizational ambitions. In 1902, they created the Commercial Corporation, which owned banks, restaurants, hotels, mines, and rice brokerages in the United States, Canada, Mexico, Panama, Southeast Asia, and Shanghai. They funded land reclamation projects in Manchuria, Argentina, and Brazil and made deals with the president of Mexico to establish public streetcar lines and housing projects. The profits were to be used to further the cause of the reformers, particularly in their publishing endeavors, although individual investors were promised dividends.[77]

Not all nationalist visions emanated from China. Some Chinese born in Southeast Asia were also interested in recovering Confucianism as a respectable national heritage. The earliest of such projects included late-nineteenth-century attempts by *peranakan* (a Malay-speaking Chinese minority that had lived in Java for several generations) elites to promote the founding of ancestral halls and reverse the trend of *peranakans* being seduced by the superstitions of Islam. This movement was eventually institutionalized in the Tionghua Huikuan (Zhonghua Huiguan) established in 1900 with an agenda of promoting education, reforming rituals, and "furthering knowledge and correctness among the Chinese in order that people might not remain ignorant or in an inferior position."[78] Later it also promoted the translation of Chinese classics into Malay, helped establish Confucian churches to compete with Christian churches and Islamic mosques, and provided scholarships for young Chinese to study in Europe or China.

In their desire to revive and reform Chinese culture in order to earn respect from non-Chinese, these overseas reform movements had much in common with the agenda of the Emperor Protection Association. A divergence of their perspectives can be seen clearly in the example of Lim Boon Keng, a Straits-born Chinese, trained as a physician in Britain. In 1898 he and Singapore lawyer Song Ong Siang established a Confucian Study Society to promote a deeper understanding of Chinese religion and reform the "superstitious" practices of local Chinese. In 1900, he also helped establish the Straits Chinese British Association "to promote among the members an intelligent interest in the affairs of the British Empire, and to encourage and maintain their loyalty as subjects of the Queen."[79] However contradictory these two projects may seem, taken together they draw from a tradition of Chinese migrant elites in Southeast Asia as cultural and economic mediators and extend it to a conviction that acceptance by local Europeans depended on widespread recognition of China as a civilized and deeply rooted culture, capable of its own transformation into nationhood and of producing its own exemplars of modern cosmopolitanism. It was a nationalism not predicated on political loyalty to China.

After 1902, the Qing government began its own program of reforms in China. Some of the most significant changes in China included the abolition of the imperial exam system and, in 1907, the establishment of provincial councils and self-government organizations. Overseas, migrants were encouraged to establish officially recognized Chambers of Commerce, and officials became more aggressive in their overseas missions and fund-raising. Ironically, the increased recognition made migrants increasingly cynical and frustrated at the weakness of the government. Medals and clothing were no longer seen as sufficient compensation for increasingly frequent contributions to officials who remained unwilling or unable to serve the practical interests of the migrants. On the other hand, the aims of the government and the Emperor Protection Association began to converge, and reformers who had once been hunted down as traitors began to collaborate with progressive officials. By 1908, the reformers—who had changed their name to the Constitutional Party (xianzhengdang) after the death of Emperor Guangxu—had clearly become part of the migrant establishment, with prominent overseas merchants as officers, and the Commercial Corporation was engulfed by the profit orientation, corruption, and petty jealousies that plagued so many other overseas institutions.

With the increasing conservatism and corruption of the Emperor Protection Association, many of its more activist and idealistic followers became disillusioned, and some transferred their loyalties to Sun Yat-sen and his revolutionary ideals. Since his establishment of the Xingzhonghui in Hawaii in 1894, Sun had been constantly traveling around the world in search of money to support his uprisings, although with much less success than the reformers. In general, he was less able than the reformers to appeal to the desires and imaginations of the influential migrants, and his emphasis on anti-Manchu race consciousness and the solicitation of contributions was often at the expense of practical organizational work. As a Christian, educated in Hawaii and Hong Kong, preaching a Western-style republic with almost none of the trappings of the imperial regime, his message appealed mostly to young Christians and radical students. With the exception of Japan—where radical students invited Sun to be president

of the Tongmenghui (Revolutionary Alliance) in 1905—and a few newspapers, Sun left few organizational legacies after he moved on and the
glow of his charisma faded.[80]

In 1910, Sun established a few Tongmenghui branches in the United
States. His fund-raising tour through the United States in the first part of
1911 was one of the most successful of his career. His usual following of
Christians and occasional sworn brotherhoods was greatly augmented by
migrants disgusted with the commercialism and conservatism of the reformers and by others who turned to Sun primarily as a way to secure resources against local competitors for wealth and prestige who happened
to be prominent Constitutional Party members. While Sun was engaged in
his fund-raising, the revolution of 1911 took place in China without his
participation. Although he was chosen as provisional president in 1912,
he handed power over to military strongman Yuan Shikai in less than two
months. His followers maintained power in Guangdong until 1914, but
the wave of support for him overseas died out quickly, and few migrants
supported his "second revolution" against Yuan in 1913.

Nationalism Abroad

Clarence Glick wrote as follows of Chinese participation in fund-raising
causes in Hawaii in the 1930s: "A migrant who gave a large donation for
famine relief in China might have been responding to three concerns simultaneously: compassion for the plight of the *tung bau* [fellow Chinese]
with whom he had come to feel a nationalistic identity; desire to gain face
with his fellow *wah kiu* [overseas Chinese] in Hawaii; and interest in
demonstrating to the non-Chinese in Hawaii that Chinese were philanthropic and humanitarian as well as commercially oriented."[81] This observation captures well the way in which nationalism had become intri-
cately woven into other migrant concerns. Although few migrants before
the late 1930s developed the total commitment to Chinese nationalism
that nationalist agitators had hoped for, its vocabulary easily intertwined
with other ties that migrants had to their homes; with the drives by associations and individuals for status, wealth, and ways to display it; and
with strategies to gain recognition from non-Chinese.

Overseas Chinese have often been considered the hearth of the Chinese revolution, but their reputation was earned more by default than intention. The spread of nationalist organizations and the internalization
of nationalist values among Chinese migrants was a constantly negotiated process. Whereas many aspects of reform and revolution certainly

appealed to the ambitions and needs of migrants—for example, by promoting commercial and industrial activity—they also came into conflict with many of the migrants' organizational and personal goals. This conflict is evident in the debate over the name for the first branch of the Emperor Protection Association in Victoria. Kang Youwei wanted to call it the Progressive Association (Zhonggou Weixinhui), with Save the Nation Association (Jiuguohui) as a secondary name. The merchant members, uncomfortable with the potential of this secondary name to annoy imperial officials, preferred the Commerce Protection Association (Baoshanghui) as a secondary name. The Emperor Protection Association (Baohuanghui) was a compromise.[82] A similar manifestation of commercial influence on nationalism could be seen in Ou Qujia's 1902 pamphlet *New Guangdong*, which couched a call for Cantonese independence in a mercantile metaphor of the nation as a corporation and its citizens as stockholders.[83]

In the early years, some Chinese nationalist visions expanded to the scale of pan-Asian solidarity, a coming global "Great Unity," or descriptions of Chinese overseas migrants as colonizers. Others shrank to the scale of Cantonese independence.[84] By 1908, nationalist orthodoxy had settled comfortably within the borders of the Qing empire as the public focus of loyalty, and many of the more transcultural and transregional versions of nationalism began to lose steam. Bicultural migrant elites had once been undisputed leaders of migrant society, accepting Chinese and non-Chinese titles and distinctions without any sense of contradiction and taking it upon themselves to lead nationalist and cultural revival movements.[85] By 1912, their very cosmopolitanism had become a cause for suspicion among ardent nationalists, as shown by a poster that appeared in Batavia: "Of what nationality is the Majoor [a Chinese official appointed by the Dutch]? Answer: Chinese and still not Chinese; native and still not native; in reality [he is] of mixed race! This bastard cannot return to China and cannot be named a European. He has no land to return to—only the Land of the Hereafter."[86]

This first great flurry of nationalistic enthusiasm had run its course by 1913 as the promise of the revolution faded. The general instability and cynicism surrounding Chinese politics over the next fifteen years meant that political parties remained small and uninfluential among migrants. But the schools, newspapers, fund-raising experience, and ideas created by nationalist organizers were still widely utilized, and ideologically devoted followers (many of them too young to have participated in pre-1911 mobilization) remained tireless in the zealous production of nationalist propaganda. Chambers of Commerce still sought recognition from various republican governments, and a stream of generals and intellectuals that represented or opposed one Chinese government or another still traveled through Chinese communities throughout the world, giving speeches, writing articles, and collecting money with great fanfare and solemnity.

The conquest of China by the Guomindang (Nationalist Party) in 1927 led to greatly increased membership abroad. This also led to greatly increased factionalism at first, but party politics quickly lost the revolutionary stridency of its pre-1927 youthful membership as anti–Chiang Kai-shek factions within the party were silenced and purged. In the 1930s, the Guomindang devoted much effort to forging links with migrant merchants, actively supporting migrant schools and newspapers in return for loyalty and war contributions. Many migrants gratefully felt that their own status abroad rose along with Guomindang successes in foreign diplomacy. Migrants and party also willingly collaborated in rewriting history as the progressive triumph of revolutionary sentiment under the unfaltering leadership of Sun Yat-sen. Patriotic mobilization reached a zenith during the anti-Japanese war from 1931 to 1945, when almost all behavior was justified by a rhetoric of patriotism, and every public event was a collection movement.[87] Scattered accounts suggest, however, that even then many migrants resented the constant demands on their time and money and the regulations that routinely extracted their contributions, and they considered the most active fund-raisers to be hypocritical promoters of their own personal power.[88]

Whether the nationalistic sentiments of migrant leaders were genuine or instrumental, they all benefited from the nationalist vocabulary of identity and ambition that could enhance rather than replace concerns for home village, prestige, and economic profit. Belonging to migrant associations began to imply more than mere embeddedness in particularistic networks. Interest in native place and family came to be seen as precisely the kind of basic affection that defined Chinese as Chinese, while the history of sworn brotherhood associations was retold as a story of persevering, anti-Manchu activism. Such sentiments often helped to revive faltering organizations and to bring more prestige to strong ones, and they contributed to an increase of native place and surname organizations around the world after the turn of the century.[89] The stated goals of most migrant organizations have always affirmed a commitment to the common welfare of the members, but a general change in emphasis occurred during the early twentieth century. In the nineteenth century, the care of the dead, mutual aid, and the organization of employment were of paramount importance to most associations. After the turn of the century, commitments to education and development in the home village and to the political fate of China became common themes.

Subnationalisms

The vocabulary of nationalism could also be appropriated for the definition of smaller groups. In 1921, Hakka associations around the world attempted to link up as branches of a single, global Chongzheng Association. These associations promoted and distributed histories of the Hakkas that were framed as a history of successive migrations, using the tropes of nationalism to construct a diasporic ethnicity. They did not see this commitment to a Hakka identity and organization as separatism but as an expression of the bonds which the Hakkas felt constituted them as exemplary Chinese (although some Hakkas denounced the Chongzheng as a form of parochialism contrary to the goals of nationalism).[90] Many surname and native place associations attempted to form similar networks after the late 1920s.[91] Similarly, in the 1920s, several sworn brotherhoods around the world linked themselves up as an international Zhigong Party, demanding political recognition in China.[92]

Nationalist activities helped create a sense of common identity, but that identity could simultaneously fragment into new and hostile ones shaped by class, occupation, and education. Nationalism created a space where migrants from South China were most likely to come into contact with students, businessmen, and diplomats from other parts of China for the first time. These interactions often transformed mutual ignorance into mutual suspicion and distaste as they learned that their varying interests in China and Chineseness were not always compatible. Students and diplomats complained that the nationalist commitment of merchants and laborers was diluted by devotion to profit, parochialism, and petty jealousies. Migrants from South China resented the arrogance of students and officials, and were extremely critical of those who appeared to be quite devoted to reform while abroad, yet used the status of returned migrant in China to join the world of corruption, dominance, and arrogance they had once opposed.[93] Neither side was willing to conform to the other's vision of what modern Chineseness should encompass.

The most significant success of nationalism among migrants was the redefinition of China as part of a world divided into a patchwork of competing units, each defined by a bounded confluence of culture, race, territory, and state. The imperial institutions of Beijing were no longer a human-cultural nexus where cosmic and moral order were maintained but just one more administrative apparatus among many throughout the world and one that desperately needed reforming. Chinese culture was no longer the universal way of being human, but just one national heritage among many. Along with this reconceptualization of China grew the conviction that the experience and status of Chinese abroad was a direct result of the status of China within the international system. If Chinese people were bullied locally, that was because China received no respect internationally. To be Chinese, anywhere in the world, was to be a representative of the motherland, to have a stake in the future of China, and to recognize the claims of China and Chinese culture over one's loyalty. Interestingly, when Chinese were most concerned with asserting their sovereignty and territorial rights, they came closest to conforming to a more traditional understanding of diaspora as a cultural entity scattered across the globe and yet linked by culture and yearnings for the homeland—a reminder that diaspora as a self-conscious identity grew along with the rise of nation-states rather than emerging in opposition to them.

Ethnicization

As increasingly hard lines of identification were erected around ideas of race, culture, and political sovereignty in the early twentieth century, behavior that appeared to express hybridity or divided loyalties became increasingly suspicious and untenable. Public choices had to be made. For most migrants, the choice to identify with China and diasporic nationalism was easy. Nonetheless, a slowly growing number of migrants chose to identify with the land where they lived, choosing to become American, Filipino, or Thai, for example. In other words, they were reorienting themselves as local ethnic minorities. This was especially true among Chinese who were born outside of China, but over the early twentieth century, growing numbers of Chinese began to cut themselves off from transnational networks, relocate entire families abroad, and identify as residents and citizens of new lands.

Such identifications tended to be extremely difficult. Regardless of his sincerity, an individual was likely to encounter racial and nationalist sentiments which made any attempts to take part in local institutions or to be accepted as a fellow national difficult, if not impossible. Such exclusions were exacerbated by physical differences, claims over migrant loyalty from China, and policies of colonial regimes and native rulers that separated Chinese into a special mercantile class or dehumanized them as alien laborers. Becoming accepted as an ethnic group—if even that was possible—was sometimes a compromise that fell short of the desired goal of complete assimilation.

Foreign-born Chinese often found themselves in a doubly difficult situation, because many migrants also indulged in a variety of prejudices against children, especially girls, who had been educated in non-Chinese schools and had adopted local ways. They were known as "brainless" *(monao)* and as "bamboo segments" *(zhusheng)*, that is, hard on the outside but hollow beneath the surface.[94] They were criticized for not sufficiently respecting their fathers or husbands, and for leading loose, frivolous lives. The rejection and marginalization of hybrid possibilities was increasingly common in the early twentieth century. Among Chinese it was closely associated with the formation of nationalist political identities.

Only after the Second World War, when further migration had been cut off and it became clear that most Chinese migrants around the world were there to stay, did ethnic identities appropriate to pluralist polities began to be negotiated. These usually emerged in some sort of hybrid formulation such as Chinese American, Filipino of Chinese descent, or *lookjin* (Sino-Thai). Such identities were predicated on the idea that it is possible to be Chinese and still belong to the national community. Many ethnic Chinese consider themselves to be locals, yet still feel they are outsiders because of cultural difference or rejection by the wider society. At other times, citizenship and local identities were assumed almost entirely for the sake of commercial interest, with little change in subjective orientation. At the other extreme, many second- or third-generation migrants rejected China and all things Chinese as representing backwardness and the social awkwardness of parents, and as generative of exoticizing and marginalizing attitudes. The details and subjectivities of these identities were very much a product of generational attitudes, local politics, and state building, drawing on cultural and organizational traits that flourished locally as well as on local histories of struggle and resistance.

Global Aspects of Ethnicity

A national rather than global perspective is most relevant to understanding the emergence of ethnic Chinese. Chinese ethnicity is a space in which the identity and meaning of being Chinese is most strongly formed by local social relations and national ideologies, where Chineseness becomes a heritage, a political status, or merely a physical appearance. Nonetheless, a national perspective is still not sufficient. At the very least, the diasporic networks and economic interests that moved laborers and merchants around the world must also be taken into account to understand the interests that shaped its members into a local community. Moreover, these interests did not always grow irrelevant as locally born Chinese began to identify themselves more completely as local ethnics. Many young Chinese ethnics, frustrated by the obstacles that blocked their attempts to integrate into local societies, turned toward diasporic nationalism as an alternative, looking back to a China they may have once scorned. Some even physically moved to China, not knowing the language or having any connections there but still hoping to use their education and skills to help "save the nation."

Continued attention to diasporic links also helps us to understand the discourses and practices used by non-Chinese to characterize Chinese minorities. Just as labor migration, migrant networks, and Chinese nationalism were embedded in economic and political relations on a global scale, so local political attitudes were embedded in globally circulating discourses of race and images of Chineseness. One of the most famous examples was the pamphlet *The Jews of the East,* written by King Vajiravudh of Thailand in 1914, in which he applies tropes of the eternally alien Jew, learned during his studies in London, to the Chinese, depicting them as inassimilable outsiders, loyal only to money. Depictions of Chinese as degraded, as parochial sojourners, as a Yellow Peril, or as scheming, insular businessmen—many of which seemed all the more accurate when observers from local perspectives viewed the diasporic activities of Chinese—had wide currency at an international level, which helped legitimize their local application all the more. At the same time, the Chinese themselves could appropriate and redeploy these images as industrious, peaceable businessmen who refrained from political agitation, contributed to local economies, and integrated local nations into global market opportunities.[95]

A comparison of recent ethnic identities with the creole Chinese identities created in earlier centuries can help highlight how ethnic identities are embedded in global historical trends. Peoples such as the *peranakans* of Java, the Babas of Malaysia, and the mestizos of the Philippines were the descendants of intermarriages between Chinese migrants and local women that began several hundred years ago. They spoke (and still speak) various Malay and Chinese creoles, yet were known for maintaining certain aspects of Chinese dress and ritual life that had long been dropped by more recent Chinese migrants.[96] As with ethnic Chinese, the formation of these creole groups was strongly situated in local political and social relations. Yet the important marker of difference tended to be cultural practice rather than race. That is, a modern ethnic Chinese may, in terms of clothes, language, and habits, be in harmony with the mainstream national culture where he lives and still be marked off as a minority, whereas a creole may be physically indistinguishable from the surrounding population yet be distinguished through cultural markers. Both *peranakan* and Chinese ethnics still exist as different groups in parts of Southeast Asia today. This distinction arose both because the new waves of migrants that began arriving in the second half of the nineteenth century were not well incorporated into limited *peranakan* networks, and because of the rise of the diasporic nationalism which often disparaged and isolated creolized Chinese as not modern, not truly Chinese, or as running dogs of the imperial powers.

Contemporary ethnicities have not emerged in regional isolation but are entwined with modern global politics. They are also built on the institutions and activities of migrants who maintained transnational networks and links to China. Neither global processes nor the more parochial concerns for village, family, and profit had an abstract existence. Both were manifested through local situations and institutions. Subsequent case studies describe some of those different manifestations.

CULTURAL FLOWS

Cultural threads run through all the networks, institutions, and identities described so far. Culture appeared in one form as the familiar language, symbols, habits, "inscribed" behaviors, and organizational principles given shape in networks, credit practices, and associations. Culture also took the form of imaginative constructions of identity such as those mobilized in nationalism or claims for ethnic identity. When successful, such constructions became aspects of migrant life that were taken for granted.

Cultural forms of organization shaped the actions and horizons of migrants, laying a basis for engagement with unfamiliar people and situations. Chinese migrants were attuned to global economic opportunities and could mobilize social and financial ties into new networks that took advantage of them.[97] Subsequent chapters describe the variety of ways in which migrant institutions also adapted to changing Chinese politics and to the environments of non-Chinese states and cities. Bonds of trust were established with people who were not Chinese. Cultural adjustments were also made in the context of more abstract global structures. One example was the growing awareness after the late nineteenth century that descent from a common ancestor was no longer sufficient to command political and cultural respect. Citizenship in an internationally respected nation-state had become a minimum requirement for recognition, both within the so-called family of nations and on the part of the local political powers where migrants resided. This also meant the reformulation of identity in the terms of international discourse, such as race, sovereignty, territory, and an objectified national culture.

At the same time as cultural forms created some level of continuity across migrant flows, those flows also served to fragment and reformulate the significance of the cultural forms. Migrants returning home from the United States impressed their neighbors by wearing gold watches and Western suits (specially ordered from Jewish tailors who were aware of Chinese tastes) that had long gone out of fashion in the United States. Up-to-date clothes that would signify to Americans that the migrant had become integrated into fashion trends would have failed to mark the migrant as a successful and cosmopolitan Gold Mountain Man back in China. Similarly, the houses and schools built by migrants were attempts to display modernization but were filled with a seemingly eclectic variety of objects selected to mark the builders as successful migrants, such as coffee that the occupants (if any) never drank, murals of open-topped sports cars in Hollywood, and swimming pools often used as fish ponds, as well as more familiar Chinese markers of prestige, such as books for families often unable to read them, rice fields at times when commercial investment was much more profitable, and elaborate ritual objects for family and communal worship.[98]

Another example of shifting meaning appears in the "modern" weddings of Chinese in Singapore during the mid-twentieth century, in which couples wore Western clothes and got married by the dozens in mass ceremonies. These ceremonies were inspired more by trends coming out of urban China than by direct contact with the British, but were still directed, at least in part, toward the British as public expressions of the modern unity of the Chinese people, although the British tended to interpret them as a holdover of traditional Eastern communalism.[99]

The process of selection and redefinition meant that the reinforcement of social and cultural boundaries was as likely an outcome of these cultural interchanges as homogenization or the blurring of boundaries. Yet these objects, like coffee and clothes, moved across boundaries in the bags of people, many of whom were surely aware of the discrepancies in their symbolic values. That is to say, meanings were damaged and reconstituted, but the men and women who transported these objects and activities consciously created and happily transgressed these discrepancies. They knew who they wanted to impress and how to impress them. If the mix of objects and activities came across as a murky symbolic chaos, it was only in the eyes of observers who drew unnecessary cultural lines. Global culture was not just a realm of homogenization but a space where cultural and political distinctions were constantly negotiated. A fedora in Zhongshan or a mass marriage in Singapore was a clear marker of Western culture, but only in the same resituated way that chop suey and fortune cookies were examples of Chinese cuisine in Chicago. Each persisted because it had a particular place in the cultural landscape, and none would have emerged if not for connections and precedents elsewhere in the world.

CHAPTER 4

Men, Ghosts, and Social Organization in South China

Migrants carried not only concrete objects like coffee, letters, and clothes across the oceans, but also less tangible assumptions, organizational practices, and desires. Economic gain was one of the prime reasons for migration, but migrant networks and institutions were not merely built from scratch in order to attain money in the most rational manner possible. They were extensions and adaptations of institutions and assumptions about social order that had developed (and were still developing) in South China. Some of these institutions, such as families and lineages, expanded and changed with the migrants. Others, like native place *huiguan* and sworn brotherhoods, were reconstituted anew in migrant communities on the basis of familiar precedents. In order to fully understand the trajectories of Chinese migrant adaptation, we need to understand a history of social organization in China.

The articulation of state and local society in late imperial China was not centered on the rule of officials and threat of armed repression—although their distant presence was indispensable for the maintenance of state interests—but on a nexus of symbolic and ritual practices mediated through institutions and individuals.[1] This vertical state-local nexus overlapped with a horizontal nexus of relationships between local groups. These relationships and practices constantly shifted over time, in the context of changing ideologies, imperial policy, economic circumstances, and local interests. The expansion and adaptation of institutions abroad is linked to history in South China as part of a single continuum.

Existing alongside this shifting social landscape were ritual practices that portrayed a timeless cosmological order. To be sure, from the perspective of an outside observer these rituals were far from eternal. They varied over time and in the interpretations of different participants. Yet, their predictability and claims to absoluteness, combined with this adaptability, made them into useful tools of rulership and the organization of human relations. More specifically for our purposes, rituals associated with the cosmological realms of men, ghosts, and gods suggest ways in which Chinese constructed relationships with non-Chinese. Chinese already had ways to account for and deal with outsiders (usually through the services of mediators) even before they left China. Prolonged contact always challenged those assumptions, but because they shaped a field for action rather than a list of inflexible rules, they could actually promote rather than restrict adaptation. What emerged was a pattern of intercultural relations that can be understood as the stabilization of distinction and mutual misunderstanding, rather than a progressive transition toward assimilation.

GUANGDONG AND EMPIRE

One of the more remarkable features of late imperial China was the high level of cultural homogeneity and stability over a vast territory, despite minimal administrative apparatus and infrequent resort to military force. By the late eighteenth century, the population of China had increased to the extent that the lowest official, the county magistrate, was expected— with the assistance of a few runners and clerks notorious for putting more effort into their own interests than those of the state—to be judge, tax collector, upholder of order, and representative of the state for an average population of about two hundred and fifty thousand.[2] This success was due in no small part to long-standing factors such as the common written language; a well-organized bureaucracy with widely recognized symbols; an exam system which accepted and co-opted ambitious young men from throughout the empire; and, as many Chinese scholars themselves insisted, tireless attention to the ordering and reordering of society through the study and reinterpretation of ancient texts and performance of proper ritual.

At the same time, the Qing dynasty—ever conscious of its own origins as seminomads from the northeast—built a consciously multicultural empire. Emperors readily adopted methods and symbols of rule that were appropriate for non-Han peoples, such as claiming to be a descendant of Genghis Kahn to the Mongols or a reincarnated Buddha to the Tibetans. Thus, coexistence of local society and the imperial government was not merely predestined by common cultural fate but a constantly negotiated process in which all sides struggled for recognition and control. Local interests were able to carve out their own spaces, assisted by imperial willingness to selectively incorporate cultural variations generated from below. On their part, local elites appealed to the recognition and symbolism of the imperial government to legitimize their own power in the face of local rivals. Cultural negotiations, however, always took place with the knowledge that the state could and would resort to physical force when it felt sufficiently threatened.

Like other regions in China, the Pearl River Delta had its own unique relationship to the Chinese state. Throughout much of the Qing dynasty (1644–1911), Canton was the only port through which tribute missions and foreign traders from the south were officially allowed to proceed. The delta was also an important commercial center in its own right. Its main exports included sugar, silk, and textiles sold abroad and to other parts of China, while cotton came in from India and the Yangtze Delta, and rice from Guangxi province and, occasionally, Siam.[3] Thus, the Pearl River Delta was an important node in the imperial state, precisely because it was a cosmopolitan link to areas beyond the empire. The services of Canton merchants were of great value to bureaucrats in Beijing. As long as tribute missions and a significant portion of foreign trade were channeled through Canton, the material interests of Cantonese elites existed comfortably with the bureaucratic order.

Despite the relatively high profile of foreigners in Canton, Cantonese commoners were noted (especially by Westerners) for their strong xenophobia. Of course, contempt is as much a form of accommodation as mutual understanding, but such sentiments must also be placed in the context of a localism that was common throughout China. Cantonese also looked upon Chinese elsewhere with suspicion, some contempt, and occasional fear. In return, other Chinese looked at Cantonese (and each other) in much the same way. This mutual distaste was often measured in terms of purity of cultural lineage and practice. By the late nineteenth century, other Chinese slandered Cantonese as "foreigners' dogs" and "Guangdong sluts," while Cantonese claimed that Chinese in the north had been contaminated by centuries of barbarian invasion and dominance, and only Guangdong was a site of truly unvarnished Chinese culture (a debate that resonates with Hakka claims of ultra-Chineseness).[4] The most passionate hostility in Guangdong, however, was reserved not for northerners, officials, or foreign barbarians, but for close neighbors who belonged to a different lineage or spoke a different dialect. Feuds involving lineages, villages, sworn brotherhoods, and subethnic groups were endemic throughout South China in the Qing dynasty, a product of increased commercialization and social mobility.

The imperial government rarely interfered in local violence unless it perceived a direct threat to its own sovereignty. The Chinese bureaucracy and imperial armies were a distant presence in the affairs of South China but rarely fell completely below the horizon of local consciousness. Cantonese villagers often spoke of the emperor and his government as a sleeping dragon: quiet and distant when not aroused but vengeful and destructive when awakened, capable of sending armies to destroy villages, lineages, and all that represented local order and human community.[5] Nonetheless, as we shall see, these units of local order all took shape in conjunction with the imperial presence, just as particular migrant networks all emerged in conjunction with larger global forces.

The interests of the imperial state and the bureaucratic order it created were complex, taking on different manifestations from different vantage points. In its most ideological manifestation—more associated with Han officials than Manchu—it was an order of centralization, cultural superiority, and agricultural stability. In this manifestation the emperor was at the center of the earth, mediating between Heaven and the World of Men. Non-Chinese people were one step further removed from this fount of civilization. Europeans and other distant peoples were barbarians from "outside the pale . . . entirely unversed in the forms of edicts and laws," and grateful to the mercy of the emperor for assisting them in their "turn towards culture."[6] According to this perspective, merchants were relegated to the lowest of the four classes of society, under scholar-officials, peasants, and artisans, and emigrants were labeled as unfilial traitors.

On the other hand, the day-to-day policies of the empire presented a flexibly practical face. Officials were aware of the necessity of tailoring diplomatic relationships to particular situations, and they took pains to develop economic policies that recognized local interests, most notably in their dealings with non-Han portions of the empire. Their choices were not always appropriate, and official communication was not always ideal, but the eighteenth century turned out to be one of the most expansive and stable periods of Chinese history. As concerns attitudes toward Chinese who traveled overseas, in practice any condemnation was implicitly, and sometimes explicitly, directed toward those who chose to reside abroad, not those who left for temporary trading voyages. Most hostility toward emigrants had roots in the legitimate, if sometimes exaggerated, fear of pirates and invasion. Officials appointed to the southern coast dealt with these traders in a variety of ways, including the writing of memorials in support of commercial activities, turning a blind eye to them, or profiting from them through open or clandestine collaboration and extortion.[7]

The different manifestations of bureaucratic order were often harmonized through ritual. Successful rites presented a facade of timeless order despite, or perhaps because of, constant adjustments to take concrete situations into account. Ritual was thus a practical method of both controlling and responding to a social world in flux.[8] It was an important complement to practical statecraft, especially when many state functions had to be delegated to other semiautonomous institutions.

Associations

Lineage and Empire

Migrant associations overseas were frequently established on the basis of native place and kinship. These organizations and the particular forms they took did not emerge spontaneously as a consequence of natural affection. The drew upon a variety of organizational precedents from China and had concrete links to some of those organizations. Overseas associations emerged from the same process by which migrants to urban and rural areas in China created merchant organizations and sworn brotherhoods. The maintenance of links to home villages was a primary function and resource for these associations.

In the villages of southeast China, lineages were one of the most pervasive organizations, structuring much of rural society. Lineages were extended kinship groups, usually claiming patrilinial descent from a founding ancestor. Larger lineages almost always held some form of corporate property, usually land, using the income for rituals, ancestral halls, and charitable activities. Like other associations, they did not merely appear as spontaneous expressions of cultural values but were adaptations to the political and social conditions of late imperial China.[9] Lineages promoted the material interests of local farmers and elites within the trappings of ancestor worship and patriline that were both long-standing aspects of Chinese daily life and activities sanctioned and supported by Qing ideology.

The proper performance of filial piety and ancestor worship marked much of what was seen as the fundamental cultivation of humanity, defining the civilized from the barbarian. Nonetheless, the proper forms of filial action and ancestor worship had long been the subject of debate and transformation. For example, the privilege of worshiping ancestors back five generations (now the standard for all family worship) was originally reserved to nobles. Similarly, extended corporate lineages were often looked on with suspicion as a potential threat to the state. During the Song Dynasty (960–1279), reference works and practical handbooks began spreading information and guidelines for proper ritual performance at home, as scholars tried to propagate moral activity beyond the confines of the elite.[10] This project included discussion of the proper forms that lineages and ancestor worship could take. A consensus gradually emerged among scholars which included many elements of a previously unformalized vernacular repertoire, such as grave offerings, charitable estates, family instruction, genealogies, and ancestral halls. During the Ming and Qing dynasties, scholars repeatedly attempted to stem what they saw as growing trends of immorality by reformulating ritual and lineage organization in order to obtain a balance between popular custom and cosmic order. By the beginning of the Qing dynasty, the lineage had emerged as one of the primary institutions through which morality was institutionalized and moral example exerted.[11]

Scholarly effort was only one influence behind the strengthening of corporate lineages at the beginning of the Qing. The commercialization and monetarization of the Chinese economy from the late Ming onwards, the general social turmoil accompanying the transition from the Ming to the Qing dynasty in the seventeenth century, and the land and tax policies of the new Qing government further promoted this consolidation. The disruptions of the transition were particularly acute in southeast China, where the evacuation of a zone of twenty-five kilometers in from the coast as a buffer against pirates was enforced from 1662 to 1681. As the Qing slowly extended its control over China, it imposed land and taxation policies aimed at breaking down the power of large landholders and encouraging the establishment of small farmer-taxpayer households. The decline of large estates worked by bonded labor, which had already begun during the commercialization of the late Ming, was further hastened by Qing laws abolishing servile labor, curbing elite privileges, and replacing corveé labor requirements with a land tax. These policies contributed to the emergence of the household farm as the primary unit of taxation and surveillance in China, as well as to increased physical mobility and urbanization. These, in turn, led to growth in the kinds of social organizations described in this chapter and to the increasing delegation of government responsibilities to these organizations and the elites who dominated them.[12]

Lineages were excellent institutions for local conflict resolution, social control, and mutual protection in periods of disorder. Other nonstate institutions could have fulfilled these roles, but lineages had the advantage of official recognition as institutions established for orthodox purposes.[13] Their cultural legitimacy and appeal to past ancestors also helped buttress land claims when the coastal zone was reopened. In the context of Qing labor and taxation policies, they were also excellent vehicles for the exercise of elite power. They brought together peasants, tenants, and landlords in the cause of mutual protection. Small households could benefit from the protection of wealthy landowners and officeholders through the lineage without having to indenture themselves. In turn, corporate lineage property and complex land-tenure rights that made it difficult to transfer land to outsiders facilitated the control of land and collection of rents, while maintaining a landscape of independent household cultivators. Both the poor and the wealthy benefited from working together to defend their land and water rights against the incursions of neighboring lineages, villages, and bandits.

As lineages became recognized as institutional manifestations of order and morality, they increasingly shaped both the past and the physical landscape. While formal kinship networks had, since at least the Song, structured settlement and facilitated mutual aid, they were now made increasingly prominent through the institution of lineage halls, common worship, corporate estates, and genealogies. Much energy and calculation was also put into the retroactive creation of a lineage in response to contemporary political needs, as a variety of possible patrimonies were selected and excluded in order to create alliances that could be beneficial in the present. Some genealogies reached aggressively into the distant past, claiming origins in North China and searching out nobility and degree holders to occupy revered places as pivotal ancestors, while any suggestion that early lineage founders were culturally assimilated aboriginals was buried.[14] Ancestors were selected and excluded not only with an eye toward imperial approval, but also in order to affect the hierarchy of relationships among local lineage branches. But even an unassailably respectable lineage history was not enough to ensure a lasting lineage. Segmentation, fusion, alliances, and internal differentiation continued as various branches became wealthy through commerce, produced imperial degree holders, reached out to subordinate neighboring branches, or resisted such subordination.

The emergence of lineages created an enduring balance between local interests and the interests of the state. The embodiment of imperially sanctioned morality in lineages both legitimized the government and lent power to the lineage leaders. This balance was personified in the mediating roles of successful scholars and officials produced by many lineages. From the state's point of view, these scholar-officials—all well educated in the classics—were charged with presenting a moral example that could mitigate the conflicts, hustling, and self-interest of the populace. From the lineages' point of view, a successful scholar meant privileged access to prestige, influence, riches, and self-perpetuation. The roles of imperial representative and filial son subjected officials to conflicting pressures, and few officials completely rejected opportunities to channel influence in the service of family and lineage, even when their role as moral exemplars could suffer as a result.

These bifurcated interests were not necessarily experienced as a conflict. Service to family and lineage on the part of a scholar-official was an expression of the same filial piety that was promoted by the state as a bedrock value. Speaking in more general terms, Frederic Wakeman wrote, "Local social organizations therefore embodied contrary principles: integration into the imperial system and autonomy from it. The dynamic oscillation between these poles created the unity of Chinese society, not by eliminating the contradictions but by balancing them in such a way as to favor overall order."[15] Idealistic scholars might have agonized over these contradictions, but they were usually forced to live the contradictions out as mediators who both embodied and dissolved that tension. Of course, the bureaucracy was aware of the subversive potential of piety and kinship and generally took pains not to post officials in their home provinces. But the checks and balances of the bureaucracy never went so far as to create a completely autonomous official class. The state was always dependent on the continued production of meritorious officials with the help of lineage and family resources, and could not afford to alienate the lineages.

As the Qing economy and population grew over the eighteenth century, so did feuds, exploitation, endless litigation, and other conflicts between increasingly powerful lineages and other groups in South China. The imperial government limited itself to moral condemnation and rarely intervened unless it was petitioned to do so or the violence directly threatened the state.[16] It was in the state's interest to accommodate the lineages and lineage elites. Despite their proclivities to fight with each other, lineages still fulfilled many of the functions of individual conflict mediation and tax collection at levels beneath the reach of the state. Magistrates even encouraged lineages and villages to resolve their own disputes and use the court only as a last resort. With the great rebellions at the middle of the nineteenth century, even much of the responsibility for raising and maintaining armies was delegated to locals. After the rebellions were subdued, the Qing continued to incorporate these potentially disruptive local power-holders into the structure of the empire through the increased sale of imperial titles and the delegation of tax-collecting and commercial regulatory power. Not only did these methods relieve the administrative burden in the waning years of the Qing, but incidents of organized rural violence also decreased by the 1880s.[17]

Lineages after the Empire

Although established with reference to the moral order of the empire, lineages remained relevant after the fall of the Qing, despite competition from other organizations and ideological attacks on the lineage system. Lineages had become rooted as a part of the daily perspective of many Chinese that was not easily discarded. Moreover, the property, social connections, and influence controlled by lineages continued to insure their relevance as social institutions, inasmuch as they could respond flexibly to new sociopolitical situations. Even during the Empire, lineages had adopted a variety of functions other than the organization of territorial settlement. For example, the lineages which ran the salt yards of Sichuan province resembled corporate business enterprises, with lineage members occupying various executive positions.[18] In the early twentieth century, the Guan lineage in Kaiping county derived much of its wealth from commercial activities, with lineage connections at home and abroad playing crucial roles in the recruitment of employees, the supply of capital, and the social connections needed to develop monopolies. Other lineages maintained corporate bases in racketeering, mercenary activities, or access to official connections.

Some of these endeavors were managed by the lineage as an institution, but more often individuals, families, and businesses utilized the services and connections of the lineage for their own benefit. Even emigration could be a communal strategy based on the resources and maintenance of a lineage. Nearly all the active male members of the Wen lineage of Hong Kong in the 1960s operated a network of restaurants throughout Britain and Europe, as well as maintaining a travel agency to Europe and an extensive range of connections in the passport bureau of the Hong Kong government, all of which were jealously guarded from outsiders. The profits made from these activities were used to maintain a traditional lifestyle in the home village that was noted throughout the New Territories of Hong Kong.[19] On the other hand, some twentieth-century lineages dropped the ritual trappings of ancestor worship in favor of a managerial structure that revolved around republican vocabularies of local self-government, rural reconstruction, progressive reform, a leadership institutionalized as a board of directors, and leaders whose prestige was based on commercial rather than landed wealth. Although the rhetoric of such a lineage could seem radical and modernizing, in practice it rarely amounted to more than an up-to-date gloss on business as usual. Political and material success, more than modernizing rhetoric, were still necessary for a viable lineage.[20]

Some lineages did not successfully adapt to changing conditions. Destruction of corporate property, changing relationships with new power holders, and challenges from competing organizations were not always successfully negotiated. Many lineages of the Pearl River Delta crumbled in the face of dwindling income during the Depression, the chaos of the Japanese occupation, and the challenges of local strongmen and other paramilitary groups taking advantage of these situations.[21] The wage labor opportunities offered by urban Hong Kong also disrupted the territory-based hegemony of many lineages in the New Territories after the Second World War. Families became more oriented toward outside job opportunities and used their new-found wealth and independent means of support to confront the old status quo.[22]

Lineages rarely flourished in urban or overseas settings. A few wealthy Chinese in Southeast Asia (or their children) tried to establish themselves as founders of lineages with corporate property, but this rarely led to more than a temporary family solidarity that disintegrated along with the family fortune.[23] In one sense, founding a lineage in this manner was going about it backwards. Starting with a founder and working down rather than reaching back into the past to legitimize contemporary claims and alliances just made a lineage more inflexible in the face of future contingencies. Moreover, the advantages of official recognition and status were not forthcoming from most non-Chinese governments. Outside of China, lineages were not so useful for maintaining local order and a tax base of independent farmers as they were in China.

Chinese organizations that were more flexible in their membership and corporate structure proved to be much more adaptable to these new situations. Perhaps most significant, however, was the fact that many Chinese migrants already felt they belonged to a lineage in their home village, even if they had been born abroad and never been to China. Many of the primary symbols of the lineage—the ancestral hall, gravesites, and corporate land—were fixed in place. Involvement in native place and surname associations abroad provided the link that maintained involvement with the lineages. This long-standing attachment to lineages based in home villages can still be seen today: much investment in the Pearl River Delta area by overseas Chinese is made with the stipulation that some money be spent in restoring ancestral halls, genealogies, and lineage consciousness among younger members.[24]

Huiguan

Lineages attained great importance as an intersection of Chinese rural life, official moral discourse, and the day-to-day familiar bonds of kinship. Some lineages reached out beyond the locales in which they were rooted, building apical ancestral halls in county towns or provincial capitals and maintaining urban schools and dormitories for the support of aspiring young lineage scholars. In general, however, other institutions emerged as more appropriate to urban settings and the needs of migrants in cities and towns, such as merchant associations, guilds, and sworn brotherhoods. Although these other institutions were less in harmony with imperial ideology than the lineages, they were equally important components of Chinese life. They were independent of lineages but still drew upon kin networks for recruitment and maintained close links to particular lineages or villages. They also drew upon the model of kinship as a legitimizing principle as well as upon a variety of less orthodox shared resources, such as native place, ritual oaths, common worship, and the search for material profit.[25]

Merchant and trade associations, often generically referred to as *huiguan*, were one of the most widespread forms of migrant association in China.[26] The earliest *huiguan* were hostels for scholars residing temporarily in Beijing. Merchant *huiguan* became increasingly prominent over the Qing. The earliest merchant *huiguan* were chartered as semiofficial organs to promote state interests in the commercial sphere, but by the late nineteenth century they had become dominated by private interests. Many crafts, services, and trading networks were dominated by people from the same native place, and *huiguan* played a critical role in protecting and promoting such monopolies. These associations were mediums through which merchants could collaborate to stabilize prices, regulate trade, limit competition, mediate disputes, and deal with officialdom. In doing so, the *huiguan* became closely linked to networks and institutions at home, and their services often expanded beyond a focus on commercial activities to a more general assortment of native place interests.

Growth of the *huiguan* corresponded with the increasing delegation of official functions such as tax collection and market regulation to their management, in part as an attempt to harness merchant energies that had grown independently of official control. *Huiguan* officials had better access to their constituencies than officials, saved them the dirty work of becoming directly involved with money and commerce, and were glad to accept the increased prestige and control that came with such responsibilities. The role of *huiguan* as native place associations was even stronger in resettlement *huiguan*, which were associations formed to organize the interests of merchants engaged in the recruitment and funding of settlers to frontiers and depopulated lands, like Sichuan province after the depredations of the Ming to Qing transition. The loans and dormitories provided by these associations involved them in extensive mutual aid activities that

served the interests of all migrants from a single locality rather than specialized trade interests.

Sworn Brotherhoods

Wealthy merchants were best positioned to maintain and benefit from
ties to home, and to attract the symbols of imperial approval. Less powerful migrants also formed associations, but these tended to be small, marginalized, or persecuted as subversive. Rotating credit associations, burial
societies, crop-watching societies, and irrigation cooperatives were common village associations that were often patronized by local elites.[27] By
the time of the Ming-to-Qing transition in southeast China, the functions of small mutual aid associations had begun to merge with traditions
of sworn brotherhood rites that drew on the rhetoric of popular novels,
magic, and apocalyptic religion. The fact that incorporation came through
initiation rituals meant that a wide variety of people could join, and these
brotherhoods were much more extensive than other mutual aid associations in their scale of membership, alliances, and common ritual symbolism. They also tended to be relatively independent of state and local
power structures.

Sworn brotherhoods in South China grew increasingly common
during the commercialization and increased labor mobility of the sixteenth to eighteenth centuries. Many of the early extensive sworn brotherhood associations were made up of rural migrants and transportation
workers coming together in mutual protection against often hostile locals. This self-protection could easily turn into predation in the form of
bandit or criminal gangs. Some sworn brotherhood associations also recruited men who were not migrant laborers but were at the margins of local power where they lived. Such organizations usually drew from several
neighboring villages and lineages, thus crossing the boundaries of officially legitimate organizations.

These societies drew upon ideologies of kinship in their internal organization, dividing themselves into master-disciple generational groups
that mirrored the father-son relationship and consistently using the metaphor of brotherly relations to characterize ties between members. Nonetheless, Chinese officials disparaged them as vehicles for the destruction of
families and obscuring of bloodlines. The government was easily alarmed
by any sign of violence from associations considered heterodox and often
responded with suppression rather than the tolerance given to the orchestrated violence of recognized lineages.[28] In their public stances, lineage elders usually joined in the marginalizing of these alternative organi-

zations, but in practice they often acquiesced and even cooperated with such organizations. Illegal profit and mercenaries to aid in lineage feuds were two possible benefits. By the mid-eighteenth century, as sworn brotherhoods became involved in some well-known local uprisings, names like the Heaven and Earth Society (Tiandihui) and the Hongmen became notorious throughout southeast China as carrying the taint of rebellion, disciplined organization, and subversive secrecy. Although the various organizations which carried these names were probably not coordinated in any but the loosest manner, groups claiming formal investiture and rights to the symbols and reputation surrounding these names (often glossed as Triads in English) became increasingly widespread.

Official distrust was not completely misplaced. Sworn brotherhoods could be more demanding of exclusive loyalty than could lineages and *huiguan,* as is evident in the dialogue of an initiation ritual of the I Hing (Yixing) Society in Philadelphia in the 1880s: "Have you a father? No! Have you sisters? No! Brothers? Only my brothers the Patriots!"[29] Indeed, the very act of initiation marked a line of separation from and even opposition to surrounding society. Violence was not integral to the constitution of sworn brotherhoods, but in many contexts they proved more willing than other groups to protect their interests by violence, especially as they had less access to legitimate means of domination. The mere knowledge by outsiders that secret rituals and procedures existed was often enough to create a mystique around sworn brotherhoods that easily translated into a sense of threat and intimidation on which they could capitalize.[30]

Sworn brotherhoods organized on principles that were independent of official patronage found their most active membership among displaced young men and could easily be used in the service of economic interests. *Huiguan* could also draw on a legacy of practices designed to facilitate the economic and social interests of migrants. Both organizations were easily adapted by migrants to areas outside of China but often with different results. Kinship and native place organizations established abroad tended to engage in transnational activities based on simple links between home village and migrant settlement. Sworn brotherhoods, on the other hand, rarely maintained links to home villages, except when involved in labor recruiting. They were primarily a means by which previously unrelated people could institutionalize newly formed relationships. As such, they often expanded to create links between different migrant communities. As we shall see below, however, the distinctions between these two types of association are only a rough abstraction, and the boundaries between them were far from clear.

Associational Ideologies

Chinese organizations of all kinds drew upon a common fund of images and organizational practices. Many of these appear in the preamble to a list of regulations for the Zhigongtang, a Chinese sworn brotherhood society in the mining areas of western Canada in the late nineteenth century:

> It is said that a well-organized society is ruled by reason and that the security and harmony of society depend on the cultivation of harmonious sentiments. The nation treats peace and prosperity as matters of paramount importance: the cangue is moistened by rain. In a hostel a friendly relationship among the lodgers is of paramount importance: the gentle breeze is important on a sea voyage. If everything is carefully planned at the beginning, there will be no regrettable results at the end. One must straighten out one's own life before one can straighten out the lives of others. . . . The purpose of forming the *Chi-kung T'ang* is to maintain a friendly relationship among our countrymen and to accumulate wealth through proper business methods. . . . Among travelers there is no distinction between host and guest. When there is a common purpose we should work together; we arrive at the principle by being aware of the basic situation; we shall not be confused or shaken by slander; we act in the name of justice. In this way our organization shall enjoy a flourishing future; peace shall reign permanently within our hostel; members who are disciplined shall enjoy living together. There is a method in the making of money; one also enjoys the profit which is inherent in the rare items one has for sale.[31]

This preamble was a typical selection of moral homilies, literary images, calls for discipline and solidarity, and promises to serve the profit motive that had brought most of the migrants to Canada in the first place. The list of regulations following it described the keeping of association records, explained the regulation of mining claims and business transactions between members, outlined the rules of residence at the association hostel (one of a network of hostels throughout western Canada), and banned excessive intercourse with outsiders. These concerns depict the Zhigongtang not as hostile to outside authority (indeed, the references to harmony and discipline were quite in line with the interests of any government official) but as self-reliant with no expectation of help from the outside.

The Zhigongtang was a large and powerful organization with a membership developed through an initiation ritual. However, smaller associations, like surname associations, rotating credit clubs, and even business partnerships used much of the same vocabulary and assumptions about organization for mutual profit. A membership and rule booklet for a small rotating credit association in Chicago in the 1930s had less recourse to allegorical language but still used a similar vocabulary of discipline and morality as the basis of its operation:

> I have heard that this kind of righteous association was established by Lord Pang [a legendary philanthropist who became a boddhisatva] in order to provide comfort in adversity and mutual aid in the creation of equally shared interest payments. This is the gentleman's great way of getting rich. This member and his close friends will exercise mutual love and assistance in closely following and implementing the regulations of this association. It must be pledged that unity will be carefully maintained from beginning to end, so that profit will not all go to one man. Nobody will fail to be moved by this lofty friendship between the members.[32]

Although individual members occasionally cheated other members, these credit associations were usually successful in generating capital for individual migrant enterprises, especially when they were under the patronage of a wealthy and well-known guarantor. This success resulted not only from their practicality, but also from the precedent of responsibility and unity called upon in the formation of the association and, ideally, embodied in the presence of the guarantor.

The proprietors of laundries, restaurants, shops, rice farms, and other migrant enterprises also organized capital, attracted workers, and harmonized potentially disruptive relationships through the organizational and moral potential offered by sworn brotherhood and kinship. For example, the partnership papers for a Chinese commercial house established in Hawaii in 1901 appealed to literary precedent in its preamble, comparing the way of getting rich through the formation of a company to the "old history of Hon. Bow Suk, in Kuang Chung times."[33] The word *gongsi*, which now means a business enterprise, was widely used in previous centuries to denote agricultural, mining, and trading collectives in China and Southeast Asia that maintained traditions of initiation, symbolism, and violence commonly associated with sworn brotherhood societies.[34] Despite the exhortations for mutual support, small businesses could not depend only on the social pressures of their relatively small memberships to maintain social control. Therefore, most migrants chose to establish equal partnerships with men to whom they were already linked through ties of kin or native place. If problems arose with kinsmen, they could be referred to the mediation of a native place or surname institution. Workers who did not have ties of kinship with the partners were usually incorporated as wage earners rather than on a profit sharing basis and often treated with suspicion.[35]

The overseas organizational attempts of the imperial state were also framed within the same general discourses, although with less emphasis on brotherly cooperation in search of profit and more on the radiating moral benevolence of the emperor in the creation of mutual aid as a manifestation of righteousness. Many overseas CCBAs were created or reorganized in the 1880s under the patronage of Chinese diplomats. Ambassador Zheng Zaoru is credited with creating the Sociedad de Beneficencia China (SBC—the local version of a *zhonghua huiguan*) in Lima in 1884 and writing the following charter:

> The benevolent thoughts of the Sage Son of Heaven generate such mercy for the common people that they even radiate across the seas. He has especially appointed an important official to establish friendship with all the countries, to inquire about the welfare of his people, and comfort them. . . . [The Chinese in Peru] did not understand the urgency of creating networks of solidarity and have not used their capital to maintain security and uphold benevolence. Therefore, it has been ordered that the men concerned establish a Sociedad de Beneficencia China. This will necessarily unify the ambitions of the many as one and make it possible to order affairs such that they may be acted upon. This purpose is deep and far-reaching. . . . The first thing to be done after the establishment of the society will be to encourage the writing of letters home [on behalf of illiterate migrants] to inquire about their relatives and express our people's longing for their roots. Then a hospital, a graveyard, and an old persons' home will be discussed, thus encouraging concerned men of the urgency of finding a way to establish them. It can then be expected that the good deeds of men who desire righteousness will increase, creating a pattern which will benefit the development of brotherly assistance, and of connections with China. This vigorous and excellent tide will spread through foreign lands. In this way, the will of Lord Zheng can be established in order to repay the mercy of the Son of Heaven in not forgetting those who are far away. As this could not be achieved through the grace of only one man, the names of those who contributed should be recorded so they may be remembered a long time.[36]

Despite the credit claimed by the emperor and his representatives, this document actually recorded not the establishment of the SBC, but the cooptation and reorganization of a previously existing association under imperial patronage. Many of the projects it suggested had already been undertaken, even before the radiating mercy of the emperor had illuminated the way. This official co-optation, however, helped to prioritize projects that pointed back to China and to encourage migrant elites to identify their interests with those of the state.

Nationalist organizers other than the Qing government utilized similar vocabularies of loyalty and mutual protection in creating their first associations overseas. Like Qing officials, they had to deal with the organizational precedents already in place and find ways of redirecting them toward their own interests. The reform leaders Kang Youwei and Liang Qichao had been quick to join fraternal societies in their travels abroad after 1898, hoping both to make connections with their members and to benefit from the reputation of patriotic rebellion associated with the sworn brotherhood tradition in China. Their dependence upon the organizational precedents of these associations is evident in the charter for a branch of the Emperor Protection Society in Honolulu in 1900: "Those who have been admitted as members are termed 'brothers'. They ought to love each other as brothers from the same parents so as to exert themselves to take necessary steps in regard to political affairs of the country. If anyone do any harm or injury to our brothers we must retaliate the same." [37] As more branches were established, the assertions of brotherhood gave way to an increasingly political rhetoric that had an eye to "strengthening the nation" and earning the respect of the international community.

Migrant Associations as Modernity

At different times and places, migrants chose to define their associations as merchant, native place, kinship, fraternal, political, or occupational groups, but in practice no hard distinctions characterized any of them. Investment pooling, profit sharing, mediation, economic regulation, labor coordination, and representation through rotating officerships were common functions of all these associations. Kinship, native place, and sworn brotherhoods were widely understood symbols by which men could be brought together as well as ideological mediums for the further enforcement of trust. In return, the very institutionalization of kin, native place, and brotherhood oaths in these associations increased their salience as factors shaping the lives of Chinese migrants.

The continuing importance of these institutions should not be understood merely as the persistence of traditional values. Even lineages, which were firmly anchored in the control of land and the legacy of the past, grew in a context of changing government policy and increasing commercialization, and have continued to adapt and include the influence of migrants living thousands of miles away. The rise of *huiguan* and sworn brotherhoods was even more closely linked to the commercialism and physical mobility of the late imperial era, reaching a zenith of importance amidst the urbanization, migration, and political turmoil of the late nineteenth and early twentieth centuries. They were an important part of general dislocations that could be grouped under the label of modernity. Their creation of extra-official solidarity, their role as mutual aid organizations for mobile people, and their frequent appeal to personal interests and profit meant that they were even more able than lineages to respond flexibly and productively in new situations outside the orbit of the Qing government.

Gary Hamilton has made a similar argument about the role of native place associations among Chinese in Southeast Asia.[38] He notes a general trend in the nineteenth century away from migrant power based on clientele networks with local royalty who granted privileges and monopolies in exchange for Chinese labor and trade services. By the end of the century, the power of migrant elites was based on the control of money and the circulation of goods within an expanding market. This shift coincided with an increase in overseas populations, the gradual urbanization of overseas Chinese migrants, an occupational shift away from laborers to petty merchants, and a replacement of sworn brotherhood associations with native place and surname associations as the primary migrant institutions. He argues that all of these changes were aspects of the growth of colonialism, capitalism, and economic activities throughout the Pacific. In terms of colonialism, this shift was a result of government penetration and suppression. In efforts to expand their control, colonial and native governments stopped dealing with and even criminalized the associations that had once dominated rural labor, trade monopolies, and revenue farms. The rituals and violence of sworn brotherhoods were increasingly portrayed as subversive, especially in comparison to the seemingly parochial and benign organizational bases of kinship and native place associations.

By the early twentieth century, the image of Chinese around the world as coolies was replaced with the image of Chinese as small shopkeepers, extending their marketing networks deep into the interiors of many lands. Urban Chinese merchants were in a position to benefit most from the increased trade and migration that came with the expansion of capitalism. Control of debt and distribution networks was rapidly becoming more profitable than control of labor. As "respectable" businessmen, they cooperated with local governments in pushing out contenders for power. They also dominated the native place and surname associations that were emerging in greater numbers. Kinship and native place links were strong and flexible means of mobilizing business connections and supervising credit relationships.

Hamilton's argument should be qualified by noting that the decline of sworn brotherhoods in favor of surname and native place associations was particular to the history of Southeast Asia. In California, *huiguan* organized the first flows of labor to the gold mines in the 1850s. As Chinese were pushed out of most laboring occupations in the 1870s, sworn brotherhoods emerged to challenge the *huiguan* hegemony, which was no longer able to serve migrant interests.[39] This qualification reminds us not to erect any absolute distinctions between the characteristics of different Chinese associations and that such organizations are always embedded in larger socioeconomic contexts. The point remains that the mobilization of "traditional" and "parochial" Chinese bonds could be a practical response to changes brought by capitalist expansion and competition.

Lineages, *huiguan,* and sworn brotherhood associations were not merely a cultural background that was transplanted and adapted to new situations abroad. They were linked and expansive organizations that reached out from China and defined a global field of activity. They were the very fabric by which migration was made possible. Moreover, their support of migrant interests was inseparable from their mediation of modernizing changes.

COSMOLOGY AND RITUAL

The coexistence of official and local institutions can be described in terms of realist politics and economic shifts. Yet tension remains despite these practical accommodations. The creation of an ideological order can often prevent this tension from bursting into open conflict. In China, ritual practice was an important means of creating ideological order. It functioned well not because it demanded conformity of perception, but because it created a space for both the coexistence and confrontation of differences.

The Importance of Form

Proper ritual and behavior were very important in imperial China, from the emperor down to peasants in British Hong Kong. Scholar-officials often started from the assumption that correct comportment was the very basis of human society. The *Book of Rites,* one of the most popular ritual reference books of late imperial China, had this to say about ritual:

> Ceremonies form a great instrument in the hands of the ruler. They
> provide the means by which to resolve what is doubtful, clarify what
> is abstruse, receive the spirits, examine regulations, and distinguish
> humanness from righteousness. To govern a state without ritual would
> be as if to plow a field without a plowshare.[40]

In orthodox ideology, rites created order in the world of men that corresponded to the order of heaven. Virtue was perfected through the performance of rituals. Status distinctions and obligations were made clear,
and stability and harmony were perpetuated. Ignorance of proper forms
signified an undeveloped intellect and low cultural level—a gap separat-
ing one from the true nature of things.

The correct ritual deportment of rulers was only the tip of the ice-
berg. Everyday social interaction in China (e.g., greetings, speech, dress,
and writing) was also highly ritualized. Widely available handbooks outlined how rites should be performed in the household; gave detailed standards of behavior for the relations between husband and wife, father and
son, and official and commoner; provided models for invitations, wel-
comes, good-byes, and other social interactions both written and oral; and
offered descriptions of the gifts appropriate to particular occasions, often
with reference to local dialect terms and customs. Public ritual events like
naming ceremonies and funerals were often choreographed all the way
down to the wording of personal conversations. Documents and petitions,
presented to mortal officials or to the gods, would only be considered if
properly drawn and sealed.

A successful ritual was a properly performed one. The meaning of
the ceremonial actions and symbols was of little importance in comparison to their correct ordering and placement. Investigators both in China
and overseas have reported that different ritual participants and social
groups often had widely differing interpretations of common symbols.
Sometimes, participants had no interpretation at all, nor any interest in
having one, usually assuming that some expert somewhere knew the correct meaning. Nonetheless, participants were still greatly concerned that
the parts of a ritual come together and proceed in the proper order.[41] This
emphasis on proper performance helped bridge the gap between imperial
ideology and local practices, creating a field within which differing interests could be articulated.

James Watson's discussions of orthopraxis elaborate on the importance of ritual form in China as a tool of political and cultural integration
across geographical and social distance.[42] He argues that many ritual symbols and procedures are common throughout China. His own research has

attempted to show the similarity of ritual procedures surrounding marriage and death that have been performed throughout China, even by Christians. This did not come about only by imitation, but also through the intervention of the state and local elites searching for recognition from the state. For many officials (as for Watson), identity as Chinese (and therefore as civilized humans) was based more on the proper performance of key rituals than on any racial or political distinctions. They made constant efforts to standardize ritual practice throughout the realm and among foreign tribute missions. This meant not only the propagation of ritual norms, but also the harmonizing of local variations and the revision of rituals that were no longer suitable to the times. The vigilance of the Chinese state against heterodoxy entailed not the monitoring of thought but the suppression of military threat and harmonization of public behavior. Even emperors patronized Buddhist sects and eclectic folk religions. If they continued to perform and promote the rituals required of their position, no contradiction existed. As long as external order was manifested through acceptance of proper symbols and individuals were fulfilling their proper roles in relation to others, the imperial government did not need to exact ideological conformity from its subjects. Merely taking part in a ritual was submission to its authority.

Watson's argument comes from the perspective of an outsider who can transcend many of the differences in ritual interpretation. Different actors within Chinese society held different views on what really held it all together. Scholars generally claimed the empire was held together through the moral virtue cultivated by rites and often assumed that conformity in ritual led to conformity in values. Local communities, on the other hand, rarely looked much further than the relationships created around particular gods, ancestors, and material concerns. They assumed that proper ritual created a relationship of mutual obligation between god and petitioner, thus effecting the granting of favors and protection. The role of brute force in maintaining the power of the imperial state was more openly acknowledged than bureaucrats were wont to do. Rambunctious local gods could even invert the norms of the imperial bureaucracy. Even single individuals could hold contradicting views on the meaning of ritual and religious matters, such as the fate of the soul after death. In various contexts, informants have told anthropologists that dead souls inhabit the ancestral tablets, pass their days endlessly in the underworld, and are reincarnated after a period of judgment, feeling little pressure to reconcile the differences.[43]

These differences highlight the importance of ritual. Different interpretations could coexist because they were rarely made to account for themselves, except by nosy ethnographers. At the same time, ritual brought these differences together in a single order. Participation in a ritual was (at least temporary) submission to the world that it created. The standardization of ritual in China did not eradicate unorthodox ritual; it was a constant process that incorporated and transformed local rituals in the name of updating and harmony. The result was not moral conformity, so much as the arrangement of order between conflicting interests.

My point is not that the elaborate development of ritual was a unique characteristic of Chinese society. The feelings and knowledge of contemporary Americans are equally shaped by etiquette and form. Legal procedure and jargon, table manners, business correspondence, job interviews, and the plot structure of fiction are just some of the more obvious examples, all with reference manuals available for guidance. Without the familiar structure of thesis and supporting arguments, academic prose such as this would convey no knowledge to its intended audience.[44] The most notable characteristic of China in this respect was the sophisticated understanding that many scholar-officials had of ritual and how to manipulate it. They knew that bureaucratic order, local solidarities, and individual desires all came together through ritual. Like associations and institutions, rituals at any moment were embedded in particular historical contexts but also provided precedents for reproduction and adaptation. Of particular interest are local rituals involving ghosts and gods which defined the relationships between inside and outside, and channeled interactions between groups.[45]

Gods

The politically integrating power of ritual came to the forefront in the official temple system and worship of gods. The worship of officially recognized and unrecognized gods provided a forum for the negotiation of social integration and differentiation. This took place both through the simultaneous existence of different interpretations and through the services of particular gods who were efficacious mediators. Imperial cosmologies emphasized a vertical structure in which local units were distinguished hierarchically along lines that were ultimately integrated at the center. The gods of households, towns, cities, and the capital occupied different levels in that hierarchy. Local communities, on the other hand, engaged in communal rituals as acts of solidarity and differentiation from other groups, including the negotiation of relationships with bureaucratic and military powers. Thus, the official pantheon did not impose a set of homogeneous interpretations. Rather, it laid out a set of widely recognized symbols that made communication, accommodation, and resistance possible.

Heaven was often depicted as a bureaucratic realm comparable to and perhaps mirrored by the bureaucracy on earth.[46] Officially, the temple system and its corresponding rituals were the keys to establishing harmony in the world of men. The emperor was at the center performing the rituals that mediated with heaven at the Temple of Heaven; city gods were worshiped by city magistrates, local gods by local communities, and the last five generations of family ancestors by individual households. In this model, the relationship between the units was a vertical one of nested hierarchy, with the increasingly numerous subdivisions spread out in relationship to the center. Order was most highly manifested at the center, and became increasingly diffuse as one moved farther away. Nonetheless, disorder was held in check by properly ranked incorporation into the hierarchy. Thus, the perpetuation of appropriate rites by suitable representatives at each level of the hierarchy was of paramount concern. Commoners were excluded from official rites performed at the city and imperial temples, and officials tended to ignore local festivals, except to criticize the wanton ways in which they were performed.

The worship of gods had a different political significance from local perspectives, where it unified groups and distinguished them from outsiders. Temples and gods were important as centers of territorial, kin, and occupational groupings, and as sources of magical power, rather than as branches of a central power structure radiating out from Beijing. Communal worship often took the form of temple fairs and processions through a local territory. The leadership and financing of these festivals were mediums for the competition and distribution of terrestrial power. The gods protected local communities against threats from the outside. Groups thus distinguished themselves by their particular relationship to a god, and their particular method of worship. These particularities were tied to specific historical memories: perhaps a temple had been established by the founder of the community, the founder himself had become a god, or a particular miracle or act of domination had tied the god and community together. The possession of spirit mediums by gods (or, more commonly in the Pearl River Delta, by ancestors) kept the past relevant through continuing dialogue. The distinction between groups was horizontal, and the rising and waning fortunes of a group were thought to be related to the powers and accessibility of the god associated with it.

Many local temple gods belonged to the official pantheon of state-approved gods, and the state was usually ready to co-opt any new god that was rising in popularity. Local groups recognized that a celestial hierarchy existed, and individuals interacted with many gods on the basis of that assumption. The more bureaucratic gods required name, address, and date of birth in order to find the file of the petitioner and consider his request. From this perspective, Chinese worship can be seen as an extension of imperial order beyond the limits of the terrestrial bureaucracy or as a process of learning the kinds of procedures needed to interact with bureaucrats in the world of men.[47] Officials often promoted ritual as a memorializing action, an orderly procedure which put the mind at ease and created morality in accordance with the order of heaven. They publicly condemned the magic, superstition, waste, and self-interest they perceived in local worship. Nonetheless, locals did not sacrifice total control of the celestial bureaucracy to the official ideology. The hierarchy itself remained stable, but the identities of the gods who filled the positions were often disputed and subject to local interpretation, as were the meanings of rituals used to worship them. Local worship was generally quite pragmatic, assuming that gods were motivated to perform favors based on the same feelings of greed and reciprocal obligation as men. Worshiping a god was not presenting tribute, as an official might have it, but making a deal or, alternatively, taking part in a nurturing exchange similar to parent and child relationships.

Another significant divergence in local and official interpretations was that the government presented the heavenly hierarchy as a structure of radiating moral example that ensured civil harmony, whereas many local representations gave it a much more military cast that emphasized the hierarchy of command and the ever present threat of violence. The city god was a prominent site for these contradictions between official and local views. For officials, he was the final dependable representative of morality and rectitude. Locals, on the other hand, often depicted him as a general in charge of a host of demonic powers, a force to be feared. These contradictions had no real ideological resolution, but neither were they totally incompatible, enacted as they were with respect to commonly shared symbols of authority.

From local perspectives, gods lower in the celestial bureaucracy were more efficacious at protecting communities and granting personal favors than higher ones because they were much more approachable and responsive to the needs of commoners. Higher gods, like great bureaucrats in the world of men, were far too distant, surrounded by red tape, and morally demanding to be of much use. The gods most often considered to be of greatest efficacy were officially recognized, but not quite orthodox enough to be completely identified with the heavenly bureaucracy.

They were often female gods, like Guanyin, a Buddhist goddess of mercy, and Mazu, a very popular goddess in coastal areas, who was not only a woman but also a virgin and thus very unfilial and immoral because she produced no sons.[48] Guandi, a very popular god in many parts of China and overseas, was a famous soldier from the novel *Romance of the Three Kingdoms* who died childless. He was considered to be the god of wealth, brotherhood, and war. As we have already seen, brotherhood and the search for riches have much in common with each other (the military aspect of migrant associations is elaborated in chapter 6) and have the potential to form power bases that could be subversive to the imperial state.

Such gods had been accepted into the imperial pantheon as a result of widespread popular worship but were rarely found in any of the higher bureaucratic positions. They had one foot in the bureaucratic system and the other foot in the popular world. They were both flexible in response to human demands and well connected in the celestial bureaucracy, and thus well suited to act efficaciously as mediators between the world of men and the underworld. Many Daoist priests also bridged the gap between officialdom and local community by asserting that their rituals involved a specialized knowledge of the procedures necessary for navigating the underworld bureaucracy, often comparing their services to those of lawyers in the world of men. They rarely earned the respect of the popular gods, but could earn a good living nonetheless.[49]

The bureaucracy was not the source of all power. Gods identified with the Buddhist tradition were also often treated with slightly more respect than those associated with Daoism because of their special connections to foreign sources of power and prestige.[50] In more peripheral parts of China, distant from the reach of the imperial state and its favors, popular gods frequently mocked and inverted official order, acting out the corruption and arbitrariness of the bureaucracy in practice. While abroad, Chinese were rarely shy about worshiping any local god they thought would be responsive to them. Local gods had local jurisdiction and the connections necessary to grant local requests. Chinese in nineteenth-century Philadelphia built small altars in their shops dedicated to the "Chinese and Foreign Lord of the Place."[51] Chinese in Bangkok have long visited a temple that houses what the Thais believe to be the spirit of San Bao He, a famous mendicant monk. The Chinese claim this name refers to the eunuch admiral Zheng He, who commanded the early Ming Dynasty fleets that sailed through the Indian Ocean. Chinese are aware of the Thai interpretation and figure that it only makes this spirit better connected and more efficacious.[52] Only small adaptations in sacrificial procedure had to be made in response to local tastes, such as not offering pork to the Islamic saints.

The simultaneous tension and collaboration between lineages and the state reappears again in relationships between local communities of worship and the imperial pantheon. The role of efficacious gods brings out the importance of mediators in bridging these tensions. Few economic and social transactions in China could be carried on without the assistance of a third party whose reputation was well known to all concerned. The third party made connections where no previous relation existed, and used his influence to guarantee the outcome. Skinner's work on the Chinese elites of Thailand in the 1950s shows in great detail the mediating role of men who were skilled in two cultural idioms. He concluded, however, that their situation was paradoxical—that these men could not persist and were vanguards of assimilation.[53] I would argue, on the other hand, that these men embodied what Wakeman called the "dynamic oscillation" between integration with and autonomy from the local state and its cultural hegemony. Indeed, recent scholars have shown that Skinner's prediction of Chinese assimilation has not come to pass, and that a recognizable Sino-Thai identity has emerged.[54] The existence of gods and men that straddled boundaries was both expected and desirable for the maintenance of local groups, a stable yet dynamic form of adaptation.

Men who could act as intercultural mediators for overseas communities tended either to be respected and central to the community or despised and marginalized—and sometimes a bit of both. While the boundaries themselves were blurred within the persons of the mediators, the profits and prestige that could be gained by controlling access across those boundaries meant that mediators had a strong interest in maintaining them. Because their prestige arose from their ability to bridge differences and ease tensions, they depended on the continued existence of those tensions and differences, however they might be defined.

Ghosts

In Thailand and other overseas countries, Chinese migrants were not trying to deal with the imperial state and its stabilizing ambitions but with the obscure and disordered habits of barbarians. Direct dealings with outsiders were risky, unprotected by the encompassing institutions and bonds of family or sworn brotherhoods. They were discouraged by lineages or associations that wanted to keep wealth within the unit and by elites who wanted to keep such interactions under their control. On the other hand, outsiders offered opportunities not readily available within more familiar relationships. In this sense, the relationship of men with ghosts is a more appropriate metaphor to describe Chinese relations with non-Chinese than the relations of men and gods. Gods (although, as we shall see, the distinctions between gods and ghosts were often blurred) were associated with the bureaucracy, order, and civilization of the Empire. Ghosts were the results of breakdowns in moral order; in this case, the order of filiality, proper ritual, and proper accommodation for death. They were tangible examples of disorder, of civilized ways in abeyance, and the hassles that arose as a consequence. Yet this very alienation from the restrictions and violence of imperial order meant that ghosts could also be more approachable and easy to deal with than gods, sometimes providing favors that would be difficult to obtain elsewhere. These favors could be obtained through the establishment of formalized and predictable relationships of exchange.

Chinese often directly applied the term *ghost* to non-Chinese, marking them as people of unfamiliar cultural practices, if not "beyond the pale" of civilization. One missionary traveling through Canton in 1835 was particularly distressed by this practice, here using the word devil rather than ghost:

> In addition to the word "barbarian," which is liberally bestowed on all
> without the pale of Chinese civilization, a more offensive epithet is
> not infrequently employed. On passing through the suburbs of Can-
> ton, or up and down the river, the cry of "foreign devil" salutes the ear
> on every side. Even mothers may be seen teaching their infants to
> point and to shout the offensive epithet as the stranger passes by.
> Some will even go out of their way or desist from their work to gratify
> their railing propensities.[55]

The term was still in common usage in 1930s Chicago. Americans were known as "Flowery Flag ghosts" *(huaqi gui)*—the Flowery Flag being a Chinese name for America—postmen as "letter delivery ghosts" *(songxin gui)*, bartenders as "bar ghosts" *(jiuba gui)*, farmers as "potato ghosts" *(shuzi gui)*, and bank tellers as "bank room ghosts" (bank-*fang gui*).[56]

Most Chinese could probably not have explained their use of *gui* as anything more than a habitual stereotype. Nonetheless, the use of this particular word draws attention to its metaphorical appropriateness in understanding Chinese views of non-Chinese, and the relationships implied by the label could be found in many of their actions. In earlier usage, *gui* was a generic term for animals, sometimes extended to denote people of alien origin.[57] It was often difficult for Chinese to observe and describe foreigners without being shocked at their disregard of the norms of human culture and resorting to images of disorder and bestial appetites. The reminiscences of a Chinese migrant in New York at the turn of the century of how foreigners had been spoken about in his home village illustrates this shock:

> I listened and heard much concerning the red-haired, green-eyed foreign devils with the hairy faces. . . . They were wild and fierce and wicked, and paid no regard to the moral precepts of Confucius and the Sages; neither did they worship their ancestors, but pretended to be wiser than their fathers and grandfathers. They loved to beat people and to rob and murder. In the streets of Hong Kong many of them could be seen reeling drunk. Their speech was a savage roar, like the voice of the tiger or buffalo. Their men and women lived together like animals, without any marriage or faithfulness, and even were shameless enough to walk the streets arm in arm in daylight.[58]

Ghosts, gods, and ancestors had all started out as men. After death, some men were promoted to the status of gods due to some mixture of uncommon virtue and widespread popularity. Ancestors were given material support in the underworld through family worship and continued to influence the well-being of the family. To become an ancestor, the dead needed money, contracts, servants, clothes, and furniture in order to navigate the underworld bureaucracy and exist in comfort. Ideally, descendants were expected to continue providing these necessities by worshiping the dead souls, as embodied in a tablet on the family altar, for five generations. Untended souls not properly incorporated into a family line would become ghosts. Ghosts wandered around the world of men, anguished, hungry, and restless, causing trouble and worry to the living. Dying with no sons who could continue the family line, dying in a foreign country, dying by suicide, drowning, or violence were common ways in which men could end up as ghosts.

The identities of ancestors were clearly demarcated, but ghosts were the spirits of individuals whose names and positions had been forgotten, entities who had no relationship with a living human. Gods and ancestors were worshiped individually, each one represented by a tablet or idol. Ghosts were worshiped in mass, anonymously. Large communal ceremonies for ghost propitiation were carried out in many parts of China during the seventh lunar month, when the gates of hell were opened and ghosts roamed the face of the earth. The offerings given to the ghosts were not later eaten by the ritual participants as in other sacrifices but were left to the local beggars. The chaos that usually ensued after the gates were opened and the beggars let in was considered to be a fitting counterpart in the world of men to the chaos of ghosts being let loose in the spirit world.[59] In their domestic worship, families put a snack or meal at some undistinguished place outside the back door to propitiate any ghost that might happen to wander by. Taiwanese informants in the 1960s said that a ghost should be treated much as one would treat a local hoodlum or policeman: "You have to give them something to eat so that they will go away and not cause trouble."[60]

Hints of such relationships could be detected in the ways that migrants dealt with non-Chinese abroad. Migrants in Philadelphia in the 1880s often told stories of the midnight visitations to their laundries of unlaid spirits that were usually non-Chinese. During the Hungry Ghost Festival, clothes, the object most frequently provided by laundry workers to non-Chinese, were burnt in laundries as sacrifices to the local ghosts.[61] A scene very evocative of the feeding of small snacks to ghosts in order to keep them in good temper was described in a newspaper account of Chinese New Year's festivities in Stockton, California, in the 1880s:

> The Chinese were well-behaved, orderly and not drunk or riotous; however, there were white drunks about Chinatown. . . . Cigars, drinks, candies, and so forth are passed to the visitors by smiling Celestials, and all is hospitality and good will. . . . When a Chinaman receives a visitor, he first offers him a small cup of tea, then a cigar, and then anything else that is about that the visitor desires.[62]

The association of ghosts with chaos was not absolute. Injuries inflicted by a ghost on the health or fortunes of living family members or people living near the site of their death were usually a means of attracting attention to their plight, with the goal of reincorporation into a worship structure through processes such as spirit marriage or adoption. In these instances, the status of ancestor or ghost was defined by integration or lack of integration into proper family relationships. Such ghosts were usually looked upon with pity more than fear, despite the trouble they caused. Nonetheless, the order created through family integration was not absolute. Souls that were adequately worshiped by one family could still be considered ghosts by the members of other families.[63] In this case, the label *ghost* just marked out a realm of outsiders not linked through kinship ties, without any ultimate implication of disorder. Such a "ghost" was still recognized to be part of the order of a different family.

Despite efforts to maintain order and boundaries, ghostliness could even penetrate the heavenly bureaucracy. Most households had altars to the kitchen god, the lowest member of the imperial hierarchy. Worshipers have described the kitchen god in a variety of ways: as a minor clerical functionary, an informant, a voyeur, a gossipy old woman, a guest, and even a suicide. Sacrifices to him were sometimes perceived as bribes that would fill his mouth and render him unable to make his report to higher-ups. In most of these cases, he was depicted more like a ghost than a Confucian official. Hardly a moral exemplar, or even an efficacious mediator, the kitchen god embodied the dissipation and corruption of imperial order when spread thin at the lowest levels.[64] More telling, however, were aspects of the ghostly world commonly depicted in a military idiom that emphasized a confluence of rigid order, threat, and the ultimate chaos of pillage and violent destruction. Many community and territorial gods, including city gods, were seen by locals as celestial generals commanding fearsome ghost armies that were far more threatening and demonic than the slightly pathetic and outcast hungry ghosts. From this perspective, the basis of bureaucratic power was not its manifestation of heavenly virtue, but its marshaling and control of potentially chaotic and destructive forces. Even gods based power on ghosts.[65]

Most ghosts, such as the spirits of dead soldiers and drowning victims, had little hope of incorporation as ancestors. Other means of differentiating themselves from anonymity were available, however, usually based on the creation of exchange relationships with humans. Some ghosts just started causing trouble to strangers and making their demands for worship known through spirit mediums. When worship was obtained, these ghosts reciprocated by providing protection to their worshipers and becoming "little gods."[66] In this sense they were in a position similar to renegade gods who had gained power by flaunting and circumventing moral standards. Many ghost shrines, particularly the burial sites of unknown soldiers, grew extremely popular because of the willingness of the ghosts to respond to petitions for personal favors without the troublesome procedures and moral requirements of the bureaucrats. Relationships with ghosts or with renegade gods who stood completely outside of the bureaucracy were based on relatively straightforward and egalitarian forms of reciprocity, accessible to anyone and uncomplicated by the demands of hierarchy and formalized morality. The unspecified nature of ghostliness provided more room for exchange than the clearly delineated structures of the bureaucracy, and the willingness of ghosts to grab any opportunity to be worshiped overcame the constraints of adhering to a moral ideology. Knowledge of the desires of ghosts and the ability to control, deploy and strike bargains with them were possible routes to wealth and power, free from the intervention of mediators.

Cosmologies of Migration

Rituals and depictions of the netherworld were arenas for the articulation of imperial control and local autonomy in China. Common symbolism did not so much reconcile differences as place them in relation to each other. The imperial cosmology arranged these symbols vertically in a hierarchical relation to the center, whereas the popular cosmology depicted the world horizontally as a collection of autonomous units struggling and negotiating for their own benefit. Conflicts rarely came to a head because integration into the imperial system was ultimately an abstract and distant process, achieved only in the person of the emperor. Daily life had to negotiate the challenges of neighbors and the immediate physical environment.

Efficacious gods, Daoist priests, and other ritual specialists acted as points of communication between different worlds, such as state and locality or the underworld and the world of men. By providing services that crossed those boundaries, they helped bridge the gap between them. At the same time, the very necessity of their services perpetuated the differences. From most perspectives, ghosts inhabited a realm of disorder and mild danger. Although official ideologues tended to dismiss belief in ghosts as degenerate local custom, the renegade status of ghosts confirmed the official ideology of the family as a basic unit of worldly order, condemning the souls who fell outside of the family as illegitimate and dangerous. Yet humans could take advantage of this renegade status by establishing exchange relationships with ghosts that could circumvent more restrictive official channels to opportunity and power. Many even suspected that official power was dependent on ghosts in the end.

This structuring of social relationships can be used to depict the experiences of Chinese migrants outside of China. Non-Chinese were often seen to embody a kind of social disorder similar to that represented by ghosts: a sphere that was threatening yet rich with opportunities and sources of power. If exchange relationships could be established with non-Chinese, profit and prestige could result. On an individual level, the establishment of such relationships was facilitated by the development of formalized methods of exchange, such as the simple vocabulary necessary for basic business transactions. Yet the disorder of ghosts could also be relative. The barbarians were members of strong and threatening states (sometimes so strong that migrants came to doubt the strength of the Chinese state) against which migrants needed to position themselves. They also had customs that could be learned. Men who became skilled in those customs could act as crucial mediators, protecting the integrity of the Chinese community through the channeling of services and favors. That is to say, patterns of social relations from China provided a template by which the increased integration of migrant communities with their surroundings would mean their identification not as individualized objects of assimilation but as a distinct corporate unit that could interact with outsiders through predictable channels of communication.

This model can help to understand much about Chinese migrants, such as the important roles of cosmopolitan elites and the ways that interactions between Chinese and non-Chinese may have been differently interpreted. Yet such a mapping of ritual order onto social behavior must be made with great caution. It becomes particularly problematic when we note that many of the rituals described here are embedded in the framework of the imperial Chinese state. Of what relevance were these rituals and cosmologies in the context of post-1911 China, not to mention overseas environments?

Ironically, the majority of the material used in this chapter was drawn from ethnographic research in post-1950s Taiwan and Hong Kong. The imperial framework of the rituals has obviously retained some significance in changing political environments. Although scholars have noted some adaptations in post-imperial times, available historical research confirms a broad area of continuity.[67] The failure of early republican governments in China has been explained in part by their inability and disinclination to engage in expected ritual exchanges.[68] Maurice Bloch has also noted the stability of ritual practices over two hundred years of political change in Madagascar. He argues that the vagueness and illogic of rituals makes it possible for their representations of power to remain stable through different actors and governments.[69] The very purpose of ritual is to depict ideologically the continuity of power despite contingent events. Adjustments are made, but the basic relationships remain the same.

Yet the large, rowdy festivals, orchestrated rituals, and territorial processions that still have symbolic and organizational importance in Taiwan and the People's Republic of China in recent years had largely disappeared from the Western Hemisphere by the early twentieth century. Most migrant associations maintained altars, but they were almost all dedicated to Guandi, which emphasizes how little attention was given to the marking of community through histories of association and reciprocity with different gods.[70] The more secular rituals of migrant associations—mostly banquets and speeches—had become the main symbolic markers of differentiation among Chinese. Traditional calendric festivals such as Chinese New Year and Mid-Autumn festival were celebrated primarily as occasions for family reunions, relaxation, personal visits, and more associational banquets.[71] Funerals of migrant elites were perhaps the largest communal ritual to be regularly encountered in the Western Hemisphere, usually as a display of the wealth and prestige of the man who died. Why were the rituals rarely reproduced abroad? Without the rituals, what happened to the kinds of social relationships that were played out through them?

Paul Siu recorded a young migrant in Chicago in the 1930s as saying, "The ancestor, if he is really a spirit, can't come over here with us, can he? This place is not suitable for him. Things in this foreign land must be different."[72] Unfortunately, the context of this comment was not enough to determine if the speaker was a believer speculating on the physics of spirit mobility or a skeptic influenced either by his experience in America or by the anti-superstition trends then popular in China. In all these cases, however, this comment assumed that Chinese religion, like the lineages, had fixed territorial moorings. Ancestors, territorial gods, and even ghosts were associated with land, gravesites, and shrines. Although the migrant had moved, his territorial base had not. Was it not pointless to perform ancestral and territorial rituals abroad when they were being performed at home, often with the continued participation of the migrants through financial contributions and decision making?

Religious practice did persist abroad in more individualized forms, regardless of whether or not the gods were able to travel across the ocean to hear personal petitions. Most patrons of temples and altars sought personal divinations and individual favors for luck in gambling and business. Similarly, graveside rituals and care for the bones of the dead continued to be performed at least until the Second World War. Belief was not gone, but the context for communal worship was. Chinese migrants and non-Chinese states had no common symbolic language by which they could engage in ritual discourses.

Even if it had been possible, it may not have been desirable to reproduce Chinese rituals in non-Chinese states. In the eyes of foreign states, the relevant units of group solidarity were not clans and villages, but ethnicity, class, or even occupation. At the level of local ethnic politics previous rituals became useless and even detrimentally divisive in the face of larger threats. Not only were the Chinese dealing with governments that cared nothing for their ritual symbolism (as was officially the case in Taiwan and Hong Kong), but also with neighbors who did not share their ritual practices. The secular associations proved more adept at adapting to these new conditions than did religious ritual. Chinese who were most attuned to local assimilationist rhetoric were even inclined to reject the usual migrant associations in favor of new ones like the Chinese American Citizens Alliance, Tayouk Tennis Club of Miraflores, or Chinese Rotary Clubs. The rhetoric and rituals of nationalism also provided a common means of interaction with neighbors and local states, although this could backfire when the loyalty of the Chinese was called into question. New Year's parades and Chinatown arches are other examples of how Chinese have defined their identity and territory in ways that local states and neighbors could appreciate. All of these approaches involved the reformulation of group solidarity and individual ambition in terms of local and global power structures.

Although this secularization of social relations can seem like a pragmatic reaction to new social environments, we may still ask about the continued relevance of rituals in China among migrants who still contributed financially to their perpetuation. Hill Gates has suggested a twist on the Chinese ritual cosmologies that may help address this issue. More strongly than I have done, she depicts two ritual ideologies in opposition to each other, sharing a common commitment to the family. Official Confucianist ideology was a manifestation of the interests of the tributary state (which includes Taiwan and the PRC). Popular rituals made up an ideology of petty capitalism that was in opposition to those states. She argues that relations with ghosts are actually an idealization of petty capitalist relations that cut across officially approved hierarchy. They represent exchange relationships entered from positions of equality, in which money is a purifying medium that opens up the lines of communication between the dead and the living. "Money subverts the rigid rules of tributary inequality, offers greater distributive justice, and thus glows with a luster brighter than virtue."[73] Thus, in the context of the imperial state, ghost worship was a manifestation of a transcultural petty bourgeoisie ideology. This suggests a variation on the idea that foreign governments merely could not understand Chinese rituals. Starting from the idea that migration itself was a family strategy in pursuit of gain, it could follow that once Chinese were abroad they could openly devote their daily lives to petty capitalist transactions. The ideology of tributary power that had compelled negotiations to take place in ritual form no longer existed as a significant force in the lives of migrants.

Difficulties arise with this explanation when we note that, even if the rituals tended to disappear abroad, the ghosts did not. More so than with ancestors and gods, ghosts were likely to be found in inhospitable places. Migrants were surrounded by ghosts and were not necessarily happy about it. Petty capitalist or not, they wanted to carefully regulate their relationships with those ghosts. Not only did migrants resist becoming ghosts themselves by dying abroad with nobody to take care of their souls, but even the experience of living abroad was akin to an experience of ghostliness in this world. In Shanghai, enormous territorial rites and festivals to feed the hungry ghosts were sponsored by native place associations on into the twentieth century, despite the objections of officials. They were instrumental in demarcating and expanding the prestige of competing native place interests, but also provided rites of incorporation that dealt with the worries of the many rootless and indigent men in the city.[74] The daily life of isolation and frustration described by Paul Siu also resonates as a kind of ghostliness on earth. Despite the potential benefits of interacting with ghosts, migration remained a risky flirtation with all the negative aspects of ghostliness.

Gates's logic might explain this as the alienation that results when petty bourgeoisie ideology is carried to its extreme. If money and exchange carried the luster of egalitarian virtue, they also brought the isolation of atomized self-interest. The main protection that migrants had against this atomization was the maintenance of networks linking them to their homes. Individuals were willing to confront the risks of the outside only if they were assured of the backing and stability of family and other corporate units. An individual fraternizing with ghosts on his own without any corporate support was likely to become little more than a ghost himself (as with the many bicultural individuals who were despised and mistrusted despite the services they performed). The ritual cosmology within which migrants were embedded must be understood on a transnational scale. Migrants were not merely relocating themselves in a new setting where ritual relations had to be reconstructed. They were entering the ghostly margins of a cosmology centered on their families in China and had to put effort into maintaining those links.

As these networks expanded, they adapted situationally to local sociopolitical contexts, as discussed in the following three chapters. The challenges of nationalism and of modernizing and localizing identities were not always successfully accommodated by these transnational networks. Also, the transnational links could be brittle, and migrants occasionally broke off and fell out of their networks. Adjustments were made, however, differently in each of the three locations, but all connected to the same economic and cultural interests in Hong Kong and villages in South China.

CHAPTER 5

Becoming Foreigners in Peru

They have come from Canton
even blind men and babes,
and now they are dressed for respect.
Today, in Peru
the Chinaman wants to be somebody.

Today many are plantation managers
and owners of shops,
and through pure plunder
have earned lots of cash.

They have earned to the point
they can kick back and grow fat.
This thing so disgraceful
is the obvious truth.
They desire to be somebody
but they never will be.

> "El chino quiere ser gente," Peruvian folksong

THE CONSTITUTION OF A BUSINESS COMMUNITY

Wu Tingfang's Agenda for the Chinese of Peru

The visit to Lima of Wu Tingfang, the minister plenipotentiary and envoy extraordinary of the Chinese Empire to the United States, Cuba, and Peru in 1909 was a significant social and diplomatic occasion for Peruvians and Chinese alike. Chinese in Peru have remembered this visit as a political and social success reflecting on them and on China as a modern nation. The Porras-Wu Protocol that resulted from this visit left little basis for such a proud memory. At best, the voluntary suspension of emigration to

Peru provided for in the protocol was a face-saving compromise which established the same status for China vis-à-vis Peru that Japan had achieved
vis-à-vis the United States with the signing of the 1907 Gentleman's Agreement. At worst, its failure to provide any realistic regulation of migration
called into question the good faith and domestic powers of both governments. But hints of failure have been overshadowed by the recognition accorded to Wu himself. His reception demonstrated that the wealthiest and
most powerful elites of Peru were willing to welcome a Chinese representative with the highest standards of civility and negotiate with him on
terms of equality. It was a public declaration that Chinese could resolve
their problems without descending to the level of the lower classes who
had looted and burnt their shops in May 1909.

Wu was a progressive official, born in Singapore, who had long been
associated with various reform factions in China. He had written the first
commercial law code for China in 1904 and had achieved solid successes
in projecting a positive image of China as a modern nation during his diplomatic career. Shortly before his departure from Lima, on 22 August,
a banquet was given in his honor. Bankers, doctors, senators, the prefect
of Lima, the captain of the police, and several Chinese businessmen attended. Wu gave two speeches, one in English and one in Chinese. The
speech in English covered the usual courtesies of thanking his Peruvian
hosts for their hospitality and their willingness to cooperate in the spirit
of civilization. The speech in Chinese was more didactic. The leading Peruvian newspaper, *El Comercio*, summarized its contents as follows:

> [Wu said that the Chinese in Peru should] try to assimilate themselves
> to the customs and habits indigenous to the country, the laws of which
> they should know and respect, dedicating themselves exclusively to
> work and the fulfillment of their obligations; that by such means,
> each man wins the esteem of his equals; that the upper and official
> classes of Peru have a good opinion of the Chinese residents, judging
> them to be of prudent and diligent character; that they should en-
> deavor to extend this opinion to the lower classes, who are the most
> impressionable and share neither the leisure nor the capability for
> analysis of the superior classes; that they engage in isolated and indi-
> vidual work, which can then be translated into collective force; . . .
> that they already live in a constitutional nation, and they should in-
> struct themselves in its legislation which is seated in the rights of man
> and society; and given that China would soon be ruled constitution-
> ally, and would be frankly following the road of progressive innova-

tions, . . . they should repay the hospitality of this country with an honorable comportment and hard work.[1]

Wu's speech presented local ethnic relations as inseparable from international relations. Harmony in both was achieved through mutual respect earned by honorable behavior. Acceptance by Peruvians was predicated on adherence to universal standards of comportment, one of which was respect for sovereignty and customs. Local customs did not deserve to be adhered to merely because they existed, but because they were part of a constitutional nation that was "seated in the rights of man and society." Assimilation to local customs was encouraged not as a process of amalgamation into local society but as a complement to isolated and productive work as a strategy for gaining respect. Wu saw strong and honorable national identities as the foundation of harmonious relations, but such identities had to be constantly adjusted in conformance to international standards of behavior and local opinion. The process of acceptance in Peru would not only serve the interests of local Chinese, but would reflect the ability of China to hold a place in the modern world.

Over the next twenty years, the migrant elites in Peru tried to live up to much of this advice. They made economic accomplishment the basis for any claim to social recognition. They presented themselves to the Peruvian public not as the representatives of Chinese associations or the Chinese community, but as the honorable managers of important companies who worked in the interests of Peru without interfering in the affairs of the people. They framed their commercial efforts in the language favored by the Lima elites who controlled international commerce and the exploitation of Peru's natural wealth. This was part of a strategy to become known as "foreigners" rather than merely Chinese. That is, they endeavored to be equated with the foreign merchants from North America and Europe, whom much of the coastal elite put forth as ideals of what Peru should strive to become. They did this by emphasizing their international commercial activities and working closely with diplomatic representatives from China.

Public statements in Peru were always couched in the rhetoric of constitutional rights. Different social groups in Peru all phrased their own interests within that rhetoric, and the Chinese were no different. In their efforts to do so, the Chinese also conformed with the tendency of the Peruvian elite to define their own modernity in opposition to the lower classes, who were seen not as the basis of progressive government but as its irrational alter ego, as suggested in Wu's low estimation of their "capability of analysis." Thus, Chinese made it clear that they represented international standards of order and modernity, and the formation of a Peru that conformed to that order. The underside of this "constitutional" order was the frequency with which Peruvian elites were willing to ignore national laws in pursuit of individual interests. Chinese also aggressively cultivated the exchange of special favors and privileges.

Merchants and Migrant Power

The presence of official delegates like Wu injected local problems with international significance. In cities like Chicago, where there was no diplomatic representation, Chinese could rarely hope to be more than another exotic immigrant group at best. In Lima they were the representatives of and were represented by a nation. The first Chinese delegation sent to Peru in 1874 to investigate of the conditions of Chinese plantation laborers was associated with the end of the coolie trade and the signing of the Treaty of Friendship, Commerce, and Navigation. The visit of Minister Zheng Zaoru in 1883–84 resulted in the establishment of a commercial agent in Lima, a system of consuls up and down the Peruvian coast, and recognition by the Chinese government of the Sociedad de Beneficencia China (SBC) as a representative organization. The first actions of the SBC included provisions to help illiterate laborers write letters to China and reestablish their connections to the homeland and a request to the Peruvian government that it be allowed to take over the implementation of a plan to register all Asians residing in the country.[2] These two projects both created a sphere of migrant autonomy as foreign nationals rather than coolies.

The close association of the SBC with the Chinese legation has been largely maintained through every change in the succession of Chinese governments over the last century. Commercial agents were regularly invited to spend vacations at Chinese-owned plantations, to act as directors of local Chinese companies, and to mediate conflicts between local Chinese. This relationship meant that it was relatively difficult to establish an Emperor Protection Association branch in Peru. The 1903 visit of Liang Qichao's brother, Liang Qitian, only succeeded in obtaining donations.[3] No branch was established until 1905, a time when increasingly progressive Chinese diplomats were more likely to be in sympathy with the increasingly conservative agenda of the reformers.

Many native place associations had come and gone in Lima in the years before and after the establishment of the SBC. The earliest and most enduring were the Gu Gangzhou Huiguan established by Siyi immigrants in 1867, the Tongsheng Huiguan for Hakkas established in 1889, and the Panyu Huiguan established in the 1880s. *Huiguan* for migrants from Zhongshan, Heshan, Huaxian, Chiqi, and Nanhai counties had also been established by the 1920s.[4] With the exception of the Longgang Association established in 1910 for the Peach Garden Oath families, the Chinese in Peru did not form any lasting surname associations. Sworn brotherhoods also existed, but apparently they never exerted much influence. In 1924, the Yingyi She, the Wanxing Gongsi founded by Fujianese, and the Yixing Gongsi made up of Hakkas were all consolidated within a reorganized Zhigongtang that had links to the international organization of the same name.[5]

By the 1920s, in accordance with the self-image of Chinese as a cosmopolitan commercial community in Peru, the nexus of power among the migrants was focused more on businesses than on native place or surname associations. The SBC was meant to be the representative organization of all the Chinese in Peru. Unlike CCBAs in the United States, its officers and active membership were not selected as representatives of other Chinese organizations but from among wealthy and prominent individuals. Accounts from the early twentieth century consistently listed a core group of prominent individuals, most of whom were Zhongshan Hakkas. Although the lists could be much longer, five men and one company topped them consistently. They were Aurelio Powsan Chia of the Pow Lung Company, established in 1889 (fig. 8); Ezequiel Chankan of Hop On Wing Company, established in 1893; Escudero Whu of the Pow On Company, established in 1897; Jo San Jon of the Cheng Hop Company, established in 1900; Javier Koo of the Kong Fook Company, established in 1910; and the manager of the Wing On Chong Company, which had been established in 1872 and was run by men appointed from Hong Kong. Their names appeared repeatedly as directors of all the important Chinese associations and businesses, including the SBC, the Chinese Chamber of Commerce, La Unión insurance company, the Chungwha Navigation Company, and the Tayouk Tennis Club in the fashionable residential district of Miraflores.[6]

Directorships and election as association officers were important in constituting the power of these men, but the commercial house each one of them owned or managed was the most crucial element of their prestige, and their names were rarely mentioned without reference to these companies. Their businesses were central nodes in much larger networks of kinsmen, fellow villagers, and other allies, all tied together through mutual interest and credit. Wing On Chong was the largest business, with its headquarters in Hong Kong and branches throughout Peru, Cuba, and Brazil. Of all the individuals, however, Aurelio Powsan Chia stood head and

Figure 8
Aurelio Powsan Chia

shoulders above the rest. His fame was described not only in terms of his financial power and social connections, but also with glowing appreciation of his generous philanthropy and unshakable moral stature. Even a blanket attack by young Chinese journalists in the 1930s on the irresponsible, self-serving attitudes of the Chinese elite in Lima made an exception for Chia and Guillermo Kongfook, his adopted son and business partner, considering them to be "among the rare people who have no enemies."[7]

Most of these powerful businesses had been founded in the late nineteenth century, often as branches of companies based in Hong Kong or San Francisco. Few ex-plantation laborers, other than labor contractors, ever accumulated enough capital to open anything more than a small artisanal establishment. The importation of foodstuffs and luxuries from China was dominated by migrants who had not gone through the plantation labor experience. From 1874 to 1904, only a trickle of these new migrants landed in Peru. Those that brought money, commercial ambitions, and strong connections from Hong Kong, China, and California found a large Chinese clientele and little competition. As these companies grew larger, they also turned to the sale and distribution of Peruvian products. Events as early as the War of the Pacific in the 1880s already revealed the different relationships that plantation laborers and Chinese merchants in

Lima were establishing with Peruvians. The laborers saw clearly that their interests were not served by the continued stability of the Peruvian elite. Thousands of them joined invading Chilean troops, especially those led by General Lynch, who was said to have a red complexion and a smattering of Cantonese learned during a term of duty in Hong Kong, which gave him at least a passing resemblance to Guandi, the God of War. Most of the Chinese provided only logistical support, but some went into battle against the Peruvian troops, often wearing masks or painting their faces. On the other hand, Chinese merchants in Lima calculated that supporting the Peruvians was in their long-term interest and gathered a contribution to the public war fund second only to that offered by the bankers. They also formed a militia to help protect the city, as well as benevolent societies to protect their own interests, but this failed to stop the massacre of four hundred Chinese by Peruvian troops in the days immediately before the entry of the Chilean troops.[8]

Throughout much of the nineteenth century, many Chinese ex-laborers continued to use the Spanish names they had been given on the plantations. Many found places in local communities as clients of powerful Peruvians—renting their land, serving their households, and having them as godparents (compadrazgo) for their children born of alliances with local women. By the end of the nineteenth century, as the commercial influence of the new migrants grew stronger, these ex-laborers increasingly began to use their Chinese names again, take an interest in migrant associations, do business with other Chinese, and marry their half-Chinese daughters off to new Chinese migrants. The use of compadrazgo continued but was now used to reinforce Chinese networks, as godparents were increasingly chosen from among other Chinese.[9] The influx of migrant capital and stronger connections to China reversed the gradual integration of Chinese into the coastal lower classes and pulled them into the networks of a migrant community. The owners of large businesses were able to channel and profit from the surge of new migrants after 1904. They set up steamship lines, struck deals with Peruvian officials, made special requests for new immigrants, and controlled the economic networks that supplied the small groceries, which were the economic mainstay of this new migration.

CHINESE IN THE CONSTITUTION OF PERU

Peruvians of all classes did not necessarily hold as high an opinion of the Chinese as Wu Tingfang had suggested. Negative images of Chinese had been circulating for over half a century and would continue to circulate for at least another half. These images had powerful effects which could be utilized by groups in Peru with very different agendas. The progressive-minded elite could use them to depict the lower classes as riddled with weaknesses, and the working classes could use them to criticize the corruption and exploitation of the elite. Discourse on the Chinese was woven into the very fabric of class conflict. The images themselves were not contested as much as their meaning was.

Many historians have described violence and racism as an integral part of Peruvian history—so much so that attacks on Chinese after fireworks displays in the central plaza of Lima by gangs of youth known as the "Knife Battalion" have been memorialized in folklore collections as part of the Limeñan tradition. One historian has characterized "pogroms against the Chinese," as the "traditional" result of labor uprisings in the early part of this century.[10] Racial discourse circulated through all sectors of Peruvian society and could be deployed as effectively by the "popular masses" as by elites, who used it to justify their domination. Like the status of *mestizos,* the status of the Chinese within this discourse was a bit unstable, drifting between the more settled categories of white, black, and Indian which dominated the social landscape.[11]

A characterization presented by José Félix Caceres of the Lima Geographical Society at the Third Pan-American Scientific Congress in 1924 brought together many of the reigning stereotypes, and can serve as an introduction to Peruvian anti-Chinese discourse:

> [The Chinese] have been a constant obstacle to our psychic and physi-
> cal well-being, due to the manifestation of their character, customs,
> temperament, and vices in repugnant excess, . . . indecent brothels;
> the gambling houses, where the "paca-piú" and the "Chinese luck"
> have sharpened the ingenuity of our Creoles for petty theft and crime;
> the opium dens; and many other iniquities. In consideration of public
> morality as well as private, the selfishness particular to them which
> has caused all of the money they have earned on our soil going to fat-
> ten the strongboxes of their mandarins without having improved any
> part of the country, not even the capital, through some notable edifice
> or humanitarian donation; the cheapening of manual labor to the ob-
> vious detriment of the Peruvian worker; the total lack of hygiene in
> the pigsties in which they live . . . their traditional hatred of the race
> and lack of altruistic sentiments, because these latter are unknown in
> their own country; and many other reasons; are powerful motives not
> only to declare that they do not exemplify the qualities we desire, but

also to ask that we be liberated this very day from this obstacle to
progress that weighs on us as one of the largest calamities we are bur-
dened with.[12]

Caceres's arguments were common to the scientific racism that flourished in Latin America in the early twentieth century. Such arguments often claimed a goal of improving the human stock of the heteroglot Latin
American nations. This usually amounted to recommendations for increased immigration of northern Europeans. The influence of other peoples was described in terms of contagion and degradation: their vices and
immorality would spread, and their offspring would weaken the genetic
stock of the nation. This threat of degradation was often amplified by
neo-Lamarckian convictions that negative traits produced by the environment could be inherited.[13] Indeed, Caceres went on to argue that some
Chinese degradation was a legacy of the nineteenth-century traffic in Chinese laborers.

Most of the images used by Caceres had been circulating since the
earliest debates over the importation of Chinese labor. Planters had considered Chinese laborers to be slightly less than human tools which could
be profitably utilized in the service of their own ambitions. Opponents
claimed that intermarriage would degenerate the Peruvian race and that
the vicious habits of the Chinese would spread throughout the lower
classes, claims that were commonly reproduced by the lower classes
themselves. In the early twentieth century, Chinese were aware of these
images and tried to disassociate themselves from the laborers of the nineteenth century. They sometimes criticized plantation owners for having
created such a degraded class, but usually emphasized that they were a
different type of Chinese, more civilized and educated than the coolies of
a previous era, willing to conform to and promote the demands of a progressive society.

In the eyes of the lower classes, the Chinese were damned by their
association with the goals of the planters. The importation of coolies had
made Chinese a key component in the elite attempt to degrade the value
of human labor. The lower classes continued to use images of the Chinese
as laborer into the twentieth century, long after it had any basis in fact.
Even after workers' propaganda began to recognize Chinese primarily as
small businessmen, they were still linked with elite hegemony, but now
as the willing henchmen of economic domination rather than the hap-
less victims they had once been as laborers. Despite their use of Chinese
to criticize the elites, working-class activists also appropriated many aspects of progressive discourse, such as the concerns for hygiene and moral-

ity raised by Caceres. The following sections elaborate the course of Chinese migration and anti-Chinese attitudes in Peru over the first half of the twentieth century.

The Aristocratic Republic

Both land and political power in Peru were increasingly concentrated in the hands of a small aristocracy in Lima during the early twentieth century. Many members of this elite were not from the older, landed families that had dominated Peru during the colonial era and had continued to dominate regional power outside of Lima. Rather, they were the children of more recent immigrants from Italy, Spain, and Chile, who had a more dynamic and rationalizing attitude toward the exploitation of agricultural lands. This aristocracy was itself plagued by internal differences, but from 1895 to 1919 many of these differences were held in check by the dominance of the Civilista Party. The Civilistas tried to build a government on the common ground of the aristocrats that were its members and who could unite to confront the growing unrest of laborers and the challenges of regional powers attempting to retain their old privileges. They promoted an economy based on exploitation and export of the natural resources of Peru, and looked to Europe for cultural fashions and material luxuries. They also perpetuated a political rhetoric based on the idea of constitutional rights, which even the most recalcitrant of local strongmen made use of to legitimize his power.[14] Nonetheless, the party was also extremely exclusive, which meant not only that few Peruvians had any opportunity to participate in the nominally democratic structures of the government, but also that the government had little effective influence beyond Lima and a few smaller urban centers. As individuals, however, many Civilistas did have influence outside of Lima, and their word could be law in the ever-expanding plantations they owned.

These plantations grew at the expense of local communities, which rarely had access to the resources necessary to defend their land and interests.[15] The largest and most self-sufficient of these plantations were located on the north coast of Peru, where most of the Chinese resided (see fig. 9). The small communities on the margins of these plantations were similar to the growing urban ghettos, in that they were also homes for the dispossessed and underemployed. They made up a growing class of coastal poor, dependent on the elite for wages and on Chinese and Italian merchants for goods.

Some of these Chinese merchants were treated with respect and spe-

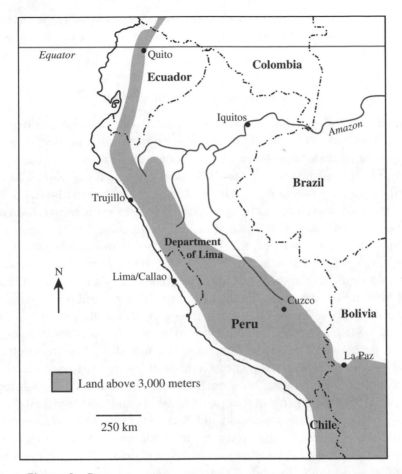

Figure 9 Peru

cial privileges, especially in small towns, where they patronized local festivals and could even hold local office. Local papers were often filled with
grateful testaments by women who claimed to have been cured by Chinese herbal doctors. Chinese further encouraged such positive images by
donating statues to local plazas, contributing to public causes, and providing fireworks for National Day celebrations.[16] On the other hand, com-
munications from the Chinese legation in Peru to the Ministry of Foreign
Relations were consistently filled with protests—which rarely received a
response—against the maltreatment of Chinese by officials, police, soldiers, and "popular masses" in all parts of the country. To some extent,
this kind of treatment could be expected by any *forastero* (outsider), espe-

cially those engaged in highly visible mercantile activities. Nonetheless, the Chinese as a group were an especially common scapegoat in local political strife.

The Rejuvenation of Immigration

The flow of independent migrants had reached a steady stream of two or three hundred a year by the turn of the century, but the dreams and ambitions of Eduardo Muelle were most directly responsible for the rejuvenation of Chinese migration after 1904. Muelle assumed the post of Peruvian Consul in Hong Kong on 3 July 1903. He brought with him not only the renewed interest of coastal agriculturists to resume the importation of laborers from Asia—which had already brought some laborers from Japan—but also a conviction that Chinese colonists would be valuable in opening up the Amazon and a belief in the promise of the great Chinese market (or at least in the promise of free trade in Hong Kong) as an outlet for Peruvian products extracted from the Amazon and other parts of Peru.[17] To achieve these three dreams, he gave his full support the Compañía Marítima Occidental, a British firm attempting to establish a shipping line between Callao and Hong Kong. He spared no effort in convincing the Hong Kong government to rethink its ban against the collective emigration of Chinese to South America (which was actually a misinterpretation of a ban against indentured migration), and "after a virtual campaign, with thousands of setbacks and discussions with the Governor and the Colonial Secretary, the license for the emigration of free Chinese to Peru [was] granted."[18] The first boat carrying Chinese migrants, the *Kensington,* arrived in Callao on 19 October 1904, with 356 Chinese passengers, including five women.[19] It turned out, however, that no Peruvians were interested in exploring the Chinese market, and Muelle's hopes crumbled after only two voyages. Except for a few samples of salt, the *Kensington* had returned to Hong Kong with no cargo, and the Compañía Marítima Occidental went out of business.

If Peruvians would not take advantage of Muelle's efforts, many Chinese were more than happy to follow up on them. Muelle had often criticized the Compañía Marítima Occidental for not having established good relations with the Chinese enterprises in Hong Kong and Lima. With the collapse of the company, eight of these enterprises decided to take things into their own hands and established the shipping company Lee Chay in February 1905. They advertised for potential migrants in the Hong Kong newspapers, and in April 1906 the *Lennox* made its first voyage, carrying 630 Chinese passengers as well as rice, medicines, foodstuffs, silks, and other staples of the migrant economy.[20] In December 1906, the Japanese company Toyo Kisen Kaisha joined the traffic to Callao, adding an extra leg to its voyages from Hong Kong to Honolulu via Yokahama.

Except during the anti-Japanese boycott of 1907, as many as six to nine hundred Chinese traveled to Peru on each boat, but none of them fulfilled the hopes of Muelle and others by taking jobs as agricultural laborers. They worked as butchers, bakers, shoemakers, and as employees in Chinese commercial houses. Most of all they opened *pulperías* (small groceries) throughout the coastal cities and towns. Subsequent Peruvian consuls in Hong Kong took stances against the continued migration of Chinese to Peru and cast aspersions on the motives of the Lee Chay company and its Chinese investors. One of them wrote that "the businessmen who occupy themselves with the emigration of coolies obtain a good return for each Chinese they send to Peru."[21] Similarly, letters in the Peruvian press accused Chinese businesses of importing Chinese laborers for exploitation in their plantations and shops. Whatever the truth of such accusations, several wealthy migrants in Peru clearly had a direct financial interest in the activities of Lee Chay, because Pow Lung and other companies sent representatives to meet migrants as they got off the boat, and the majority of new migrants were able to find jobs working for other Chinese or for themselves.[22]

As described in chapter 2, the arrival of the *Montrose* with 774 passengers in July 1910 convinced Peruvian authorities that the Porras-Wu Protocol of 1909 was ineffective. The resulting scandal and crackdown made this the last voyage sponsored by Lee Chay. The subsequent restriction of migration opportunities meant that false documents, assumed identities as returned migrants, and special permissions to work as employees in Chinese companies in Peru began to carry a high market value. Peruvian consuls accused Chinese in Hong Kong of speculating in Peruvian resident passports, Peruvian citizenship papers, and false titles of kinship for children. Newspapers in Hong Kong and Canton advertised migration positions to be sold to the highest bidder. When the Ministry of Foreign Relations instituted stricter controls over proof of Peruvian citizenship, they claimed that "the interest of the Chinese in nationalizing as Peruvians disappeared."[23]

The market in migration rights was facilitated by the connections of influential Chinese with corrupt consuls and port officials. Each of the six Peruvian consuls that served in Hong Kong from 1913 to 1920 left their posts plagued by accusations of venality and dishonesty. The most common accusations, by both the Ministry of Foreign Relations in Lima and the Chinese in Hong Kong, were of demanding exorbitant fees and selling visas to the highest bidders. Within days after arriving at his post in 1915, consul Salvador Cavero was already predicting and making excuses for his own decline, writing to the Ministry that, "in the circumstance of finding oneself so far from home, so poorly financed, and in the midst of an element so likely to make unscrupulous proposals of all kinds, I am referring to the Chinese element, the honor of the official can easily weaken if he is not exceptional, and once he is on the slope, nobody can know where he will stop."[24] Others never ceased protesting their honesty throughout their appointment. One of them reached apocalyptic tones in his protests against denunciations in the Hong Kong press, writing that the Chinese were "vile and offensive, and do not consider for an instant the good name of the Government, nor of its representative, dragging his name and reputation through the dirt until his desires are crowned; but some day they will be made to feel the weight of justice, and the rectitude and justice of the Peruvian Government will be shown to them in this form."[25] This consul was much criticized by his successor for the scandalous state of the records he left behind.

Luís Alvarez, who took over as consul in 1917, sent a relatively detailed description of the mechanics of corruption back to the Ministry in Lima. He began by noting how all the other consuls, ship accountants, and authorities in the colony were talking of the "business and thick profits that had been made in this consular office" and by the officials in Callao. He went on to describe how, upon his arrival, he had found a Chinese in his office who told him he was the "Secretary of the Consulate." Within a short time, the consul learned that this man was a wealthy partner in a commercial house in Hong Kong who was well known by shipping company officials and who "associat[ed] on a par with persons of the European colony here, and enjoy[ed] the protection and confidence of a South American colleague." Candidates selected for emigration by the commercial houses were presented by him to the consul along with an appropriate gratuity. The result was that "there have been officials who shortly after arriving have felt themselves to be virtual sultans, and have proceeded capriciously."[26] Several other consuls hinted that accusations in the local press were not the expressions of indignation by righteous Chinese they appeared to be, but attacks by competitors who felt they were not receiving an adequate amount of favoritism. At one point, several Chinese companies even asked the Chilean consul to represent them in approaching the Peruvian consul with their complaints over how he was allowing other Chinese businesses and the Chinese Chamber of Commerce in Hong Kong to control his affairs.[27]

Smuggling of migrants was another important means of entry that depended on extensive support networks and the corruption of other Latin American consuls. As the entry of Chinese into Ecuador was extremely difficult, most surreptitious entry into Peru came via Chile, Bolivia, and up the Amazon from Brazil.[28] Both Bolivia and Chile had restrictions against Chinese immigration, although Chile allowed a periodic quota of Chinese to enter upon payment of a high entry tax. According to the Peruvian consul, the Bolivian consul seemed free to charge whatever price he liked to grant Bolivian visas. Several Peruvian consuls complained that the large majority of the Chinese who obtained visas to these two countries eventually ended up in Peru, "the promised land." However they got to Peru, the paths of Chinese migrants were paved by a dense network of connections and exchanges.

Enemies of Hygiene

Strong anti-Chinese sentiment was already available to greet the 356 Chinese passengers on the first direct steamer from Hong Kong in 1904. The *Kensington* had the misfortune to arrive toward the end of a bubonic plague epidemic in Lima. The plague was widely believed to have originated in Asia and had resulted in the establishment of an invasive public health apparatus.[29] The *Kensington* was met at the port in Callao by doctors charged with its fumigation and police posted "to prevent that the people should assume a hostile attitude against the Chinese."[30]

In the following days, representatives in both chambers of the legislature presented laws to prohibit the collective immigration of Asians. In response, factions of plantation owners presented their own proposals to allow Chinese immigrants to be brought over on the condition that they signed four-year contracts and would be repatriated after the contracts were fulfilled. The planters repeated an argument they had made over a half a century earlier, that the Chinese were a "necessary evil" if Peru's resources were to be developed.[31] Neither side got its way, but the Ministry of Foreign Relations felt it wise to discourage any pretext for more controversy. In early 1905, Consul Muelle was already counseling Lee Chay representatives in Hong Kong that it was not prudent to carry so many Chinese passengers on its first voyage. The company responded with the same arguments that Muelle had already used to convince the Hong Kong Government to allow emigration—that Peru and China had a treaty that guaranteed free immigration, and none of the migrants had signed contracts.[32]

Most opinions against the arrival of the Chinese amounted to the conviction that they were a degenerate and noxious race that would debilitate the physical and moral strength of the country by contaminating

Peruvian blood, spreading their pernicious habits and pushing Peruvian laborers out of their jobs. Images of social contamination were complemented by a preoccupation with health and hygiene. All the Chinese on the first voyage of the Lee Chay ship *Lennox* were required by Consul Muelle to obtain certificates of health before embarking, although this did not avert a minor panic over the fear of bubonic plague and other diseases when the ship docked in Callao.[33] Muelle's requirement was made law on 12 June, 1907. Two months later, on 12 August, another decree stipulated a fee of five pounds for the certificate. The consul responded approvingly that "Asian emigration will diminish considerably [which] will obligate the Chinese company to suspend its voyages."[34] Clearly, the authorities considered this to be a measure not only against viruses carried by the Chinese but against the Chinese themselves. After the hoped-for decrease did not occur, the fee was raised to ten pounds in February 1908. This time the consul was not so optimistic that it would have any effect on migration, writing that it was not the passengers themselves who paid for the tickets and fees, but the Chinese commercial houses to which the Chinese were indebted upon arriving in Peru.[35] The only complaint recorded from the Chinese was that the certificate was demanded of all Chinese subjects "without distinction of class and social condition."[36]

Although concern over hygiene and contamination—by germs, immorality, and interbreeding—was spearheaded by the scientifically oriented elite, it garnered widespread acceptance among other classes. Two labor unions, the Confederation of Artisans and the Assembly of United Societies, were convinced that plantation owners were responsible for the importation of Chinese, and appealed to the president of Peru in 1906 to halt it. They insisted that "the yellow race has only contributed to Peru hybrid descendants, who are weighed down with vices and physical defects too numerous to mention." They also claimed that by competing for the jobs of Peruvian nationals, the Chinese were threatening "the improvement of the national race and its future prosperity."[37]

Newspapers were filled with anti-Chinese articles and letters, reaching such a point in 1907 that the Chinese legation presented a memorandum to the Ministry of Foreign Relations complaining of the "general and systematic slander against the Chinese in the press." The memorandum also noted an increasing frequency of unjust treatment and detention by local authorities and of attacks against Chinese establishments and individuals by soldiers and the people, and stated that, "even if the police are aware of the things that happen, they adopt no means to prevent them."[38] The *Fray K. Bezón,* a publication with anarchist sentiments, was established in 1907, devoting much of its space to a systematic series of jokes and attacks on the Chinese.[39] In early 1909 the standard of cleanliness in small Chinese restaurants was a common target of criticism in several papers, which often accused the Chinese of eating and serving rats.[40] In 1917, the *Ilustración Obrero (Worker's Illustrated)* suggested openly that hygiene requirements were an ideal excuse for official harassment: "The Inspection of Hygiene should make its authority felt. With this purpose in mind, we judge that this municipal organ should be able to initiate its work by obligating all small Chinese industrialists to obtain their respective certificates of health to continue performing their services. As it will be humanly difficult to fulfill the requirement, we are sure that there will be at least a fifty percent decrease in these monopolies, and our people will be able to return to set up their diverse businesses."[41]

Enemies of Labor and the Riot of 1909

Labor practices associated with Chinese migration were also frequently attacked. The 1913 requirement that Chinese children traveling to Peru obtain passports and proof of kinship was accompanied by accusations published in *El Comercio* by the consul in Hong Kong that hungry and homeless children were being purchased in Hong Kong by Chinese businesses in Peru to be sent across the ocean to work for them.[42] In one of the few public responses by the Chinese in Lima in those years, T. Pousan Chia wrote a letter to *El Comercio* denying the allegations, adding that "this would not be possible in a place like Hong Kong where the culture has reached an appreciable level of development, influenced by the English element, open to the commerce of all nations, and where the human and liberal laws of the Republic of China are observed with the utmost strictness."[43] This response, with its emphasis on rule of law, commerce, and civilized behavior, echoed both the sentiments expressed four years earlier by Wu Tingfang and the contents of the more concentrated image-building efforts that the Chinese in Peru would embark on in the 1920s. Nonetheless, accusations that wealthy Chinese in Lima were importing other Chinese to work as virtual slaves continued through the 1910s. The desire to recruit their own indentured laborers was openly admitted by the plantation-owning elites of Peru, thus creating an ideal opportunity for workers' groups to conflate the actions of their enemies.

Urban working-class dissatisfaction and hatred of Chinese came to a peak in the riot of 9 May 1909. The riot started as an open rally of the Workers' Party in the streets of Lima. The participants yelled *vivas* to Nicolás de Piérola and Augusto Durand—two provincial politicians with reputations for patriotism, *machismo,* and rebellion—and "Death to the

Chinese!" Speakers blamed the government for having brought the Chinese into the country to work cheaply when Peruvians themselves had no jobs. After the speeches, the crowd was led to the residence of de Piérola, "mistreating any Chinese who happened to pass by." Not finding de Piérola at home, they began to shout, "Down with the Chinese!" and then separate into small groups that spread to all parts of the city to attack and loot Chinese shops. The police estimated that "almost all the Asian stores were threatened by the people." The claim for compensation presented four days later by a commission of Chinese merchants counted twenty-four looted stores.[44]

Competition for jobs and excessively inflated prices in the stores were suggested in the newspapers as motivations for the hostility but do not account for the specificity of attacks against Chinese. No Italian shops were attacked, although they were as numerous as the Chinese shops. As far as competition for jobs was concerned, very few Chinese were actually employed in laboring occupations. The highest concentration of Chinese in any manual occupation in 1908 were the 223 Chinese shoemakers, who made up less than 10 per cent of the 2,253 shoemakers in Lima in 1908. The only manual occupation they dominated was street sweeping, where 132 Chinese nearly monopolized the 141 available positions.[45] Chinese were singled out more as a highly visible symbol than as a critical threat.

The government also singled out the Chinese as a convenient scapegoat in their attempts to smooth over the threat of the organized and belligerent lower classes. After the riot, the Chinese legation quickly demanded that the Peruvian government take immediate measures for the compensation and protection of Chinese subjects.[46] The Peruvian government responded with uncharacteristic haste but not with the kinds of measures that the Chinese had hoped for. Within five days of the riot President Leguía, noting that "public opinion has openly manifested itself adverse to Chinese immigration," issued a decree requiring that Chinese migrants could enter the country only when carrying five hundred pounds sterling on their person.[47] The decree was later explained to Wu Tingfang as a means to pacify the demands of the workers and prevent similar disorders in the future.

The mayor of Lima, Guillermo Billinghurst, acted even more quickly and sensationally than the president. Billinghurst was an anti-Leguian politician with populist pretensions and a strong base among the workers, which was unusual in urban politicians of the day.[48] The misfortune of the Chinese created an irresistible opportunity. At three in the afternoon of 11 May, two days after the riot, Billinghurst ordered the immediate destruction of the Callejón Otaiza. The Callejón was a building, or conglomeration of buildings, built around a courtyard within which more than five hundred Chinese were thought to live and do business. It had often been a target of newspaper critiques and invasions by the sanitation police over the previous five years. Billinghurst justified the destruction not only as a long-planned hygienic action against the "squalor and perversion" that were believed to exist inside, but also as the first in a projected series of public works designed to create employment and improve living conditions in the city. During the destruction, many Chinese remained in the Callejón until "the dust billowing from the darkened walls threatened to asphyxiate them," while crowds gathered outside the Callejón looking for jobs and yelling *vivas* to Billinghurst.[49] In place of the Callejón a "decent and clean street that deserves to carry the name of the Mayor" was built. By 13 May, Billinghurst had begun to search the outskirts of Lima for a suitable location to which Chinatown could be moved, "and subjected to the necessary vigilance of the hygiene inspection." It was never found.[50]

As Wu Tingfang later noted, none of these measures seem to have been particularly successful in pacifying the workers, for on 29 May, at least eleven more Chinese shops were looted in the disturbances surrounding an attempted revolution by the sons of Nicolás de Piérola. Many observers believed the violence would have been even more serious if not for the widespread belief that the Chinese had been buying guns to protect themselves.[51] The election of Billinghurst to the presidency in May 1912 was also accompanied by the looting of a few Chinese stores. The financial compensation promised to the Chinese in the wake of the 1909 riot was a lot slower in coming than the scapegoating responses. In March 1911, twenty-two months after the riot, the Peruvian government offered to pay 30 percent of the reclamations requested by the Chinese commission. Even this small amount was probably only offered in recognition of the international ceremony surrounding the visit of Wu Tingfang, and the Chinese accepted it as "proof of a spirit of cordiality."[52]

In the Context of Indians and Europeans

Some upper-class observers, like the editors of *El Comercio*, claimed to understand the "legitimate disgust" that the "most modest social classes" felt toward the Chinese, but they criticized the violence used to express anti-Chinese feelings as an offense against "national decorum."[53] The upper-class dislike of the Chinese was related not so much to economic insecurity as to social insecurity. They believed not only that the Chinese presence provoked threats and disorder on the part of the lower classes, but that their habits threatened to further corrupt the already substandard morals

and virility of the workers and indigenous population. Such fears were expressed with increasing frequency as the Peruvian elite became more concerned with how the people who lived within the territorial limits of Peru
could be integrated as the citizens of a Peruvian nation.

At the turn of the century, many Peruvian intellectuals were increasingly convinced that a united and constitutional Peruvian nation-state
could not be asserted without a solid basis of racial and cultural homogeneity. Yet attempts to define or create such a basis were confounded by a
belief in the unchanging nature of racial groups, buttressed by the increasing use of biological vocabulary. Some despaired that these racial distinctions were insuperable. Others found hope for the creation of a Peruvian identity through *mestizaje,* although often on the condition that
more immigrants of Northern European stock were necessary to add
strength and vitality to a mixture that would otherwise be dominated by
Indian and Asiatic blood. Attempts to promote European immigration
were largely ineffective. As old Chinese workers died out at the end of the
nineteenth century and the export of plantation products grew increasingly lucrative, many coastal plantations began to turn toward the Andes
as a source of labor and Indian communities as sources of land. The appropriation of Indian land and proletarianization of their labor were accompanied by an ideology promoting the rapid incorporation of Indians
as citizens of a consolidating nation.

A 1905 circular sent to all the departmental prefects offered a succinct summary of official goals at the time. It began by criticizing absurd
local obligations and fees imposed on the Indians and declaring that all
Peruvians should be equal before the law, because

> Our indigenous peoples still preserve latent in them all the valuable
> qualities that allowed the Incas to organize them into a vast and pow-
> erful empire. . . . This is not only an attempt to realize a civilizing
> work of uprooting a considerable number of beings from dejection,
> but also an attempt—and this is the interesting aspect of the prob-
> lem—to have them participate actively, as a factor of progress, an ele-
> ment of production of incalculable force.[54]

The increased interest in the Indians led to their becoming a "problem," and to pose them as a problem was to suggest that they could be
solved. Indians were increasingly described in terms of malleable cultural
differences rather than fixed biological ones. Solving the problem was a
project aimed not only at the Indians, but also at the displacement of local powerholders by the central government. Indian culture was often portrayed as the legacy of colonial degradation, something which could be

reversed by the eradication of "feudal" land relations, education, moral cultivation, and determined, positive action. Practical education programs usually began with training in hygiene and led to lessons in Spanish, love of country, and the biographies of national heroes. Other measures to incorporate the Indians included the destruction of collective communities (seen as obstacles to progress and private property), the building of roads into the mountains, and the encouragement of migration to areas in need of labor.

Public discussion about the relationship of Indians to the nation and which of their qualities should be selected for nurturing, reform, or extermination were an integral part of defining the Peruvian nation-state.[55] Some people did not agree with the more aggressive and socially disruptive measures taken by the government and plantation owners to turn them into individualistic worker-citizens. They created pro-indigenist groups which aimed to protect the Indians against the white elite through the discovery and preservation of their culture and history. Nonetheless, their agenda began with many of the same assumptions made by the government. A 1909 speech by the prominent Pro-Indigenist Society member Dora Mayer demonstrates many of these assumptions, as well as the marginal position of the Chinese in these debates over the nation:

> The conservation of the indigenous race is a duty for many reasons. It is not important that the Indian belongs to an inferior race. Even if he did not have any intelligence, he would have to be cared for: a good housewife takes care to preserve the most modest objects in her house; she does not permit a single broom to be mistreated, because it is of use to her. The Indian is not less than a broom. He is useful to us and he must be cared for. . . . I add that if the gentlemen [in the audience] are partisans of the suppression of the Indian, they must also believe themselves to be better off by cutting off their feet and hands. The races of color, the Chinese, the Blacks, the Indians, are the feet and the hands of the white. The Europeans are better for ordering than for working as soon as they leave their climate. As soon as the army of Saxons, which some persons here hope for as much as the coming of the Messiah, erupts over us through the Panama Canal, the new colonists will bring Asians in great quantities to carry out the tasks of industry. And the Asians in bondage cannot compete with the aborigines who are made of the clay of the native land.[56]

The Chinese were not only inferior, but alien as well. While they could be of some use to developing Peru, the convenience they offered was not a substitute for putting one's own house in order first.

Other commentators saw the Chinese as a more direct threat to the project of uplifting the Indians. If not worrying about the physical degeneration brought about by intermarriage, they worried that the vicious habits and cultural degeneration of the Chinese would spread to the Indians, hindering any attempts at moral reform. A tightening of opium licensing laws in 1916 was preceded by a public campaign concerned with precisely this question. A report produced by the Office of Public Assistance in 1916 proposed many of the requirements for the ventilation, hygiene, surveillance, and exclusion of women and non-Asians from the opium dens that would later become law. To justify the proposed measures, the writer of the report argued that

> everything leads one to believe that opium addiction would find
> unique conditions of acclimatization in Peru if permitted to reach the
> Indian. Our aboriginal race, which possibly has distant ancestral rela-
> tions with the Asian, is, like them, congenitally and hereditarily dis-
> posed to the dreams and indolence which are artificially excited by
> the intoxication of opium. The Indian now only knows the drunken-
> ness of alcohol and the stimulus of coca, and we see the customary
> abuse of both, but it is indubitable that if opium came to be known
> and accessible, he would become an opium addict, just as he is an
> alcoholic and a coca addict, and he would docilely and voluntarily
> encounter and acquire one more morbid opportunity to accelerate
> the process of organic and moral decadence of which he is already
> victim.[57]

As this report suggests, few were concerned about the effects of opium on the Chinese. They were considered irredeemable in their subjection to the drug, and the only concern was that their vices not spread. Nonetheless, the adoption of restrictive measures in 1916 did not help much in alleviating these fears, for in 1918 the Lima press continued to be scandalized by the patronage of opium dens by white men and women.[58]

Even positive depictions of the Chinese were situated primarily as commentaries and critiques of other groups in Peru. In his observations on the riot of 1909, leftist intellectual Manuel Gonzales Prada argued that popular anti-Chinese feeling had been artificially stirred up as a political tool and that the majority of poorer Peruvians harbored good will to the Chinese, whose humble and persevering ways made a favorable contrast to the insatiable greed of European immigrants.[59]

Like the Indians, the Chinese were constituted as bearers of racial characteristics, but they were alien ones which could be isolated or cleansed from the national body rather than incorporated. The relative lack of positive social action focused on the Chinese actually gave some room to maneuver, especially since the practice of Peruvian nation-building was never so clear-cut and efficient as the ambitions of its rhetoric. The Chinese occasionally fell victim to hygiene and morality campaigns, but they were just as likely to be granted realms of delimited autonomy in such matters, as the attention of reformers and officials was directed toward the creation of citizens out of other human material.

CHINESE AND THE REPUBLIC

Justice in Trujillo

The complex relationships of Chinese with local communities, which ranged from roles as victimized outsiders to respected residents, could be seen in the coastal city of Trujillo, about three hundred miles north of Lima. In the first half of the twentieth century the Chinese population in this city averaged about one thousand individuals, about 5 per cent of the total population. Chinese enterprise in this city centered on *pulperías*, butcher shops, small bars, bakeries, pig farms, and a monopoly of the pawnshop industry. They played a very important if not dominant role in the provision of goods and finance to the poorer residents of the city. They were also constantly exposed to the surveillance and petty extortions of a variety of municipal inspectors and police, resulting in frequent fines for infractions of hygiene laws, doing business on Sundays, inaccurate weights and measures, and unlicensed liquor sales.

The administrative suits considered by the Trujillo government for the years 1900 to 1920 are dominated by Chinese contesting the imposition of inspection fines, in a proportion far greater than the 30 percent of new business licenses granted them over those years. The Chinese themselves were quite aware of the discrepancy, and they—or, to be more precise, their lawyers—were often quite eloquent in demanding their constitutional rights while accusing the municipal government of "antagonizing the Asian Colony, and acquiring funds for the Municipal Government at the cost of our work and industry." One suit claimed that "there are no violent and often arbitrary methods which have not been employed to humiliate us."[60] Often these suits reproduced images of the Chinese as uncultured aliens in order to draw a picture of predatory health inspectors who fell upon victims who were ignorant of their rights and how to defend themselves. Sometimes this image was given a historical dimension as the Chinese attempted to turn the accusations back on the hypocrisy and cruelty of the Peruvians in bringing them there in the first place: "The majority of the members of the Chinese colony were brought here by these same Peruvians to work on their land, and now, weakened by the work and the demands, when not invalids, they are still not able to return to their Motherland to bury their remains."[61] Such invocations of the past were rare, however, and most Chinese tried to distance themselves from any association with coolie labor and a lack of culture.

Characterizations of the Chinese as helpless and unaware may have been accurate in individual cases, but the Chinese as a whole were much more active in defending their interests through confrontation with the local government than any other group in Trujillo. Not until the late 1920s were Chinese administrative complaints eclipsed in number by the suits of middle-class Peruvians annoyed at being fined for traffic violations. More common than images of ignorant victimhood were Chinese self-portrayals that drew attention to the positive status conferred by Peruvian legislation and international politics, to the material benefits brought by their presence, to laws promising equal treatment of foreigners, and to the 1874 treaty which had abolished the coolie trade and guaranteed the free pursuit by Chinese of commercial activities in Peru.

Some struggles against particular regulatory legislation continued for years and were referred to Lima for resolution. A fight against stricter pawnshop regulation lasted from 1903 to 1909. The Chinese made an appeal to international standards by calling upon Wu Tingfang for help during his visit in 1909, who forwarded their complaint to the Ministry of Foreign Relations. The case was finally resolved in Lima in 1910, largely in favor of the Trujillo government but with some concessions to Chinese objections.[62] A similar struggle over the attempt by the city government to remove Chinese-operated pigsties from the Trujillo city limits was resolved in Lima in 1911, largely in favor of the municipality again.[63] The Chinese had better luck contesting the enforcement of legislation than the legislation itself. Complaints brought to the municipality by individual businesses were frequently rewarded with reduced or canceled fines. Indeed, despite their occasional blanket condemnations of the motives of the Trujillo government, the Chinese generally found their interests could be well served by appealing to its sense of enlightened justice.

Identity in Trujillo

Prejudiced enforcement of hygiene laws contributed to the public constitution of a Chinese identity by singling them out and creating a cause around which to mobilize. The common struggle against health inspections, however, was still far from sufficient to forge solidarity among the

Chinese. In fact, the rhetoric of modern hygiene and rule of law within which health legislation was embedded could also contribute to social divisions among the Chinese, as some migrants tried to distinguish themselves from the degradation and misfortune of others. This attempt to make distinctions could be seen in the shifting public images presented by migrant associations.

The new wave of Chinese migration to Peru in the twentieth century was accompanied by a proliferation of Chinese institutions, as local SBCs began to appear in towns up and down the coast.[64] These associations were usually organized with the stated goals of developing unity, providing aid, and offering representation on behalf of the local Chinese community. In practice, the achievement of these goals was qualified by the interests of the wealthy merchants who held office in these associations. When the Trujillo government attempted to enlist the services of the local SBC during the bubonic plague scare of 1904, the local Chinese as a unified community suddenly slipped through their fingers. The city was concerned that the many Chinese beggars on the street were a medium of infection and asked the Chinese community to take up the responsibility of removing them to a confined location. Their first attempts to contact the Chinese community through the SBC met only with responses by individuals who claimed to no longer be president of the association or to represent the Chinese as a whole. Eventually, several individuals presenting themselves merely as a group of influential merchants with no connection to the SBC or any other representative organization formulated a response:

> The Inspection proposes to commit the Asian Colony to bear the cost
> of these beggars for three months, but it seems it did not take into ac-
> count that the Colony is not a Society of Charity, nor are its members
> personally obligated to respond to obligations other than those which
> are related to the preservation of each one of us. If, then, each of us
> enjoys complete independence, responsible for the support of his fam-
> ily through his own actions and work, we would be doing wrong to
> commit ourselves to this, and [doing wrong] to the interests of the rest
> of the Asians in responding to such external necessities to which we
> are not obligated by any law, either individually or collectively.[65]

Thus, the merchants justified their own freedom from responsibility as a claim for the rights of all Asians to be considered in terms of the individual rights recognized by Peruvian law. Of course, the city's request was very ill-timed, coming in the midst of a particularly severe hygiene inquisition against small businesses and the beginning of the legal campaign against the pawnshops owned by the elite. Moreover, most of the beggars were former plantation laborers, precisely the group against which the merchants were trying to distinguish themselves as educated and well-to-do businessmen. The bubonic plague threat exposed the fragility of the ties that ran across different migrant networks and interests. Nonetheless, two weeks later the merchants compromised a little, offering to assist in the production of a large theatrical show for the benefit of plague victims. It was a form of charity that linked them more with the Trujillo bourgeoisie than with exotic, impoverished aliens.

Monopolizing Vice in Lima

The Chinese of Lima were more successful in presenting a public face of solidarity than those in Trujillo. Although I have found hints that Chinese nationalist politics were a source of tension, and a general tendency for Hakkas and Siyi migrants to move in different circles, such rifts never penetrated the appearance of unity. Most differences were enveloped in silence, and little documentary evidence is available to trace them. Even if the image of harmony did not accord with reality, the maintenance of such an image was still a remarkable achievement by the more powerful Chinese.

Struggles over the control of gambling and opium that accompanied the imposition of restrictive laws after the turn of the century are a rare case where Chinese differences are recorded in the public record. The concern to restrict opium and gambling was part of a larger interest on the part of nation-building Peruvian elite in the creation of urban order. Gambling, opium smoking, and "degenerate" activities in general were widely perceived by Peruvians as congenital and irrepressible aspects of Chinese culture (who blithely ignored how plantation owners had always provided their laborers with opium, not only because they believed it made the Chinese work harder and rebel less but also because its sale channeled much of their wages back into their own hands), and laws were designed to contain them as isolated spheres of Chinese activity. On their part, many Chinese were aware of the monopolies and profits that could be obtained by cooperating with the government in enforcing limited restrictions and pushing out competitors.

The licensing of opium, gambling, and prostitution had already begun in 1906. Larger prostitution and gambling establishments were mostly licensed out to non-Chinese, while lower-level gambling establishments and the sale of opium were managed by Chinese. The administration of licenses and regulations was put up for auction each year by the municipal government, and the winning bidder was always Chinese. Aseng and Company, Auctioneers and Collectors of Special Police Fees and Licenses, successfully bid for the Lima licensing monopoly of 1909 and promptly began efforts to replace the existing gambling licenses with licenses for establishments of its own choosing. When Aseng presented the monthly licenses for approval, the subprefect of Lima noticed that all the names were different from those on the register of existing gambling establishments and refused to put his seal on them, admonishing Aseng not to be involved in managing gambling houses. Aseng subsequently made out licenses to the previous establishments but refused to hand them over to the representatives who came to collect them. Aseng explained itself by claiming that the representatives were not the real owners of the houses, making dark hints about the very existence of these owners and the sinister interests manipulating the legitimate practice of gaming in Lima for their own illicit purposes. The company also attempted to argue that because these houses were legally closed while these licensing problems were being resolved, there was nothing in the law to stop them from granting the licenses to new proprietors. This tactic was blocked by the prefect of Lima, but Aseng continued in its attempts to dislodge the existing establishments by raising the licensing fees, demanding the deposit of larger guarantees, upgrading the status of the houses to higher licensing categories, and imposing a multitude of fines for technical infractions. The existing gambling houses attempted to go over Aseng's head by appealing to the prefect with the claim that Aseng owned the houses to which it wanted to grant the new licenses. In March, the office of the prefect reversed its previous attitude and supported Aseng in all its attempts to impose extra fees and fines, noting that it did not matter who ran the gambling establishment so long as Aseng could pay the amount of money it had promised to the government.[66]

Even before Aseng had gotten gambling in Lima firmly under its control, it had turned its attention to the rest of the Republic. The original charter for the collection companies only mentioned specific jurisdictions in a few provinces and for particular kinds of gambling houses—the specifications of which suggested that the original intention was only to regulate gambling in areas where there was a large Chinese population. In February Aseng requested that its jurisdiction be extended unambiguously to all the departments in the Republic and to all classes of gambling establishment, and the government agreed.[67] Notably, Aseng did not request that its jurisdiction be extended to all the brothels in the Republic as well, a vice with a much higher level of non-Chinese proprietorship and patronage, and with which Aseng maintained much more congenial relations. On the other hand, tactics of usurpation were immediately extended to the gambling houses of Trujillo. At first, the Trujillo Chinese refused to accept that Aseng's agent, Ricardo Peréz, had any jurisdiction in Trujillo, saying that they had always received their licenses from local pawnshop owner Li Chi (also known as Yec Li). The municipal government of Trujillo supported the local proprietors, ruling that Aseng could only collect fees and not replace houses. Aseng was able to secure the more powerful support of the prefect of Lima with the argument that they were providing the government with three times as much revenue as the previous collectors. Even so, they could not dominate the Trujillo market as easily as the one in Lima, and in 1910 they were still trying to put another of their own houses in place by taking advantage of a gap provided by the transfer of ownership of another local house.[68]

Aseng and Company acted as collectors for five years. The collection monopoly was then granted to Yec Lee and Company from Trujillo in 1914, and to Tomás Yui Swayne in 1915. By Swayne's time the collecting monopoly was not as lucrative as before due to increased municipal interference. Whenever his actions were criticized by other Chinese, Swayne argued that the government should support him because nobody else wanted to act as collector since stricter gambling laws had reduced the opportunity for profit.[69] In 1916 the restrictions on gambling, opium, and prostitution were tightened and aimed more specifically at limiting these activities as specifically Chinese threats against the moral constitution of the city. At the beginning of the year, Chinese operated eight licensed opium dens, and nine Chinese stores had permission to sell opium. After a series of raids on unlicensed gambling and opium dens, the Peruvian government reduced the number of establishments permitted to sell opium to four and promulgated a host of restrictions that included stipulations for hygiene and methods of operation as well as restrictions against the entry of non-Asians. Licensed gambling establishments in Lima were also reduced to four. The collection company was eliminated, and the operation of establishments in Lima was granted to one Chinese entrepreneur in gambling and one in opium, both of whom were very enthusiastic in seeking out and notifying the police of illegal gambling and contraband opium.[70]

Although the control of vice in Lima was an area of intense conflict between Chinese, it never degenerated into the open violence common in other Chinese migrant communities around the world. The plantations and mercantile companies owned by migrant elites of Peru already offered a significant source of wealth and domination that did not depend on the control of gambling and vice. Their struggle depended not so much on the deployment of violence as on the ability to invoke the threat of violence controlled by the Peruvian state—an ability achieved by adhering to administrative procedure, developing special relationships with officials, and perpetuating the perception that Chinese affairs were unique and could be properly regulated only by other Chinese. In the 1920s, the Peruvian government finally consolidated its gradual penetration into the regulation of vice by taking control of the distribution of opium and banning gambling completely. This had two effects on the Chinese. One was the final delegitimization of activities that had come to be associated with Chinese and the public disassociation of Chinese elite from any involvement in their practice. The other was to bind Chinese elite closer to various members of the government who could protect illegal activities.

BECOMING COSMOPOLITAN IN THE ONCENIO

In a message to congress during his first presidency in 1911, President Augusto Leguia proclaimed, "With a clear vision of the future, the government has imperturbably followed the path of progress, and nothing will be able to divert it from this path. Peru, with its almost inexhaustible natural resources, only needs the general and conscientious cooperation of its social elements to become a respected and prosperous state."[71] This was the standard vision of the Civilista government of those years, but not until a military coup in 1919 led to Leguía's second rise to power were comprehensive efforts made to impose that ideal beyond the small circle of Peru's coastal elite. The eleven years of Leguía's second presidency, known as the Oncenio, were also a relatively golden age of influence and prestige for many of the Chinese merchants in Peru who were able to mobilize local and international resources in response to Leguía's ambitions.

Leguía rode into office in 1919 on a wave of social turmoil and bitterness against the cliquishness and elitism of the Civilistas and their inability to firmly confront social problems. Through a committed disregard for democratic practices and institutions, Leguía was much more able to act upon visions of an integrated Peruvian nation producing wealth which could be sold to the world. His government built roads into the mountains, purged local strongmen, encouraged foreign investment in the systematic exploitation of natural resources, developed registration and conscription policies designed to involve more closely all residents of Peru in nation-building projects, erected buildings and monuments in the capital, and negotiated with neighboring countries to clearly define the national borders. This wide embrace of the modern world facilitated the rise of progressive social and political organizations, which were careful to establish popular educational programs.

On the other hand, the implementation of modernity also included techniques for the repression of internal opposition. Even the generous welcome shown to foreign investment was tempered by registrations of foreigners, laws designed to expel pernicious aliens, and a strong paranoia about foreign infiltration in affairs of state. The consequence of this conditional commitment to openness and change was that the drive for a modern, integrated Peru resulted mostly in the increased ability of Peruvian elites and foreign enclaves to access and exploit Peruvian resources for the benefit of themselves and international markets. Some provincial elites expressed their dissatisfaction with Leguía's policies through their congressional representatives, while others resisted his invasive policies through rebellions in the early 1920s. Urban intellectuals constantly complained of nepotism, patriarchalism, disregard of democratic procedure, plutocracy, and the toleration of corruption practiced by his administration, all to little effect. Objections were systematically repressed and ignored, rebellions were defeated, congress made impotent, and intellectuals imprisoned.[72]

Leguía took an opportunistic approach toward Asian immigrants. He had been directly involved, through his position with the British Sugar Company, in the importation of the first batches of Japanese contract laborers after the turn of the century. Many people suspected he had a similar interest in the importation of Chinese, but his connections there were much different.[73] As president in 1909, he had acceded to the victimization of the Chinese in the name of preserving social order by promulgating the first anti-immigration decree. He explained to Wu Tingfang that this action was only undertaken in order to mollify the workers but that he personally had no belief in the inherent inferiority of any race and supported the advancement of all peoples through education.[74] If, during the Oncenio, his government never publicly promoted the Chinese cause, the actions of his officials suggested that the ability of Chinese to reproduce the political rhetoric of the New Fatherland and act as sources of profit to individual officials was indeed more important than skin color in obtaining political patronage.

Immigration During the Oncenio

The common ground of material profit forged between the Chinese elite in Peru and Leguía's supporters was clearly apparent in Chinese migration practices during the Oncenio. From 1909 to 1919, every consul in Hong Kong felt compelled to send at least one communication to Lima expressing his strong opposition to the "danger" of Chinese immigration, a protestation of loyalty that few Leguian consuls felt compelled to make. In defending themselves against accusations of corruption, some Leguian consuls even went out of their way to defer to the Chinese in Peru, writing comments like, "The Asians of this place [Hong Kong], who are in their own country, are not the peaceful individuals we know in our own; . . . once they are outside of the jurisdiction of the Republic, they remove their masks and begin their destructive work, most of all that which can serve their ambition and personal profit."[75] Such observations had their roots as much in the personal and professional problems of the consuls as in any deportment on the part of the Chinese, but they nonetheless reflected the esteem that Chinese were beginning to enjoy among some sectors of Peruvian society.

Before 1919, most fraudulent migration through Callao had primarily taken the form of altered return certificates, paper sons, and the corruption of lower-level Peruvian officials. By 1919, a system of multiple photographs, improved communication and record keeping, and passports put in care of ships' accountants had made the fraudulent practices of the previous ten years more difficult.[76] Fortunately for potential Chinese migrants, the Oncenio produced new opportunities for semilegal migration. The special permits granted to Chinese companies to replace their employees provided the foundation of these opportunities. Before 1919, permits had been limited and not created any significant administrative problems. The Chinese legation was expected to investigate each request and present a final list to the Ministry of Foreign Relations, which approved it and forwarded it to the consul in Hong Kong. The number of permits never exceeded one hundred for any year prior to 1920, and everyone involved took pains to create an appearance of rectitude. The Chinese legation in particular often remarked how much smaller its final list was compared to the number of requests it received. If the actual distribution and use of permits was still subject to fraud and corruption, it was of little concern to the government, because the total number of permits granted was closely regulated.

During the Oncenio, this formal procedure was put aside, and the granting of permits increased dramatically. Four hundred and six permits were authorized in the first eight months of 1922, many of which were written and signed by prominent supporters of the Leguian government, such as congressional Deputy Manuel Quimper, founder of the newspaper *El Tiempo* (which had once been notorious for its outspoken anti-Chinese stance but now included pro-Chinese pieces and advertisements); Deputy Ernesto Devéscovi and the famous doctor Enrique Basadre, both connected to the interests of the Peruvian Steamship Company; Minister of War Germán Luna Iglesias; ex-Prefect of Lima and Minister of the Navy Octavio Casanave; and the two sons of the president, Carlos and Augusto Leguía Swayne, who were widely rumored to be involved in gambling and the distribution of opium in Lima.[77] Chinese to whom such permits were granted merely presented themselves to the consul in Hong Kong with a signed letter which said, "Certified by [name of prominent person], who has guaranteed the honorable conduct of the named [Chinese persons] and their condition as merchants." Then the consul compared the names with a list sent by the ministry and granted the visa. As could be expected with the multiple origins of the permits, confusion was unavoidable, and the blame for misunderstandings generally fell on the heads of the consuls. The Chinese in Hong Kong were more reserved in their accusations against the consuls than previously, now allowing high officials in Lima to exert the bulk of the pressure.[78] Despite the occasional delays, the future of migration under this permit system looked promising enough that Chinese merchants in Lima established the Chungwha Navigation Company in 1921, with stockholders in Chile, Panama, Mexico, Honolulu, Shanghai, and Hong Kong.[79]

The rise in Chinese immigration was again accompanied by an increase in public anti-Chinese sentiments, which had never disappeared since 1909 but had become somewhat more muted. The general strike of May 1919, which set the stage for the Leguian coup in July, was the occasion for another outburst of looting, albeit one more indiscriminately directed at petty merchants of all races. The financial reparations by the Leguian government to the Chinese were made in only nine months, much more quickly than after 1909.[80] In the 1920s, however, Chinese immigration and the corruption that surrounded it gained new significance as a wedge that could be used by anti-Leguian congressmen in their generally futile struggles against the president. By 1922, the institutions of civil society were once again suffused with anti-Chinese sentiment. Labor organizations like the Anti-Asian Patriotic League presented petitions to their representatives in congress. Letters, editorials, and articles against Chinese immigration filled the newspapers.[81] A law requiring the closure of Chinese medicine shops was promulgated in June of 1922, citing the need to protect gullible women from unscientific charlatanism.

A widespread belief emerged that Chinese immigration was not proceeding in accordance to the Porras-Wu Protocol and that corrupt bureaucrats were to blame. In July 1922, the Callao authorities refused to allow the Chinese passengers of the Japanese vessel *Anyo Maru* to disembark. The Chinese Commercial Agent, Tsung-Yee Lo, immediately obtained a personal audience with Leguía, during which he appealed to the rights of immigration guaranteed by the Porras-Wu Protocol. Leguía's personal intervention led to the Chinese being able to disembark "without delay."[82] Despite this presidential interest, the Ministry of Foreign Relations ordered the Hong Kong consul to grant no more visas allowing Chinese to travel to Peru (an order he seems to have interpreted loosely).[83] In November 1922, the House of Deputies sent a special commission to investigate the status of the Chinese who had just arrived in Callao on the steamer *Ginyo Maru*. Their report stated that of the 106 Chinese on board they allowed only 16 to disembark, including 13 men with return passports issued by the Chinese legation in Lima, 2 children, and 1 woman, who did not require passports according to the protocol. Otherwise, they interpreted the Porras-Wu Protocol as a total prohibition of all new migration, noting that the other passengers did not know Spanish, were not familiar with Peru, and had defective passports. They concluded with a proposal for legislation that would, "from this moment cut off all Asian immigration." The law was approved without discussion, but with "great applause."[84]

Again the Chinese Commercial Agent obtained an audience with Leguía.[85] The proposed law was never presented to the Senate, but Chinese migration was suspended for nearly two years until June 1924, when it was reinitiated through clandestine diplomacy. In March of 1924, the Chinese legation had sent a communication to the Ministry of Foreign Relations requesting it to live up to an oral promise that, after Congress was in recess, Chinese who had previously resided in Peru would be permitted to return. In July, the Ministry authorized its consul in Hong Kong to visa the passports of three hundred Chinese who knew Spanish, whose return would be distributed over the next three voyages. Fifty more returns were authorized in August, as well as 120 special permissions for new arrivals. These authorizations were justified partially "with a view to maintaining the existence of Chung Wha [Navigation Company]." This crack in the dike led to a flood, and by 1925, Chinese migration to Peru exceeded the levels of 1922. More than 1,300 migrants left Hong Kong between June 1924 and August 1925, at least 549 of whom carried special permissions issued by the Chinese Legation and approved by the Ministry of Foreign Relations.[86]

Public Image

The willingness of the Leguiístas to support Chinese migration was based on more than just a mutual interest in illegitimate profit and a taste for intrigue and personal favors. The Chinese also cooperated in the production of similar visions about the modernization of Peru. Whatever journalists, congressmen, and labor organizations thought of the Chinese and their unsuitability for Peruvian society, the migrants found a comfortable niche in the Leguian vision of the "New Fatherland." Basadre described the characteristics of the New Fatherland as a desire for the "miraculous realization of progress" and an exaltation of practical politics over the "vague, the diffuse." "Practical politics" in action tended to mean a toleration of high levels of personal enrichment by the political elite (although Leguía himself was believed to be quite honorable) and a strict public order that originated in strong government. The concrete goals most strongly promoted by the New Fatherland were a spirit of commercialism, the growth of a middle class, material progress, and urban development.[87] In such a political environment, the Chinese could develop a much more vigorous public response to the attacks made on them than they did in the previous decade. They were in a good position to present themselves as a group willing and able to fulfill the Leguian demand for progress, international commerce, and the full utilization of the natural resources of Peru.

In the 1920s, Chinese frequently contributed to the debate about them in the Peruvian press. The most common tactic was to compare Chinese migrants favorably to other migrants, selecting judiciously from all the readily available stereotypes. The Japanese were a favored foil, with several writers complaining that Japanese migrants had largely been spared for no good reason the public opposition that had arisen against the Chinese. As a letter sent by a Chinese to *El Comercio* put it, the Japanese "do not represent to the Republic a laborious element, patient and docile, like the Chinese, but a rebellious and dangerous factor which feels itself supported by the cannons of its homeland."[88] Another tactic was to emphasize the services provided by Chinese merchants and businessmen in distributing cheap goods and providing employment to the poor. A full-page advertisement for the Wing On Chong Company published in *El Tiempo* on New Year's Day, 1923, began with a long discourse on the values of international trade. It pointed out how Chinese business had contributed to the development of a maritime traffic which traded South American raw materials for Oriental silks and porcelain and had added greatly to the national treasury through tariff payments. The role of the Chinese was given an anti-imperialist twist by depicting Chinese commerce as preferable to

that of other foreign colonies because the Chinese only acted as intermediaries between foreign producers and Peruvian buyers and did not force
any unwanted products on the market. The article also argued that the success of Chinese-run agricultural enterprises in Peru had proven that Peruvian workers could produce just as much as Europeans, given an efficient
and humane management willing to pay adequate wages. The willingness
of Chinese to contribute to the development of Peru was due not only to
their inherent sense of generosity and gratitude, but also to the rising prestige and self-awareness that accompanied the transformation of China
into a modern nation:

> These [Chinese commercial] houses have understood that the energies
> of the foreigner should not be limited only to the deed of carving out
> a fortune to attain personal well-being, but should also be applied to
> the benefit of the country which has furnished this fortune. That is
> why there is no activity where the action of well-organized Chinese
> capital has not been felt, not with the object of dominating, but with
> the disinterested object of repaying the hospitality and generosity
> which the nationals of this beautiful country have given. . . . Chinese
> commerce has now entered a stage of progress which speaks well of
> the advantages which the new men, who make incarnate the ideals
> of the renovation transforming China since the revolution, bring to
> the colony. . . . These men . . . have reorganized commerce on foun-
> dations of efficiency which it did not have before. They do in Peru
> what they have done in their homeland, in order to extract all of the
> benefit possible from contemporary civilization, but with a spirit of
> cooperation in which respect for the country in which they labor is
> united with the desire to return the benefits which the country has
> offered them.[89]

Articles such as this attempted to promote the Chinese in the racial hierarchy of Peru to the level of the white coastal elite, while still claiming a
certain sympathy for the interests of Peru which other foreign merchant
colonies did not have. The suggestion that China was successfully under-
going a revolutionary transformation into an efficient, modern nation
implied not only that Chinese merchants brought managerial skills and
access to commercial opportunity, but also that they had a memory of
foreign domination which translated into affinity with other dominated
peoples and experience in overcoming that domination. They were to be
a progressive and humble elite which actually lived up to the modern, humanitarian ideals that were promised but not delivered by other elites.

In 1924 the Chinese repeated many of these points in a book distributed to members of congress, entitled, *The Chinese Colony in Peru: Representative Men and Institutions: Its Beneficial Action in the National Life*. It was intended "to convince congress of the importance of having a Chinese colony among us as an element of progress, as a factor of order, and as a stimulant of the national energies, now that thousands of Peruvian workers are already at the service of Chinese agricultural enterprises, where they are always treated with all manner of consideration."[90] It contained biographies, descriptions of Chinese-owned businesses and plantations, advertisements for Chinese and non-Chinese firms, and essays emphasizing the low rates of delinquency and mendicancy among the Chinese. In many ways the book promoted the importance of thriving commerce in building a strong nation even more than the desirability of having the Chinese in Peru. The dedication of the book to "the illustrious statesman" Mr. Leguía asserted,

> Our country, hospitable because of the excellence and the enthusiastic welcome of all initiative by nationals and foreigners, which tends to increase commercial and industrial activity, has Mr. Leguía as its most genuine representative. With the singular commercial vision which has distinguished him since his youth, Mr. Leguía has understood that the economic future of the country depends in large part on taking advantage of all the living forces that contribute their fertile initiatives, their capital, and their energies to the end of placing Peru in the first rank among the countries most distinguished by a high level of economic activity.[91]

The Chinese who produced the book underlined their links to international commerce but downplayed any links or loyalties to a foreign government of the kind for which they had criticized the Japanese. They also discouraged perceptions of local Chinese institutions as organs of political power and social control independent of the Peruvian government. The book claimed that the SBC had been reorganized as the Central Chinese Society and was no longer an organization providing regulation and political representation but a forum for the social gatherings of men committed to performing humanitarian acts: "The idea could not have been more brilliant, because when converted into a social group, the humanitarian acts of the Sociedad de Beneficencia China will naturally be more frequent and effective; and because the idea of charity is born more freely and spontaneously from the social gatherings than from committees charged with practicing it in organized form."[92] Similarly, the Chinese newspaper, *La Voz de la Colonia China,* founded in 1911 as an organ of political factions in opposition to Sun Yat-sen, now represented itself as an organ of the "independent mercantile interests" of the Chinese community, which was "little by little putting itself in direct contact with Chinese commerce in the capital and the rest of the Republic, and progressing rapidly in connecting itself to the social interests of the colony and its commercial interests, which find themselves represented and defended in *La Voz*.[93]

Dora Mayer, whom we saw fifteen years earlier characterizing the Chinese as the feet and hands of the whites, now made her own contribution to this outburst of positive publicity with a book entitled *China, Silent and Eloquent: A Homage from the Chinese Colony to Peru: Motivated by the Centennial of Her Independence* (and she probably wrote, under the pen name Zulana, the long advertisement in *El Tiempo* quoted above). This book offered a romanticized version of Chinese civilization and history which challenged her earlier position on the greater suitability of the locally rooted Indians to be cultivated as members of the Peruvian nation by asking, "Is it possible to believe that the barbarian Zulu or Inca Indian is more assimilable than people of the classical secular civilization of Asia?"[94] She also distinguished the recently arrived Chinese migrants from the coolies of the previous century as more cultured, educated, and like the "respectable foreigners" from Western Europe and the United States.[95]

The Chinese also followed the practice of other foreign colonies by contributing to the monumental statuary of Leguian Lima. For the centennial of the Independence of Peru in 1921, funds were collected from among all the Chinese to have a marble fountain built in Italy and shipped to Lima (fig. 10). The sculpture on top of the fountain depicting a woman surrounded by several children was meant to represent nature protecting the many races of mankind. The young boy on the left of the fountain and the young woman on the right were meant to symbolize Peru and China. Each of these figures held jars from which streams of water cascaded into a larger basin, where they mixed into a single current, signifying that, "The rice and silk of the Yangtze had arrived at the margins of the Amazon, and coffee and sugar from the valley of Chanchamayo had approached the mouth of the Yellow River."[96] The fountain arrived in 1924, in time for the centenary of the Battle of Ayacucho, and was presented to the city in a grand ceremony attended by Leguía, his ministers, and several important Chinese merchants. Aurelio Powsan Chia and Escudero Whu were granted the Order of the Sun in recognition of their efforts.

Figure 10 Commemorative Fountain for the Centenary of the Independence of Peru. (Author's photograph)

Effects of Chinese Efforts

The Chinese media campaigns did have some effect on Peruvian attitudes. The illustrated weekly *Variedades,* which had been one of the greatest cheerleaders of the destruction of the Callejón Otaiza in 1909, now noted with approval that the top hats and tuxedos worn by the Chinese to the many respectable functions they were invited to attend gave them a demeanor of "aristocracy and distinction."[97] Banks printed advertisements in Chinese on the front pages of Peruvian newspapers, stressing their convenient connections with financial institutions in Hong Kong and Shanghai. Chinese even attained a certain a level of respectability among the Europeans and North Americans in Lima. An article in the English-language weekly, the *West Coast Leader,* compared the Chinese in Lima favorably to those in San Francisco and to the native population of Peru. It remarked that the plantations operated by Chinese were "models of scientific cultivation. The labor is Peruvian, and the welfare of the peons is studied in every way." The most notable cause for compliment, however, was the remarkable ability of the Chinese to assimilate into Peruvian life:

> The Chinaman does not assimilate himself with ways that are disorderly and unmethodical, and cleanliness is to him very near akin to godliness. . . . He has not sought to bring China to Peru or to live in an isolated aloofness. On the contrary, he has adapted himself to his Peruvian surroundings to a greater degree than any other immigrant. The Chinese merchant or working man goes about his affairs in exactly the same manner as the business man or laborer from any other part of the world. . . . Taken by and large, there is no more industrious and law-abiding element in the country.[98]

Perhaps the most fascinating conflation of the interests of the Chinese with the interests of upper-class Lima and international commerce were the reports which appeared in the Chinese and English-language press of Hong Kong in 1923 and 1924 that anti-Chinese riots in Lima were being suppressed by United States Marines.[99]

The alliances and conflicts established by 1922 repeated themselves through the rest of the Oncenio. The struggle of congress and labor against Leguía's support of Chinese migration began another cycle in August 1925, when the authorities in Callao only allowed 18 of the 258 Chinese passengers of the *Bokuyo Maru* to disembark. As in 1922, their release was obtained through clandestine diplomacy. This time the Chinese commercial agent made a deal with the minister of government, the minister of foreign relations, and the chief of police in Callao "to extra-officially permit the excluded passengers to find their own means and methods of disembarking, but not in Callao, with the promise that they would not be pursued by the local authorities."[100] In the end, however, they were taken to Panama, where they awaited the efforts of the legation to secure their entry with new special permits, an alternate farce which had also been suggested by the Peruvian ministers.[101] In October, the 194 passengers on the *Rakuyo Maru* disembarked only through the intervention of President Leguía, and Chinese immigration was again suspended.[102]

This suspension meant the end of the Chungwha Navigation Company, but not the end of Chinese migration to Peru. As with the previous suspension, migration was resumed after several months with a concession to the Chinese legation for a limited quantity of returning Chinese and special permits, this time restricted to twenty-five Chinese per boat. In December 1926, the legation suggested a rigorous procedure for the granting of special permits that would give it "complete and strict control over the new Chinese, in order to assure their quality."[103] The proposal was quickly accepted by the Ministry of Foreign Relations and led, once again, to the highest numbers of immigrants since 1908, reaching a peak of 1,233 in 1929, 795 of whom came with special permissions. Far from assuring the quality of new migrants, the legation even granted special permits without specifying the names of the migrants to whom they were granted.[104]

After Cosmopolitanism

The Collapse of Respectability

Chinese became undesirable aliens once again with the fall of Leguía in 1930. Whatever identification the Chinese had achieved with the Leguian government had suddenly become a political liability. The military coup led by the populist Luís Sánchez Cerro brought a vision of the Fatherland quite different from the Leguian one. One worker remembered the triumphant entry of Sánchez Cerro into Lima as a kind of euphoria: "Everybody was a Sánchezcerrista. Blacks, whites, *cholos*. The people cried, they applauded, they embraced him. . . . I have never seen anything like it."[105] He notably did not include Asians in his vision of "everybody." Yellow skin was on par with foreign capital and connections to corrupt and autocratic Leguian officials as anathema to this new vision of the Fatherland.

One of the first acts of the new government in 1930 was to impose a total ban on the entry of all Asians, including naturalized citizens and those who had families in Peru. The ban on Japanese, who were backed by a strong government, was partially lifted after three weeks, but the ban on Chinese remained in force for nearly two years.[106] The only concession granted the Chinese government was to allow it to maintain the fiction that migration had been suspended voluntarily by China in accordance with the Porras-Wu Protocol. A quota of twenty permissions issued each month to Chinese who had not been out of the country for more than two years was in place by 1935, and ratified with a new protocol in 1941.[107] Other new laws included a prohibition on the sale of herbal medicine in December 1930, stricter anti-gambling laws in March 1931, several local laws prohibiting the establishment or sale of businesses to foreigners, and the native employment law of April, 1932, which required that at least 80 percent of the workers in any business be Peruvian. Other

Figure 11 Statue
in Honor of the Four
Hundredth Anniversary
of the Founding of Lima
(Author's photograph)

than some objections against the native employment law, the Chinese
usually gave way in the face of the uncompromising ideological fervor in
support of these regulations, agreeing that they were necessary to avoid
more popular disturbances. They also continued with some attempts to
ingratiate themselves with the new government, such as another contribution to the public statuary of Lima made in 1935 in honor of the four
hundredth anniversary of the founding of the capital (fig. 11). This time
two bronze sculptures were offered, one of a peasant with Indian features
leading oxen and one of a group of llamas, which appealed to Peruvian
nationalism more than to international brotherhood.[108]

The Legacy of Respectability

It is difficult to gauge the extent to which images of the Chinese as a sophisticated and mercantile foreign colony actually circulated through Peruvian society. The Leguian government, the Chinese legation, and the
migrant elite had found common ground both in rhetoric that justified the
migration of honorable and commercially oriented Chinese and in the financial rewards that came from the channeling of such migration, but it
would be difficult to argue that the Chinese shared in any but the smallest
part of the status granted to Europeans and North Americans. The image-

building campaign had clearly backfired by the 1930s, but it did have some strong, long-term effects. Both Chinese and non-Chinese in Peru today have little memory of the powerful anti-Chinese sentiments common earlier in this century, and images of Chinese as honorable and diligent workers, skillful merchants, and immigrants open to assimilation into Peruvian society are now widely accepted. These images are inseparable from contemporary political strategies, but support for them has been drawn from readings of publications produced by the Chinese decades ago.

A commemorative volume put out by the Chinese community for the centennial anniversary of the SBC in 1986 reproduced these tropes of friendship, harmony, and integration. One passage on the history of the Chinese in Peru echoed the advice of Wu Tingfang seventy-seven years earlier in describing success and interracial harmony that consisted of each person maintaining his proper place:

> The Chinese did not trust Peruvian workers. When they needed a partner, they always hired their compatriots. If they needed merchandise transported, they hired local people. Because of this relationship, the life of the Chinese was always within the circle of their countrymen, and they did not have conflicts with anybody. They nurtured their own strength, and never tried to steal Peruvians' "rice bowl." This is why even though the Chinese of those years were the victims of some discrimination, they never were victims of hatred or exclusion. This is because the Chinese never had any conflict with Peruvians in industry, business, or matters of profit, and the great majority of Chinese upheld the public order and conformed to the rules.[109]

The American anthropologist Bernard Wong also looked through this rose-colored history in his comparison of Chinese assimilation in Lima and New York in the 1970s. He argued that the Chinese in Peru assimilated much more successfully because "the Peruvians are used to co-operating with people of many different cultures in the economic and social spheres. There is no desire to maintain a superior race or the homogeneity of a ruling racial group. Their racial attitudes are tolerant, and their economic and social structures are pluralistic."[110] One significant difference between Wong's depiction of Chinese integration and the rhetoric produced by the Chinese is that Wong understands the process of acceptance as incorporation into an egalitarian pluralism (the populist pluralism that did emerge under Sánchez Cerro had little place for the Chinese), whereas the Chinese, both then and now, clearly understood that they were negotiating their way up a racial hierarchy. Much of their economic success was based on exploiting the gap between the white elite and non-white lower classes, but they wanted to shake off the negative associations with the lower classes that had originated in their days as plantation laborers and still persisted through their extensive, small-scale retail interests. Their claim to acceptance was not a claim to become Peruvian but to be considered as respectable foreign residents capable of productively exploiting the material and human wealth of the country.

CHAPTER 6

Exotica and Respectability
in Chicago's Chinatown

Chinatown is exotic—exotic, not because it is a colony of Chinese,
but because it is a colony of Chinese in an alien land.

   Ruth Soong, *A Survey of the Education of Chinese Children in Chicago*

Chinese in Peru occasionally attempted to isolate their activities into a
distinct sphere of uniquely Chinese interests. Their status was also limited by the negative perceptions surrounding their history as plantation
laborers and a general discourse favoring all things European and white.
Nonetheless, in the 1920s, the migrant elite attempted to climb the Peruvian social hierarchy by drawing attention to their modernizing ambitions, transnational and domestic business activities, and their status as
foreign nationals. These attempts were not entirely successful, but, as the
observations in the *West Coast Leader* show, they still managed to project
an image that was different from that in the United States, where Chinese
were seen as dirty and isolated. The *Leader* suggested that it was the Chinese themselves who were different, but Chinese in Peru moved through
much the same transnational networks as those in Chicago. Rather, migrants and migrant institutions interacted with local environments, creating images and activities that facilitated their transnational interests in
accordance with the possibilities and constraints of local concerns. Chicago presented a situation in which social mobility was more difficult,
and it was more in the interest of the Chinese to fortify their limited
spheres of local autonomy.

   During the early twentieth century, Chinese in Chicago built an
increasingly sequestered Chinatown and Chinese economy. They established spheres of residence, gambling, laundry regulation, and social control free from the interference of government and gangsters, and later attracted a clientele for restaurants and curio shops by manipulating images

of the exotic oriental. The migrants and migrant elite in Chicago were no less sophisticated than those in Peru, but the social context of Chicago and the weight of historical precedent in the United States created a situation in which they were less able to mobilize transnational resources in a bid to move up the local status ladder. Links to China and migrant associations could rarely be presented as anything more than the parochial attachments of immigrants. At the same time, migrant associations formed the nexus of power in Chicago rather than businesses. Competition and anti-Chinese attitudes made it difficult for Chinese to gain great success as businessmen. Within this context, Chinese on the West Coast had built a complex of powerful associations in the nineteenth century. The precedents and organizational strength of these associations continued to shape Chinatowns that emerged in the eastern United States after the turn of the century.

The condition of Chicago as a polyglot migrant frontier at the cutting edge of global industrial society actually helped to isolate the Chinese. Not only did the wealth of Chinese in Chicago not measure up to that of the most successful Chinese in Peru in absolute terms, but whatever commercial importance they did attain was completely overshadowed by the modernizing glory of Chicago. In Peru, Chinese could also develop a status as foreign nationals with diplomatic representation, whereas in Chicago they could never be anything more than one of many struggling immigrant groups, and a strange and marginalized one at that. Even when local migrants did have the resources to appeal to the Chinese legation in Washington, the history of Sino-American relations offered only a legacy of accumulating humiliations. Revolutionary transformation and the modernization of China were, at best, only amusing sidebars in Chicago newspapers.

The difficulties of obtaining wealth were one consequence of the weight of anti-Chinese history in the United States. Not only were anti-Chinese activities in the nineteenth century much better organized in the western United States than in Peru in the nineteenth century, but the racial gaps that Chinese had been able to exploit as middlemen in Peru were unavailable. As a result, Chinese were successfully excluded from many lucrative occupations in the United States. Opposition to Chinese also resulted in the formation of a strong and defensive institutional structure that continued to shape migrant politics in the eastern United States. Given these strong institutional resources and potential difficulties of economic diversification, fortifying the borders of an isolated enclave was the best strategy available for a migrant elite to consolidate its power. In this context, ties to home and to strong transnational credit networks were not mobilized as cosmopolitan commercialism but as a narrow parochialism which helped shape migrant isolation. Similarly, limited potential resources meant that conflicts among the migrants were more divisive and violent, and dominance, when achieved, was much more complete. In a city that had become a laboratory for the development of assimilation theory, the Chinese offered an image of old world traditional bonds. To paraphrase Ruth Soong, Chinatown in Chicago was exotic—exotic, not because it was a colony of Chinese, but because it was a colony of Chinese that had become invested in a status quo.

I focus here on a period of particularly intense conflict among Chinese migrants in Chicago between 1904 and 1912. This conflict is interesting not only for its open violence and undisguised hostility, but for the insight it provides into the way that migrants negotiated a dense intersection of kinship networks, Chinese nationalist politics, Chicago municipal politics, local economic interests, feuds between nationwide sworn brotherhood societies, and public identities as respectable local merchants. These struggles culminated in the relocation of Chinatown in 1912 and the consolidation of a predominant power faction. This faction combined a local numerical predominance based on kinship networks and control over migration opportunities with the resources provided by a multi-city sworn brotherhood association and privileged access to local law enforcement. With the rise of this faction, control was consolidated under migrant elites who presented themselves as sophisticated local businessmen capable of providing exotic pleasures to a city of consumers and of representing their peaceful and unique ethnic constituency to otherwise uncomprehending outsiders. At the same time, they never completely suppressed the images of violent retribution, inscrutable intrigue, and insularity that clung to them and had effectively discouraged gangsters, unions, politicians, social workers, and other competitors from interfering in their turf.

THE LEGACY OF THE WEST

The "Companies"

In its reporting on the Chin Wai murder trial of 1908, the *Chicago Tribune* wrote that one would have to go back two thousand years for "a knowledge of ancient Chinese history . . . necessary to a proper understanding of the case."[1] Two thousand years was certainly excessive, in keeping with tendencies by both Chinese and non-Chinese to mystify Chinese social organization, but the reporter was correct in sensing that the context of the murder was more complex than just the economic struggle over control of gambling described by the prosecuting attorneys. We probably need to go back only about fifty years and as far as San Francisco to develop an understanding of that context. I have already mentioned (and much has been written on) the ways in which discrimination pushed Chinese into marginalized service occupations like household service, laundries, and, to a lesser extent, restaurants. Although the profits to be gained from these occupations were limited, laundries in particular were easily adaptable to eastward expansion because of the low start-up capital and vast potential clientele in towns and cities throughout the United States. The lack of diversification in this migrant economy made it easily contained and regulated, which, in turn, discouraged new attempts at diversification.

The organizational structure of the Chinese in Chicago was also linked, through precedent and direct institutional connections, to the history of Chinese associations on the West Coast. Sworn brotherhood societies, native place associations, political parties, kinship groups, and the CCBA were all established in Chicago by migrants aware of the models provided in other American cities. Some of these organizations were affiliated with larger institutions elsewhere, and others were just reproductions of familiar forms. Reproduction did not mean cloning, however, and slight differences in institutions and the relations between them always emerged as they moved across North America.

The beginnings of Chinese migration to California in the 1850s were quickly dominated by native place *huiguan*. These *huiguan* provided the usual mutual aid services, such as mediation, a place to stay, and care after death for people from the same part of China, but their original purpose was to serve and regulate the interests of merchants channeling migrants from Chinese villages to the gold mines of the Sierra Nevada. Migrants had their passage funded by a credit-ticket system in which they borrowed money for their passage and either worked directly for the man who loaned the money or were held to a fixed repayment schedule until the balance and interest were repaid. Although the *huiguan* were known as Chinese "companies," they did not directly earn profit so much as help manage the investments of the recruiters and employers who did. In this context, mutual aid became a form of social control in which migrants were met by *huiguan* representatives as soon as they stepped off the boat, quickly distributed to branches set up near the gold mines, and forbidden to return to China unless they had paid a fee and cleared all of their debts. As the gold mines were exhausted, the *huiguan* retreated to more circumscribed activities in San Francisco, but the transnational recruitment networks they initiated to take advantage of the gold rush still channeled laborers into railroad work, agriculture, and canning factories throughout the nineteenth century. Many employers preferred to deal with Chinese labor because they were efficiently mobilized and controlled by responsible Chinese foremen.[2] The responsiveness of these networks to non-Chinese industry could still be seen in 1924, when the Chinese consul in Vancouver remarked that whenever the Canadian Pacific railroad needed laborers, it could easily "tell someone here, who tells someone else in China. Over there they start a sort of new immigration society and send over so many men."[3]

Violence between migrants in California was present from the beginning. In the 1850s, the largest incidents were between *bendi* and Hakkas. By the late 1860s, lines of conflict had broken from precedents set in China and revolved around the competing interests of *huiguan* in the United States. With the end of the gold rush, many *huiguan* came to be associated with particular occupations or other economic interests in San Francisco, and they formed, split, fused, and regrouped with amazing fluidity in the early years as these spheres of control were negotiated. In 1862, the Consolidated Chinese Benevolent Association was formed in San Francisco as a centralizing institution intended to promote harmony within the Chinese community and present a unified front in dealings with non-Chinese. The CCBA was popularly known as the Six Companies because it was established at a time when six *huiguan* were in existence. Its functions mark the extent to which *huiguan* had already developed beyond merely organizing business and labor. Its membership included representatives from each of the *huiguan,* and offices were to be rotated between these representatives, although the distribution of representation was violently debated over the next decades as various *huiguan* grew and declined in size and power. The arrangement nonetheless impressed the Qing government, which delegated some formal diplomatic responsibilities to the Six Companies in the 1880s and used it as a model to promote the establishment of similar organizations in other countries. On their part, the *huiguan* also imported degree holders from China to act as presidents, although they rarely amounted to much more than figureheads. In this way, the Six Companies positioned itself at the nexus of interaction among the kin and native place organizations, the Chinese government, and the non-Chinese world.

CCBAs, native place, and surname associations were soon set up in communities around the western United States and in New York, following the examples of those in San Francisco. The San Francisco institutions claimed most of these new associations as branches but generally left them to act independently, although when local associations had a serious dispute they could not handle, they often referred it to San Francisco for mediation. Thus, local associations could potentially be part of two hierarchical networks, one leading up from small family associations to the local CCBA and another leading to larger branches in other cities. These latter networks also served as channels through which merchants could cultivate and maintain dispersed connections and arrange lodging for less wealthy members when traveling.

"Fighting" Tongs

The rapid growth of Chinese population in California, an economic depression, and the completion of the railroad projects brought many unemployed Chinese to San Francisco in the 1870s, and conflicts came to a peak.[4] Migrants increasingly criticized the *huiguan* as exploitative institutions that defended the interests of merchants without providing the legal and other kinds of protection they promised in return. The surname associations that grew over this decade were smaller organizations that often offered better personal services and participation but still tended to emerge under the influence of ambitious merchants. Although they sometimes came into conflict with the *huiguan,* they generally tended to integrate themselves as subdivisions of those larger institutions. On the other hand, the sworn brotherhood societies that rose in the 1870s positioned themselves as a clear challenge to *huiguan* dominance.

The tongs (I follow the practice of calling sworn brotherhoods in the United States *tongs*—a romanization of the Chinese word meaning "hall"—to emphasize the particularities of their development here) depicted themselves as egalitarian institutions supporting the interests of the working man in the face of merchant exploitation. Their initiation rituals and rhetoric of loyalty and sworn brotherhood removed them from the hierarchies of family and place that structured the *huiguan* and surname associations. They also provided a means for tighter organization and discipline. Whereas other associations were forced to accept anybody who fit the unrigorous qualifications of name or hometown, the admission rituals of the tongs provided for selectivity at all levels of membership, as well as a mystifying initiation with the potential to heighten the sense of inclusion and difference from outsiders. These rituals were accompanied by written by-laws and well-defined internal organizational hierarchies.[5]

The first tong in San Francisco had been established in 1852, but the early ones tended to restrain the scope of their interests and were not significant on the migrant political scene. Their importance developed within the context of an increasing hostility between Sanyi and Siyi migrants. Although Sanyi migrants were fewer, they controlled much of the migrant economy and were politically dominant in the Six Companies. The numerically superior Siyi migrants were mostly laborers unable to develop significant power as individuals or through their institutions. The tongs' outspoken anti-merchant rhetoric and activities led to a strong identification with Siyi interests. They were therefore excluded from representation in the Six Companies and disparaged as disreputable groups of outlaws, as Chinese merchants cooperated with non-Chinese in propagating images of "fighting tongs," "dens of hatchetmen," and "highbinders." The activities of tongs often lived up to these images, but so did the activities of many surname associations and *huiguan*.

The disrepute surrounding the tongs grew with the criminalization of gambling and prostitution. Before 1877, police did not include the San Francisco Chinatown within their regular jurisdiction, and vice establishments could openly pay five dollars per officer per night for protection. The extension of police jurisdiction in 1877 was just one of many attempts to "clean up" Chinatown, both physically and morally. In addition to constituting the Chinese quarter as a unique racial problem, these movements also pushed vice underground, as payments and protection took on an aura of corruption and bribery. Conscious of their roles as representatives of the Chinese community and respectable merchants, *huiguan* officers disassociated themselves from these practices as much as possible, and the tongs stepped into the void. Individual *huiguan* leaders continued to own many of the establishments, but protection was organized by the tongs.[6]

By the 1880s, violent tong wars had become a significant aspect of migrant life in San Francisco. Some of the hostilities could be described as class conflict, such as the battles of tongs against the wealthy Wong clan and the Six Companies or the celebrated war against the Sanyi Huiguan, which ended with the killing of the powerful, American-educated Sanyi gangster Little Pete in 1896. Many wars, however, were between the tongs themselves. They often started on emotional public pretexts of wounded honor and indignation, such as a stolen woman or a slap in the face, but the conquest of protection territory also provided practical economic motivation. These wars developed into cycles of revenge that continued through the first years of the twentieth century, often following a standard progression from insult to negotiation, battle, and resolution, which included a banquet and formalized peace treaty.[7] The Zhigongtang (not connected to the network of fraternal associations carrying the same name throughout the mining communities and railroad camps in the Pacific Northwest and Canada) was established in the 1880s as a forum for the reconciliation of these differences, a sort of Consolidated Benevolent Tong. As the Zhigongtang had no other representational or economic functions to bind it together, it was much less successful than the Six Companies, and by the early twentieth century it had become much more interested in Chinese politics than in mediating local conflicts.[8]

The dominance of the Six Companies was most severely challenged in 1893, after it failed to have the Geary Act requiring the registration of all Chinese laborers in the United States declared unconstitutional. Not only was this a great loss of face for the Six Companies, but it was one more instance in which the United States government bypassed the mediating services of the CCBA to establish direct control over migrants. A boycott of Sanyi businesses and a new rash of wars pitting the tongs against the *huiguan* flared through the West Coast Chinatowns. The Six Companies identified itself with the cause of public order and attempted to enlist the San Francisco police to fight on its side. It was a losing battle, however, and the struggle resulted in the removal of many Sanyi businesses to Mexico and a reorganization of the Six Companies so that representation was based on the numerical size of a *huiguan*, a change which led to Siyi domination. Despite the reorganization, Six Companies prestige among the Chinese was impaired by the struggles. The persistence of Americans in treating it as the legitimate organ representing the Chinese community contributed greatly to whatever status it regained.

Despite occasional outbursts, armed conflict between Chinese migrants on the West Coast declined in the first decade of the twentieth century. A variety of factors coincided with this growing peace. The Chinese Peace Association was established as a federation of tongs working together for mutual harmony, similar to the Zhigongtang thirty years earlier. It is sometimes given credit for fostering cooperation and reducing violence, although if the founding date of 1913 is correct, it was more a result of reduced hostilities than a cause.[9] More ideologically motivated interpretations have credited the nationalist movements and revolutionary agitation after the turn of the century as laying the groundwork for a sense of unity among the migrants. Reformers and revolutionaries all emphasized how internal divisions were detrimental to the greater goal of establishing China as a respected modern nation. This view ignores how the enmity between competing nationalist groups and their supporters often exploited and aggravated previously existing differences within migrant communities. It also ignores the concurrent rise of tong violence in the eastern United States.

A more likely explanation was the reorientation of the Chinatown economy. With the rebuilding of the San Francisco Chinatown after the earthquake of 1906, tourism was a growing source of income. Previously, non-Chinese who entered Chinatown with the intention of spending money and enjoying themselves were mainly in search of gambling, opium, and prostitution. As vice districts were driven underground, Chinese merchants began to consider the possibilities of attracting non-Chinese patronage to restaurants and curio shops. Plenty of money and an improved public reputation could result from restricting vice to a Chinese clientele and keeping it out of the public eye. The previously hostile division between tong and *huiguan* became an amiable division of duties. Merchants careful about their images avoided any public association with the tongs or claimed to have joined tongs only for self-protection. Behind the scenes, merchant capital and tong organization worked together in the maintenance and extraction of profit from vice. By the 1920s, tongs were often seen as rigidly controlled by businessmen with their eyes on the bottom line, and many Chinese had begun to romanticize the tongs of the previous century as brotherhoods of noble braves fighting together for honor and self-protection. The tongs of the 1920s were not seen as less dependent on violence, but as exercising that violence in acts of coldly calculated and cowardly assassination.[10]

Entrepreneurial Tongs

Just at the time that West Coast violence was dying down, tong violence in the eastern United States bloomed, and Chinese nationalism was swept up in its wake. The new breed of entrepreneurial tongs proved well suited to the goals of accumulating wealth and influence within the younger and less organized Chinatowns of the east. Most of them had very small populations in the nineteenth century, usually focused around a handful of village networks. Most native place and surname associations in the eastern United States date back no earlier than the late 1890s, consciously modeling themselves upon organizations in San Francisco. By this time, the western *huiguan* were no longer flexible vehicles of merchant influence but had become somewhat static vehicles of symbolic prestige for their officers. Moreover, most of the migrants to the eastern United States were from Taishan county, which usually meant, if the San Francisco model were to be followed, only the establishment of a Ningyang Huiguan, with the few migrants from other parts of China banding together in a Liancheng Huiguan (Allied Association) as a counterweight to Ningyang power.

These broad-based eastern *huiguan* were unable to articulate any coherent interests within the community. The aggressive tongs, newly reorganized around commercial interests, could much more actively and flexibly promote the interests of their leaders in the context of these growing Chinatowns. As they grew more powerful, the tongs even pushed aside CCBAs as the dominant organizations in most eastern Chinatowns. Even the powerful New York CCBA—which had been established in 1883 with a membership of prominent merchants rather than *huiguan* representatives—was forced to allow tong representation in its councils, although it did not submit as completely as other eastern CCBAs to the centrality of tongs as the dominant Chinatown organization.[11]

Although evidence is scanty, the first organizations created by Chinese migrants to the eastern United States seem to have been sworn brotherhood associations. Most of the Siyi men in Philadelphia in the 1880s belonged to the Yixing Association, which the wealthier Sanyi men held in contempt.[12] A branch of the Zhigongtang was established in New York by the 1890s, and various sources have mentioned other fraternal societies that existed in New York around the turn of the century.[13] One Chinese source from the 1920s dated the establishment of the Chinese Free Masons (a common reference to the Zhigongtang) in Chicago back to 1881.[14] By 1905, however, the On Leong Tong (Hall of Peaceful Conscientiousness) and the Hip Sing Tong (Hall of United Victory) had begun to displace all these organizations and become the most powerful Chinese institutions in the eastern United States.

The Hip Sing Tong had been established in San Francisco in the 1870s, purportedly by a scholar who had failed in business. By the 1890s, it had developed a reputation for aggressive expansionism, tight organization, and the ready acceptance of Christians into its ranks, for which it was sometimes known as "the Church."[15] A branch was established in New York around the turn of the century. The On Leong Tong first appeared in New York some time before 1903, led by local migrants who perceived the arrival of the Hip Sing as a threat to their interests. It was probably a reorganization of one or more previously existing fraternal associations. Tom Lee, the "Mayor of Chinatown" and a deputy Sheriff of New York County, was the public figurehead and patron, although Louie Yong Hock and Moy Dong Yue, "The Silver Tongued Orator," are generally credited as founders.[16]

Although the two tongs were similar in their goals and forms of organization, a popular distinction arose between them which defined the Hip Sing as an organization made up of working men and the On Leong as an organization of merchants. Sources sympathetic to the Hip Sing have claimed it was a more democratic organization, which resulted in gunmen who were more daring and less likely to harass innocent bystanders without provocation. The On Leong Tong, on the other hand, was widely considered to be a wealthier tong dominated by merchants and restaurateurs who felt threatened by the arrival of the Hip Sing.[17] It was a distinction of rhetoric more than fact, that probably had roots in the timing of their establishment. The rhetoric of democratic brotherhood that had surrounded the growth of tongs in nineteenth-century San Francisco seems to have clung to the Hip Sing, whereas the On Leong was founded in the early twentieth century, when the image of respectable local merchants had once again become more potent than that of egalitarian brotherhood and loyalty. Despite these popular perceptions, each tong commonly characterized itself to white reporters as an "association of respectable merchants," while accusing the other of being a "den of highbinders."

Without the competition of effective native place associations, On Leong and Hip Sing quickly moved beyond the limited activities of their western predecessors and became locked in an intense territorial rivalry throughout the east, not only over the protection of vice operations, but over the right to collect from all Chinatown businesses. In cities with smaller Chinese populations, such as Milwaukee, Cleveland, and Indianapolis, one tong would usually dominate, but in larger cities they would hold competing territories. The On Leong also extended its operations into Hip Sing territory in the Southwest, and violence between the two tongs occurred as far away as Mexico.[18] At first, the various branches of the Hip Sing and On Leong were loosely allied through a system of common symbols and mutual recognition. Traveling members could expect assistance from branches in other cities, and local branches could even make appeals to the resources of other branches, but activities were rarely coordinated. Over time, their organizations became much more centralized. The On Leong formally unified around 1910 as a federation under national officers and with annual meetings. The older Hip Sing had to overcome more deeply entrenched local interests, but in order to remain competitive it also coordinated itself as a federation in 1918 at a San Francisco convention.[19] Hostilities originating in a single locale could then quickly spread across the nation.

Bureaucratic Tongs

The On Leong and Hip Sing each developed a dedicated military branch in the service of the central organization, which facilitated their expansion. As mentioned in chapter 4, sworn brotherhoods often had a military aspect, although not all of them were committed to military organization. The violent history of tongs in the United States, however, had made it a standard feature by the time of the On Leong and Hip Sing. The control that tongs had over the lives, deaths, and loyalties of its members can easily be exaggerated, but, as early as the 1880s, the vocabulary of loyalty and brotherhood had already been supplemented by an explicitly hierarchical military rhetoric. A letter to a Zhigongtang soldier in the Northwest in 1888 was much less egalitarian and mutual-aid oriented than the Zhigongtang rules quoted in chapter 4, leaving little doubt as to his subservient place in the scheme of the organization:

> It has been said that to plan schemes, and devise methods, and to
> hold the seal is the work of the literary class, while to oppose foes,
> fight battles, and plant firm government is the work of the military.
> Now this tong appoints salaried solders to be ready to protect its mem-
> bers and assist others. This is our object. All, therefore, who undertake
> the military service of this tong must obey orders, and without orders
> they must not dare to act. . . . When orders are given, you shall ad-
> vance valiantly to your assigned task. Never shrink or turn back upon
> the battlefield. You must be punctual and use all of your ability for the
> good of the Commonwealth.[20]

The letter went on to outline the financial compensation that would be provided to him or his family in the case of injury or death.

These soldiers were just one part of well-developed tong bureaucracies. An ex-tong officer in 1930 described the internal organization of a tong as composed of three groups: the officers who directed the military actions and handled the daily affairs of the tong, the elders who acted as advisors, and the ordinary members from whom the "armed guards" were recruited. The office of interpreter was especially important because it had the exclusive responsibility of dealing with outsiders. Important decisions were made at joint meetings of elders and officials. A committee of twelve elders was also established to act as a tribunal for the settlement of all grievances. This committee was also responsible for raising funds in case of war, often providing the money out of their own pockets and getting it back by a levy on all of the members.[21]

Even if this ex-officer's description of tong organization was somewhat sensationalized (published in a book entitled *Tong War!*), it still shows some of the advantages a prominent Chinese merchant could gain by joining. The ready-made structures of hierarchy, discipline, and paramilitary corps were easily put to the service of building commercial monopolies and territorial control. Domination through a tong could easily bypass the much more difficult process of building up networks and alliances through kinship, debt, and the constant manipulation of social relations. Tong affiliation, however, also came with negative aspects, such as their poor public reputation. One of the first steps taken by the On Leong and Hip Sing in the east was to reject the word *tong* in favor of names that often included references to workers or merchants (although, in accordance with popular distinctions, the On Leong has stuck with the English name "On Leong Merchant's Association," while the Hip Sing eventually settled on "Hip Sing Association"). This image renovation was part of a larger attempt to appropriate the images of public benevolence and inclusive membership enjoyed by CCBAs and *huiguan,* and to take over their functions of business regulation, conflict mediation, and public representation.

The minutes from the annual national Hip Sing conferences in the 1930s read like meetings of the board of directors of a joint stock company specializing in tribute extraction.[22] Concern with the efficient accumulation of profit and the management of territory was expressed through a vocabulary of morality and gratitude. References to egalitarian brotherhood and democratic procedure were mixed in with hierarchical expressions of generosity and gratitude. Prospective brothers *(kunzhong)* were to be given a careful background check and a trial membership period in order to determine if they were "virtuous and law-abiding types" *(liangshan fenzi)*. Weekly payments from businesses were called "incense and oil contributions" *(xiang you yin),* and the five-hundred-dollar fee required to open a new business in Hip Sing territory was demanded as gratitude to the tong for having "endured ten thousand difficulties and persisted unflinchingly through a hundred troubles" *(qian xin wan ku, bai zhe bu nao)* in making the opportunity possible. Modern republican rhetoric was also thrown into the mix, as branches from throughout the United States each voted for a "congressman" *(yiyuan)* who would be sent to the national conference. Other common topics included membership dues, the setting of extortion prices and payment deadlines, the distribution of profits throughout all the branches, the naming of a national "foreign affairs" *(waijiao)* representative, the granting of scholarships to children of members, donations to universities in China, and solvency qualifications for officers.

At the fourteenth annual meeting in 1931, regulations were drawn up for a new Chinatown being formed in Newark, New Jersey. A set of eleven rules demarcated the territory of the new Chinatown, set monthly fees and tong membership requirements for businesses established there, made provisions for extra funds to be collected in the case of "harassment by Western officials" *(xichai nao luan),* made schedules for the repayment of start-up loans, and declared that tong members who started businesses outside the territory and any outsiders who caused trouble inside the territory would be regarded as enemies. It did not own any businesses, but worked closely with the Yongli Company in making start-up loans available to individuals and partnerships. Three-tenths of the "incense and oil contributions" would go to the central tong office in New York, one-fifth to the local branch, and one half to the Yongli Company. Despite the extensive regulations, local branches still acted with a certain amount of autonomy. One of the justifications for creating a new set of rules for Newark was that nobody was following the old rules in other Chinatowns anyway.

Tongs in the United States had become merchants of protection that assumed the form of tribute-extracting regimes. Individual tong members often had a large financial interest in gambling houses, lotteries, prostitutes, smuggling, and opium, and the tong itself may occasionally have owned a few shares in such enterprises, but most of the power of the tong came through dealing in protection. The services they offered to businesses and individuals under their protection included prevention of police raids, exclusion of competitors, mediation of disputes backed by the realistic threat of enforcement, and the promise not to victimize the patrons themselves. Their resources included the connections they cultivated with police, politicians, and the courts; the armed men under their control; and, perhaps most important, their reputations for taking revenge and enforcing agreements swiftly and ruthlessly. The isolation of the Chinese in American society was an asset that facilitated the tongs' rise to power, which they actively nurtured. By establishing firm boundaries around Chinese activities and monitoring interaction across those boundaries, they set themselves up as overlords and indispensable mediators. They also provided stable conditions which both fostered and circumscribed the extent of Chinese economic activities.

CHINESE IN CHICAGO

In the City of Progress

From the late nineteenth century through the 1920s, Chicago was known around the world as a showcase of the goods and ills of modernity. Progress and poverty, towering buildings and crumbling ghettos, mass production and insular neighborhoods of displaced peasants existed side by side. Observers, investigators, and activists of any persuasion could find something there to capture their interests, fuel their visions, and ignite their moral fires. Except for the attention directed by a few University of Chicago sociologists toward what they perceived as the more exotic specimens in this social laboratory, the Chinese tended to get lost amidst this seething metropolis. Too many other causes, spectacles, stories, juxtapositions, injustices, and inspirations competed for the attention of onlookers and residents. As a result, Chinese migrants in Chicago generally escaped the fate of migrants on the West Coast, who sooner or later became the objects of one or another project of public scrutiny, reform, or rejection. Any public attention the Chinese in Chicago did attract was usually as one of many diverting pieces of exotica inherent to a big city like Chicago: an interesting shopping excursion, an amusing sideline to the normal glut of crime and delinquency that backed up the Chicago courts, or another bit of color in the circus of Chicago politics. A typical example occurred in 1924, when ex-mayor Bill Thompson launched his boat, the "Big Bill," on his ill-fated journey to the South Seas to find the elusive tree-climbing fish: "More fascinating than the customary political harangues . . . were the antics of a band of Chinese who rushed through the craft beating tom-toms and making weird noises designed to chase the devils away."[23]

No legislation was ever passed against the Chinese in Chicago, and I have seen no newspaper article criticizing their presence in the city. When the newspapers editorialized about the "Chinese problem," it was as a distant difficulty in faraway states. There was some opposition to Chinese students in the public schools in early 1900s, partly due to their advanced age, but such students were still commonplace in the 1920s.[24] There was also some calls for police crackdowns after flare-ups of tong violence in the 1920s, but the only instance of organized anti-Chinese activity was motivated by an event that took place in New York in June 1909, when the murder of a Christian English-school teacher by her Chinese lover generated a brief wave of sensationalized press reports and local alarm directed at Chinese Sunday schools located in residential districts of Chicago. An English school on the South Side was invaded by police, and a few incidents of Chinese being arrested for approaching white girls for reasons as innocuous as the desire to offer an umbrella took place. More often than not, however, newspaper editorials condemned unjust treatment of the Chinese. Many teenage girls—the purported objects of the Chinese threat—seemed more thrilled than terrified; groups of them sought out Chinatown tours in New York and watched Chinese men on their way through the alleys to and from English school. The attention proved to be short-lived, and active displays of prejudice soon faded.[25]

The average Chicagoan was no more tolerant toward Chinese than anybody else in the nation. Day-to-day racial divisions could be seen even among Chicago dance hall owners who wanted to discourage Asian patrons (who were predominantly Filipino): "Our patrons are high-class people. They won't go to the same places where these Chinks or whatever they are go. . . . No really white guy is willing to go in and dance with these Chinks or Japs or whatnot."[26] What was different about Chicago was that the Chinese were rarely taken into account in the formulation of issues involving reform, hostility, and distinction. The bulk of the attention went to investigating, categorizing, and assimilating the masses of white European immigrants and to creating hard and fast boundaries against the growing black population.[27] Chinatown took up a relatively limited area, Chinese residents were dispersed throughout the city; they made no attempt to move beyond laundry and restaurant businesses and did not fit into the major black and white racial division that came to structure most racial perceptions and policy in Chicago. As with the few Mexican migrants in the early twentieth century, Chinese seemed to live in the cracks.

Bachelortown

The setting of the Chicago Chinatown before 1912 offers a physical metaphor for how the Chinese in Chicago got lost in the melee of larger concerns. It occupied a block of South Clark Street between Van Buren and Harrison, just south of the central business district (known as the Loop; see fig. 12). The multiple reputations and notoriety of Clark Street strongly overshadowed the Chinese presence. An 1894 article referred to it as "that 'Midway Plaisance' of thoroughfares. . . . Here the representatives of almost every nation under eastern and western skies mingle in the heterogeneous throngs which ceaselessly, day and night, walk the pavements."[28] Local ward boss Bathhouse John Coughlin referred to this block as the "greatest little old stem in the world," meaning that it was an attractive place for transients and "sporting" men interested in gambling, sex, intoxication, and cheap lodging.[29] Indeed, the bulk of Clark Street's fame, and the attraction that brought visitors from around the Midwest, arose from its position as a main thoroughfare of the "Levee," the largest vice district in one of the most "wide open towns" in the United States.

Like many other Chinatowns throughout the world, the Chicago

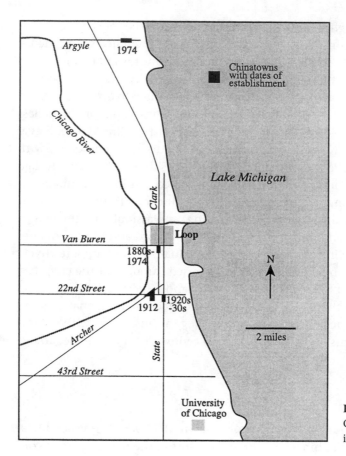

Figure 12
Chinatowns
in Chicago

Chinatown in this period was not a residential district so much as a collection of stores, dormitories, and recreational venues that served a dispersed Chinese population. The Chinese establishments provided services exactly like the other businesses with which they shared the street. Gambling halls and brothels were concentrated directly south and east of the Chinese. Chinese businesses and association halls shared buildings on Clark Street with the Salvation Army, bars, flophouses, pawn shops, barbers, dime museums, and oyster bays run by a variety of ethnic groups. The Hip Sing Tong shared a building with the "Deutsches Gast Haus," an Italian grocery, and Harrison's lunchroom (fig. 13). Black Mushmouth Johnson's gambling house, famous for clientele of all races and bets as low as a nickel, was right next door to one of the earliest Chinese restaurants, the Bow Wo Fung. The Kenna Saloon, headquarters of Hinky Dink Kenna, John Coughlin's partner as ward boss, was one story below the King Yen Lo, an upscale restaurant with a citywide reputation. What the denizens

Figure 13 Headquarters of Hip Sing Tong, Clark Street, 1907. (Source: Chicago Historical Society, DN #5285)

of Clark Street had in common was that, except for the prostitutes, they were bachelors attracted to the area for entertainment and cheap lodging. Political and reform pressures gradually forced the brothels and gambling houses farther and farther south in the period from 1897 to 1909, but the flophouses and bars remained along with the Chinese on Clark Street between Van Buren and Harrison at least through 1912, when the expanding central business district and rising property values constituted a more unstoppable threat.[30]

Colorful accounts of turn-of-the-century Clark Street usually depicted the Chinese as merely one more example of Levee decadence. One reminiscence described them as "the most respectable, or rather the least disreputable, part of the Levee."[31] The most common reference was atmospheric: the smell of opium wafting up from the basements. The activities on Clark Street drew constant attention from reformers and moralists. The same discourses of hygiene and morality that were elsewhere conflated with constructions of race were here focused on the depiction and condemnation of a promiscuous lifestyle, and investigations usually ignored the Chinese in favor of flashier attractions like elegant brothels, gigantic beer mugs, enormous black madams, and other colorful figures like Bathhouse John and Hinky Dink.

Coughlin and Kenna represented the First Ward—which included the Levee and the Loop—in the Chicago city council from 1892 to 1936.[32] They were commonly considered as two of the "gray wolves," politicians who tirelessly maintained Chicago's reputation for graft and corruption. Coughlin was also famous for his loud clothes, awful poetry, and pockets full of nickels which he shared liberally with everybody he passed on Clark Street. Kenna was much more reserved and thought to be the brains of the ward. From within the confines of the Kenna saloon at election time, he coordinated the packing of the local flophouses with voters from throughout the city, the stuffing of ballot boxes, and the provision of mugs of beer and shots of whiskey as the payoff for favorable votes. Their efforts were rewarded by the "boodle"—kickbacks and bribes that came with the granting of public works contracts—available to them after taking office, although Coughlin and Kenna had a reputation for not taking "the big stuff" and preferring to cultivate good relations with the mayors.

Reform-minded citizens consistently attacked such local bosses for fostering patriarchal dependence and a lack of civic morality. Other writers have romanticized them as a buffer against the exploitative and invasive practices of a cold, heartless society, depicting them as always ready with personal attention, sympathy for the common man, an open pocket, and perhaps even a job for friends in need. Beyond moral posturing and personalized favors, Kenna's and Coughlin's power also depended on the systematic organization of services most in demand in their ward. Not only were they tireless in making deals and fighting legislation that threatened the segregated vice district in Chicago, but they also established a fund to buy off police and politicians, to send prostitutes with tuberculosis to the sanitarium, and to keep lawyers on retainer if any of their constituents got in trouble. Most of the money for the fund was collected through mandatory contributions levied on brothels, and protection was given in return only if food and liquor was purchased from approved merchants. Such stipulations mirrored the kinds of arrangements established by Chinese surname, native place, and sworn brotherhood associations.

Being ineligible for citizenship, the Chinese could not vote and were therefore of little political interest to Coughlin and Kenna. This was probably in Bathhouse John's mind in 1894 when, as a new alderman trying to build his image in the city council, he scapegoated the Chinese by introducing anti-opium laws into the city council and organizing vigilante groups to raid Clark Street basements. He professed shock at seeing "young American girls in the arms of Chinamen whom I knew to be as degraded as any human beings ever become," and continued with the warning that, "So long as those who know nothing of the habits of the Chinese pamper them and raise the cry of persecution whenever an effort is made to raid their dens, they will feel comparatively secure. As for me, I know their methods, and opium smoking don't go in the first ward." [33]

This negative attention marked an uncharacteristic low point in relations between the Chinese and local politicians. As Coughlin and Kenna became more secure in their position as local vice lords in succeeding years, they developed a peaceful coexistence with the Chinese, which was almost certainly based on contributions to the Kenna-Coughlin protection fund, as the Chinese were often able to secure the use of lawyers held on retainer there. By 1905, Kenna even found a use for the migrants in his political campaigns. Republican mayoral candidate Harlan had attempted to besmirch the virtuous demeanor of Democratic candidate Edward Dunne by questioning his relationship with Kenna. In response, Kenna "got old King Yen Lo, the manager of the Chink joint on top of my place on Van Buren Street, to write the answer. I don't know what he said, but if it is anything like I told him it's a peacherino." The broadside, written in Chinese characters, was printed up in green ink and distributed throughout the first ward. Whether or not King Yen Lo expressed any insight into the relationship of Kenna and Dunne is unknown, but the form of the response shows the gap between issues that were considered serious in first-ward and citywide politics. [34] Local Chinese proved useful again when the municipal government began police raids with the intention of closing down the Levee for good. Businesses closed for liquor violations sometimes reopened behind documents and licenses issued to Chinese companies, such as when Freiberg's, a notorious bar and dance hall, and favored hangout of Coughlin and Kenna, reappeared as the Hop Ling Company in 1915. [35]

The powerful rackets of Chicago also tended to leave the Chinese in peace. The gambling rings controlled by men like Michael MacDonald and Monte Tennes around the turn of the century created a system of fees and regulation as rigorous as anything the municipal government could devise: "[Tennes] established systematic exclusion. Anyone wishing to enter the gambling business had to apply to this ring. The man and the location would be investigated, the leading gamblers in the city would be asked to approve the applicant, and if disapproved he would be placed upon the 'dead list.'"[36] Chinese houses appeared to be free from this interference, possibly having made arrangements with the rings as a collectivity. Even the Allied Laundry Council—one of the most vigilant rackets in Chicago, violently devoted to assuring that no laundry would undercut the prices they set for the city—seemed to leave the Chinese alone, although they energetically organized laundries run by members of other ethnic groups. The common perception was that Chinese were "poison" to racketeers, their tight insularity preventing successful interference by outsiders.[37]

CONFLICT AMONG THE CHICAGO CHINESE

The Rise of the Moys

In 1926, Moy Dong Chew, by then frequently referred to as the "patriarch" and "historian" of Chinatown, recalled some of his first impressions of Chicago in the 1870s to Ting-chiu Fan, a Christian Chinese graduate student in the School of Social Services at the University of Chicago: "[The residents of Chicago] never said to me that the Chinese have got the perfection of crimes of four thousand years. They never asked me whether or not I ate rats and snakes. They seemed to believe that we had souls to save and these souls were worth saving. The Chicagoans found us a peculiar people, to be sure, but they liked to mix with us. I was destined not to return to my fatherland, I thought."[38] Moy was a chronic politician, and everything he said must be evaluated as part of a calculated strategy of social relations. Over his nearly fifty years as one of the most prominent Chinese in the city, he was instrumental in the development of Chinese public relations and social organization. In further conversations with the graduate student, Moy continued to emphasize souls, the mild but unobjectionable exoticness of the Chinese, the friendly but limited interest that non-Chinese had in the Chinese, and a commitment to establishing himself as a citizen of the city. It was a conversation that could be expected coming from a businessman attempting to promote and maintaining his sway over a limited and specialized niche. Of course,

Moy's comfortable role as a spokesman and his vision of the role of the Chinese in Chicago cannot be taken for granted. It emerged from an energetic power struggle in the decade before 1912, during which the vocabulary used by Chinese to depict unity and difference was much more varied and unstable.

Both numerically and socially, men of the Moy surname have dominated the Chicago migrant community since their arrival. Moy Dong Chew arrived in Chicago in the mid-1870s, followed shortly afterwards by his brothers Moy Dong Hoy (Sam Moy) and Moy Dong Yee. They bought a shop in the Loop from a man known as Opium Dong, which they called the Hip Lung Ying Kee Company. They moved the store to a small concentration of laundries on South Clark Street in 1884, and it became the nucleus of the first Chinatown in Chicago. For years, this shop was a focal point of Moy power and identity, referred to in Chicago newspapers as "the center of Chinese society." Reporters routinely visited it in search of Moy Dong Chew—who had taken on the identity of the company and was often known as Hip Lung—if they wanted a "representative" opinion from the Chinese community or a colorful description of New Year's festivities. By 1928, about eight hundred Moys lived in the city, making up a quarter of the Chinese population.[39] Numerical superiority and their early presence were important factors behind their power, but such advantages could be maintained only through constant attention to alliances and access to outside resources.

A conflict in 1893 highlights some of the social resources the Moys could draw on in Chicago. That year, Wong Aloy (who in 1904 would become interpreter for the Bureau of Immigration) had allegedly been beaten by some Moys as part of a feud between the Wong and Moy families. Wong Chin Foo, who had studied American law and spoke "choice" English, came from New York to pursue Wong Aloy's case in court. His learning was sorely tested against the extensive Moy connections in the city. Shortly after his arrival, Wong told reporters that he had just visited State's Attorney Kern, and had come to the conclusion that "it is impossible for any Chinaman in the City of Chicago who is not friendly to the Moy family to obtain justice through [State's Attorney Kern]." He reported having told Kern that he did not believe the rumors to the effect that "whatever Sam Moy or Hip Lung did they were all right with the state's attorney," and that Kern had replied, "You may believe them. It is true. . . . I have my information from Sam Moy, who is a resident of Chicago, and I prefer his testimony to yours. Moreover, I want you to understand that if you prosecute Sam Moy or Hip Lung, you prosecute me. Those men are my friends and in no case will I prosecute them." Kern later justified his attitude to a reporter by making a frequently formulated distinction between respectable Chicago residents and troublemaking outsiders:

> In my opinion Wong Chin Foo is an adventurer. He came to Chicago at this time, I think, for the purpose of stirring up a quarrel among the Chinamen that he might reap benefit from it. As I understand from Hip Lung, whom I have known for a number of years as a prosperous merchant and peaceful man, he is considered a professional mischief-maker, who travels about among his people in an ostensibly self-sacrificing manner for his personal profit. I think I understand China-men thoroughly, and believing that Wong Chin Foo had come here to create trouble in Chinatown, I thought the surest way of averting it would be to read the riot act to him. I told Wong Chin Foo that if it had been a white man in the case he would have been fined $25 and the case disposed of long ago. They are making a trivial matter the excuse for a bitter factional fight.[40]

Wong was not immediately discouraged. He saw a ray of hope in his perception that the "financial power of [the Hip Lung Company] is the secret of its influence over civil courts" and that Moy Dong Chew was at the moment financially crippled after sending eight thousand dollars to aid his connections in Canada who had gotten into trouble smuggling Chinese into the United States. On his part, Moy Dong Chew accused the Wongs of raising six hundred dollars for his assassination and of offering to withdraw prosecution on payment of five hundred from the Moys. I do not know the results of this particular tussle, but Kern would continue to be a friend of the Moys for decades. In 1912 he was owner of a new, three-story building occupied by the Hip Lung Company.[41] When the Moys gave him the confidence to present himself as a man who "understands Chinamen," they acquired not only a legal and financial patron but a public promoter of their trustworthiness and prosperity as members of the Chicago commercial community.

Two Types of Integration

Wong Chin Foo had long been an advocate of assimilation into American society and cultivated the same kind of cosmopolitan demeanor as the Chinese elite of Peru in the 1920s.[42] His activities provide a point of contrast from which to better understand the kinds of personal relationships and ethnic boundaries cultivated by the Moys. Wong was a tireless promoter of assimilation and Westernization when talking to Chinese, and of Chinese culture when talking to non-Chinese, occasionally presenting himself as a "Buddhist missionary" who criticized the hypocrisies and religious intolerance of Christians. He traveled widely about the country giving speeches, publishing articles in English, asserting the value of Chinese as quality immigrants and potential American citizens, and engaging in debates in which he defended the value of Chinese culture against a host of criticisms large and small—including the accusation that bothered Moy Dong Chew of being snake and rat eaters. In 1892 he had formed the Chinese Equal Rights League of America to fight against exclusion, and to demand "an equal franchise for the Americanized Chinese of the United States."[43] Although Wong was an unusual character among the migrants, he was not a complete outsider in Chicago, despite the claims of State's Attorney Kern. In 1881, he had even helped the Moys persuade the mayor to use his influence to stop the prosecution of minor gambling and opium use at the Hip Lung Company. He had also led three Moys, one adult and two children, to the criminal court for naturalization as American citizens, which proved to be impossible in view of recent precedents in New York and California against citizenship for Chinese.[44]

In 1893, shortly after his legal conflict with the Moys had brought him back to Chicago, Wong began producing a handwritten bimonthly newspaper called the *Chinese American,* which was a revival of a paper of the same name he had published in New York a decade earlier. The opening issue proclaimed in English, "[This paper] especially will appeal to the members of the Americanized Chinese of this country who understand the English Language and love the institutions and civilization of America, and are willing to cast their life lots with us here instead of with the people of China." It then criticized migrants who did not invest more money in their businesses in America, continued to wear Chinese clothes, and engaged in traditional practices, saying their behavior was "not a proper way for followers of confusion [sic] to do."[45] The English section also printed one of Wong's speeches against the exclusion laws and praised a group of Chinese merchants who had put up ninety thousand dollars to establish a booth at the World's Colombian Exposition when the Chinese government failed to do so. The booth included a "Chinese temple and joss house" and a panorama of "Chinese Heaven and Hell," so that visitors could "see all and save a trip to China." The investors had also learned an "expensive lesson" about what was lacking in the display and were "going to place some pretty Chinese ladies within their various departments shortly." The Chinese section included international news, with a special emphasis on conflict between Japan and China; national news, with criticisms of the Geary Act and the Six Companies for failing to successfully oppose it; local Chicago news; exhortations to study and learn; pieces of gossip from China; stories of miraculous events, like women who gave birth to pigs and rocks, and the doctors who cured them; warnings about counterfeiters and fraudulent business schemes; and explanations of American culture.

Despite his enthusiasm and eclecticism, Wong was unable to develop the influence among other migrants or the practical mutual understanding with non-Chinese that the Moys had. Wong's calls for Americans to respect Chinese culture, and for Chinese to assimilate into American life while maintaining selected aspects of Chinese culture were idealistic and in the spirit of American liberalism, but they served the practical needs of only a handful of his contemporaries. Newspapers published in English and the encouragement of large investments in the United States are only two of the most obvious examples of how Wong's agenda was irrelevant to most migrants. The average migrant, linked to a family in China and embedded in migrant networks was likely to find Americanization risky, if not impossible or undesirable. The practical alliances in the service of day-to-day interests offered by the Moys were much more responsive to the immediate interests of the migrants, although this responsiveness was ultimately self-seeking and limited migrant horizons.

Between them, the three Moy brothers divided the labor necessary to establish themselves at the center of the social and economic networks which ran through the migrant community in Chicago. As an officer for several important migrant organizations and the head of an important import and export company, Moy Dong Chew was a key figure in Chicago migrant politics. He was often sought to act as a guarantor or to safeguard the money and valuables of kinsmen. He also maintained extensive connections throughout the United States which facilitated his many immigrant smuggling projects. Moy Dong Hoy was most active in establishing practical relations with the non-Chinese world. He could frequently be found at the Bureau of Immigration testifying as to the respectability of one person, the kinship of another, the financial status of somebody else, which business transactions he had witnessed, and whose money he was holding in safekeeping. The agents were pleased by his ability to produce information and documentation that easily conformed to bureaucratic requirements. They added weight to his statements by describing him to the Washington office as a well-known and "respectable local merchant." Moy could even get immigration officials to send telegrams to the border requesting that they expedite the entry of his friends.[46] The third brother, Moy Dong Yee, spent much of his time in Hong Kong, China, and the Hip Lung branch in San Francisco, where he established and confirmed business connections, made sure that money invested in village affairs was suitably deployed, and looked out for family business interests. He was not always successful in imposing the will of the Moy brothers, as in 1905 when thirty thousand Hong Kong dollars sent to China for the establishment of a school had to be returned to the United States because nobody could agree on where to build the school.[47]

Their cousin Moy Dong Mow, known as Charlie Kee, was also an important part of the Moy establishment. He had run a cigar store in Chicago since the 1880s but made his home at the Hip Lung Company along with the three brothers. He was also one of several Moys who were hired as interpreters for the Bureau of Immigration around the turn of the century. He accompanied special agent Greenhalgh on an undercover tour circuit of the United States from 1898 to 1899 to investigate Chinese immigration cities and ports throughout the country, carrying a letter of introduction from Moy Dong Chew. He was also an important middleman in the citizen discharge scam in upstate New York in 1903–4, working with white lawyers both to facilitate the connections between them and the Chinese and to shake down and threaten Chinese who were not willing to pay the fees. By 1907, he and Greenhalgh had quit the bureau and were suspected of traveling the country representing themselves as agents in order to extort money from other migrants.[48] As late as 1914, two years after Kee was murdered in Seattle, investigators on the Gulf Coast still despaired of establishing any kind of efficient border controls against Chinese smuggling, in large part because of the pernicious influence of the "Moy ring."[49] Smuggling not only produced profit but helped contribute to the numerical dominance of the Moys in Chicago, as well as link many migrants to the brothers through bonds of debt and obligation.

Moy versus Chin

By the turn of the century the Wongs had pretty much fallen out of the picture as pretenders to local power in Chicago, but the Chin family network was mounting an even larger challenge to Moy influence in Chicago and the Midwest. By the end of the nineteenth century at least five Chin merchants in Chicago were wealthy enough to establish households with concubines brought from China.[50] By 1907, Chin F. Foin was the most prominent Chinese restaurateur in Chicago and a pioneer in upscale Chinese dining (see fig. 14). He had arrived in the United States in 1892 at the age of fifteen and come to Chicago in 1895. By 1905, he was the owner of the King Yen Lo above Kenna's saloon, and by 1912 he and his four brothers owned five restaurants in Chicago. It was said that he spoke

Figure 14   Chin F. Foin, with his wife, Yoklund Wong, 1903. (Source: Chinese Immigration Case Files, C-440. Chicago District Office, Records of the Immigration and Naturalization Service, Record Group 85)

German fluently, belonged to an exclusive social club, rode horseback, was the first Chinese in Chicago to own an automobile, and "was a good all-around American."[51] He counted Chinese ministers, prominent Chicago socialites, and Kang Youwei among his acquaintances and friends.

Tongs and Chinese political parties both emerged as areas of conflict between the Chins and Moys. The Chicago branch of the Hip Sing Tong was established by 1905, and the On Leong by 1907.[52] One story about the establishment of the On Leong tells of the arrival of a Hip Sing representative from San Francisco to establish a new chapter in Chicago. On his way to the proposed meeting hall he got lost and stopped in a store owned by some Moys to ask directions:

> Innocently, he explained his mission. The store keeper called in several other of his Moy kinsmen, who listened to the man's story of how he had brought the flag, seal, and book of oaths from San Francisco for the purpose of forming a tong there, and they became incensed. They jumped to the conclusion that they were being harmed, that a new tong was being formed to combat them. Therefore, the new tong had a bitter enemy even before it was founded in Chicago.[53]

Apocryphal as this story may be, it nonetheless captures well how new tong chapters were quickly embedded in local disputes. In fact, the identification of Moys with the On Leong already had a long history. The Portland, Oregon, Hip Sing had put a price on the head of Charlie Kee in 1899, and New York On Leong founder Moy Dong Yue was most likely a cousin of the three brothers. By 1907, the conflict between Moys and Chins centered on the control of gambling, and what better way to obtain resources for such a battle than to join a tong of national scope with long experience in such battles?

The Moys and Chins were also attracted to the local Emperor Protection Association as a platform from which to build and extend their prestige. An Emperor Protection Association branch was established in Chicago in June of 1903, a month before Liang Qichao (who devoted more space in his memoirs to the sights and modernity of Chicago than to local Chinese) passed through the city. Moy Dong Chew was the first president of the local branch, but the Chins would play a more important role in association activities and attract more recognition from the prominent reform leaders.[54] Kang Youwei passed through Chicago on 23 May 1905, attracting a crowd of four hundred Chinese to his speech criticizing the exclusion laws.[55] Later that year, Kang and his associate Tom Leung began to solicit capital from investors across America and China to establish a new restaurant as part of the Commercial Corporation. The original plan was to find a location near Leung's residence in Los Angeles, but Chin F. Foin recommended a site he had located in the Chicago Loop. Kang and Leung took Chin's advice and made him manager. He supervised all aspects of design and decoration, including the importation of expensive fittings from China, and the new King Joy Lo promised to be even more splendid than the old King Yen Lo above Kenna's Saloon, which had established Chin's reputation as a restaurateur.

Kang Youwei himself took an interest in the naming and decor of the restaurant, and was there for the opening in May 1907. During that visit he distributed many articles of imperial clothing in return for donations, and many local migrants had their pictures taken in them.[56] Chin F. Foin continued to enjoy a heady stream of social successes in the months right after the opening, not only among other migrants but also among Qing officials sympathetic to the reformers and among local Chicagoans sympathetic to a luxurious dining experience. He achieved a major social coup in November, when the acting Chinese minister and many prominent Chicagoans attended the naming ceremony of his one-month-old baby at the King Joy Lo. The baby was named Theodore Chungow Chin,

Chungow being the name suggested by the previous minister, and Theodore the name suggested by the acting one in honor of President Roosevelt's willingness to mitigate the rigors of exclusion enforcement.[57]

The King Joy Lo was plagued with scandal nearly from the start. That same November investors were already wondering when they would see some return on their investments. Tom Leung, the manager-in-absentia in Los Angeles, was accused of inefficient management and of using $160,000 he had borrowed from the Commercial Corporation for his own purposes. The delay of profits from the King Joy Lo also led to delays in the establishment of other Commercial Corporation enterprises and to the general aura of corruption and disenchantment gradually adhering to the Emperor Protection Association. Kang Youwei interpreted Leung's behavior as a betrayal of his trust and claimed to have fallen sick for months due to heartbreak.[58] The scandal was concurrent with aggressive attacks on Chin interests in Chicago as their relations with the Moys broke down to a state of naked, unmasked hostility. Local papers noted that Moy Dong Chew played a prominent role in the Chinese reception committees for Minister Wu Tingfang's visit to Chicago in May and June of 1908, as Chin F. Foin and the King Joy Lo receded from the limelight. Wu turned his attention to matters of state and sent his secretary to help straighten out problems that had arisen in the Emperor Protection Association.[59] The secretary quickly found himself immersed in a conflict that ranged far beyond the concerns of Chinese reform politics. In response to accusations surrounding the King Joy Lo scandal, the Chins were accusing Moy Dong Chew of not having used his moral influence as president of the Emperor Protection Association to forestall the establishment of the On Leong Tong the previous year, and both sides repeated the accusations that were part of a widely publicized trial that month, in which the Chins accused Moy Dong Chew and his brother of the murder of a fellow clansman.

Murder

The event that most clearly marked the degeneration of local struggles into irreconcilable hostility was the murder of Chin Wai in October 1907, just months after the establishment of the King Joy Lo and the On Leong Tong. Fortified by Hip Sing power and Reform Association prestige, the Chins had challenged the Moy dominance of local gambling in the summer of 1907. The Chin lawyers later claimed that "Hip Lung . . . attempted to form a Chinese gambling trust with himself at the head, and when he met opposition, instead of resorting to underselling, secret agreements, and rebating, he simply decided to kill off a few of the independents as an object lesson."[60] The Chins had accompanied their opposition with a propaganda campaign, circulating proclamations calling upon all the Chinese of Chicago to resist the tyranny and extortion of Moy Dong Chew and establish an "open" Chinatown. Moy Dong Chew justified his dominance to white reporters by claiming that he had been responsible for keeping highbinders and hatchetmen out of Chicago for twenty years.

Moy Dong Chew and his son Frank were victims of assaults and threats in August and October. The atmosphere on Clark Street grew so tense that many merchants were afraid to venture from their stores, and even the Chicago press noted the tension.[61] Early in the evening of 16 October, Chin Wai was shot and mortally wounded near the corner of Clark and Van Buren (right next to the Kenna Saloon). Police who had heard the gunshots chased and captured Harry Lee, a Christian laundry man from Forty-third Street, as he attempted to hide on the Hip Lung Company premises.[62]

Chinese willing to share their opinions with the press in the days before and after the murder echoed Moy Dong Chew in blaming the murder on a society of highbinders which had descended upon Chicago. They drew these images from newspaper articles at the turn of the century that frequently offered a vague and seamy vision of "highbinders," which wavered between describing them as united in a single predatory nationwide network and as uncontrolled, unorganized delinquents. Chinese in Chicago did little to either refute or clarify these images because, either way, they worked to conveniently dissociate their own respectable commercial image from hints of illegal activity. They emphasized that the violent offenders all came from outside of Chicago, particularly from Boston, where tong violence had resulted in an enormous police raid in 1903 which had made that city notorious throughout the nation.[63]

Because the Boston violence was also part of the Hip Sing–On Leong rivalry, some Chinese accused the Hip Sing Tong and others the On Leong as being the real source of the highbinders. Members of each tong also insisted that theirs was a "respectable merchant organization" made up of locals who had a strong interest in peace and stability in Chicago.[64] While posting bail for Harry Lee, Frank Moy commented on what a "hard-working man" Lee was, and on Chin Wai's unsavory reputation as "a known highbinder [who] belonged to the Boston branch of the society."[65] Despite many other such attempts to displace scrutiny, the indictment against Harry Lee was changed in January to charge Frank's father and uncle, Moy Dong Chew and Moy Dong Hoy, with having personally shot Chin Wai.[66]

The Trial

The Moys and Chins drew from different social resources in organizing forces for their upcoming court battle. The Moys made use of the networks and alliances most associated with South Clark Street, hiring Robert E. Cantwell, one of the lawyers held on retainer by the Coughlin-Kenna fund, to lead their defense team. He had a reputation for successfully defending the seemingly hopeless cases of many well-known criminals. He was also known for a melodramatic and quarrelsome flair, for being a "friend of people higher up," and for having been convicted of contempt of court and assault, including one on an assistant state's attorney.[67]

The Chins also worked through First Ward connections, but followed them further afield in their search for legal talent. The most famous member of the Chin prosecution was ex-mayor and future governor of Illinois, Edward F. Dunne. Dunne had a progressive reputation—earned in his campaigns as county judge against corporate bribery and tax evasion—as "a living symbol of justice and humanity," a "defender of the underdog," and as one who loaded his administration with "long-haired friends and short-haired women."[68] Although an enemy of corruption, Dunne was not strongly associated with the moralistic brand of upper middle class reform that had been the bane of the Levee for so many years, but with a more widely based brand of populism which appealed to working-class voters. His successful 1905 bid for the mayorship had been greatly assisted by the support of Kenna and Coughlin (and the green-inked broadside). It was an unlikely alliance which had broken down quickly when Dunne pushed for the enforcement of saloon closure on Sundays and authorized a few raids on gambling establishments. The loss of First Ward support was crucial in his failure to gain reelection in 1907, but only months after the election he was once again involved in the affairs of South Clark Street as he accompanied two Chinese on a high-profile visit to the death bed of Chin Wai. On the way to the hospital, they made sure that reporters noticed their stop at the Harrison Street police station to request two detectives to escort them as protection against bad elements who might not want them to hear what Chin had to say.[69]

Despite their choice of lawyers, the Moys did not lack connections with men of moral stature equal to Dunne's. Their supply of well-known gentlemen to act as character witnesses included Dunne, as well as Chicago banker, upper-class reformer, and ex-Secretary of the Treasury Lyman Gage, who had held office in 1898 when the Treasury Department was aggressively prosecuting a smuggling ring linked to the Hip Lung Company.[70] Despite the presence of such respectability, the trial was plagued with scandal before it even started. It took an unusually long time to select a jury, and accusations never stopped circulating as to the integrity of the jurors, many of whom were "men of wealth and high business rating" in Chicago. One juror was claimed to have been seduced by a pretty woman from New York into trading his vote for a kiss.[71] After the trial Cantwell and his key witnesses, John Moseland and politician H. H. Stridiron, who claimed to have seen the murder and that the murderer was not any of the accused, were themselves accused and convicted of perjury. Stridiron left the country in July in an attempt to flee justice, but later turned himself in.[72]

The perjury evidence came too late to influence the verdict. The Moy brothers and Harry Lee were acquitted on 17 June 1908. Shortly after the verdict they gave a great banquet in honor of all who had assisted them, at which a Chinese orchestra played the "Star Spangled Banner" along with various Chinese tunes.[73] The Chins were distressed. They had put their necks on the line by asking for the death penalty, although they had backed down from this demand as the trial began to turn against them. Many Chins closed their businesses and left the city in fear of Moy reprisals.[74] Other Chins did not give up, and weeks after the verdict Dunne was once again in their service accusing the police of conspiring with the Moys to harass Chins with vagrancy arrests on Clark Street.[75] Later, in 1909, the Chins took advantage of a growing sentiment in the municipal government to push vice underground and again cooperated with Dunne and the police in raiding Clark Street gambling houses.[76] Violence burst out again in 1911, shortly after the festive opening ceremonies of a new Hip Sing headquarters at 358 South Clark Street. By the end of the year, two On Leong members had been shot in Chicago—one was killed and the other hospitalized.[77] Charlie Kee was shot in the back in Seattle in March of 1912, in what was reputedly a dispute over opium smuggling. By this time, however, the Moys had already begun preparations for their trump card: the relocation of Chinatown.

The Move

In February of 1912 it was announced that Chinatown would move two miles south of the Clark Street location to the intersection of Twenty-second and Archer. Many of the Clark Street leases were due to expire in the next three months, and forty ten-year building leases on Twenty-second Street had been arranged at a cost of over fifty thousand dollars. Plans were also made for the erection of new buildings, the addition of ornate balconies and facades to the old ones, and the construction of a temple for what was to be "the most complete Chinatown in America." [78] Not all the Chinese businesses and associations took part in the move. The Hip Sing Tong and a few shops allied around it remained on Clark Street. Nonetheless, by the first of May, the majority of the Chinese had followed the Moys to the new location, leaving behind only a few posters hung on the walls denouncing the Hip Sing as a den of hatchet men "that have come out into the open for the first time." [79]

The move had been encouraged by the expansion of the central business district and the rising rents and threats of demolition that accompanied it. Other bachelor-oriented establishments on Clark Street also gave way to the erection of skyscrapers. Even Hinky Dink Kenna was forced out in 1911 when the building that housed the Kenna Saloon and the King Yen Lo was purchased and slated for demolition. A newspaper article entitled, "Progress Menaces Dink's Throne Seat, Death Knell for Chinatown," reported that upon hearing the news, "The little boss was too overcome for a moment to speak. . . . 'I guess de first ward's goin' south. . . . First it was Custom House place. Now dey want Chink town." [80] As far as the Chinese were concerned, the move was not a flight but a carefully planned and executed relocation. Even arranging the leases at Twenty-second and Archer was accomplished with a remarkable amount of crafty planning, aimed both at befuddling hostile property owners and forestalling Hip Sing interference. Public announcements originally stated that Chinatown would be relocating at Wabash and Twenty-second, resulting in protests by local residents. It was an elaborate ruse, because Wabash and Twenty-second was where the brothels and gamblers who had been neighbors of the Chinese on Clark Street had reestablished themselves after being chased south by raids a few years earlier. They were probably the last group of property owners in Chicago who would spontaneously organize to object to a Chinese presence. While attention was diverted to that area, leases were quietly signed with building owners in a residential area a few blocks west at Archer. [81]

The move provided the opportunity for a new start away from the unsatisfactory Clark Street gambling situation, which had been subject to Hip Sing interference and increased city-sponsored raids aimed at eradicating vice. During the move, some low-ranking On Leong members had acted on their own initiative to establish a clear-cut monopoly on Twenty-second Street. With the assistance of attorney Charles Hille, who had earlier worked with Dunne in the 1909 Clark Street raids against the On Leong, they struck a deal with Mayor Harrison to allow limited gambling within the new Chinatown, provided that absolutely no police payoffs took place. When they presented this plan to the rest of the tong, Frank

Moy and the other officers were infuriated, responding to the unautho-rized negotiators with physical violence. The officers suspected that by ar-ranging this deal, which undermined their established informal arrange-ments for protection, these men were expecting some kind of special payoff or, even worse, were attempting to usurp tong leadership. Lick-ing their wounds, the renegades presented their plan at the national On Leong conference that year, but the tong backed the Frank Moy fac-tion. Gambling flourished in the new Chinatown via payoffs channeled through the usual Moy connections.[82]

In the years to come, the new Chinatown and the On Leong would flourish, dominating the site in a way never achieved on Clark Street. The new Chinatown was in a much more isolated location than Clark Street, with railroad lines and vacant lots demarcating clear boundaries on three sides. Most non-Chinese businesses moved out over the next twenty years, and the new Chinatown became completely dominated by Chi-nese businesses. It survived the widening of Twenty-second Street in 1922, erecting new buildings and slowly pressing south down Wentworth Street. Chinese families even began to move into the surrounding residential neighborhood. In contrast, the Hip Sing territory on Clark Street appeared more and more abandoned. Some sources even claimed that the On Leong continued to rent Clark Street buildings and leave them empty to con-tribute to the appearance of desolation.[83] The Hip Sing attempted to re-juvenate its territory in the late 1920s by sponsoring a new Chinatown at Twenty-third and State Streets, about a half mile east of the On Leong Chinatown, but was not successful. By 1931, the Chicago Hip Sing Presi-dent, Li Weiyang, was requesting the national Hip Sing congress to find a means of putting pressure on local businesses that refused to repay the loans he had given out for start-up capital. By the early 1940s, the Hip Sing and a few businesses associated with it had retreated back to South Clark Street.[84]

The move became a fertile source for interpretations of the history of Chinese in Chicago. A Chinese student at the University of Chicago in the 1920s suggested that the move occurred in 1912 because that was the year of the Chinese revolution and the "progressive" Chinese felt they had to move away from the more conservative reformers.[85] Ting-chiu Fan, who got much of his information from Moy Dong Chew, took a dif-ferent nationalist slant that downplayed internal schism by pushing the move back to 1905. He argued that the anti-American boycott in China that year had engendered anti-Chinese feelings in Chicago, which had led to rent increases on Clark Street and the creation of tongs and other mutual aid societies for self-protection against whites.[86] An interpretation offered decades later by an ex-Chicago resident in Communist China was even more explicit in blaming 1905 rent increases as a racist conspiracy by the white Chicago bourgeoisie.[87] An immigration inspector who had been posted in Chicago after the move localized the 1905 boycott as a Chicago protest against rising rents on Clark Street.[88] A young Moy studying at the University of Chicago in the 1920s was able to conflate ethnic politics, Chinese factionalism, and the enthusiasm of students for mass movements all into one explanation. He repeated the inspector's idea of a local boycott, but brought the date back up to 1912 and claimed it was led by the local CCBA over the objections and defiance of the renegade Hip Sing Tong.[89]

Almost all of these explanations reflected the expanding consciousness of Chinese in Chicago by interpreting the move in terms of political events linked to a national or even global scale. I would argue, however, that the move was primarily a bid for local hegemony. Rent increases were a factor, but not a determining one—the Hip Sing and a few shops remained on Clark Street until the 1970s. More to the point was that a move away from the expanding business district and the Hip Sing offered a level of isolation and autonomy that fostered On Leong dominance. On Twenty-second Street, the Chinese had a corner of Chicago all to themselves.

THE CONSOLIDATION OF THE CHICAGO CHINESE

After 1912, Moy Dong Chew started delegating many of his responsibilities to Frank, who became the personification of On Leong dominance through the late 1930s. Frank (whose immigration records claim he was born in Portland, Oregon) had married a local, non-Chinese woman and had a home in Hyde Park near the University of Chicago. Local Chinese were impressed by his gold chains and tailored suits, and by how he was driven to the front door of the On Leong in his four-thousand dollar black Lincoln.[90] Non-Chinese knew him as the Mayor of Chinatown, and one reporter said he was "as hospitable as a Southern Colonel."[91] His death in 1937 was reportedly due to "overexertion in patriotic activities," a reference to his involvement in anti-Japanese fund raising. The funeral boasted a procession of over three hundred autos.[92] He lived a high-profile life with wide connections, yet even today old Chinese still speak of him with hesitancy and a touch of fear. The skills of men like Frank Moy in accumulating friendships and status symbols recognized by both Chinese and non-Chinese were an important part of the boundaries and protection being wrapped around local Chinese.

The growth of the new Chinatown was part of the increasing domination of the On Leong Tong. The success of both was manifested in 1927 with the erection of a massive tong headquarters near the corner of Twenty-second and Wentworth. It was soon known as the "Chinatown City Hall," a title usually reserved for local CCBAs. A 1931 article in the *Chicago Tribune* quoted a prominent migrant as saying the On Leong "pretty completely directs the economic, political, and social life of Chinatown."[93] This domination meant first of all that gambling operations and business territory were made more stable and secure from outside interference. It also marked a transformation in the activities and self-image of the tong. The collaboration between tongs and merchants in San Francisco that had arisen with the growth of tourism after 1906 was taken one step further in Chicago, where the main organ of merchant interests was the On Leong Tong itself. The On Leong went beyond merely asserting that it was an association of "respectable merchants," and tried to fill the role of charitable and representative Chinatown organization. In achieving this, the On Leong did more than just perform the usual mediating, benevolent, and legal functions of a CCBA. It also presented a public face to non-Chinese as a group of businessmen actively marketing their specialization in oriental delights.

Why a Tong?

The limitations of the Chinese economic role in the United States meant that individual Chinese, unlike those in Peru, were rarely able to claim recognition based on their positions as successful, independent businessmen. Whatever prestige individual Chinese in the United States could attain among non-Chinese was strongly based on a reputation as a representative of the Chinese community. Migrant associations played a key role in defining that Chinese community and legitimizing individual claims to represent it. As a manager of the Hip Lung Company, Moy Dong Chew had earned some public recognition. Backed by the On Leong, Frank Moy became the Mayor of Chinatown. Idealistic but poorly connected men like Wong Chin Foo could gain publicity, but were much less successful in exercising influence. The legitimizing power of these associations had roots in their importance in organizing the earliest flows of migration (whereas migration to Peru was organized by white planters) and was maintained through the success of the Six Companies and other CCBAs in placing themselves at the nexus of complex associational networks and portraying their interests as identical to those of the local Chinese community. As the Chinese moved east, the political significance of migrant associations was maintained, but tongs replaced CCBAs as the dominant institutions. The Chicago On Leong was a model example of this transformation, so successful that by the 1920s it was an anchor point in the national On Leong system. Why did the tong prevail over *huiguan*, family, business, political parties, and occupational guilds as a vehicle for the consolidation of Moy power in Chicago?

In brief, tongs offered more flexible alliances, superior resources, and an organizational structure easily put in the service of the economic interests of its leaders. The *huiguan* of the 1850s had offered similar benefits, but by the twentieth century they had become somewhat ossified in their actions and structure. Surname and native place organizations were limited in their range of membership and consequently in their ability to centralize power and represent the migrant community as a whole. Large-scale labor mobilization was no longer a primary source of wealth, although great profits still came from smuggling and the sale of papers. Consequently, strong connections in China were no longer as critical as connections with officials and underground networks. Moreover, after the upheavals of the late nineteenth century, the *huiguan* had surrendered much of their direct involvement in economic affairs and developed pretenses toward broad representation. In Chicago, almost all the migrants came from Taishan county, and all could make some claim to representation in the local Ningyang Huiguan. Rotating officerships and little selectivity regarding membership made such a *huiguan* difficult to mobilize as an effective organizational tool under the dominance of a single clique. A brief burst of *huiguan* creation took place in Chicago in 1911 "to fight against Moys," but none of them lasted very long.[94] By the early twentieth century, surname and native place associations had become much more relevant as institutions for the maintenance of small-scale mutual aid and links to villages in China.

A CCBA had been established in Chicago in 1904 but was merely a figurehead institution through most of its history. It had little influence over the conflicts before 1912, and after the move to Twenty-second Street the On Leong began to perform the community-wide mediation and regulation that usually belonged to the CCBA. In the 1920s, most migrants would only accept CCBA mediation if Moy Dong Chew and Toy Fong (a wealthy merchant who had only resided in Chicago sporadically before the late teens) were present, suggesting how power was vested in the CCBA only at the pleasure of powerful men.[95]

Chinese political parties after the turn of the century also offered avenues of prestige that reached out beyond the local migrant communities and village-based migrant networks. These organizations, however, lacked a stable financial basis other than the solicitation of funds from migrants. They tended to demand too many contributions without providing enough in return, and attempts like the King Joy Lo to develop a stable source of income could prove fruitless under the stresses of individual and local interests. As the Emperor Protection Association crumbled under the weight of scandal, Sun Yat-sen's revolutionary movement finally gained momentum as he passed through Chicago at the end of 1909, early 1910, and again at the beginning of 1911. The second Tongmenghui in the United States was established during his 1910 visit, with most of the dozen or so original members—more than half of whom were Moys—being Christians. His visit in April 1911 was a much more significant event, coming on the heels of an unprecedented show of support in New York, which had resulted in the public humiliation of the New York CCBA president. He was met at the train station by leaders of the Hip Sing, the On Leong, and the Zhigongtang.[96] By the following February, however, the Chicago Chinese were already using the Chinese New Year's celebration to celebrate the ascension of Sun's rival Yuan Shikai to the presidency (including homage to George Washington for good measure). The Chicago Moys and the Hip Sing both remained supporters of the Constitutional Party into the 1920s, but interest in political organizations as a source of status was largely deflated by the failure of the 1912 republic.[97]

Tongs, on the other hand, were open to people of any surname, from any native place, and even of any race, while at the same time being selective about who would be initiated. Thus, tongs were ideal vehicles through which a group like the Moys could institutionalize alliances with other families and individuals while retaining control of the institutional structure of officers, elders, and common members. Tong affiliations also offered access to resources outside of Chicago, especially after they were formally confederated into a nationwide organization, while still respecting the autonomous control of local branches over nearly all local business activities. These resources included ready access to armed men and a commitment of nationwide resources to the regulation and exploitation of economic activities. Migrant elites could focus tong resources to their benefit in local situations, or use the tong as a forum to pursue their ambitions beyond the limits of the local migrant community.

Benevolent Tongs

On Leong and Hip Sing members continued to murder each other in Chicago after 1912, more as an aspect of nationwide conflict among the tongs than as a consequence of local struggles. Even the nationwide war of

1924, which originated in factionalism in the Chicago On Leong branch, is best understood on a national scale. Chin Jack Lem had been one of the renegades who tried to establish a new gambling arrangement with the mayor in 1912. Despite that failure, he rose quickly within the Chicago branch, building a career out of his reputation for ruthless violence. At the 1924 national On Leong meeting in Pittsburgh, Chin was expelled along with New York founder Moy Dong Yue and other members who supported the Constitutional Party and were known as the "conservative" faction. Leaders of the "progressive" faction that had taken over included Lee Toy of Chicago, who was elected national president and national interpreter for the tong that year. They had reportedly won the 1924 election through "American" vote-canvassing tactics, which meant handing out flyers at the door and attempting to bypass the usual practice of a previously orchestrated consensus. When Chin Jack Lem and some of his followers joined the Hip Sing in New York, violence erupted throughout the United States.[98]

The extension of rivalries based in the Chicago On Leong to a national scale reflected not only the increasingly tight relationship between the branches, but also the extent to which local challenges had been subdued in Chicago. As local power was consolidated, the On Leong became the main stage for power struggles, and individual ambitions could be directed outward toward national influence. The On Leong freely sent inspectors to Clark Street to make sure that no On Leong members were gambling there, but Hip Sing members were afraid to go without armed escorts to Twenty-second Street to take part in CCBA meetings.[99] The Chins had forsaken the Hip Sing as well. By the 1920s, most of the prominent Chins who had not left Chicago had drifted over to the new Chinatown and became involved in the On Leong.[100] That the Chicago Hip Sing retained any autonomy at all was more a result of the nationwide balance of power than any local tolerance on the part of the On Leong.

Control of gambling always remained the primary basis of On Leong power, both financially and socially. The creation a secure space for gambling activities was a crucial aspect of the undisputed territorial monopoly of the On Leong. During the four years from 1905 to 1908, 2,239 Chinese were arrested in Chicago (a number amounting to well over half of the entire Chinese population), 64 percent for gaming violations.[101] In the eleven years from 1914 to 1925 (excluding 1919, for which I have no data), only 1,913 Chinese were arrested, a decline in the yearly average of nearly 70 percent. Of 484 convictions, only 11 percent were for gaming, and those were said to have been gamblers in small, independent houses that did not pay protection to the tongs. Of the other convictions, 24 percent were for disorderly conduct, and 18 percent for prostitution, activities which usually took place outside of tong influence, although the 9 percent for concealed weapons may have had some connection with the tongs.[102]

One migrant recalled, "When we talk about gambling, this is connected to the American police, because it was them who arrested gamblers, it was them who indulged and protected gambling, and it was also them who used gambling to stir up fights among the Chinese."[103] This observation was accurate in pointing out the significance of local police indulgence, but not in evaluating the results. When collaboration between municipal and tong officials over gambling went smoothly, as was the case in Chicago after 1912, the local Chinese community was not disrupted so much as enclosed within a barrier. The interests of non-Chinese in segregating the Chinese resonated with tong interests in dominating them. The less access that average Chinese had to outside opportunities, the more the tong elite could earn profit and prestige by interposing themselves between migrants and the non-Chinese world.

The rise of the On Leong also corresponded with a more general shift in the political relations of the city as a whole. When the Moys left Clark Street in 1912, the neighborhood was already disappearing, both physically and socially. As vice was pushed underground in the early twentieth century, its open protection by politicians like Coughlin and Kenna became a thing of the past. Independent crime syndicates grew in their place, reaching full flower during prohibition. This shift accompanied the rise of big business, not only as a source of profit and patronage for gangsters and politicians, but also as a model of organizational efficiency. The new criminal was an organization man, and profit was the measure of success.[104]

Tongs were changing with the times. In abandoning Clark Street, the Moys disentangled themselves from neighborhood political relations and found an isolated location in which the tong could be the final authority, retaining its own legal staff and making its own deals with city officials. The tong itself had also attained a level of organizational strength and profit orientation unknown in the nineteenth century. Chinese merchants in the United States had always engaged in a range of activities that might be considered conspiratorial, illegal, or exploitative in certain situations. With the On Leong, however, the criminal tong and respectable Chinese merchant association became one and the same. At the turn of the century, Chinese merchants had interacted flexibly with local politicians and vice entrepreneurs. By the 1920s, they had developed a coherent institutional identity for themselves as local businessmen. Their most high-profile interactions with non-Chinese no longer appeared as special friendships, but as open commercial and public relations encounters. At the same time, they never restrained the violence and flow of cash that continued to underwrite the less public side of Chicago business. The main thing that tongs lacked was respectability as legitimate organs of migrant representation, but the Chicago On Leong was a pioneer in developing that respectability.

Respectability and Exotica

Although the Chicago On Leong was closely linked to nationwide tong activities, locally it attempted to dissociate itself from tong activities and legitimize its domination as a representative and benevolent businessman's community center in the style of a CCBA. Moy Dong Chew told Ting-chiu Fan in 1925 that tongs were growing weaker in the United States and that none of the respected Chinese belonged to them. Fan's thesis did not even refer to the On Leong, but only to a "Chinese Association" that was "a branch of a national organization in North America" that provided social services, arbitrated disputes, certified documents, maintained order, and represented the Chinese.[105] A University of Chicago student from North China claimed the On Leong was primarily an arbitration agency.[106] The Moy sociology student who had credited the CCBA for moving Chinatown felt compelled to recognize the existence of unsavory activities among the Chinese in Chicago, but shifted the blame away from the On Leong by explaining how the legitimate leaders of the On Leong were occasionally "put to shame due to the malpractices of some of the black sheep of the colony who have learned the tricks of lower-class American politicians in the ward."[107] Susan Lee Moy's 1979 master's thesis continued this tradition of describing the Chicago On Leong as the sum of its charitable and commercial activities, but she was perhaps a bit less romantic when she suggested that it was also "the only organization with power and money enough to carry on large community projects."[108] The establishment of the On Leong as the local Chinese government even included attempts to rewrite history by appropriating some of the past glories of the Chins. Within a year after Chin F. Foin's death in 1924, Moy Dong Chew assumed credit for the King Joy Lo by pushing its establishment back to the 1890s as the first chop suey house in Chicago and implying that he and Minister Wu Tingfang had established it as a joint effort to improve the lot of local Chinese.[109]

Journalists visiting the On Leong in the 1930s were impressed by the "intelligent, courteous, and educated business men," who received

Figure 15 Wentworth Street and On Leong Tong Building, 1952. (Source: Chicago Historical Society, ICHI-04881; photograph by J. Sherwin Murphy)

them.[110] The most notable manifestation of the rise of a local Chinese business community was the increasing commodification of Chineseness in and of itself as a salable product. Sophisticated On Leong businessmen increasingly marketed a product of mild oriental exoticism. The On Leong building was probably the most visible example of this Chinese public identity (fig. 15). Its solid, heavy form and dominating presence evoked the power of the On Leong, while the jade-colored trimmings and pagoda-shaped turrets offered an exotically seductive lure which could be seen for blocks around.

Restaurants were at the core of this economy. Turn-of-the-century restaurateurs like Chin F. Foin had made much of their profit from American-style meals, but by the 1920s, they were tapping into a growing market of customers searching for something different yet unthreatening, like Chinese American chop suey and fortune cookies. The food was served in an atmosphere of vague oriental exotica embodied in names like Golden Pheasant Inn, Bamboo Inn, Peacock Inn, Canton Tea Garden, and Oriental Garden, and in a spectrum of decor that included gaudy red and gold interiors, pointed reed hats, and cuneiform typefaces meant to appear as if written by a Chinese brush to bamboo and thatched grass lobbies serving "Polynesian cocktails." Some Chinese earned money giving tours of Chinatown to diners leaving the restaurants. By the late 1930s, these tours were even sponsored by the WPA, and a receptionist was kept in the lobby of On Leong Tong building to welcome visitors.[111]

If Frank Moy was a symbol of rising On Leong dominance, Gerald Moye personified its mature public face as head of a benevolent local business organization selling the tastes and sights of the Orient. Moye, a long-time president of the Chicago On Leong after Frank's death, was a lawyer educated at the University of Illinois and a partner in the firm Moye, Gleason, and Dillon. He had also managed a small tourist attraction called the Ling Long Museum in the 1930s, which offered a panorama of the "Highlights of Chinese History and Chicago's Chinatown." The descriptive pamphlet for the museum began with a brief summary of Chinese history, in which the Chinese Republic received most of the attention, and then asserted that the Chinese in Chicago were the inheritors of this noble historical legacy. It quickly made a point of diffusing any suspicions that this legacy might be a threat to American sovereignty by stating that "there is really no political set-up in Chinatown. We do not have a 'mayor' or a 'city hall." It continued by explaining that "tongs are simply merchant associations, and are strictly of American origin . . . [consisting of] well-educated men . . . [making] efforts toward philanthropic goals rather than confined to rivalry." This image of civilized behavior stopped short of the aim of total assimilation into America with the assertion that Chinatown was still independent and "self-governed by Chinese without political alliances, through the cooperation of the different associations."[112] The pamphlet concluded with an invitation for outsiders to visit a tourist trail which included stops at the On Leong building, the Methodist Church, and the larger souvenir shops.

In many ways, Gerald Moye was finally putting into practice Wong Chin Foo's vision from over forty years before of the Chinese as a dedicated commercial community deploying selected aspects of Chineseness as a basis for integration into American society. By the 1920s, Chinese in both Chicago and Peru were actively promoting positive images of themselves as Chinese. In Peru, this Chineseness was expressed primarily as membership in the Chinese nation, based in part on claims of racial and cultural affinity, but also modeled after prestigious European colonies defined by their cosmopolitanism and modernity. The Chinese in Chicago, however, defined their qualities as a group not so much in terms of international standards as in terms of local material interests and institutions. These qualities included their ability to take care of themselves, get along with their neighbors, and provide attractive products from far away to local consumers.

Tongs had few links to any particular locale in China and (except for the Zhigongtang, which tried to involve itself in national politics in China rather than local hometown issues) most of their goals and resources were focused on local interests outside of China. Their networking across North America was a form of collaboration designed to fortify the interests of local branches. Thus, local affairs and access to the non-Chinese world were easily dominated by tongs, which helped perpetuate the status quo of laundries, restaurants, and gambling. Direct links to China primarily involved profits from smuggling migrants (or, more likely, from the protection of smugglers). Once in the United States, however, these migrants were generally left to their own means. The tongs only "protected" local enterprises; they were not the nodes of business and credit networks, because such networks always reached ultimately beyond North America and beyond tong surveillance. This was unlike the elite businesses in Peru that could channel migrants all the way from Hong Kong and into their extensive local business networks. Migrant elites in Peru both profited from transnational networks and publicly drew upon them as a means to upward mobility. In Chicago, however, organizations and small businesses other than the tongs continued to make up the fabric of transnational networks, which remained strong along with the relatively high proportion of new migrants. Local power was left to the tongs, which had developed in conjunction with the racism and economic opportunities of North America. They could not, however, develop the connections necessary to dominate transnational networks. Rather, they cooperated with those networks to orient migrants in such a way as to perpetuate the local isolation upon which tong domination was built.

Continuing Patterns

The On Leong building still marks the entrance to the Twenty-second Street Chinatown. It was raided by federal agents in the late 1980s for gambling and closed for several years but has now been occupied and renovated by a Christian social service organization. A plaque installed in the doorway in 1993 to recognize the building as a historical monument praises the community-building aspects of the On Leong:

> The business association that commissioned this building was instrumental in creating Chicago's Chinatown in 1912. The building housed various meeting halls, a school, a shrine, and the association's officers.

Its design was derived from the architecture of the Kwangtung region of China, the ancestral region of many of Chinatown's residents.

The conflicts of Chinatown history receive less public acknowledgment than the benevolent merchant facade, but they are still evident today. When the federal government bought out the Hip Sing property on Clark Street in 1974 to build a parking garage and prison, the Hip Sing moved eight miles north to Argyle Street. With funds donated by the Nationalist government in Taiwan, it purchased several buildings and made plans for a beautiful mall complete with fountains and pagodas.[113] The plans for the Argyle Street Chinatown were as ambitious as those that accompanied the move to Twenty-second Street but were much less successful. The new Chinatown was saved from obscurity only by the waves of Southeast Asian migrants who came to Chicago in the 1980s. The Twenty-second Street Chinatown remains almost exclusively Chinese; many residents can trace their networks back to migrants who arrived much earlier in the century, while Argyle Street now boasts businesses with signs written in at least five languages.

Patterns of violence also persisted. Four years after the Argyle Street move, some old men gambling in the Hip Sing building were brutally attacked by a youth gang affiliated with the On Leong. Chinese statements to the media provided denials and assertions similar to those heard in 1907: that the perpetrators were outsiders from New York, that they victimized the Hip Sing because the Twenty-second Street Chinatown was too close-knit for freelance criminals to operate in, and that the tongs themselves were only involved in social and charitable activities.[114] The less public side of this continued legacy of tong domination can be seen in observations made to a white reporter by a Chinese merchant in New York in the 1980s:

> [Extortion] is the cost of doing business here. Maybe 1 percent of places getting extorted are unhappy. It's status quo. I'm upset now because we're in the first phase of disorganized crime. It's so serious it's terrifying. Those kids come in. We have no one to negotiate with. You can't b.s. your way out, or make a deal. This is new. In eighty years, this is new. We don't know who they are—it's not the same guys each time. We think it's free-lance kids. Vietnamese don't respect anybody. Things are changing. . . . I know the management of the tong that controls my street, its general, and its lieutenants. To save face, I'll complain to its second rung, not the top. The kid gets taken care of. . . . I'm for tranquillity. I'm not looking for reform. I'm typical, I think. Chinese are the richest people on earth, you know. All these guys out

EXOTICA AND RESPECTABILITY IN CHICAGO'S CHINATOWN............................223

there are getting rich. They don't view themselves as enslaved by
gangs and associations. The IRS enslaves me, not the gangs.[115]

For this merchant, the tongs were more legitimate than the United
States government in their claim to govern and extract tribute. He expressed a belief that Chinese success depended to some extent on security
from outside interference. This was not necessarily an accurate assessment of his best interests. Different assessments of the best interests of
Chinese communities are evident in the resistance of the Chinese Hand
Laundry Alliance against the New York CCBA in the 1930s, in the demands for rights of citizenship by Chinese American Citizens Alliances,
and in the activities of social service organizations that have emerged
since the 1960s. Nonetheless, the continued relevance of this merchant's
assessment is based on the success of tongs and other migrant associations in monopolizing contacts with non-Chinese and directing the Chinese toward networks that link them more strongly with China and other
Chinese.

CHAPTER 7

The Auspicious Legacy of the
Ancestors in Hawaii

Most Chinese in Peru and Chicago in the early twentieth century were born in China, and their experiences were strongly linked to global migrant networks. In Hawaii, by the 1930s, as many as half of the Chinese were locally born. They had little experience with the physical act of migration and were more likely to conceptualize their future primarily in terms of Hawaii. Nonetheless, the precedents and institutions created by earlier migrants, the reputation of the Chinese nation, and the opportunities offered by transnational networks continued to shape their activities and public relations.

By the 1900s, China-born migrants in Hawaii had achieved even more recognition as successful businessmen than the Chinese in Peru in the 1920s. In Peru the image of the cosmopolitan businessman adhered only to a handful of elites. In Hawaii, the image of the respectable merchant was shared by a much larger spectrum of Chinese engaged in a variety of small-scale retail and wholesale activities. They were well integrated into the Hawaiian economy and experienced less competition over the control of segregated economies. As in Peru, the Chinese in Hawaii had close relations with diplomatic representatives from China and made direct links between the international status of China and their own local status. The stronger social status of Chinese in Hawaii, however, meant that even though the Chinese had close relationships with Chinese officials, they were not so dependent on official representation, and these relationships were often quite stormy. In the early 1900s, Chinese nationalist politics was the most public site of conflict among Chinese in Hawaii. The struggle for political recognition surpassed economic interests, native place, and surname alliances as the issue that defined competition among the Chinese.

By the 1920s, with the failure of the republic and the rise of a strong locally born generation, Chinese increasingly defined themselves in terms of Hawaii as a coherent ethnic group in a multicultural society. Interest in the struggles of Chinese politics was replaced by a less partisan interest in the rise of China as a modern nation. Interest in the old migrant associations was also revived in the 1930s as markers of local ethnicity and immigrant heritage. Local Chineseness was critically shaped by American patriotic rhetoric. The public agenda of the federal government, which promoted the United States as a land of immigrants and freedom that was hostile to patriarchal and elitist domination, provided guidelines for appropriating aspects of the Chinese past and presenting them as a local ethnic heritage. It also offered a vocabulary that could be used strategically to compete for status with other groups on Hawaii.

BEFORE ANNEXATION

The Early Chinese Presence in Hawaii

As agriculturists, merchants, and financiers, Chinese created and dominated many of the networks that connected rural Hawaii with Honolulu and plantations with villages in the nineteenth century. As merchants, they distributed a variety of consumer items imported by the large Chinese and *haole* (a word referring to Caucasians other than Portuguese and Spanish immigrants) firms in Honolulu to villages and plantation laborers throughout the Islands, and they provided capital and tools to Chi-

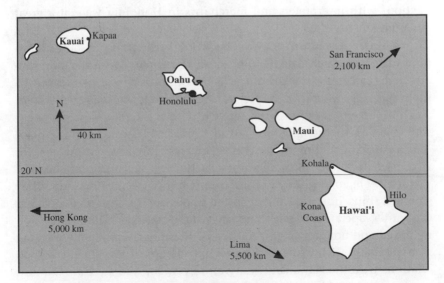

Figure 16   The Hawaiian Islands

nese rice growers. They cultivated good economic relations with both
haoles and Hawaiians; among the former, they found reliable markets,
suppliers, millers, and financial connections with the former, and from
the latter they obtained favors from the royalty, a pool of temporary laborers, and steady customers for their shops. They collected and shipped
locally grown produce back to Honolulu, often on terms of barter and
credit with Hawaiians that few haoles would have been willing to grant,
but which were secure investments for the Chinese, who were better integrated into rural life. As rice and taro planters, Chinese also reclaimed
and utilized land owned by themselves, haoles, and Hawaiians.

Some rice-growing districts were so heavily populated by Chinese
migrants that they could appear to be independent of other Hawaiian social structures, with water buffalo and fruit trees imported directly from
China. As late as the 1920s, many rice farmers continued to be perplexed
by the behavior of white landowners and tax collectors. The visits of Chinese or Hawaiian tax collectors and landlords were social events, a time
for food, smoking, and the reinforcement of social ties. White landlords,
on the other hand, were an enigma. When they visited their lands, they
could only speak of contracts and avoided other displays of mutual commitment. They often knew nothing of farming and cared little for socializing. The autonomy of Chinese agricultural districts, however, depended
precisely on the links to markets, money, and services provided by Chinese who successfully merged into non-Chinese Hawaiian life. When the
need arose to deal directly with the haole owners, planters who had connections with interpreters and merchants in Honolulu were at a great
advantage.[1]

Chinese agricultural activities had roots in the ability of some prominent Chinese to ingratiate themselves and intermarry with the local royalty in the early nineteenth century. Their connections and spouses earned
them special economic concessions and access to land usually kept out of
reach of foreigners. As businessmen, Chinese were among the many entrepreneurs who attempted to take advantage of Hawaii's strategic place
on trans-Pacific trading routes and its status as a reprovisioning port for
whalers. The three Chinese commercial houses, Samsing, Hungtai, and
Tyhune, were among the most important businesses in Honolulu. They
supplied ships, imported and exported goods and luxuries to China and
California, operated bakeries, ran inter-island transportation routes, and
managed and financed sugar and rice plantations, occasionally working
in partnership with white businessmen and companies. They had good
relations with the Hawaiian royalty and even enjoyed a certain amount
of respect among the rather exclusive haole community in Honolulu.[2]

Following the examples of the Americans and Germans in Hono-lulu, the Chinese merchants threw a great ball in 1856 to honor the marriage of King Kamehameha V and Queen Emma. Although some participants were patronizing and astonished at the Chinese ability to throw such a successful party, most praised it as a successful social event and took pride in the cosmopolitan atmosphere it lent to Honolulu society.[3] The ball was successful largely because of its embellishment of Western social forms with smatterings of exotic detail. Elaborate Chinese costumes, beautifully presented food, and dance cards written in romanized Cantonese impressed all who attended as tasteful, intriguing, and exotic variations on the standard grand ball. Chinese merchants were also invited to social affairs thrown by haoles, and cosmopolitan pride can be seen in comments such as this from the *Pacific Commercial Advertiser* about a soiree held by the British consul-general in 1861, which noted "a striking and characteristic feature of our polyglot society—the presence of our leading Chinese merchants, than whom His Majesty does not possess more faithful and devoted servants, as honored guests."[4]

Even in the increasing anti-Chinese atmosphere that arose between the late 1860s and the 1880s, Chinese retained much of their political clout. Although Hawaiians often allied with haole immigrants in opposition to Chinese, this rarely interfered with cordial personal relations in day-to-day life. This was also true at the highest levels of government. King Kalakaua, who reigned from 1874 to 1891 after running for election on a platform of "Hawaii for the Hawaiians" and "Preserve and Increase the Race," was remembered by many Chinese as a "friend of the Chinese," and his reign was a golden period of Chinese influence in the Kingdom.[5] Chinese lobbyists filled the halls of Congress, offering gifts and banquets to receptive Hawaiian congressmen, assuring that many proposed anti-Chinese measures never passed into law. In 1882, Commissioner of Immigration Armstrong wrote, "Everywhere the King goes he is welcomed by [Chinese]; flowers are strewn in his pathway; satin banners with Chinese dragons greet him at every turn; . . . the walls of the city are always covered with Chinese emblems, and no one knows what they mean. . . . It is a very uncomfortable condition to live under."[6]

Armstrong's discomfort reminds us that Chinese political influence was inseparable from growing stresses within the Hawaiian government. Haoles were increasingly dissatisfied with Hawaiian rule and were making ever-bolder attempts to control policy. Chinese were a haole concern not only as potential laborers or "undesirable" immigrants, but also because of growing rumors and fears that the Chinese government had designs on Hawaii and may even have been planning a naval invasion. Attempts to sign a treaty between China and Hawaii were undermined by haole opposition, and attempts to establish a Chinese consulate were delayed several years until 1881. Kalakaua's 1879 investiture of the merchant Chun Afong as a Hawaiian noble and member of His Majesty's Privy Consul was done in part as compensation for failed diplomatic negotiations.[7]

In the end the close relationship of Kalakaua and prominent Chinese led to the besmirching of both of their reputations by the opium scandal of 1887. After the Hawaiian legislation restored a licensed opium monopoly in 1886 at a set price of $30,000, a Chinese rice planter named Aki claimed Kalakaua had accepted $71,000 from him in return for the license but then granted the monopoly to Chun Alung, a China-born son of Chun Afong, who had taken part in the first Chinese educational mission in Hartford, Connecticut, in 1872, accompanied Yung Wing to Peru in 1874 to investigate the conditions of Chinese plantation laborers, received a degree at Yale, and had recently left his post as assistant to the Chinese envoy in Washington, Chen Lanbin. Kalakaua insisted he had thought the money from Aki was just a gift and that no commitment had been promised in return. Aki took the case to court, which determined that the king could do no wrong and thus could not be sued. This financial immunity did not translate into political immunity. Kalakaua attempted to counteract criticisms and gossip about the affair by buying the *Pacific Commercial Advertiser,* using money provided by Alung, who had agreed to finance the purchase only after Kalakaua blocked an attempt to raise the Chinese landing fee from two dollars to ten. Such efforts were in vain. The opium scandal remained one more justification used in the 1887 haole uprising that led to haole control of the legislature and a new constitution that revoked suffrage for all Asians not born on the Islands, including those who had naturalized.[8]

The Rise of the Haoles

The rise of anti-Chinese attitudes in Hawaii was closely linked to the rise of haole power. Although far from united in their opinions, missionaries contributed greatly to the early fund of negative images of Chinese on the Islands. In their zeal to educate, nurture, and civilize the Hawaiians, they often depicted the Chinese, with their opium and gambling, as a negative moral influence on the impressionable Hawaiians. They believed the lack of Chinese women led to the corruption of Hawaiian women, while Chinese cleverness and lust for profit deceived the Hawaiians into acting against their own best interests. Their opposition to Chinese was not absolute but closely linked to their conceptions of the nuclear family as a basis of Christian civilization. Although they occasionally opposed Chinese immigration, they were just as likely to call for the immigration of Chinese women, which they believed would result in families that were more likely to treat Hawaii as a home. Indeed, as early as the mid-nineteenth century, the offspring of unions between Chinese men and Hawaiian women had come to symbolize the future of Hawaii, not only as a sign of emerging Chinese-Hawaiian hybridity, but also because of their ability and eagerness to conform to missionary ideas of what respectable Hawaiian society should be like. Missionary teachers in Hilo commented that the Chinese-Hawaiian girls "were the best educated, the most fluent in English, the neatest housewives, and the most likely young ladies," and predicted of both girls and boys that they were "destined to occupy stations of great influence."[9]

By the 1880s, anti-Chinese activities in Honolulu had received a shot of energy from the growing community of haole artisans and from newspapers claiming to be the organs of the working class. Their propaganda accused the Chinese of pushing the Hawaiians out of employment and found receptive ears among Hawaiian voters and politicians who were excellent allies in presenting anti-Chinese bills to the Hawaiian congress. The series of immigration bills which led to the near cessation of Chinese immigration 1886 has already been outlined in chapter 2. After that year, the legislature considered a new series of bills aimed mostly against Asian property and economic influence. One of the most offensive to the Chinese was a bill requiring that all business accounts be kept in English, Hawaiian, or a European language, which was pushed past King Kalakaua's veto to become law in 1888. Several laws restricting Chinese land ownership also passed over the next few years. None of these measures, however, brought with them the same level of bloodthirsty popular participation and demagoguery that had shaped the anti-Chinese movement in California. Many of the earliest attempts to pass migration legislation were against labor migration in general, rather than specifying Asians. Hawaiian resistance to all forms of immigration was linked to their hostility against the planters who promoted it and the regime of disciplined labor and profit they were trying to impose. Haoles and Asians were two sides of the same problem in the eyes of Hawaiians: the white men took away their land in the country, and the Asians their employment in the towns.[10]

In Peru, the thirty-year gap between the end of the labor trade and the resurgence of Chinese migration had made the popular link between elite exploitation and the spread of urban Chinese artisans and traders somewhat implausible by the early twentieth century. In Hawaii, however, the rising influence of haole planters and money following the sugar boom that came with the 1876 treaty of reciprocity with the United States was very closely linked to the local status of Chinese. Not only did the sheer number of Chinese migrants imported to work on the plantations arouse local resistance, but they also lacked the wealth necessary to present the cultured image cultivated by the merchants, and ex-plantation workers were seen as flooding urban retail and artisanal trades with unreasonably cheap competition.

Equally significant was the decline of the monarchy and missionary influence, and its replacement by a rising haole oligarchy.[11] The inefficient social structures and relatively tolerant attitudes of earlier governments—to the point of actively promoting racial hybridity—fell aside in the face of a labor regime that was ideologically dependent on the maintenance of racial distinctions. As their wealth increased, haole planters no longer depended so much on cultivating good relations with Hawaiians in order to make their fortunes; instead, they justified their exploitation as part of the natural order of things. This rapidly consolidating haole oligarchy, made up mostly of the descendants of missionaries and merchants linked together in a multistranded web of marriage, education, social clubs, and friendship, was increasingly exclusive. Armed with biological arguments about the inferiority of nonwhite races, they were also increasingly contemptuous of the ability of nonwhite peoples to govern their own affairs. They became more openly rebellious against government policies they perceived as contrary to their own interests, and projected their own interests as the true "interests of Hawaii." By the late 1880s, cynics and supporters of the oligarchy both commonly asserted that the only morality on the Islands was that determined by the needs of sugar.

The prejudices of the haole oligarchy were entangled in a slightly different set of fears than were the prejudices of the Hawaiians, haole artisans, and earlier missionaries, although clearly based on the same common fund of negative images and stereotypes. Their initial motivation in promoting images of the Chinese as a degraded race arose from their interest in the continued immigration of easily controlled laborers. Later, with the availability of Portuguese and Japanese laborers in the 1880s, many planters changed their attitude toward the Chinese and came to dislike them as troublemakers (as happened with other ethnic groups that were perceived as too numerous). As haoles became increasingly convinced that their destiny as white men was to rule and bring order to the Islands, their primary concern was not the economic competition or moral influence of the Asians, but their fear that a predominance of Asians would make it difficult to remake the Islands in their own image. The decline of the native Hawaiian population through disease and intermarriage supported popular theories of racial succession and evolution, but the Asian population was less accommodating, showing no signs of giving way demographically. The belief that Asians were not yet capable of exercising or appreciating democracy made this persistence seem all the more threatening and ominous.[12]

Rising haole ambitions came to a head in the brief revolution of 1893, in which the last remnants of the monarchy were overthrown, and the Republic of Hawaii was created. One of the unfulfilled goals of the revolution was immediate annexation to the United States, in the hope that American influence could buttress haole civilization against the swarming brown men beneath them. Failing that, laws were passed forbidding the Chinese to naturalize. Nonetheless, despite a common contempt of the Asians, the haole elite was still divided over how they should be incorporated into Island life. Whatever opinions the planters held about the Asians, they still needed them to work their fields, and they generally believed that the less educated and more dependent the laborers, the better. Other instigators of the 1893 revolution were professionals and merchants from Honolulu who were unwilling to support planter interests on many issues, including Asian immigration. The vision of illiterate, Asian coolies bound to the plantation regime was exactly what the professional haoles feared most in their vision of an Americanized Hawaii. In their view, if Asians were to be admitted at all, they needed to be educated and amenable to controlled participation in a democratic state. A compromise was reached in which quota of five thousand Chinese laborers a year was admitted on the provision that they return home after their contracts expired.

Negotiating Political Shifts

Despite their political troubles, Chinese migrants flourished in Hawaii in the years between the Reciprocity Treaty of 1876 and annexation by the United States in 1898. They increased in number, their economic strength grew and expanded, they became entrenched at the nodes of many local power networks, and a significant minority decided to settle their families (or at least part of their families) on the Islands. The stipulations of the Reciprocity Treaty worked together with the declining native population to create opportunities that led to the entrenchment of Chinese interests in the Islands. Both Chinese and haole planters grew financially and socially independent of the Hawaiians. The new waves of Chinese immigration promoted by the government in the wake of the treaty were intended to serve sugar interests but also worked to the benefit of Chinese companies, which not only profited from the traffic in laborers itself, but from channeling their labor into the production of rice, which had become duty-free in the United States. The decline of the Hawaiian population left disused taro fields and swamplands for reclamation as rice paddies, often in remote areas where Chinese could achieve wealth and power with almost no competition. Much of the wealth of Chinese companies and individuals in Honolulu was based on their extensive networks and holdings in rural areas.

Public Chinese response to the anti-Chinese movement was rare before 1887, but when Chinese channels to high-level official influence were cut off by the haole control of the government, the Chinese immediately began to respond to anti-Chinese measures with mass meetings, petitions, legal action, increased security, bribery, and revolution. A Bao'an Ju (Self-Protection Bureau) was created in 1887 and solicited wide participation and contributions to the struggle against anti-Chinese agitation. A handbill posted by the society called for contributions, drawing from examples across the Western Pacific to assert that the Chinese needed to transcend their existing divisions (Hakka-*bendi* conflicts were rampant) and act in concert against the threats confronting them:

> We Chinese in Hawaii left our home villages to make our fortunes. At first we lived peacefully and happily, but later on conflicts arose among ourselves as we cut each other's skins. And because of this weakness we were frequently subject to foreign exploitation. . . . If we are not harmonious among ourselves and do not promote friendship among our countrymen, how can we protect our property and life? This is why the establishment of a Protective Bureau in Hawaii is the most pressing need. Remember the massacre of Chinese in Peru, also the driving out of Chinese in Los Angeles and the burning of stores there. Beware that we don't fall into the same trouble.[13]

The handbill did not locate the source of the threat in the anti-Chinese sentiments of Hawaiians, or even in the haole oligarchy, but only in the "Foreign Worker Party" *(Waiguo Gongdang).* Despite their new tactics of mass mobilization, the Chinese still did not want to antagonize their old patronage networks.

Some of the money collected by the Bao'an Ju was used for physical protection, including the purchase of rifles and hiring of watchmen. The organization also attempted to forestall the necessity of battle through legal and political channels. They had the 1888 legislation requiring all business records to be kept in Hawaiian or European languages declared unconstitutional by the Supreme Court. Later that year, mass meetings, petitions, and bribes to congressmen helped defeat a proposed constitutional amendment that would have allowed the Legislative Assembly to forbid the employment of Chinese in any occupation except the production of rice and sugar, deny them the right to own land, and block them from remaining in the country for more than six years. More public meetings and legal action blocked proposed legislation in 1894 that would have prohibited Chinese from entering mercantile or mechanical trades and resulted in an anti-foot-binding law being declared unconstitutional in 1895. They were less successful in regaining the suffrage denied them by the constitution of 1887, regaining voting rights only for Chinese born on the Islands. This loss was especially galling because suffrage had been returned to Japanese residents that year on the same terms as for the haoles.[14]

A few Chinese even collaborated in the unsuccessful, pro-monarchy rebellion of 1889 led by Robert Wilcox, but this alliance did more harm than good, because further restrictions on Chinese rights during the Republic were often justified by the suspicion that Chinese were contributing to other "counterrevolutionary" movements. Moreover, this alliance of Chinese migrants and Hawaiian royalists was not promising for the Chinese, since the kind of nationalism that fueled the uprisings was generally no more accepting of Chinese immigration than it was of haole dominance. In the 1890 elections, Wilcox's Hawaiian Political Association formed a coalition with the haole-dominated Mechanics' and Workingmen's Political Associations, two parties that had little in common other than a conviction that Hawaii should not be overrun by Asians.[15]

This period of open conflict between Chinese and the rulers of Hawaii was brief. By the time of annexation in 1898, a strategy of conciliation and emphasis on common mutual interests was more common. If racial destiny was one pillar upon which the oligarchy rested its claim to rule, private property and wealth was the other. In the months before the 1887 haole uprising, assertions that the brown man was not fit to govern his own affairs were entangled with statements like this one in the *Hawaiian Gazette:* "Advocates of universal suffrage may put forward what specious ideas of human equality they please, but it stands to reason the necessity of government lies as much in property rights as anything else. Life and property are the two principal wards of organized government, as they are the only stakes which we have to pledge in defense of established order."[16] The pillars of property and race tended to support each other. The property requirements for suffrage effectively excluded many nonwhite groups from the vote, and racist laws further hindered them from ever acquiring property. At the same time, biological and evolutionary theories were used to explain haole dominance and superior wealth as part of the natural development of racial difference. It was a vicious circle that the oligarchy had no intention of ever straightening out.

Yet, the glorification of property and sugar interests as fundamental national values provided a window of opportunity for Chinese integration. It was a minuscule window, to be sure, but accessible via a genre of commercial republicanism similar to that exploited by the Chinese in Peru. A reputation as respectable merchants was certainly not sufficient for entry into the haole oligarchy, but still raised the status of Chinese in comparison to other local groups. Moreover, social order based on wealth and hierarchy easily intersected with the interests of most migrants. The search for wealth was what drew most Chinese to Hawaii in the first place, and the accumulation and proper use of this wealth was a key marker of status for Chinese migrants around the world. By the late nineteenth century, Chinese nationalists had begun to explain the low status of China in the modern world as the result of its commercial weakness and technological inferiority. The ability to attain wealth was increasingly accepted as a marker of status. The superior treatment accorded to Japanese migrants throughout the Americas after the turn of the century confirmed the importance of wealth as the route to respectability.

Of course, given that international prestige was also deeply entangled with racial and cultural discourses, wealth was rarely a sufficient basis for respect as an equal. Given that racism also permeated more egalitarian and leveling democratic rhetoric, however, the window of opportunity offered by Hawaiian commercial republicanism was larger than that offered by populist democratic movements that opposed propertied interests. Populist democratic rhetoric was an integral part of the most belligerent anti-Chinese movements in California, Peru, and Hawaii. In populist visions, Chinese were a degraded people incapable of assimilation, and they were further stigmatized as tools of the capitalist to exploit and degrade the working man. Nothing short of the complete exclusion of Asians would do if an egalitarian and homogeneous society were to be attained. That is, democracy was understood as a national quality. The more the Chinese might attempt to integrate themselves economically, the more they would be rejected as subversive competitors or alien exploiters.

Promoters of commercial republicanism, on the other hand, depended on growing intercourse with the outside and the maintenance of class and racial distinctions. Thus, even though the subjugation of a controllable work force was in their interest, they also welcomed the rise of middlemen who could facilitate commercial interactions across class and racial divides. In places like Peru and Hawaii, where a small, white elite dominated a large population of a different color, the ability of Chinese to conduct themselves as respectable merchants helped to place them slightly above the subjugated masses. In places like Chicago or California, which aspired to a common culture or individualistic egalitarianism, Chinese were often rejected as different or excessively parochial and backwards. In places like Peru, Hawaii, or even the southern United States, where ruling groups did not hope to forge a common culture and hierarchy was more acceptable, Chinese were more able to occupy an intermediate status.

In Peru, Chinese positioned themselves as international merchants. In Hawaii, they deployed a commercial identity even more effectively than in Peru, but as the basis of a local ethnic identity and heritage. Chinese in Peru avoided drawing attention to long-term local roots because they did not want to link themselves to the coolie legacy or hoi polloi of the lower classes. The Chinese in Hawaii, on the other hand, could use their history as businessmen and their role in the early development of sugar to portray themselves as pioneers and builders of an emergent Hawaii. This image gained strength after annexation, when a fund of patriotic rhetoric backed by the power of the American state became available. The Chinese could use the image of the groundbreaking pioneer in portraying themselves as avid Americanizers from the very moment they landed on the Islands, and they could also select from the more populist strains of American republicanism in order to challenge the more exclusive Americanizing visions of the oligarchy.

URBANIZATION AND CHANGING CHINESE ASSOCIATIONS

From 1900 to 1930 the proportion of Chinese who resided in Honolulu increased from 35 to 71 percent. The rice economy was in decline, taking with it the rural economic networks that were the basis for much Chinese wealth. This shift coincided with a rise in the proportion of locally born Chinese counted by the census, which grew from 15 to 72 percent. Thus, much of this increased urbanization was due to locally born Chinese and new migrants settling in Honolulu, and the rural Chinese population was increasingly dominated by aging migrants without families. Chinese in Honolulu were involved in a variety of small- to medium-sized retail trades, service occupations, and a slowly rising number of semiskilled and professional occupations. The rural networks that had once isolated the

Chinese under the protection of wealthy mediators and financiers gave way as many of the new Honolulu businessmen learned to deal with haoles on their own. Chinese began to learn English rather than Hawaiian and to move their businesses and residences away from Chinatown, dispersing them throughout the city.[17] These changes did not lead to the dissolution of the Chinese identity but to its reformulation from local village and kin networks into a national group and then a local ethnic group.

As the Chinese in Hawaii became increasingly integrated into Honolulu society and self-consciously American in their outlook, the bases of recruitment for their associations appeared to grow increasingly particularistic, developing from the sworn brotherhoods common in the late nineteenth century to the native place and political organizations formed at the turn of the century and then to the surname associations created from the 1920s to the 1960s. The aims and significance of the associations also changed. Whereas the older associations were oriented toward the immediate needs of employment and companionship, the turn-of-the-century associations were designed more to channel influence back to China. Later associations were primarily markers of ethnic identity in Hawaii. Global flows of goods, money, and people continued to be integral parts of these new institutions, but the nodes of these networks were increasingly centered in Hawaii.

Hongmen Associations

The first known noncommercial Chinese association in Honolulu was the Manoa Lianyihui, founded in 1854 to provide for burial and care of the migrant dead. Over the next hundred years several more burial societies were established by different native place groups in different parts of Hawaii. Of more significance politically were the sworn brotherhood Hongmen Associations established throughout rural Hawaii.[18] The first of these societies for which there is any record was the Tongxing (mutual progress) Gongsi, founded in 1869 by Hakkas in rural Oahu. By 1910, at least thirty more had been established. Admission usually entailed an initiation ritual and the swearing of an oath in which the initiate promised always to aid his brothers in need and not betray anyone to outside authorities. Many gathered enough money to build clubhouses that were often the only two-story buildings in the area and could serve as gambling halls, opium dens, altars, fairgrounds, and schools.

The creation of Hongmen societies was usually sponsored by wealthy

Chinese merchants. They gained prestige by erecting clubhouses and acting as officers and mediators, and profited from them as institutions for the recruitment and distribution of agricultural labor. In the 1880s, sugar planters often accused the Hongmen of helping Chinese to escape their contracts by sheltering those who had fled the plantations and buying them out of their contracts. Little conflict occurred among these Hongmen. Most of them tended to be the only Chinese associations in isolated villages and rice-planting districts, where most of the residents, if not from the same village, at least spoke the same dialect. More than one Hongmen sometimes arose in places with a greater diversity of migrants, such as in Kohala on the Big Island, where Christian Hakkas joined together with *bendis* to form an association in competition with another Hongmen made up of non-Christian Hakkas. Although many Hongmen had been founded in order to institutionalize local power, the lack of local competition meant that they usually functioned as centers for the entertainment and companionship of isolated men rather than as weapons for protection and profit.

The Hongmen disappeared as the Chinese moved to Honolulu after the turn of the century. As the interests of migrant elites became focused less on the organization of Chinese labor and more on developing business contacts and gaining individual respect as Honolulu merchants, the support of associations like the Hongmen became less relevant to them. The Hongmen that survived in rural areas became more and more oriented toward charitable services for the old migrants who had stayed behind. Some of the clubhouses were made into residences for aged migrants, some became homes for the wealthy migrants who founded them, and some served as resorts for Chinese travelers from Honolulu, but most were abandoned in the end.

A few Hongmen associations attempted to negotiate the changing social landscape by capitalizing on the anti-Qing reputation of the Hongmen and hooking up with nationalist movements after the turn of the century. Emperor Protection Association leaders had joined local Hongmen in 1900, as did Sun Yat-sen on Maui in 1903. Both joined for the purpose of developing practical connections (for Sun, this translated into legal assistance from the San Francisco Zhigongtang when he attempted to enter the United States as a Hawaii-born citizen the next year) although eventually they resisted too close an identification with these migrant organizations.[19] Resentful of this rejection, these politicized Hongmen began to produce their own newspapers and political agendas. In 1913, two of the remaining Hongmen in Honolulu consolidated into one association, taking the Zhigongtang name in 1919 and later becoming active in the international Zhigong Party.[20] Hongmen and the Zhigongtang were never very influential as political associations in Hawaii. Only the Guo An (Ket On) Association, which was the new name of the Tongxing Gongsi after it moved to Honolulu in 1899, remained consistently active throughout the twentieth century, primarily as a social club.

The United Chinese Society

The United Chinese Society (UCS) was founded as an organ of merchant and diplomatic interests in November of 1882 and remained a central stage for migrant ambitions as the Chinese urbanized after the turn of the century. Like the SBC of Lima, it was a reorganization of a previously existing association, this time under the auspices of Minister Chen Lanbin. His visit was partly in response to complaints by local Chinese about Chun Afong, who had been appointed as the Chinese Commercial Agent in 1879. He was accused of masterminding a virtual slave trade in Chinese that worked in favor of local *bendi* interests at the expense of the Hakka. After his visit, Chen gave local merchants one thousand dollars to erect a meeting house and assigned two commissioners who were familiar with the Six Companies in San Francisco to help organize the UCS in Honolulu. The reorganized society was intended to offer an organized response to rising anti-Chinese activities, smooth over tensions between Hakkas and *bendi,* and act as a conduit of communication with the Chinese government. It also served to replace the consul general, which had been established the previous year. In response to the unwillingness of the Hawaiian government to sign a treaty with China, Li Hongzhang, the Chinese official in charge of negotiations, demoted the consulate from an appointed organ of the Chinese government to a representative body selected by local merchants, who would have to make their own negotiations with both the Chinese and Hawaiian governments.[21]

The UCS was unlike the Six Companies (but similar to the SBC and the early New York CCBA) in that membership was granted on the basis of individual prestige rather than to representatives of other associations. The first members were twenty-five prominent Honolulu merchants. This meant that the rural Hongmen were ignored in favor of urban merchant interests (although their interests were not always distinct). On the other hand, a strong effort was made to assure equal representation to Hakkas and *bendi.* The prominent *bendi* merchant C. Alee was the first president, and the Christian Hakka Goo Kim was made vice president, positions they held until 1890. The president and vice president also held concurrent positions as Chinese commercial agent and vice–commercial agent to Hawaii.

Many Hawaiian officials and legislators feared that the UCS had subversive or extraterritorial ambitions. Formal recognition and incorporation as an association under the laws of the kingdom were not granted until the UCS agreed that the minister of the interior and the Board of Trustees could approve the appointment of all officers, and that minutes of all UCS meetings would be provided to the government in English. Despite these initial suspicions, the government proved more than willing to delegate responsibility for the enforcement of its new immigration restrictions to the UCS. As of 1887, passports for Chinese leaving Hawaii with the intent to return were issued by the commercial agent for a fee of five dollars, two of which went into the UCS treasury and became one of its most important sources of funds. Thus, the merchants who ran the UCS had their status and control over migration formally recognized by both the Hawaiian and Chinese governments.

Village and native place associations began to appear in Honolulu after 1890 and continued to arise through the 1950s. The majority of them were established by migrants from districts and villages in Zhongshan county. The 1892 law allowing for a quota of five thousand laborers a year led to a burst in the Siyi population of Hawaii, and the Siyi *huiguan* was established 1897, later splitting into the Yiyi Tang in 1901 and the Gangzhou *huiguan* for migrants from Xinhui in 1907.[22] One stated function of these associations was to take over the mutual aid and socializing functions of the declining Hongmen societies. Yet burial associations already existed to take care of the dead, and guilds were replacing the Hongmen to provide for the concerns of employment. They were also relatively inactive in providing formal representation for their constituencies, never pressing for formal representation in the UCS or acting as an important base of factionalization in Honolulu. In San Francisco, the native place associations had been the basis of Six Companies power. In Honolulu they were adjuncts to UCS power, spreading merchant influence deeper into the Chinese community in Hawaii and then beyond to villages in China.

Building the Chinese Nation and Dividing the Chinese

The UCS seems to have succeeded in reconciling the Hakka-*bendi* feuds that plagued the Chinese of Hawaii through the 1880s. C. Alee and Goo Kim continued to dominate the association until 1902. Over the next decade, however, UCS officerships became much less stable as Chinese wealth moved away from isolated rural fiefdoms and concentrated in

Honolulu. By 1912, struggles to control the UCS had become openly hostile, to the extent that association activities were suspended from 1916 to 1919, pending resolution of a dispute between two competing slates of officers claiming legitimate election. The issue that most divided the two sides was the political future of China. The noisy and well-promulgated ideological hostilities easily drowned out any other pretext for conflict.

Unlike Peru or Chicago, Honolulu did not give rise to a single dominant person or clique. The extensive economic opportunities throughout the Islands in the late nineteenth century meant that nobody had been able to dominate flows of migration and economic activity. Even in Honolulu after the turn of the century, migrant fortunes were based less on the control of other migrants through credit, extortion, or the financing of migration than on direct economic relationships with the greater Honolulu society. Thus, migrants did not struggle so violently over economic domination, nor were the lines of conflict drawn around kinship, native place, or direct economic competition. Correspondingly, the structure of migrant institutions in Honolulu was never so well articulated and involved in the daily lives of migrants that it could facilitate domination. Most kinship and native place assistance was still relatively informal, and more prominent merchants had clients with a variety of surnames and dialects.

It was relatively easy for a Chinese to operate a reasonably successful business in Hawaii while remaining aloof from political entanglements. Social involvement was necessary, however, to translate that wealth into prestige. The successful merchant who did not devote time and money to organizations and fund-raising was generally looked down upon.[23] Located in the middle of the Pacific Ocean, Honolulu was a prominent site for the early organizing activities of the Qing government, reformers, and revolutionaries. Competition for recognition in Chinese politics led to a highly factionalized migrant community.

Sun Yat-sen founded his first revolutionary organization, the Xingzhonghui, in Honolulu in 1894 "to promote the interest and uphold the dignity of China." It attracted about fifty young men, a good portion of whom were Hakkas and Christians or had been classmates of Sun during his days at the Iolani School. Many of them had also been involved in the 1889 Wilcox uprising. The association collected six thousand dollars for Sun to instigate an uprising in China that year and held military drills in the yard of the Reverend Frank Damon (who later claimed that the overthrow of the Qing in 1911 was "God-ordained for the advancement of humanity," and even took some credit for it, claiming that "I had the honor to place in Sun Yat Sen's hands a copy of a volume on American democracy which I believe has been the foundation for his propaganda for a constitutional government in China.")[24] In 1896, in the wake of his failed uprising, Sun returned to Hawaii to find that the military training had been discontinued, and the former Xingzhonghui members received him with somewhat less enthusiasm. Although the impact of the Xing-zhonghui at the time of its founding was minimal, it attained much greater significance later as some Chinese in Hawaii sought to claim a revolutionary heritage.

Interest in Chinese politics was rekindled on a much larger scale in 1900, when Liang Qichao spent nearly half a year in Hawaii. He established a branch of the Emperor Protection Association in Honolulu, helped found the *New China News (Xin Zhongguo Bao)*, and traveled around the Islands giving speeches, engaging in debates, and establishing more association branches. Association officers claimed that from 80 to 90 percent of the migrants on the Islands joined, including many former Xingzhonghui members. This organization lasted much longer than the Xingzhonghui, although contact between the migrants and prominent reform leaders quickly dwindled and transformed into mutual suspicion after Liang's departure. Liang even avoided visiting the Islands in 1903 on his return from a tour of the United States, claiming that the Emperor Protection Association there was evil and a "national humiliation," which may well have been a way to divert attention from his own mishandling of contributions.[25]

A Chinese consul was posted in Hawaii after annexation in 1898. Goo Kim continued as vice-consul for several years, and officers of the UCS were all appointed as members of the consular staff, but their political agendas often conflicted with that of the consul. Even though many of his staff were Emperor Protection Association members, the first consul, Yang Weibin, aggressively persecuted all association activity in Hawaii. He successfully opposed incorporation of the Emperor Protection Association under the territorial government and had the viceroy of Guangdong imprison the family of a man who had housed Liang Qichao during his stay in Hawaii. The president of the Honolulu Emperor Protection Association, Wong Leong, was harder to punish because he was a Hawaii-born American citizen, and his family was in Honolulu. Yang settled for having the tablets from his lineage's ancestral hall confiscated, causing lineage members to demand that Wong pay the redemption money. Yang later promised nonreprisal to any migrant who filed a $5.25 certificate with the consulate swearing that he belonged to no society opposed to the Chinese government. The last straw was when Yang announced his intention to send $9,500 of the $25,000 in relief money collected by the UCS for the victims of the 1900 Chinatown fire to Beijing to help finance the continued reconstruction of the Summer Palace. The destruction of the palace by British forces in 1860 and the frequent misuse of funds in its reconstruction from the 1870s on made it a potent symbol of Qing weakness and corruption. The UCS, led by C. K. Ai and assisted by Secretary of State Hay, appealed to the Chinese minister in Washington for the impeachment of Yang and succeeded in having him recalled in 1902.[26]

Hawaii was an important center for the development of debates between reformers and revolutionaries. During his visit to Hawaii in 1903, Sun was impressed by the effects of Liang Qichao's journalistic activities and started to become more active in developing his own propaganda. By 1905, many Chinese in Hawaii had become frustrated with the remoteness of the leaders of the Emperor Protection Association. The arrival of revolutionary newspaper editor Loo Sun from Hong Kong at about this time and the founding of the revolutionary *Liberty News (Ziyou Xinbao)* in 1908 kept political debate in the public eye. The *Liberty News* soon competed with the *New China News* as a key organ of Chinese revolutionary propaganda in the Western Hemisphere, and the two papers never tired of spitting invective at each other. Political opponents twice attempted to have Loo Sun thrown out of Hawaii on immigration charges. The first attempt was based on technicalities in his admission status, and the second tried to have him deported as an anarchist on the basis of articles he had written praising the recent assassination of a Japanese prince. The *Liberty News* writers claimed that the group attempting to have him deported was made up of the Chinese consul working in conjunction with the Emperor Protection Association, and later revolutionary histories claimed that Wu Tingfang and several prominent Hawaii merchants had personally helped him beat the charges.[27] The competition extended to education, and two new Chinese schools opened in Honolulu within four days of each other in February 1911: the Minglun School (fig. 17), with a reformist agenda, and the Huamin School, with a revolutionary agenda.

By 1911, the Chinese consuls had become deeply enmeshed in this web of local conflict. They had also been deeply involved in the immigration process since 1906, when the consul asked the Immigration Bureau to notify him immediately if any Chinese were refused admission, so that he could assist in arranging an appeal.[28] They were also often involved in property disputes brought to the UCS for mediation, not only as respected judges but also as partisan supporters of interested parties,

Figure 17   Minglun School, circa 1915. (Source: Old Chinese Immigration Case Files, 1903–15, case number C-1983. Honolulu District Office, Records of the Immigration and Naturalization Service, Record Group 85. National Archives and Records Administration—Pacific Region [San Francisco])

occasionally threatening to use their influence to terrorize the opposition's family in China.[29] Consul Liang Guoying (fig. 18), who took his post in 1910, brought the scandal and conflict surrounding the consulate to a peak. Although the *Liberty News* routinely accused him of working hand in hand with the Constitutionalists, in the end he managed to unite most of the factions in Hawaii against him. The two acts which most offended the local Chinese were his intention to conduct a census of all the Chinese in Hawaii, requiring that each person counted pay a $1.25 enumeration fee, and his sending a list accusing seven Honolulu migrants of being "dangerous revolutionary characters" to the viceroy in Guangdong. The negative reaction was so universal among the local Chinese that the UCS formally requested Liang to retract his charges.

When the *Liberty News* printed the full text of Liang's report to the viceroy, revealing that his insinuations about the loyalty of the migrants in Hawaii were much broader than previously realized, a large public rally was held, and the UCS petitioned the Chinese minister in Washington to have Liang removed. The increasingly besieged Liang brought a libel suit to the Hawaiian courts against individuals he thought had slandered him

Figure 18
Liang Guoying, Chinese
Consul in Hawaii, 1910.
(Source: Edgeworth Col-
lection, Bishop Museum,
Honolulu, Hawai'i; Neg.
CD 24917-XS 16939)

in the mass meeting. He lost the suit, and the judge criticized him for using methods "foreign" to American values. Pleased at Liang's defeat, many
Chinese further denounced him for having brought internal problems
into the American courts for judgment by outsiders in the first place. The
Liberty News expressed a mixture of glee at seeing Liang embarrassed by
the judge and opposing lawyers and resentment that American imperial-
ists could so easily humiliate a formal representative of China. The Chinese minister in Washington asked Liang to resign in early 1911.[30]

After the Revolution

The unity of the migrant response to Liang Guoying rolled over into
widespread support (or at least lack of public objection) for the revolution
of 1911 and the establishment of a republican government in China. The
momentary suppression of political differences and the mixed reaction to
Liang's humiliation in court remind us that involvement in Chinese politics reflected not only a concern for personal prestige or even a nationalist concern for the fate of China, but also an awareness of the way that
the status of China reflected on their local status as an ethnic group. Un-

fortunately, the good feelings that came with an internationally respected republic were short-lived. As the unity of the republic quickly crumbled, so did the unity of the Chinese in Hawaii.

In 1911, the Chinese Chamber of Commerce had arisen as a new platform in the competition for prestige and had already sowed the seeds for later discord. The establishment of Chambers of Commerce as the representative organs of migrant communities around the world had been promoted by the Qing since 1907. The push to establish chambers was renewed as the Qing tried to revitalize its relations with Chinese migrants in the final months of its reign. The government provided the bylaws and constitutions of these chambers and delegated to them the authority to work with the consuls as intermediaries between Beijing and the local migrant population. Two competing chambers arose in Hawaii. One was the Chinese Merchants' Association *(Zhonghua Zongshanghui)*, formed in August 1911 by the same men who were officers in the UCS. The rival Overseas Chinese Merchants' Association *(Huaqiao Shanghui)* was established a few months later by followers of Sun Yat-sen, inspired by the revolution then occurring in China.[31] In the UCS elections of December 1912, followers of Sun Yat-sen packed the hall with newly registered members and got themselves elected into control of the society.

The ousted officers tried unsuccessfully to contest the elections in the territorial courts, but they were more successful in blocking recognition from China. By the time the new Republic of China got around to giving some attention to overseas Chinese, conservative military strongman Yuan Shikai had already taken power from Sun in China. His government recognized the Chinese Merchants' Association as the legitimate Chamber of Commerce in Honolulu, and its newly appointed consul ignored the reception arranged for him on 1 January 1913 by the revolutionary UCS. The consul also replaced the former role of UCS officers in the consulate with an Advisory Board made up of the conservative ex-UCS officers, who were concurrently members of the National People's Constitutional Party, a reorganization of the Emperor Protection Association ordered by Yuan. They were responsible for investigating all the complaints and immigration matters brought before the consul and thus recaptured much of the power they had previously exercised through the UCS.[32]

The group of men ousted from the UCS leadership—many of whom had been staunch Constitutionalists in opposition to the revolutionaries —readily embraced republicanism after the revolution, but their republicanism was firmly opposed to Sun Yat-sen and his supporters. In 1913, a forty-eight page booklet in English, entitled *Chinese in Hawaii: A Resume of the Social, Industrial, and Economic Progress of the Chinese in the Hawaiian Islands, with an Historical Sketch of the Events Leading to the Foundation of the Chinese Republic,* was published "to Commemorate the recognition of China as a Republic by the United States, and the Friendship which has long Existed between the Two Great Nations of the East and the West." [33] It was a clearly partisan publication insisting that Yuan Shikai was "the only strong man fitted to establish the new republic on a firm footing." It gave credit to Sun and his followers for instigating the revolution, only to criticize them for turning against Yuan in the second revolution of 1913, thus "endangering the life of the young republic, and so losing the prestige they had gained, only to become wanderers on the face of the earth." [34]

Individual Accommodations

The greater part of *Chinese in Hawaii* was devoted to promoting the Chinese in the eyes of non-Chinese. Many individuals were quoted as urging the Chinese in Hawaii to bury their factional differences—both in politics and business—and work together. On the one hand, this can be interpreted as the supporters of Yuan pressuring the followers of Sun to concede their loss. Yet such calls gave these conflicts a different tone than the conflicts in Chicago, where factions always strove to completely discredit each other, and only outsiders ever called for compromise. Factionalism in Chicago developed a wide social base through violence, migrant institutions, and concrete economic interests. The process of struggle and its outcome directly affected all the local Chinese. In Hawaii, however, the causes and effects of factionalization were comparatively abstract. The relentlessly dogmatic drawing of lines that accompanied nationalist discourse in Hawaii stood in contrast to the flexible political leanings of most individuals. The newspapers and a handful of devoted partisans made up the core of political factions, but the support they received from political parties was contingent and fickle, determined more by opportunistic ambitions and changing political winds than by the relatively less flexible bonds of kinship, credit, or sworn brotherhood. Almost anyone who traveled the Islands giving speeches in Chinese, be he a revolutionary, reformer, or Christian missionary, was bound to attract the attention and contributions of entertainment-starved migrants.

Two of the most prominent Chinese at the turn of the century, Chu Gem and C. K. Ai, are good examples of the ways in which individuals could flexibly negotiate migrant politics. Of the two, Chu was more of a

Figure 19
Chung Kun Ai, 1913. (Source:
Old Chinese Immigration
Case Files, 1903–15, case
number C-633. Honolulu
District Office, Records of the
Immigration and Naturaliza-
tion Service, Record Group
85. National Archives and
Records Administration—
Pacific Region [San Francisco])

practical politician.[35] His biography in the 1913 booklet called him the
"Merchant Prince" and described him as "possessing probably the widest
acquaintance of any Chinese in Hawaii, honored and trusted by all." He
liked to boast that he had never been sued. He had long been a follower
of the reform parties, was a "staunch supporter" of the Minglun School,
and backed the pro-Yuan *Huaxing Bao (Flourishing China News).*[36] He was
president of the UCS several times from 1906 to 1921 and leader of
the conservative slate during the split of 1912. He was also president of
the Chinese Merchant's Association from its founding until 1918 and a
founder and long-time president of the Siyi *huiguan.* On the other hand,
he also fought for Loo Sun's right to reside in Hawaii as an editor, helped
to obtain land for the revolutionary Huamin School, led the struggle
against consul Liang Guoying, and collected funds to assist former consul Zhang Zuofan, who had been arrested in China for plotting against
Yuan in 1913. He was also an investor in the City Mill run by C. K. Ai
(fig. 19), a prominent supporter of Sun Yat-sen who referred to Chu with
respect in his autobiography.

C. K. Ai was a Christian Hakka who attended Iolani School with Sun
Yat-sen, with whom he used to steal mangos, swim, and beat up Hawaiian kids. He was an original member of the Xingzhonghui and later became treasurer of the Emperor Protection Society upon its founding in
1900 and president of the UCS from 1902 to 1905. He lost his enthusiasm

for the reformers in 1905, when he was snubbed by Liang Qichao during a visit to Japan to inquire about the fate of contributions sent from Hawaii. He later became a sponsor of the *Liberty News,* which earned him the enmity of more die-hard reformers. In an interview with the Bureau of Immigration in 1915, Constitutionalist Party President Wong How said, "I know that all the merchants and all the good people favor Yuan Shikai's government." When confronted with the fact that the prominent merchant C. K. Ai did not favor Yuan, he responded, "Do you suppose C. K. Ai got money he is high class; what does C. K. Ai know about China? . . . I think that kind of people no good for China, no good."[37] Another merchant was more cautious in his estimation of Ai when he remarked that "his speech and his acts seem to belong to the Nationalist [revolutionary] Party, but I don't know."[38]

According to his autobiography, Ai had tired of Chinese politics by 1915 and devoted more of his efforts to directly promoting Chinese interests in Hawaii. His desire to contribute to the economic development of the republic had been frustrated during a trip to China in 1913 by what he saw as the shortsightedness and petty greed of republican officials and businessmen. Upon his return to Hawaii, he became a cofounder of the Chinese American Bank in 1916 and the American Chinese Federation of Hawaii in 1917. He also worked hard to modify the exclusion laws, moving from an interest in promoting the immigration of Chinese rice plantation laborers that began during his days as a UCS president to a stronger interest in overcoming the travel difficulties of Hawaii-born Chinese. After some business failures in the 1920s, Ai grew increasingly devoted to his Christianity. This devotion coincided with a rekindling of interest in his home village, as was common among many older migrants. He supported charitable activities directed toward China, including the Unbounded Faith-Love Mission, and started the C. K. Ai Foundation "to aid in the preservation of Chinese culture, with particular reference to the villages in the area around Xishan Village, China, which was the ancestral home of the Trustor."[39] Such generalized charity was less involved with subscription lists and lineage interests than with clothes drives and missionary activities, and it drew attention to the status of its instigator in Hawaii.

Ai's conversion to Hawaii-based issues was an example of a more general decline in revolutionary passions in the decade after 1912. Many revolutionaries disliked the thought of plunging China into a civil war, and supporters of Yuan Shikai were put off by his attempts to install himself as emperor. The succession of governments in Beijing after Yuan's death in 1916 inspired little loyalty from anybody. By 1920, the old UCS officers were reelected, and a close working relationship between the UCS and the Chinese Merchants' Association was established. Over the next twelve years they gave their allegiance to the Beijing governments, although the instability of those governments meant that in practice this allegiance was little more than loyalty to the idea of a Chinese Republic. Even without close support from China, the local status of these two associations as the most important Chinese institutions in the Islands grew stronger. By 1926 the Chinese Merchants' Association had changed its English name to Chinese Chamber of Commerce in Honolulu, and extended its membership to include all substantial merchants who cared to register. They also unveiled plans for the construction of a new building, which, when completed in 1929, had a direct corridor to the UCS chambers, physically symbolizing how indistinguishable the two organizations had become.

The rise of the Guomindang to national power in 1927 led to some shuffling of political alignments in Honolulu, but not with the level of hostility manifested after 1911. Through the late 1930s, two competing Guomindang branches existed in Hawaii, a pro–Chiang Kai-shek faction and a leftist, anti-Chiang faction centered around the *Liberty News*. For many migrants, however, the rise of the Guomindang was an opportunity for Hongmen members, Constitutionalists, and supporters of the northern governments to admit the eclipse of their respective causes and throw their support behind an ambitious new government which made concerted and effective efforts to woo the wealthy migrant elite and had attained a high level of international respect. The rise of the Guomindang also meant the rewriting of migrant history as the valiant struggle of Sun Yat-sen and his masses of supporters in Hawaii to overcome the wrongheaded deceptions propagated by the reformers. Much of the previous factionalism was swept under the carpet, whereas selected events like the founding of the Xingzhonghui and the struggles against consul Liang Guoying were recalled with pride for decades.

The Guomindang victory over political loyalties was, to some extent, built upon the indifference of the migrants. Chinese in Hawaii had become more committed to defining themselves as an ethnic group. The circulation of Chinese-language newspapers had dropped to less than a thousand by the late 1920s, and many observers noted that only old, China-born migrants were still interested in the ideological differences and home town gossip recorded in their pages.[40] The Chinese nation was no longer relevant as an immediate source of political contention, and local migrants were happy to grasp any image of China as earnestly striving to take a place in the modern world.

FROM HISTORY TO HERITAGE

Annexation

Most of the haole oligarchy on Hawaii welcomed annexation because it guaranteed a market for Island produce and promised to add institutional backing for their project of cultural control. Annexation had some disadvantages, however, and two of the most serious drawbacks revolved around Asians. The first was related to the sugar planters' desire for inexpensive, controllable labor. The Chinese exclusion laws were immediately extended to the Islands after annexation, and the planters had no reason to believe that the free entry of Japanese and Korean labor would be allowed to continue for much longer. Fortunately for the planters, the colonization of the Philippines by the United States in 1898 opened a new source of migrants against which it was highly unlikely any that new barriers would be erected. Nonetheless, rice and sugar planters continued to petition Congress for a modification of Chinese exclusion through the 1920s, as they came to fear the growing Japanese and Filipino populations.

The second drawback of annexation came with the Organic Act of 1900, which established the territorial government of Hawaii and extended United States citizenship to all individuals, including Asians, born or naturalized on the Islands. The Americanizing efforts of the United States Congress were far more extensive than many haoles were prepared for. Although haoles were divided over the desirability of more Chinese immigration, they were more unified around the conviction that Chinese and other Asians should be restricted to the plantations and not allowed to take part in the affairs of the Islands. Unfortunately for them, the Americanization project of the federal government did not want simply to support the continued dominance of the haole oligarchy. It wanted to undermine what it saw as the less desirable characteristics of elitist local power structures and impose its own lines of direct control. Asians turned out to be the unintended beneficiaries of this project. Congress insisted that the letter of American democracy be upheld in Hawaii; all citizens of every race were given the vote, and democratic and juridical precedent were followed to the extent that several bills presented in the Hawaiian legislature to limit Chinese occupational activities were rejected, despite widespread haole support. These moves toward encouraging the participation and inclusion of Asians came more from a position of fear and besiegement than from tolerance. Federal representatives reasoned that if Asians were not actively assimilated, Hawaii would become a colony like Singapore, Hong Kong, or the Philippines, where the ruling elite was a minority among the Asian masses.

The fears of the haole oligarchy that enfranchisement would create undue Asian influence on local politics were considerably exaggerated, especially in the case of the Chinese. In 1902, only 143 Chinese were registered to vote. The number of Chinese voters did not begin to reflect the significance of the Chinese population in Hawaii until 1930, when the 4,402 Chinese registered to vote amounted to 8.4 percent of the voting population. Even then, only 48 percent of those eligible to vote that year actually voted, the lowest percentage of all ethnic groups, and they tended to support the ruling haoles by voting Republican.[41] Even the Japanese, who had greater influence both through sheer number of voters and through labor organization, which exploded into the great strikes of 1920, never came near to the takeover envisioned by haole alarmists. The Hawaiians, on the other hand, did make a brief attempt for power in 1900. That year Robert Wilcox ran for and won the position of Hawaiian representative to the United States Congress as the candidate of the Home Rule Party. By 1902 the oligarchy had reorganized itself within the Republican Party and recaptured congressional representation with the election of their candidate, Jonah Kalanianaole Kuhio, a member of the Hawaiian royalty. Using their considerable wealth to distribute patronage, offer bribes, and provide extravagant election parties, the Republican Party dominated representation to Washington and elective positions within Hawaii over the next four decades, until the imposition of martial law in 1941.

As far as Chinese legislation was concerned, Home Rule would not have been much different than Republican dominance. Although Hawaiians were generally more cordial to the Chinese on a daily basis, they shared haole political fears when it came to Asians. Republican Representative Kuhio was beholden to the interests of his patrons in the sugar industry, but he occasionally felt that as a member of the Hawaiian royalty he should also uphold the spirit of Robert Wilcox. One of Wilcox's platforms that Kuhio refused to abandon, despite his patrons, was the intention to cut off Asian immigration, block Asian economic opportunities, and pass legislation that facilitated homesteading and the acquisition of government jobs by Hawaiians. Sometimes he even promoted haole homesteading as preferable to Asian immigration, despite the common perception that the haoles had already stolen the land from the Hawaiians. Such a position was, in part, based on the fear that too many Asians in Hawaii might lead to the loss of self-rule and the imposition of a military commission on Hawaii. It was a threat often evoked by the oligarchy, and it worked in subduing political challenges from Asians who, as we will see below, would have lost access to the political tool of egalitarian American rhetoric.

The Imposition of American Hegemony

Despite the fears of an Asian takeover, most local haoles continued to perceive Asians as little more than servants or laborers, despite their extensive commercial activities. Most books and articles by visitors and residents on the Islands barely mentioned the presence of Asians. A well-known haole in 1910 said that the "Asiatics" in Hawaii had the same impact on the institutions and customs of the Islands as did "the cattle of the ranges," and five years later an observer from the federal government noted that the haole leaders thought of the Japanese, Chinese, and Koreans "primarily as instruments of production." [42] Racial issues were generally not mentioned in polite company, which obscured the pillar of racism that helped buttress haole power.

New haole migration from the mainland—settlers and military personnel—brought cruder and more direct expressions of racism as well as a distaste for the haole oligarchy and their comfort with the social hierarchy of Hawaii. This new population of middle-class whites shared neither the advantages and exclusive networks of the haole oligarchy nor their often patriarchal attitude toward Asians as children who had to be carefully watched over. They were much more inclined to see Asian merchants as a subversive threat to their own livelihood and less likely to play along with the polite racial etiquette that pervaded much public discourse in Hawaii.

The most influential bearers of these new attitudes were the haoles who came with the new federal agencies as administrators and officials. Although taking positions next to the oligarchy as rulers, they did not share the same sense of a destiny deeply enmeshed with the past and future of the Islands. They saw the oligarchic system as a feudal vestige that needed reform and democratic civilizing just as much as the masses of brown men. At times this difference in political and moral vision led to an all-out attack on the corruption and laxity that had allowed so many Asians to arrive in the first place. Circuit Court Judge Estes denied all but one habeas corpus case of Chinese refused admission by the Bureau of Immigration put before him in 1900, often on the basis of technicalities or hesitating testimony. When he demanded that a claimant for American citizenship must "prove by a preponderance of the evidence that he was born in these Islands," he went against not only precedents of lax enforcement set by previous Hawaiian governments, but also judicial precedent established on the mainland, where it was the duty of the Immigration Bureau to prove that claimants presented to the court were not citizens.[43] He did, however, succeed in setting a local precedent so strong that few Chinese attempted to appeal to him in succeeding years. In one decision he summarized the motivation behind his work, a simultaneously egalitarian and racist vision of Hawaii's future as an inalienable part of the United States, which showed great unfamiliarity with the economic conditions of Chinese in Hawaii:

> Chinese laborers come to America to work only . . . and not to become a part of the body politic; they rarely bring their families with them or encourage American home life; they are always Chinamen in America and not Americans; they live apart here as in China. It thus seems dangerous to the American republic to admit on an equal footing with American labor, these vast hordes of Chinamen who neither love this country nor assimilate with its civilization. The presence of such a people tends to create class and racial distinctions, and tends also to lower the standard of American manhood, by placing beside them, competing in the field of labor, a different race of men, who know nothing of the free institutions and only seek our shores for a temporary advantage.[44]

Although not stated explicitly, Estes's attack was directed as much against oligarchic sugar interests as against the Chinese. It was firmly in the tradition of crude connections made between cheap Chinese labor and degrading capitalistic monopoly that had fueled many anti-Chinese labor organizations in California.

Twenty years later, this same egalitarian vision was in vogue among federal immigration agents in Hawaii, but the explicit racism had given way to local practices of racial etiquette. In 1921, a Honolulu immigration inspector made an (unsuccessful) plea to the secretary of labor on behalf of a Chinese named Yong Yee who was about to be deported for polygamy. Estes's unproblematic incorporation of Hawaii into the sovereignty of the United States was now replaced by an almost apocalyptic vision of the continuing struggle to impose righteous justice. The agent blamed the Hawaiian agricultural-political complex not for having allowed the Chinese into the Islands but for having exacerbated the undesirable morality of the Chinese, who, in turn, still retained the potential for redemption under the tutelage of American democratic institutions:

> [The Chinese] were kept under a paternal industrialism in which they were permitted to follow the practices which were customary in their own country. . . . Following their own customs among themselves, to themselves doubtless there was not the sense of moral turpitude that would obtain in similar cases of one of our own social order to which these laborers were not made to conform to any extent. The elements of moral stability were subordinated to the maintenance of the satisfied, ignorant, laboring class. The land was practically permitted to be polluted for profit. It is now the task of our government to put right in the place of rot. Immunity for Oriental laxity must pass; but in view of the past and endeavoring to bring about a better state of affairs, it would seem that justice might be tempered with mercy. Yong Yee was simple, honest, and direct in his admissions, and his conduct must have been due to the ignorance which was abetted by those in power in this community in years past. He may have regarded himself, if still under the domination of old ideas, as without sin, when before annexation many like unto himself were practically so treated. However, the law came with annexation, and for him sin revived, and he, like others, was deported. . . . Had the enlightening officials of these islands before annexation placed moral considerations before material, I am of the opinion that this Chinaman would have had the knowledge and felt the necessity of conforming to the higher conditions and methods of conduct which are deemed necessary by us to the stability and welfare of the State.[45]

In this context, the appropriation of a vocabulary of Americanization by Chinese was useful not only as a way to project a positive image of themselves, but also as an appeal to the support of outside power against a haole oligarchy invested in perpetuating the inferiority of Asian residents. The oligarchy had wrapped itself in the cloak of American culture, thus making conformity to American ideology the standard for respect in Hawaii. Nonetheless, the United States also brought a critique of the oligarchy that could easily be used by less powerful ethnic groups to claim a stronger progressive and egalitarian heritage on the Islands than the haoles. As a result of the simultaneous political power and social abstraction of democratic ideology in Hawaii, becoming American for Chinese on the distant islands would become easier than in the United States.

Accommodation to Exclusion

The Chinese met annexation with a memorial prepared by the UCS for the commissioners assigned to investigate conditions on the Islands. Much of the memorial attempted to demonstrate the economic importance of the Chinese to the development of Hawaii and the extent to which they had adapted to local customs through intermarriage, naturalization, land reclamation, and conversion to Christianity:

> [The Chinese] have contributed very largely to the revenues of the country and their progressive influence, from knowledge gained here, has been beneficially felt in their own land. To them is due a share of the credit for the prosperity of Hawaii today, in consequence of their labor developing the sugar and rice plantations, the fruit farms and vegetable gardens, and the great shipping business and commercial relations with the Orient, of which they were pioneers. To them Hawaii has become endeared as their adopted home by the kindness and fair treatment of many years, and their long sojourn here has been marked with amity and the absence of all discordant influences. In commercial and social life they have been respected and esteemed, and they have constituted a peaceable and law-abiding portion of the community.[46]

The memorial also requested right of transit for Chinese from Hawaii to the United States, no legal discrimination, and that immigration rights be granted to Chinese workers for rice plantations, Chinese clerks for their businesses, and the wives and children of Chinese residents. A ten-point appendix was attached arguing why exclusion should not be extended to Hawaii. The main arguments were that laws should be applied flexibly to local conditions, and the situation in California that had called for exclusion did not apply in Hawaii. They argued that singling out Chinese from all other nationalities for exclusion "has the effect of lowering China in the eyes of the world," and that the Chinese presence on Hawaii was actually beneficial because they were law-abiding, "minded their own business," did not compete with white labor, got along with the natives, and possessed enterprising qualities that the natives lacked. These images and arguments were presented repeatedly by the Chinese over the next three decades. They were similar to the images produced by the Chinese in Peru in the 1920s. The one significant difference was that the Chinese in Hawaii emphasized how thoroughly they had settled in Hawaii and made it their home.

Annexation got off to an inauspicious start for the Chinese with the bubonic plague prevention measures that led to the great Chinatown fire of 1900. In the long run, however, immigration and opium were the only two issues that ran contrary to Chinese interests. Before annexation, laws against the importation of opium were not vigorously enforced, and the drug was a common aspect of migrant life, offered as a matter of course to guests, friends, and temporary workers on the rice farms. Federal enforcement after annexation severely affected the supply and price of the drug, forcing many addicts to quit and many merchants to lose an important source of profit.[47] Dislike of anti-opium measures was generally kept quiet, however, whereas exclusion could be protested publicly.

The first wave of Chinese protests against the exclusion laws in Hawaii from 1900 to 1905 generally included complaints against rigorous and humiliating treatment of "respectable" merchants, while admitting the value of restricting "undesirable" classes. C. K. Ai was a local leader of the 1905 anti-American boycott, even though his City Mill had won the contract to build the local immigration offices and detention quarters in 1903—a job on which he claimed to have lost five thousand dollars.[48] By the middle of the decade, protests focused on the argument that the Islands would benefit economically from the immigration of Chinese agricultural laborers. The UCS often worked with sugar planters in writing petitions to the United States Congress and the Department of Commerce and Labor requesting a modification of the exclusion laws. In 1915, the Rice Grower's Association even sent a delegation to Washington for a congressional hearing. This movement was finally a dead issue in 1921, after even an attempt by sugar interests to play up the specter of the Japanese menace in the wake of the recent sugar plantation strikes could not procure the admission of Chinese laborers.[49]

Most public statements against exclusion were carefully tailored to show that Chinese were more than willing to conform in most other aspects of Hawaiian life and Americanization. The 1913 booklet quoted above, *Chinese in Hawaii,* was a typical vehicle for such imagery. An article entitled "Chinese Labor Problem" explicitly addressed the issue of the exclusion laws, asking why the Chinese were made to bear the brunt of mainland prejudice when, "as a race they had never disturbed the balance of power. They had not meddled in politics; they were peace loving and law abiding, and all they had ever expected was the right to engage in commerce and trade without molestation."[50] The article expressed the hope that the emergence of China as a democratic nation-state would lead to a reduction in the "indignities" the Chinese were forced to suffer, but most of all it emphasized how the exclusion laws hurt the local economy, arguing not only that the rice and sugar industries would benefit if Hawaii were exempt from the enforcement of the exclusion laws, but that "the development of other natural resources of the Islands which require cheap labor to place them on a paying basis will be materially hastened."[51] The introductory article attempted to make a connection between the economic significance of Chinese and their cultural contributions to Hawaii:

> No better indication of the industry of the Chinese can be found than the fact that from the most humble beginnings, many have acquired beautiful and comfortable homes which in all respects are on a par with those of the most cultivated persons of other races. Pianos and other musical instruments are found in their houses, and many of their sons and daughters are accomplished musicians. They are patrons of the arts, acquiring paintings and statuary, and are constant in attendance at theaters.[52]

In 1908 a Chinese Information Committee was set up under the auspices of the UCS to propagate ideas favorable to Chinese immigration, with the Reverend Edward W. Thwing as chairman and principle propagandist. The committee put out a weekly newsletter in English that was distributed in Hawaii and to government agencies in Washington. The articles repeated the whole range of pro-Chinese images that had been in circulation since 1898 and added a few new themes of their own, all of which would become standard fare for Chinese publications over the next sixty years. One of these additions included the story of how the Chinese had taught King Kamehameha I how to organize his port, charge tariffs, and more fully integrate Hawaii into the international market at the beginning of the nineteenth century, thus initiating the entrance of Hawaii onto the international stage. The strongest emphasis was always placed on the commercial respectability of the Chinese, their contributions to the wealth of the Islands, and their potential as a link to an extensive international market. Chinese affinity with local cultural and political institutions was also a significant theme. The success of the local Chinese baseball team was a particularly fertile topic:

> In the appeal of the Chinese of Hawaii to the American people on behalf of a limited immigration of Chinese to Hawaii, the athletic spirit may not be an unimportant factor. In a country where the athletic spirit is as vigorous as in America, where it plays as important a part in the life of the country as it does there, and where the chief magistrate owes not a little of his popularity to his athletic spirit, a basis of common interest could be found. . . . With the common bond of athletics

recognized, much of the prejudice that has existed in the past is likely to give way, and open candid minds to new information and new considerations on the questions involved in this desire to permit a limited Chinese immigration to the Hawaiian Islands.[53]

By and large, Chinese made a show of welcoming American institutions after annexation. They even began to accommodate themselves to the exclusion laws as it became increasingly clear they would not be modified. The basis by which exclusion was made palatable could be seen as early as 1911, when Yong Got, the president of the Hilo Tongmenghui, was unable to reenter Hawaii after a trip to China because somebody had reported to the Immigration Bureau that his Hawaiian birth certificate was false. This incident provided yet another opportunity for the *New China News* and the *Liberty News* to hurl invective at each other. The opening salvos of the debate by the *New China News* focused on what it saw as the hypocrisy of Yong's involvement in Chinese politics while claiming to be a citizen of the United States. The paper waxed particularly satirical in portraying the opportunism of Yong's claim to American citizenship: "China is weak, America is strong. He doesn't recognize weakness, just strength. He understands the state of the world. Scholars, ancestors, and descendants will all take him for a sage."[54] The reformers went on to criticize Yong's use of a false birth certificate because it had made the immigration inspectors suspicious, so that they might begin deporting people.

In response, Wen Xiongfei, the America-born editor of the *Liberty News,* wrote an editorial entitled "Emperor Protection Association acts as loyal official to the American Government." It argued that the reformers were collaborating with the enforcement of exclusion by turning Yong in to the immigration officials and were thus traitors not only against China, but against the good reputation of the Chinese in Hawaii:

> Only Hawaiian birth certificates get good treatment from the American government. . . . The American government's treating the Hawaiian born so well is a result of the Hawaiian overseas Chinese having created these conditions for themselves. The natives born in San Francisco all know about the special privileges of the Hawaiian born, and want the same privileges. Why can't they get them? Because of the big smuggling industry. The people involved in it attack each other daily. If it is not A attacking the legitimacy of B's certificate, then B is attacking the witnesses for A's certificate. . . . We Chinese have caused the laws to be stringently enforced. Since I have come to Hawaii, I have noticed that the Hawaii officials treat the Chinese well here, not like

in California. We cannot fail to put forth the good reputation of the
Chinese here as a reason for this.[55]

The article made no attempt to show that Yong Got was born in Hawaii,
but proceeded with a long diatribe about how the Constitutionalists did
not care for the good reputation of the locally born Chinese, but only
cared about money and inducing persecution by foreigners. The argument was strong enough to put the *New China News* on the defensive,
claiming that others had unmasked Yong's birth certificate before they
did and that they would never have voluntarily called attention to such
an incident.[56] This exchange revealed a tacit understanding that matters
of practical immigration should take precedence over ideological vendet-
tas and also showed the extent to which maintaining a public image as
law-abiding citizens could supersede all other concerns.

This growing willingness to comply with exclusion reached an extreme in an article by Hawaii-born lawyer Ernest S. Ing, published in English and Chinese in a 1929 volume of self-promotion put out by the Chinese, entitled *Chinese of Hawaii*. Ing argued that in light of the great
benefits offered by residence and citizenship in the United States, exclusion and the inability to naturalize were only minor inconveniences. He
emphasized how Chinese citizens resident in Hawaii were "alien friends,"
who shared many of the rights of citizens and owed a temporary allegiance to the United States of America. He further remarked that

> living under these advantages and restrictions, the civil status of the
> alien Chinese cannot be said to be oppressive, though far from being
> enviable. . . . If our Chinese-American citizens suffer any hardships
> through restrictions imposed upon their alien relatives, this is on ac-
> count of the disadvantages growing out of the operation of the immi-
> gration and naturalization laws of the United States and does not dero-
> gate from the value of their citizenship.[57]

Ing reduced exclusion to an unfortunate historical circumstance
which did not adequately reflect the status of local Chinese, discounting
the discrimination and suspicion that also existed in Hawaii against locally born citizens of Asian extraction. As late as 1933, the governor of the
territory wrote, "Our citizens are largely of oriental blood and for the most
part are recognized as aliens until the contrary is proved."[58] It is unlikely
that Ing was ignorant of such attitudes. He was, instead, just proceeding
one step further in a strategy that Chinese had followed since annexation—that of manifesting extreme loyalty and devotion to democratic

and commercial institutions in order to gain peace and acceptance. This step was consistent with a growing trend among Chinese in Hawaii to interpret their migrant past within the American framework as a heritage of pioneering immigrants dedicated to the building of America.

ANCESTORS FOR AMERICANIZATION

Ethnic Associations

As a generation of Hawaii-born Chinese came of age in the 1920s, they reinterpreted their past from within the framework of American nationalism and began to revive and create many immigrant associations as vehicles of that interpretation. The Chinese were redefining themselves as ethnic groups in the context of multicultural Honolulu, and Chinese associations were the markers of that ethnicity. Village associations continued to be founded through the 1950s, and many of them continued to sponsor the building of schools, ancestral halls, and public works projects in home villages in China, but this interest began to carry a flavor of charitable volunteerism. Contributors to these projects were concerned less with bolstering their status in the eyes of villagers in China and more with promoting the image of Chinese in Hawaii as a humane and generous people.

The shift in orientation toward Hawaii emerged more clearly in the surname associations and the large Zhongshan and Hakka *huiguan* founded after the 1920s. The emergence of these associations also marked the rising participation of the locally born. On into the 1970s, China-born migrants continued to be more involved in village associations and the locally born in the surname associations.[59] These new associations no longer emerged primarily from the context of migrant mutual aid and links back to China; they now centered around picnics, bridging the generation gap, historical preservation, and relations with neighboring ethnic groups. They were often created with the explicit goal of providing a site for social activities and networking opportunities, and professionals like dentists or merchants used them to build clientele. For example, the Mao family association founded in 1931 claimed that its purpose was "to bring together the old and young," to help and advise those in distress, to remember the hardship and struggles of the pioneer Maos, and "to keep pace with the American standard of living and to develop better American citizens," this last function perhaps being fulfilled by the maintenance of a vacation resort outside of Honolulu for members.[60] They also functioned as constituencies for individuals who wanted to use them as stepping stones for entry into other Chinese associations.

The Hakka and Zhongshan *huiguan* had no strong links to China and were very much products of perceived interests in Hawaii. Before the 1920s, most Hakkas had been strongly involved in organizations like Christian churches, the YMCA, the Chinese-English Debating Society, nationalist organizations, and the long-lived Guo An Association, and they did not feel the need for a formalized organization that explicitly revolved around being Hakka. Several locally born Hakkas talked about forming the Renhe *huiguan* around 1911, but it only met informally until 1921. It was unable to get together funds to erect a clubhouse—a crucial marker of associational prestige—until 1937, when it also changed its name to the Chongzhenghui and linked itself to the world network of Hakka associations under the same name. The clubhouse emerged long after the association was of any use in providing practical mutual aid services to migrants. The aims behind it could be better appreciated in the opening ceremonies, to which leaders from all of the other native place and kinship associations were invited. Speeches were given in Cantonese rather than Hakka, and the main topics were the speakers themselves, their accomplishments, and their contributions to the Chinese community.[61] More than anything, the Chongzhenghui was a platform for ambitious Hakkas to gain face and integrate themselves into the larger migrant community. Similarly, in 1950 all of the district and village associations from Zhongshan came together to establish a Zhongshan *huiguan*. As most associational services were already being provided by the smaller associations, there was little necessity for its creation other than to invest its members and representatives with a status equal to those from the Siyi and Hakka *huiguan*.[62]

Only three surname associations had been created before the 1920s: a Lin association in 1889, a Huang association in 1906, and a Longgang Gongsuo, for the Liu, Zhang, Guan, and Zhao surnames in 1919. These early associations had purposefully sought memberships and officers that spanned the district boundaries of Zhongshan, in the hope that they could serve to resolve disputes between people from different districts. A few more associations were founded in the 1920s, and a handful continued to be established in each decade through the 1960s.[63] Many of these associations had a strong interest in maintaining ancestral halls in China and in editing and publishing family genealogies. In fact, family researchers in the 1980s occasionally found that all the remaining genealogy books for their lineage were to be found in Honolulu.[64] This interest,

however, was often less of a filial interest in the maintenance of a patriline than an attempt to establish a pedigree as the descendant of a genuine immigrant family, as is evident in the public statements accompanying the reorganization of the Lin family association in 1931:

> About one hundred years ago people of our clan with a pioneer spirit,
> and progressive mind, crossed the sea and came to this place from
> Kwangtung. We, the posterity, should revere the pioneer spirit of our
> clan people, which can rival that of Columbus and Magellan. If we
> don't have an organization to bring our clan people together, friend-
> ship will be diminished, and we'll treat each other as strangers. It is,
> therefore, evident that our clan needs an organization to bring all of
> our people together. . . . We must have past history as a model for the
> present. . . . Since the establishment it has now been several decades.
> As time goes by, all the deeds [the founders] have done are buried. All
> the records have been lost.[65]

The ancestors appealed to were not those who had founded the Lin family several generations back in China but the immigrant pioneers who, as
Columbus and Magellan had supposedly done for the Europeans, had
forged a place for the Lins in Hawaii.

Many of the new surname groups strove for a broad membership
beyond the descendants of a single lineage and residents of a single village. The president of the Gu family association explained the rationale
behind this in 1966, writing, "With the Goos, historically they came from
different villages. We felt that we were Chinese by heritage and basically
Goos, so whether we are of the same village doesn't matter. . . . We would
like to base it on the American system where you are of German or Italian ancestry but basically American."[66] Belonging to a Chinese family association not only integrated individuals into the Chinese community,
but provided them with an immigrant heritage that linked them to America more than the homeland.

Sociologist Clarence Glick wrote in 1938 that Chinese associations
in Honolulu were losing vitality and becoming less relevant.[67] Tin-Yuke
Char echoed this evaluation in the 1950s, adding that many associations
only continued to exist because of the income from the land and buildings they owned.[68] In the 1970s, anthropologist Judith Morrison also recorded a general belief among the Chinese that the associations were losing vitality and that young people in particular were not interested in
them.[69] From her longer historical perspective, however, she did not take
this judgment at face value. Glick also removed this evaluation from the
version of his dissertation published in 1980. Focusing her attention on

the native place associations, Morrison argued that even when they did not engage in any significant charitable or communal activities, their existence as the institutional representation of a particular group was still meaningful, both in relation to other Chinese and as a marker of Chinese ethnicity which distinguished them from non-Chinese. While agreeing with Chinese observers that the native place associations in Honolulu primarily attracted the interest of older men, she argued that this was a reflection the human life cycle rather than an associational life cycle. These old men still recruited successful, middle-aged businessmen to act as officers because of the prestige and connections they could bring to the association. Most of them accepted the positions willingly, despite previously having had more interest in associations such as the Chinese Civic Association and the Rotary Club, reflecting an awareness of the important role of the associations in creating their own positions in Honolulu's multiethnic business community.

Morrison's observations were a reformulation of arguments made in the 1930s by Clarence Glick and Romanzo Adams. They argued that on an emotional level the associations emphasized a common cultural heritage, and on a practical level the network of banquets, inaugurations, and commemorations attended by officers of the various groups fostered a concrete sense of connection. Moreover, status granted to the immigrants through the associations often translated to status in the eyes of other ethnic groups. Summarizing his understanding of the relation between migrants and associations, Glick wrote,

> The activities of the migrant brought him formal, highly valued recognition from China; they brought him the more personal esteem of the other members of the Chinatown community; and, finally, as these Chinese activities secured recognition from the dominant island groups, the migrant who achieved "face" in Chinatown was raised in the esteem of the interracial society. . . . In a sense, assimilation of the migrant into a Chinatown society meant at the same time accommodation to a larger interracial society of which Chinatown was an integral but distinct part. To the extent that the migrant willingly participated in the emerging interracial society, he did so in the role of a recognized member of a distinct racial and cultural group.[70]

Even older migrants who had not reoriented their consciousness in terms of Hawaii adapted to the localization taking place around them. In their old age they wanted to enjoy the trappings of the status in Chinese terms, such as wearing the clothes of Manchu officials in birthday ceremonies performed for their honor and arranging for elaborate funerals with around-the-clock wailers, mourning clothes, public processions, the burning of paper money, servants, horses, and cars for use in the underworld. Significantly, they did not feel they had to go back to China to enjoy these things. Families had taken root in Hawaii, and death on the Islands was no longer a threat of ghostliness. As one old man remarked about his desire to be buried permanently in Hawaii, "I want to be there with my children, and my children's children."[71] It was possible to establish a new patriline, based on the efforts of the founding ancestor. Of course these funeral rituals, as well as other rituals that continued to surround Chinese New Year and marriage ceremonies, did not have the same significance as in China. Most younger participants were ignorant or even scornful of what they saw to be the superstitious beliefs underlying their performance. Yet, many still took part in them as a part of their heritage. These rituals became ethnic markers in much the same way as the surname groups. As in China, differing interpretations did not matter so much as the way in which common participation drew boundaries and forged orderly social relationships.

Racial Succession

The work of sociologists like Adams and Glick is useful not only because of its insight into the Chinese community in Honolulu, but also because the Chinese themselves began to draw on their theories in creating a place for themselves in Hawaiian society. By the 1930s, with the increasing arrival of servicemen and other haoles from the mainland, cracks were appearing in the racial etiquette of Hawaii, and a popular impression of the mixed races of Hawaii as a breeding ground of delinquency was beginning to emerge. On the other hand, scholars who had been attracted to the Islands as a successful experiment in melting-pot democracy helped preserve racial etiquette in the face of increasingly open racial tension by depicting Hawaii as an example of smooth racial relations and amalgamation. Many Chinese were quick to latch on to these models and attempt to make them into social reality.

Funding from sugar planters made possible the research of Stanley Porteus that led to the book *Temperament and Race* in 1926. It was a pioneer of race research in Hawaii, and the strongest academic voice in support of inherent racial difference. It was the definitive application to Hawaii of theories which attempted to describe personality as the biological properties of racial groups, working from the assumption that "the place in the community that each racial group attains will be determined, not by the weight of the environmental handicap, but rather by the mental, temperamental, or character traits which each possess." [72] Thus, for Porteus, it was natural that the Chinese had a status inferior to that of the haoles in Hawaii. Although they were intelligent, it was only a practical intelligence based on the desire to accumulate money. They were still desirable residents, however, because they were "unlikely to scheme for the advancement of their group" and each had "all the virtues of a useful citizen without the embarrassing ambition to be one." [73] That is, the Chinese kept to their place under the terms of Island racial etiquette.

The Chinese and the missionaries who often represented them in the petitions and pamphlets written at the beginning of the century had often cooperated in producing such a judgment. Their emphasis on economic contributions to Hawaiian history and their unwillingness to interfere in local affairs had seemed very opportune in light of their desire to obtain the entry of more Chinese migrants while diffusing fears of an Asian takeover. Most of their hopes for political status were pinned publicly on the recognition of China as a modern nation-state. By the 1920s, however, the failure of the Chinese republic and a growing awareness of the limit to upward mobility inherent in the racial characterization of the Chinese led to a search for new explanations of their position in Hawaii. Newer sociological theories that explained the status of local ethnic groups as the result of universal historical and environmental processes rather than internal characteristics found quick favor.

A group called the Overseas Penman's Club put out a slew of commemorative and promotional volumes and yearbooks during the 1930s. For the most part, they contained the usual hodgepodge of statistics, biographies, accounts of funds collected to "save China," business directories, brief histories of associations, and advertisements that have filled Chinese commemorative volumes throughout the world. Yet the descriptions of the cultural and economic significance of Chinese in Hawaii marked a slight change from earlier publications in Hawaii. Their first publication in 1929, *The Chinese of Hawaii,* had a Chinese section largely devoted to the new task of promoting the legacy of Sun Yat-sen and rewriting the history of the Chinese in Hawaii from the perspective of the Guomindang. The English section, on the other hand, was much more attentive to redefining the Chinese experience in Hawaii in terms of popular American discourses of hardy pioneering, cultural pluralism, and eager modernization. It was dedicated "to the spirit of progress which has characterized Chinese life from the days of the earliest pioneers; to the future of a Chinese community in its service to all in this territory."

In addition to the articles written by Hawaii-born Chinese professionals on the usual topics of athletics, churches, and economic success, it included an article by Romanzo Adams entitled "The Meaning of the Chinese Experience in Hawaii." It was intended as a reinterpretation of the Chinese presence on Hawaii that emphasized "the special circumstances under which they have lived and thus [made] them more understandable to others on the basis of our common humanity."[74] He argued that, until recently, Hawaii-born Chinese "seemed to desire unrestricted social relations with Caucasians, but what they really did want was a satisfactory social life on the American plan with people of similar education and interests, and most of such persons, for the time being, happened to be Caucasians."[75] As more and more Chinese received an American education, however, they were able to forsake haole companionship and create networks and associations among themselves without giving up their claim to be truly American. He argued further that the love of China taught in the Chinese-language schools should be encouraged, because it instilled in children the values necessary to be able to love the United States as well. Adams concluded with homage to the immigrant heritage that echoed the opening dedication, asserting that "when the immigrant generation shall have passed away, their posterity will erect to them memorials in lasting granite. In literature their achievements will be celebrated, and their virtues will be recounted for the instruction of youth."[76]

Adams saw this ethnic solidarity of educated Chinese as a temporary phase. In other writings he made it clear that he was a strong advocate of intermarriage and total integration, and showed more awareness of haole discrimination against the Chinese. Chinese, however, latched onto this vision of an identity that was simultaneously Chinese and Americanized. The nature of this identity was developed more extensively in the second volume of *Chinese of Hawaii* in 1936. In this volume, the Chinese and English sections were much more similar, centered on two economic and educational histories of the Chinese in Hawaii written by Kum Pui Lai and Paul Kimm-Chow Goo. With the help of copious statistics, these articles presented a celebration of Chinese success in Hawaii shaped by theories of ethnic succession then being pursued in Hawaii by sociologist Andrew Lind. As explained by Lai, ethnic succession meant that "success in cultural adjustments of the immigrant groups in Hawaii seems to vary with their length of residence, numerical size, and group solidarity. . . . This 'graduation' from the rural plantations to the business houses and then to professional occupations in the cities of Honolulu and Hilo appears to be duplicated by each group after a period of labor in the sugar camps and pineapple fields."[77] Thus, as the Chinese were the first group to arrive after the haoles, this theory claimed a status for the Chinese as the second most integrated and important group in Hawaii (native Hawaiians were not taken into consideration by this theory, except as the unfortunate victims of succession).

From the perspective of ethnic succession, nothing more than the timing of Chinese arrival in Hawaii was necessary to explain their status as a unique Hawaiian ethnic group. Chinese success on the Islands was due to their having come together as Chinese, but the influence of Chinese culture and connections to China could be taken into account or ignored at will, depending on the context. Thus, Paul Kim-Chow Goo could assert of the Chinese that "their characteristic traits of industry, providence, thriftiness, endurance, love of peace, and patience were important in their struggle to rise to the top against resentment, prejudice, and misunderstanding, which in time gave way to better understanding, and a more friendly spirit ensued," without necessarily negating his claim that other ethnic groups in Hawaii, "like the Chinese, are all the products of the same general ground pattern, and they proceed on the same general uniformity of progress."[78] He could depict the Chinese as inherently noble and industrious while avoiding any of the biologically racializing implications of such a mode of characterization because they were contingent cultural qualities rather than deterministic traits. The status of Chinese in Hawaii was now determined by environmental and historic factors. Whereas much assimilation theory on the mainland required the breaking down of group identities as a basis for assimilation into the cosmopolitan and individualistic larger society, racial succession provided a basis for pluralistic integration as a group with a particular local history.

Ethnic Consolidation

Mui King-Chan, the Chinese consul in Hawaii, wrote an article entitled "The Chinese as Builders of Hawaii" for a 1937 issue of the *Pan Pacific* magazine devoted to the Chinese in Hawaii. In it he transformed the process of ethnic succession into a dramatic procession: "Huge obstacles in the way of foreign language and culture and strange environment were fought and conquered through the dogged patience and persistence of each succeeding generation. From farmer to merchant and merchant to leader the Chinese progressed."[79] This article was jumping ahead of itself. The Chinese had been stuck on the plateau of merchant for over four decades, and in 1937, describing Chinese as leaders was more wishful thinking than empirical observation. In 1938 Lind himself noted that ethnic succession on the Islands was no longer as dynamic as it once was, appearing to have hit a kind of status quo. The number of professional and leadership positions at the top was limited and had already been filled by haoles, leaving fewer avenues of mobility for those on the bottom.[80] Adams often explained this impasse as a result of haole discrimination and decried it as an unfortunate barrier to complete integration. The haole oligarchy dominated the largest business interests in agriculture, shipping, wholesale distribution, and department stores, and they cooperated closely to exclude all economic and political competition, leaving only smaller retail concerns and a few selected products to the Chinese.

The Chinese also took part in the reproduction of this stagnant status quo. Few Chinese writers acknowledged racial restrictions on the development of Chinese economic life, preferring instead to underline their contributions, commitments, and general acceptance in Hawaiian society. They presented themselves as satisfied with their second rank on the ethnic totem pole and tended to adhere to the racial etiquette of the Islands, rarely posing challenges to the haoles or any other ethnic groups for that matter. Unlike the Japanese and Filipinos, they were never involved in strikes or political opposition to the haoles, and even during the anti-Japanese war they generally restrained themselves from participating to the prevailing discourse of fear and prejudice against the Japanese on the Islands (although they untiringly attacked the ambitions of the Japanese government).[81] They held a precarious position and worked hard not to disturb it.

In economic activities, ethnicity and ethnic associations facilitated the consolidation of business connections and the protection of those interests from the interference of other groups. Chinese had a very clear sense of what kinds of merchandise were part of the Chinese economy, such as poi, tea, and fish, and few Chinese were willing to invest in products like coffee or pineapples, which were believed to be dominated by other ethnic groups. Yet within this Chinese economic sphere relations were shaped more by intense competition than cooperation. Occasional attempts to set up committees for business regulation and price control generally met with failure. Frustrated or ambitious Chinese businessmen would occasionally talk about the "need to modernize" as a criticism of other Chinese businesses for their tendency to hire managers and employees on the basis of family ties rather than competency, their reluctance to adopt more efficient management techniques, and their unwillingness to depart from the exclusively Chinese business networks.[82] Nonetheless, even sophisticated financial institutions like the Chinese American bank, established in 1916, and the Liberty Bank, established in 1922, tended to reinforce a segregated Chinese economy in Honolulu.

Many children of Chinese and Hawaiian parents preferred to publicly identify with the Chinese rather than the Hawaiian side of their an-

cestry in deference to the higher status of the Chinese and common beliefs that Chinese were more diligent and had more business skills, even
though many of them had been raised only by their Hawaiian mothers
after their Chinese fathers had returned to China, died, or abandoned
them. Many even embroidered their family histories to assert that their
fathers or grandfathers in China had been doctors, scholars, and other
men thought to be of superior quality. On the other hand, growing ethnic consciousness meant that Chinese were increasingly less likely to accept Chinese-Hawaiians into their networks and associations, unless
"personal character or family connections" recommended them.[83] Race,
migrant past, and economic niche were becoming one and the same.

Many educated young Chinese with professional ambitions were
unable to achieve their goals, given the limited opportunities available in
Hawaii and were more likely to feel the glass ceiling placed on their advancement. Finding so few chances in Hawaii to exercise their professional skills, many moved to the mainland or, more commonly, to China
in search of employment (where they were known for their talents in
baseball and ukulele playing). From 1924 to 1931, 911 more American
citizens left for China from Hawaii than returned.[84] Many of those young
Chinese had developed a sincere sense of patriotism for America and
American values during their education in public schools, accepting
George Washington, Thomas Jefferson, and English constitutional liber-
ties as their own personal heritage.[85] Nonetheless, as Romanzo Adams
told his Chinese readers in 1929, Chinese enthusiasm for America and democracy often faded quickly after the young graduates found that what
they had learned in the integrated halls of the school was not necessarily
the reality of work and economic competition they had to deal with
when they left. A visit to the mainland and the experience of more open
racism there often left a deep impression on many Hawaii-born Chinese.
One student in the 1920s told how bad experiences while studying in
California had made him rethink his feelings toward China and Hawaii:
"While I am being more and more Americanized—adopting more and
more American customs, habits, and ways of thinking—I am also feeling
more sympathetic to China." He considered going to China to begin his
career, but was not certain he could fit in there, either, because he had
also been rejected while trying to mix with students from China in California.[86] This dilemma was common among many young Chinese in an
era when identity was closely tied to national inclusion. A common response was the development of a pluralist alternative through the reinforcement of Chinese ethnicity in Hawaii.

In the context of Hawaii, the goals of "Americanization" were difficult to distinguish from "modernization." Both included a taste for social recognition and acceptance, a high standard of life surrounded by technological conveniences, and a commitment to national patriotism rather than what were seen as parochial cultural attachments. As such, the process of taking root as a Chinese ethnic group in Hawaii was not much different from the experiences of other Chinese migrants around the world. The most significant differences in Hawaii were the transformation of connections to villages in China into distant heritages and the fact that access to modernity was not dominated by a small elite. As Americans, all young Chinese felt that modern life should be within their reach.

Chinese Migration and the Early-Twentieth-Century World Order

I want to be able to rely on you, [my father] who inked each piece of our own laundry with the word "Center," to find out how we landed in a country where we are eccentric people (Maxine Hong Kingston, *China Men*).[1]

There is no East here. West is meeting West. This was all West. All you saw was West. This is The Journey *in* the West. I am so fucking offended. Why aren't you offended? . . . These sinophiles dig us so much, they're drooling over us. They think they know us—the wide range of us from sweet to sour—because they eat in Chinese restaurants. . . . What's so "exotic"? We're about as exotic as shit (Wittman Ah Sing, complaining about reviews praising his staging of an old Chinese novel, in Maxine Hong Kingston, *Tripmaster Monkey*).[2]

I'm tired of all this Chinese this, Chinese that. You people, you think gambling, extortion, corruption are kosher? Because it's a thousand years old? Well all this thousand-year-old stuff, it's a lot of shit to me. This is America you're living in, and it's two hundred years old, so you better get your clocks fixed. You're not special, and you're not beyond the law, any more than the Puerto Ricans or the Polacks. So we're all going to obey the law the way it says (Lieutenant Stanley White, in *Year of the Dragon*, a Dino de Laurentiis film).[3]

American children hear no stories about ghosts. They spend a dime at the drugstore to buy a Superman comic book. This "Superman" is an all-knowing, resourceful, omnipotent hero who can overcome any difficulty. . . . Superman represents actual capabilities or future potential, while ghosts symbolize belief in and reverence for the accumulated past. As much as old Mrs. Park, trying to lessen the distance between east and west, might lead me over to the corner of the living room to look at faded photographs, it was the Redfield's little boy who showed me the heart of American culture, and it lay in Superman, not ghosts. . . . How could ghosts gain a foothold in American cities? People move about like the tide, unable to form permanent ties with places, still less with other people. . . . In a world without ghosts, life is free and easy. Americans can gaze straight ahead. But still I think they lack something, and I do not envy their life (Chinese anthropologist Fei Xiaotong, 1943).[4]

Like the disjunctive, nation-based histories discussed at the opening of this book, the preceding quotations illustrate some of the difficulties in establishing common ground for a discussion of Chinese migration. Unlike those histories, however, these observations were produced from within a single nation—the United States—reminding us again that movement and intermingling are as much a part of modern history as the construction of nation-states and national heritages. Although they come together to create a vision of diversity, each statement revolves around a single crude distinction between East and West that has been a cornerstone of conceptualizations of world order in the twentieth century.[5] Their varying perspectives on that distinction—rejecting it, questioning it, and accepting it—combine to make it somewhat intangible: a shifting distinction between inside and outside.

Wittman Ah Sing and Stanley White both strive for Chinese integration into America by commenting on how the exoticization of Chinese isolated them from the mainstream. Yet they respectively accuse non-Chinese and Chinese for perpetuating that isolation. Both of them could make a good case for their accusation, and neither wanted it to persist, yet they occupy little common ground. The young girl in Kingston's *China Men,* on the other hand, was just beginning to perceive how her "center" could be at the margins of something else. She, herself, was a site within which definitions of inside and outside were shifting.

Chinese anthropologist Fei Xiaotong described his experiences during a visit to the United States in 1943 for a series of newspaper articles published in China. He characterized the East-West divide as one between tradition-bound China and forward-looking America, a distinction that he would develop further that year in his book *Earthbound China*. The distinction was partly inspired by experiences such as his visit to a Chinese restaurant in Washington, DC, where waiters speaking Taishan dialect served chop suey (a Chinese-American creation that could be literally translated as "miscellaneous chopped-up things") and chow mein ("fried noodles") to be eaten with a knife and fork and accompanied by ice water (occasioning Fei's hypothesis that Americans complained Chinese food was hard to digest because of the great invasion of congealed grease caused by drinking cold water rather than warm tea). While consuming the meal, he watched a Cuban singer and "half-naked women doing Spanish dances" to the accompaniment of jazz music, all presented by a man of Southern European ancestry. His impression was, "Truly bold! A young culture!"[6] He failed to mention that the entrepreneurs who had brought this cornucopia together were Chinese themselves.

Fei retained ghosts as a symbol of disorder but reversed the location of ghosts and order. Now, ghosts marked encrusted layers of tradition and familiarity in China, while the young United States, despite its freshness, was the site of a somewhat sterile and alienating order. He commented that living in brightly lit American rooms "gives you a false sense of confidence that this is all of the world, that there is no more reality than what appears clearly and brightly before your eyes. . . . [Americans] think of the unknown as static, waiting for people to mine it like an ore, not only not frightening, but a resource for improving life in the future."[7] In contrast, life in China was engulfed in the textures of the past. He did not write of ghosts literally as the presence of dead spirits, but he preserved the sense of an intangible specter of the past that inhabited and affected the present. A difference, however, between Fei's ghosts and those of south China peasants was that Fei's ghosts did not represent the vague threat of outer chaos. Rather, they were the thick encrustation of past events that made up the very core of being Chinese, perhaps even of being fully human. "Life in its creativity changes the absolute nature of time: it makes past into present—no, it melds past, present, and future into one inextinguishable, multilayered scene, a three-dimensional body. This is what ghosts are."[8]

Fei conflated China, ghosts, and the past on one side of the East-West divide, and America, order, and the future on the other. His own life spanned both sides. Although he had originally undertaken his own intellectual and physical journeys as a search for universal standards, within ten years they had produced an elaborate assertion of difference. He had been drawn into Western academia by a desire to apply the universal light of scientific knowledge to China. He attended lectures by Robert Park in China in 1932—which he said had "determined the course my life has taken"—and then studied with Bronislaw Malinowski in London. His depictions of America as a bold, young culture recalled Park's depiction of

American cities as a site of heteroglot modernity and emancipation from the bonds of culture, while his tradition-bound China offered a finely textured opposition to that modernity that resonated with the rich accounts of cultural holism created by men like Malinowski. He later began to suspect that scientific knowledge had its own cultural underpinnings and that the light of science was insufficient to illuminate aspects of Chinese life that could never be understood without being Chinese. That is to say, Fei's development as a cosmopolitan, migrating individual was inseparable from his increasingly eloquent and systematic construction of differences.

Even though hard to pin down, the differences that are the subjects of the opening quotations were real, inasmuch as they were social discourses that shaped social activity. China as traditional, Chinese as exotic, an America under the rule of law and science, Americans as fresh and vibrant: these ideas have all shaped the imaginations and lives of people in the twentieth century. Yet these distinctions do not map out a set of discrete units with discrete histories that fit together to form a systematic whole. Each speaker was attempting to define or rearrange those distinctions. The young girl from *China Men* was trying to make sense out of her confusion, while Fei Xiaotong had made sense of his via an elaborate anthropology of oppositions. Wittman Ah Sing and Stanley White wanted to abolish the distinction through denial. Taken together, they suggest that the distinctions themselves are not the place to start in understanding the history of Chinese migration; rather, they are the threads of interaction.

Chinese, Peruvian, American, and Hawaiian

It is difficult to extricate the particular histories of Chinese in each location from the more general processes of Chinese migration. The search for a stable environment in which to do business, the formation of associations, and the striving for respect via the manipulation of Chinese nationalist and local discourses were broadly similar in all three locations. Yet the last three chapters have been devoted to explaining how these processes worked out uniquely in each situation. What, if anything, about the experiences and institutions described in this book was particularly Chinese, Peruvian, American, or Hawaiian (or Midwestern or Limeñan, for that matter)? What is the significance of these differences and their relationship to a broader panorama of Chinese migration?

At the simplest level, all migrant experiences were parts of these respective national histories merely by virtue of having happened within their boundaries. Yet asserting participation in a national history is not the same as describing how the experience and identity of a Zhongshan migrant in Honolulu were different from those of his younger brother in Lima. The development of national histories is as much an ideological process as a given physical or cultural fact, and inclusion always brings certain consequences, certain reformulations of the past which can obscure broader links. For example, it has been easy until recently to exclude Chinese from United States history by briefly citing their cultural differences and propensity to sojourn. This is no longer the case, but claims for inclusion are often made at the expense of ignoring links to China and transnational networks that shaped much of migrant life. When those links are acknowledged, they are generally seen as parochial connections to a traditional past which Chinese have readily broken away from in becoming American.

Chinese in Hawaii have been sucked into this American history by virtue of annexation. By the 1930s, being Hawaiian had become an ill-formed concept. It could mean identification with native Hawaiian tradition, resistance to American hegemony, an emergent creolization, or a local variation of being American. Recent Asian American histories have tended to choose this third alternative, as did Hawaii-born Chinese after the 1920s. In fact, Chinese in Hawaii were self-consciously "Americanizing" at a greater rate than those in the United States. This is not surprising, because one of the benefits of "Americanization" in Hawaii was precisely that it was a discourse brought in from outside and could be selectively appropriated. Aspects of liberal democracy and the virtues of a pioneer immigrant heritage could be used to discredit the haole oligarchy and buttress Chinese status vis-à-vis other ethnic groups in Hawaii.

In Peru, the sociocultural content of a national history has been subject to more intense debate than in the United States. Within these debates, the history of the Chinese has been used as material for attempts to forge a multiethnic "popular" or "creole" identity out of the tangle of peoples that made up the coastal underclass, as an example that shows the ability of a liberal legal system to preserve justice across cultures and as an example to highlight social disjunctions that deny the very existence of a national history.[9] The Chinese in the 1920s, as we have seen, saw their own best means of integration to be identification as foreign citizens and cosmopolitan merchants. That is, they promoted international legal and commercial standards rather than blood or cultural blending as the basis for national participation. Thus they threw in their lot with a particular sector of Peruvian society. This strategy was successful in helping Chinese elite go beyond the coolie heritage and eugenicist theories of the 1920s, but it did not serve them well after the rise of a populist government in 1930.

If these national/regional histories are understood as processes of becoming, Chinese clearly participated in each of them. They interacted with expanding states and have been objects and protagonists of debates about national identity. To what extent was this also a process of becoming Chinese? None of the activities described in this book were unique to the Chinese. Many other peoples have migrated as laborers and traders, set up transnational networks, become involved in criminal and entrepreneurial activities, sent money home, and returned home themselves. They have also helped construct nationalist identities, built immigrant enclaves, negotiated ethnic identities, and sought acceptance as locals and citizens. We may be able to identify differences of magnitude between groups in the intensity of nationalist sentiment, frequency of trips home, long-term viability of transnational families and networks, amount of commercial success, or the influence of migrant associations. In the final analysis, however, the Chinese were still migrants, following a variation in the set of experiences lived out by many other migrant groups.

Yet, from the perspective of participants who made up these networks and communities, being Chinese could be the most significant fact of their social existence. Participation in migrant activities both depended upon and produced Chineseness. A person was Chinese by virtue of the fact that he moved in networks channeled though Hong Kong, Shantou, or Xiamen, and back to villages in which they or their ancestors were born. Symbols and oaths of solidarity are common among many peoples, but the particular details and symbols used to mobilize association and bonds of trust among Chinese, such as the names of villages, surnames, ritual oaths, and fictional kinship bonds derived from well-known stories, were irrelevant, if not unintelligible, to non-Chinese. Similarly, although nationalism developed simultaneously among many different peoples around the world, the community of people willing and able to be accepted as Chinese nationals was limited. From another perspective, the barriers created by discrimination and racialized conceptions of Chineseness by others often assured that even people who wanted nothing to do with Chineseness had no choice but to be treated as Chinese. This was especially true in the Western Hemisphere, where Chinese were marked off by distinct physical features. The ethnic identities created in this way were different from cultural or practical solidarities but could still result in a sense of unique heritage, often shaped by experiences of marginalization or resistance. Participation in all these experiences and processes made people Chinese in some form or another, although none were particular to the Chinese.

The Early-Twentieth-Century World

"Americanization," "Chineseness," *huaqiao,* and the production of other labels and identities are inextricable from historically specific methods of marking difference and building solidarity. Those methods are part of larger patterns of global order that emerge at particular moments in world history. The two aspects of that history most relevant here are the increasing density of global economic networks and the emergence of nation-states and national identity as the main markers of political, cultural, and social recognition around the world.

The networks and associations of Chinese migrants were based on patterns of mutual aid and association in China. These patterns crystallized during the mobility and commercial growth of the sixteenth through the eighteenth centuries into familiar forms such as lineages, sworn brotherhoods, and merchant *huiguan.* The resilience and flexibility of these forms facilitated expansion along channels of economic opportunity both within and outside of China. They facilitated the spread of Chinese laborers in the late nineteenth century and the later spread of retail and service businesses built on dense networks of credit and finance. They also became sites for the reproduction of migration that were relatively independent of any specific, local economic conditions. As important nodes of migrant networks embedded in an expanding world economy, Chinese migrant associations continued to grow stronger and more pervasive in the early twentieth century as they adapted to specific niches. For example, the tongs that emerged in the eastern United States were well-suited to maintaining a narrow ethnic specialty in laundries and restaurants. The centrality of import-export houses and corporate directorships in Peru corresponded with the high profile of internationally oriented merchants in the national economy. Village and surname groups persisted even among locally born Chinese in Hawaii as markers of ethnic identity and platforms for economic networking.

The political and ideological rise of nation-states also shaped this history. By the early twentieth century, it was apparent that neither migrants nor anyone else could gain respect internationally without a strong nation-state to back them. A national state that took part in internationally recognized diplomatic procedures and had a powerful military could advance merchant interests and protect migrants against local hostility. The creation and viability of such a state was difficult without the grassroots cultural work of creating a unique national heritage and identity. The development of a feeling of common fate could both galvanize potential citizens into concerted political and economic action and justify international claims to self-rule and autonomy. Awareness of the utility of official and military backing was nothing new. It was apparent in the early influence of Qing officials on Chinese networks in the late nineteenth century, including their sponsorship of CCBAs and Chambers of Commerce after 1905. The sense of total inclusion within a national state, however, did grow in the early twentieth century. Its general effects were evident in the rise of overseas Chinese nationalism, increased investments in China beyond the village, and the development of a diasporic *huaqiao* consciousness.

These larger shifts that spanned migrant networks are only one aspect of the rise of international consciousness, which took different forms in each of the cases in this book. Chinese in all three locations moved through an ideological landscape of Chinese nationhood, local nationhood, eugenics, class, economic interests, and cultural difference. These aspects came together differently in each location, revealing a variety of possible manifestations of similar global conditions.

In the early twentieth century, a Peruvian "nation" was still poorly defined and riven by increasingly hard ethnic divisions. Chinese migrant elite were aware of these divisions, and threw their lot in with the factors of cosmopolitan modernity. They developed close relationships with the Chinese consul, stressing their status as foreign citizens of a modernizing nation and their participation in international commercial networks. They consistently appealed to the reigning discourse of liberalism and constitutional rights that had shaped Peruvian politics in word, if not in fact, since the 1820s. This both served to identify the Chinese with the forces of global modernity and to lift them beyond the eugenic and racializing discourses surrounding the debates over Peruvian citizenship and "racial stock," which only had the potential to drag them down. The Chinese claimed local acceptance based on foreign citizenship and commercial skill. These claims were inseparable from the assertion of a transnationally applicable modernity.

In Hawaii during the years immediately after annexation, Chinese migrant elites became deeply involved in Chinese politics, partly in the hope that a revived and republican China would generate increased local respect. As the promises of the revolution faded, the role of the Chinese nation in local Chinese lives also faded. By the 1920s, many had turned toward the United States for inspiration. "Americanization" became indistinguishable from "modernization" in the statements of many Chinese. At the same time, they drew upon mythologies of pioneer immigrant groups and theories of ethnic succession—sprinkled with a touch of genetically determined diligence and intelligence—to claim a relatively high status in the local ethnic hierarchy. As ethnic lines were more clearly drawn, many locally born Chinese also began to conceive of their lives in terms of cultural conflict. Notably, the poles of conflict were usually American and Chinese, as forms of Hawaiian or "pidgin" identity became increasingly less attractive. Some of these young Chinese tried to make a career for themselves in China, but for the bulk of them, local ethnic identity within a national context was the most common form of resolution.

In Chicago, Chinese were effectively excluded from any significant recognition or integration into the nation for a number of reasons: racism and exclusion from citizenship, the relative insignificance of the Chinese economy (which blocked self-representation as cosmopolitan merchants, which was possible in Peru), low numbers of locally born Chinese, and the historical process whereby associations used force and protection to maintain a limited yet well-defined ethnic niche. Even though Chicago was as heteroglot as Hawaii or Peru, a sense of what it meant to be "American" was much more clear-cut than the contours of local identity in the other locations. This left little room for negotiation, other than forging a marginal niche as local exotica. Local elite did present themselves as well-heeled local businessmen, an identity that was promoted by graduate student Ting-chiu Fan. But Paul Siu described another side of the Chinese situation, in which they were lost in a gap between two cultures. Migrant associations and transnational networks in Chicago appeared as markers of parochialism and isolation. The relationship between Chineseness and modernity or assimilation (which often amounted the same thing) was generally perceived as an opposition, occasionally transcended by a few forward-looking businessmen. In practice, however, the creation of scattered isolated enclaves was just as much a product of industrial progress as was the emergence of undifferentiated individualism. The Chinese grew *in* to Chinatown during the early twentieth century, not out of it.

Chinese Migrants as Moderns

This idea of the "modern" can offer a foothold by which to negotiate the multiple forces shaping Chinese migration. I understand modernity in a loose sense here, referring not so much to debates over the nature of modernity (in comparison to something like postmodernity), as to various ways in which migrants understood contemporary local and world trends and attempted to keep up to date with them. Chinese migrants in the early twentieth century engaged in activities and self-representations to earn respect in the eyes of each other, the non-Chinese they interacted with, and "international opinion." These included a variety of often contradictory images: Chinese migrants presented themselves as supporters of education and economic change in their hometowns, as representatives of a respectable and economically powerful republic, as wearers of patent leather shoes and high heels, as cosmopolitans, as individuals experiencing liberation or cultural conflict, as successful businessmen, as Americans, and as bearers of Chinese culture and its traditions of diligence, intelligence, democratic incorporation, and exotic allure. All of these images were deployed as interpretations of widespread early-twentieth-century discourses of nationalism, assimilation, individualism, or commercialism, and they could be generalized as an attempt to reach toward the "modern."

Of course, even self-consciously modern Chinese still engaged in ostensibly "premodern" activities, such as the maintenance of a patriline, membership in sworn brotherhoods, personalistic networks, the accumulation of symbols of imperial power, geographic mobility as a family-oriented economic strategy, and struggles for status according to village norms (although we must remember that many of these practices took form during the "early modern" commercial growth of Late Imperial China). Some of these practices were self-consciously crystallized as "tradition," yet all of them continued to be entwined with, to be transformed, and even to flourish as part of Chinese migration in the modern world. Some aspects of these activities were of the kind that Bourdieu would describe as "inscribed" through early childhood socialization, and others were much more consciously appropriated, negotiated, and deployed as responses to new environments. The participation of Chinese migrants in a modern, nation-based world order was not a transformative disjuncture but a complex array of shifts and partial shifts.

Some of the most apparently "unmodern" of those inscribed cultural principles were the institutions, rituals, and constructions of ghostliness discussed in chapter 4. Chinese embarked on their migrations under the auspices of institutions that would structure their experiences abroad and brought conceptual patterns of social relationships that allowed plenty of room to incorporate unfamiliar people.[10] Outsiders—as ghosts and government—presented both threat and opportunity. Group solidarity was forged for mutual protection, while access to opportunities was maintained through formalized and predictable rituals of interaction and exchange. Encounters with outsiders would take the form of gradually formalized difference rather than eventual homogenization. Ritual specialists and mediators were often required to properly negotiate these boundaries. People like Aurelio Powsan Chia and the Moy brothers were precisely such prestigious mediators, whose influence depended on the maintenance of a distinct Chinese group which they could protect.

Of course, the particularities of Chinese rituals had little efficacy outside of China, and it is hard to argue convincingly that Chinese still shaped their relationships with non-Chinese based on the underlying principles of these rituals. Yet migration did not mean the end of these rituals, because most migrants were still connected via associations and family to altars and lineage halls in China where they were still performed; they did not become things of the past which migrants left behind as they moved through the modern world.

Moreover, the efficacy of rites lay not only in their common symbols, but in their ability to persist and continue to order social life by encompassing mutual misunderstandings and adapting to new forces and actors. That is, encounters of migrants with the modern world did not just lead to the destruction of ritual as a vestige of premodern tradition. Rather, the new relationships formed by Chinese with the rest of the world can be fruitfully understood as involving a reconfiguration of ritual ordering. Participation in rituals created group solidarity at the local level in China via the development of relationships with particular gods and ghosts. It also ordered hierarchical relations throughout the empire via official rites that incorporated newcomers and, in effect, tolerated local misunderstanding, so long as that misunderstanding was veiled under proper comportment. Thus, neighbors who were distinct and oppositional at ground level came together at a higher level of imagination, symbolized by the empire and its apex in the emperor (although some groups, like sworn brotherhood societies, had an ambiguous relationship to the empire).

The emerging world order within which Chinese migrants were moving can be understood on similar terms. Nations, ethnicities, and cultures are arrayed against each other. They each have the practical solidarity of daily encounters and submission to common political hegemony. They also rally around internationally recognized symbols like flags, language, and heritage. The details of these symbols and governing institutions are always different, yet the fact of their existence is common to all nations. They are mediums by which nations are made mutually comprehensible and brought together within a larger "family of nations." No single apex corresponds with the Chinese emperor, but a similar and often unarticulated sense of ultimate belonging within the natural structure of the human race still prevails. That structure is the mosaic of discrete cultures and sociopolitical groups that make up most concepts of world order, from the United Nations to the area studies structure of history departments. Each of those units is still riven by differences and conflict, but the general effect of this world order is to make all of those conflicts appear as internal affairs rather than aspects of a global structure.

In the cases studied here, it is clear that the Chinese born in Hawaii had come closest to completely conceptualizing themselves in terms of ethnicity, heritage, nation, and blood. But these categories were also used by local restaurateurs and cosmopolitan merchants in Peru and in Chicago, who presented their differences as inseparable from claims for inclusion. They all made claims to exemplify international standards of comportment, both as possessors of unique heritages and as practitioners of commercial activity that demanded recognition and protection as a universal human right. Despite these self-representations, they continued to live their lives through diasporic networks that often seemed subversive to the nation-states to which they addressed these appeals.

Like Chinese-Hawaiians, Fei Xiaotong believed the transcultural rule of law and science promoted within the international system to be much clearer and more orderly than a localized world of ghosts and tradition. His life experience shows, however, that having become socialized into this new discourse by no means meant that boundaries between Chinese and others had been erased. Rather, they had been reformulated and transposed. The presence of the past was an inseparable part of the modern—both as a foil to modernity and as the material from which it was built.

Late-Twentieth-Century Shifts

Chinese migrant history continued to change through mid-century in conjunction with shifts in world history. The establishment of the People's Republic of China in 1949 severed many migrant networks that had already been weakened by the Depression and the Second World War. The division of the government between Beijing and Taiwan also created confusion and uncertainty among proponents of diasporic nationalism. Migration and the circulation of goods and money reached a low point. The Cold War and postindependence rise of Southeast Asian nationalism put further pressure on Chinese to orient themselves to the lands in which they lived. For a short period, individual nations began to dominate the circumstances of being Chinese migrants. Of course, Chinese also took part in defining the terms of these national inclusions. For example, localization movements such as the Asian American movement have been very successful in directing the standard of national inclusion away from total assimilation and toward pluralist and "multicultural" acceptance of locally oriented Chinese.

Over the past thirty years, however, transnational links among Chinese have reemerged more strongly than ever. These new and reemergent links may be usefully described as diasporic entrepreneurialism, or even as the emergence of a global bourgeoisie, as these networks become increasingly identified with economic power and modernity in the Pacific.[11] Some commentators have even seen them as a new form of deterritorialized economic organization, and even a new form of identity.[12]

Regardless of any unprecedented transformations that are taking place, these flows follow many of the routes and networks built up over past centuries, even as they transform those networks. They may now be described more accurately as a web rather than a set of radiating grooves, with new cities like Vancouver, Taibei, Sydney, and New York overshadowing earlier nodes like Hong Kong, Singapore, and Xiamen. As in earlier networks, the family is still a basic institution, but these families are now cut off from the household in China and less interested in the maintenance of the patriline. They are more concerned with assuring the material survival of the nuclear family by taking advantage of opportunities for economic activity, education, and political stability around the world. Geographic dispersal is still common, and the ability to maintain connections across large distances and political boundaries is still an important source of profit and strength, but the altar and household as anchors for the family in space and across time have largely disappeared.

Other remnants of shared cultural behavior also remain and even facilitate the practical reconstruction of networks. People previously unfamiliar with each other can discover that they speak a similar language, eat similar food, have ancestors from nearby villages, and can read each other's body language. These similarities help them to feel they know what to expect and when they can trust each other, thus laying the groundwork for business deals, social encounters, and extended relationships in which differences in personal experience can gradually be overcome and replaced with an even richer texture of common practices and attitudes.

Along with these day-to-day encounters come assertions of the timeless and unbreakable heritage of a "Greater China," which are reminiscent of early-twentieth-century nationalist claims. A recent journalistic account of Chinese migration used one of the most succinct expressions of this constructed cultural heritage as its title, *Sons of the Yellow Emperor*.[13] Many of these assertions have emanated from China, as it tries to attract the money of wealthy Chinese migrants. The assertion of a "Confucian ethic" of thrift, diligence, and family values that underlies recent Chinese success is another prescription of this unity. Confucian family values are often formulated in terms much closer to the campaign speeches of an American presidential candidate than anything a Confucian official would have understood as family. This only underlines, however, the way in which the past is constantly entwined with the present.

Participation in this realm of diasporic culture and economic opportunity often entails the resinicization of individuals who had taken on local identities. This could include sending children to learn Mandarin or the revitalization of cultural performances such as the lion dance. It is also driven by a claim that to be Chinese is to be modern, to be at the cutting edge of economic and cultural globalization. We must also emphasize, however, that to the extent that such a diasporic culture exists, it is far from universal and is in many ways a class-based ideology. Only a small portion of people who identify themselves as ethnic Chinese have the means, language skills, and inclination to take part in this diasporic culture, and many resist it as an infringement on hard-won local identities.[14]

These developments are part of an ever-shifting flow of historical circumstances. If we trace the history of overseas Chinese networks no farther than the brief predominance of nation-based identities at mid-century, we can only see them as a disjunctively new phenomenon, ultimately shaped primarily by global circumstances. If we root them in the idea of a timeless "Confucian ethos" we have no way to understand the intervening twenty-five hundred years, not to mention the ways in which ideological discourses are constantly appropriated and redeployed. Rather, the recent rise of diasporic networks can only be understood in the context of a shifting history, shaped by the constant interaction of Chinese migrants, local histories, and global trends.

Ai, Chung Kun	鍾工宇
Alee, C. (Ching Lee)	程利
American Chinese Federation	中美聯合會
Bank-*fang gui*	房鬼
Bao'anju	保安局
Baohuanghui	保皇會
Baoshanghui	保商會
bendi	本地
Chankan, Ezequiel	陳群
Char, Tin-Yuke	謝廷玉
Chen Lanbin	陳蘭彬
Cheng Hop	正合
Chia, Aurelio Powshan	謝寶山
Chin F. Foin	陳宏勳
Chinese American Bank	中美銀行
Chinese-English Debating Society	中西擴論會
Ching You Hoong	程友雄
Chiqi	赤溪
Chongzheng Hui	崇正會
Chu Gem	趙錦
Chun Afong	陳芳
Chungwha Navigation Company	中華航運公司
danjia	蛋家
Duanfen	端芬
Enping	恩平
Fei Xiaotong	費孝通
fen gong	分工
Gangzhou Huiguan	岡州會館
gongsi	公司
Gongyan Bao	公言報
Goo Kim (Goo Kim Fui)	古金輝
Goo, Paul Kimm-Chow	古錦超

Gu Gangzhou Huiguan	古崗州會館
Guan, Liu, Zhang, Zhao	關劉張趙
Guandi	關帝
Guanyin	觀音
gui	鬼
Guo An (Ket On) Association	國安會館
Guomindang	國民黨
he ban	合伴
Hehe Huiguan	合和會館
heigui	黑鬼
Heshan	鶴山
Hip Sing Association	協勝會
Hongmen	洪門
Hop On Wing	合安榮
Hua County	花縣
Huamin School	華民學校
huaqi gui	花旗鬼
huaqiao	華僑
Huaqiao Shanghui	華僑商會
Huayang Xinbao	華洋新報
huiguan	會館
Hungtai	恆泰
jinshanzhuang	金山莊
jiuba gui	酒吧鬼
Jiuguo Bao	救國報
Jiuguohui	救國會
Jo San Jon	何壽康
Kaiping	開平
kejia (Hakka)	客家
kefei	客匪
King Joy Lo	瓊彩樓
Kong Fook	廣福
Kongfook, Guillermo	張志仁
Koo, Javier	古鏡福
kunzhong	昆仲
Lai, Kum Pui	賴金佩
Leung, Tom	譚張孝
Li Weiyang	李偉洋
Liancheng Gongsuo	聯成公所
Liang Guoying	梁國英

Liang Qitian	梁啟田
liangshan fenzi	良善分子
Liberty Bank	自由銀行
Lin Family Association	鄰德堂
Longgang Association	龍岡公所
Loo Sun	盧信
Manoa Lianyi Hui	萬那聯義會
Mau Family Association	毛氏同鄉會
Mazu	媽祖
Meihua Xinbao	美華新報
Minglun School	明倫學校
Minxing Bao	民醒報
minzhong tuanti	民眾團體
mounao	冇腦
Moy Dong Chew (Moy Tong Joy)	梅宗周
Moy, Frank	梅鴻起
Nanhai	南海
Ningyang Huiguan	寧陽會館
On Leong Merchants' Association	安良工商會
Panyu	番寓
Pearl River	珠江
Pow Lung	寶隆
Pow On	寶安
qian xin wan ku, bai zhe bu nao	千辛萬苦，百折不撓
Qiaosheng Bao	僑聲報
Renhe Huiguan	人和會館
Samsing	三盛公司
Sanyi	三邑
Shunde	順德
shuzi gui	薯子鬼
Siyi	四邑
Situ Meitang	司徒美堂
Sociedad de Beneficencia China	中華通惠總局
songxin gui	送信鬼
Taishan	台山
Tanxiang Shan	檀香山
Tiandihui	天地會
tong	堂
Tongmenghui	同盟會
Tongsheng Huiguan	同陞會館

Tongxing Gongsi	同興公司
Tyhune	黃帝桓
United Chinese Society	中華總會館
Waiguo Gongdang	外國工黨
waijiao	外交
Wanxing Gongsi	萬興公司
Wen Xiongfei	溫雄飛
Whu, Escudero	鄔子才
Wing On Chong	永安昌
Wong Aloiao	王羅有
Wong Leong	黃亮
Wu Tingfang	伍廷芳
Wuyi	五邑
xichai nao luan	西差撓亂
xiang you yin	香油銀
Xiangshan	香山
Xianzhengdang	憲政黨
Xinghua Bao	興華報
Xingzhonghui	興中會
Xinhui	新會
xinju	信局
Xinning	新寧
Xin Zhongguo Bao	新中國報
Xishan	西山
Yang Weibin	揚蔚彬
Yec Li (Li Chi)	益利
Yingyi She	英義社
Yixing (I Hing)	義興
yiguan	衣館
yinhao	銀號
Yiyi Tang	以義堂
yiyuan	議員
Yong Got	揚吉
Yongli Company	永利公司
Zhang Zuofan	張作藩
Zhaoluo	肇羅
Zheng Zaoru	鄭藻如
Zhigongtang (Chee Kung Tong)	致公堂
Zhigong Party	致公黨
Zhonggou Weixinhui	中國為新會

zhonghua huiguan	中華會館
Zhonghua Zongshanghui	中華總商會
Zhongshan	中山
zhusheng	竹升
Ziyou Xinbao	自由新報

BZTZ	Bilu Zhonghua Tonghui Zongju, ed., *Bilu Zhonghua Tonghui Zongju yu Bilu Huaren, 1886–1986.*
CAT	Causas Administrativas, Grau Regional Archives, Trujillo, Peru.
CCBA	Chinese Consolidated Benevolent Association.
CCCF	Chicago Chinese Case Files, Records of the Immigration and Naturalization Service, Record Group 85, National Archives, Great Lakes Region, Chicago, Illinois.
EBP	Ernest Burgess Papers, Regenstein Library Special Collections, University of Chicago.
HCCF	Hawaii Chinese Case Files, Records of the Immigration and Naturalization Service, Record Group 85, National Archives, Western Region, San Bruno, California.
HKE	Hong Kong entradas, 1900–1937, Archives of the Ministry of Foreign Relations, Lima.
HKS	Hong Kong salidas, 1900–1937, Archives of the Ministry of Foreign Relations, Lima.
INSC	Subject Correspondence, Records of the Immigration and Naturalization Service, Record Group 85, National Archives, Washington, DC.
LCE	Legación china entradas, 1900–1937, Archives of the Ministry of Foreign Relations, Lima.
LCS	Legación china salidas, 1900–1937, Archives of the Ministry of Foreign Relations, Lima.
MIP	Prefectural Records of the Ministry of the Interior, National Archives, Lima.
RCGI	*Annual Report of the Commissioner General of Immigration.*
SBC	Sociedad de Beneficencia China, Lima.
UCS	United Chinese Society, Honolulu.

CHAPTER ONE

1. "Lee K. K.," EBP, box 137, folder 6.

2. Siu 1987: 124.

3. Basch, Glick Schiller, and Sztanton Blanc 1994: 8 notes that contemporary migrants rarely describe their own experiences in terms of the transnational circuits that the authors use to understand them, but in terms of the nation-state.

4. S. Chan 1986: 369.

5. Huang Jianchun 1993: xi–xii (my translation).

6. S. Chan 1990, and 1991: 63–66, 96–67.

7. Anderson 1991; Okihiro 1994; Takaki 1989; Wong and Chan 1998. For comparable perspectives from Southeast Asia, see Suryadinata 1997.

8. Wang Gungwu 1981 discusses the implications of *huaqiao* history. Wang Gungwu 1998 and Yang 1995 offer suggestions about how to grow beyond this perspective. L. Wang 1995 also notes the competing claims of American and Chinese historiography, but argues that Asian American Studies is an alternative to these dominant paradigms.

9. Wang Gungwu 1996; Woon 1981.

10. S. Chan 1986: xx. A. Chan 1981 has argued that the sojourner is an orientalist construction with no basis in reality.

11. S. Chan 1986: xx; Glick 1980.

12. S. Chan, 1991: 35. Whitehead 1998 explicitly argues for the inclusion of Hawaii as part of the history of the American west.

13. Similarly, Mountz and Wright 1996, and Rouse 1991 argue for an understanding of contemporary Mexican migration in which the social space between geographically separate residences has collapsed. In the context of rural-urban migration in Peru, Altamirano 1980 and 1984 offer excellent critiques of analyses produced by development theory agendas that make a strict division between urban and rural society. He offers his own historical-structural approach that focuses on continued circulation. Chirot and Reid 1997, Hamilton 1996, Ong and Nonini 1997, Ownby and Heidhues 1993, Trocki 1990, and Tu 1991 situate Chinese migration in larger transregional and comparative contexts.

14. Wallerstein 1974–89. For an application of world-systems theory to the Pearl River Delta, see So 1986.

15. Sahlins 1988.

16. E. Wolf 1997: 6.

17. Along these lines, Grew 1993 outlines prospects for research in world history, Thomas 1991 develops the idea of "entanglement," and Wolfe 1997: 413 suggests that "Europe and its others were co-produced in and through their unequal interactions."

18. For example, see Bodnar 1985, Bonacich and Cheng 1984, and Wyman 1993. On the other hand, Thistlewaite 1964 makes a notable attempt at a global perspective on migration.

19. P. Siu 1987: 297.

20. P. Siu 1952: 42.

21. Ibid., 39.

22. Ibid., 42–43.

23. P. Siu 1987: 295

24. Ibid., 3.

25. Park 1914: 607. The continuing influence of these ideas can be seen in Takaki 1989: 18: "In their trans-Pacific odyssey, [Asian immigrants] 'crossed boundaries not delineated in space.' Their migration broke the 'cake of custom' and placed them within a new dynamic and transitional context, an ambiguous situation 'betwixt and between all fixed points of classification.' They reached a kind of geographical and cultural margin where old norms became detached, and they found themselves free for new associations and new enterprises. . . . Energies, pent up in the old country, were released, and they found themselves pursuing urges and doing things they had thought beyond their capabilities." See also Chan and Ong 1995: 525.

26. S. Chan 1998, McKeown forthcoming, and H. Yu 1998 describe how sociological constructs shaped the identities of Asian American academics in the early twentieth century.

27. Tilly 1990: 87–88.

28. Bhabha 1990; Cheah and Robbins 1998.

29. Behdad 1997 discusses these processes in the context of the United States.

30. Geyer and Bright 1995, Mazlish 1998, and Mazlish and Buultjens 1993 argue for global history as a framework from which to understand the unique processes of globalization that have occurred over the past two centuries. Foner 1997 critiques this assumption.

31. Castells 1996; Harvey 1989; Offe 1985.

32. Marx and Engels 1992: 22.

33. Appadurai 1996; Featherstone 1990; King 1997; Palumbo-Liu 1997; Robertson 1992. Ong 1999 argues that the gap between cultural and political economy approaches should be bridged, but still focuses predominantly on cultural themes.

34. Although terms such as *post-Fordism* and *disorganized capitalism* are common in cultural approaches, they refer primarily to cultural phenomena, with little grounding in economic shifts.

35. See the first incarnation of the journal *Diaspora*, vols. 1–4, 1991–95; Clifford 1994; Hall 1994; and Ong and Nonini 1997.

36. Baumann 1997, R. Cohen 1997, and Gilroy 1993: 205–12 are more sophisticated examples of using the Jewish experience as model.

37. R. Cohen 1997: 26; Safran 1991.

38. Stratton 1997 argues that the Jewish experience also needs to be interrogated and better historicized.

39. R. Hsu 1996; Kim and Lowe 1997; Koshy 1996.

40. Tan 1997: 28. See also Dirlik 1996 and Sau-ling Wong 1995.

41. Koshy 1996: 319.

42. See the more recent incarnation of *Diaspora,* vol. 5, 1996 onward, especially Tölölyan 1996 and Vertovec 1997. Also R. Cohen 1997 and McKeown 1999a.

43. B. Wong 1978 and the ensuing debate in Thompson 1979, Daniels 1983, and B. Wong 1985 illustrate the concepts of culture that shape comparative assimilation research.

44. Bourdieu 1990: 53. The concept of *bricolage* in Lévi-Strauss 1966 is also useful in describing how cultural structures are constructed by drawing relationships between whatever material is at hand.

45. Bourdieu 1990: 54, 60.

46. Benton 1996: 285.

47. Ibid., 288.

48. Bourdieu 1991a: 163.

49. Sahlins 1981 starts with a systemic view of culture of the kind criticized by Bourdieu, yet he is much more successful in conceptualizing intercultural encounters. His idea of the "structure of the conjunction" argues that local cosmologies extend to embrace the world, making a place for everything they may encounter but readjusting themselves in the process. However, this approach provides little place for the relevance of hybrid individuals and few means by which to conceptualize histories of global order.

50. Palumbo-Liu 1997: 13.

51. Bloch 1989 also criticizes Bourdieu with the argument that different ideologies can be incorporated in the same ritual. See McNeill 1998 and E. Wolf 1956 on the importance of mediators and the construction of common channels of communication.

52. Robertson 1992: 135.

53. Robertson 1992: 61.

54. Wallerstein 1990 develops this idea in a discussion of the contradictions within the idea of culture.

55. Many personal and contingent factors also shaped the choice of these three locations. I did my graduate studies in Chicago, which made it a convenient place to do research. This book first took form as a research paper for a seminar in American Immigration History. I later reworked that paper into a comparison between Chicago and Hawaii as part of a course with Marshall Sahlins on the history of Hawaii. Theoretical issues raised in that course have continued to shape this book. The choice to go to Peru was made much more consciously. I had wanted to do some work on the relatively unknown Chinese communities in Latin America and the Caribbean. After much preliminary research, Peru seemed to offer the best archival access and richest base of secondary material. That I also wanted to visit Peru was more than incidental in the decision to do research there. If I were to start over, however, I might choose northern Mexico, because the strong links between Chinese in Mexico and California would help support my focus on the importance of extra-local networks.

CHAPTER TWO

1. S. Chan 1986; Saxton 1995

2. Sayler 1995 offers the most comprehensive and accurate description and analysis of the exclusion laws.

3. McClain 1994: 219.

4. Sayler 1995: 65.

5. RCGI 1924: 30; 1925: 23–24; 1930: 29–30.

6. RCGI 1920: 48. Sayler 1995: 125 notes that as early as 1909 the bureau considered the Chinese to be a "disappearing problem." Such statements made up recurring cycles of bravado and frustration.

7. INSC 52600/48: "COMPILATION from the Records of the Bureau of Immigration of Facts Concerning the Enforcement of the Exclusion Laws," 88–97; M. Hsu 1996: 112–30; and RCGI 1916: xvii.

8. INSC 53560/225, memorandum to the Secretary of Commerce and Labor, 15 October 1913.

9. INSC 52600/48: "COMPILATION," 136–58; RCGI 1904: 139, 1907: 108, 1910: 149–50.

10. My own calculations, based only on claimants to native-born citizenship who made a trip to China, counts a minimum of six male children born to every Chinese woman residing in the United States before the fire.

11. RCGI 1907–24. See also McKeown 1999b.

12. W. Chen 1940: 453, and many poems in Hom 1987.

13. W. Chen 1940: 422.

14. Asian American Studies Library. Judy Yung Collection, "Immigration Inspector #3": HC 0413, box 1, file 49.

15. RCGI 1907–24.

16. T. Char 1975: 36–37, 54–55, Glick 1980 1–4.

17. Glick 1980: 7–12; Kuykendall 1963: 119, 136.

18. Chen Ta 1923: 115–18; Kuykendall 1963: 136–78; Lydon 1975.

19. Glick 1980 19–21, 29; Chinese Bureau 1896.

20. Glick 1938: 129; Governor of Hawaii 1903: 15–16; Reinecke 1979: 56.

21. RCGI 1907–24. Fraudulent Hawaiian birth certificates were often used for entry into the United States. In the years immediately prior to 1924, a scheme emerged whereby immigration officials in Honolulu would hold up a sign with the number 1,350 during the entry interview. This was the amount the migrant would have to pay if he wanted admission as a citizen. Officials who uncovered this ring claimed that many of these Chinese then made their way to the mainland. Transit statistics show 110 Chinese a year traveling steerage class from Hawaii to the mainland in 1923 and 1924, up from an average of less than 40 in most other years. See W. Chen 1940: 306–9; National Archives and Records Administration, Western Region, Files 1300–23000, 1302–4873, and File #18, "CONFIDENTIAL from District Intelligence Officer, 14th Naval District to Director of Naval Intelligence, 4/3/24," in binder labeled "Chinese Stuff"; and Governor of Hawaii 1915–24.

22. Glick 1980: 10.

23. Kuykendall 1963: 121–22, 140.

24. Similarly, when British Caribbean colonies in the nineteenth century paid a bounty of twenty dollars for each wife brought to the Caribbean, less than one in four male migrants were accompanied by women, whom they often deserted soon after arrival; see Look Lai 1993: 47–48, 97.

25. Glick 1980: 12, 238. Merry 2000 describes the impact of missionary-influenced family regulation and how it was supplanted over the second half of the nineteenth century by planter interest in the acquisition and regulation of labor.

26. General Superintendent of the Census 1897: tables 8 and 9.

27. RCGI 1907–24.

28. It is difficult to compare rates of alliance with local women in different locations because few were registered, and little concrete evidence is available. Although Hawaiian women were known for their readiness to intermarry, alliances with Indian and black women were probably equally common in nineteenth-century Peru. Although there were no antimiscegenation laws in Illinois and New York, intermarriages—mostly with Polish, Irish, and black women—were relatively infrequent. McKeown 1997: 232–38 shows that Chinese intermarriages in all three locations dropped significantly around 1900 and were more likely to involve Caucasian or part-Caucasian women. Adams 1929 argues that a mere handful of Hawaiian-Chinese intermarriages in the nineteenth century could account for the more than five thousand mixed Chinese-Hawaiians by the 1920s.

29. Millones Santagadea 1973: 64–66. Flores Galindo 1990: 57–68 notes that by the late eighteenth century, the Spanish word for Chinese, *chino,* was widely used in Peru to refer to the children of unions between blacks and Indians. This usage could possibly be traced to the Quechua word *china,* which literally meant a female animal but was also used to refer to a young woman in a somewhat lewd manner.

30. Rodríguez Pastor 1989a; Stewart 1951.

31. They also tried to bring Chinese from California; *El Peruano,* 22 April 1875; Stewart 1951: 210–14.

32. McKeown 1996: 70–72; Ruíz Zevallos 1993: 103–9.

33. Before 1911, senior Chinese diplomats were appointed to a jurisdiction that included the United States, Peru, and Spain (and Cuba, after independence in 1898). They usually resided in Washington DC, but Zheng Zaoru had visited Peru in 1886.

34. *Wu Zhiyong* 1909: 4, 8, 14, 28.

35. HKE 20 May 1915: 42; 19 July 1919: 55.

36. McKeown 1996: 63.

37. *Boletín de Relaciones Exteriores* 124 (1936): 80–82; LCE 6 July 1936; LCS 30 September 1936.

38. Fan 1926: 39–43; Wilson 1969: 61–66.

39. P. Siu, "9/2/38," EBP, box 137, file 6.

40. P. Siu 1987: 23–39; Wilson 1969.

41. *Chicago Record-Herald,* 19 December 1909: 5; *Chicago Tribune,* 20 July 1908: 1; 29 January 1911: 2.

42. Soong 1931: 10 counted 160 Chinese restaurants in Chicago in 1930.

43. Kagawa 1983; Leong 1936: 195–200; P. Siu 1987: chs. 15 and 16.

44. Gonzales 1989; LCE 13 September 1884; Rodríguez Pastor 1989a: 114–34.

45. BZTZ: 55–56, 86, 93–94; Hu 1988; Rodríguez Pastor 1989b.

46. BZTZ: 61.

47. Rodríguez Pastor 1989b: 98; Lausent 1983; Lausent-Herrera 1988.

48. De Trazegnies 1994: 483–84; Lausent-Herrera 1997; Rodríguez Pastor 1994: 31–32.

49. Glick 1938: 32, 1980: 18, 48, 66. A minority of the contracted laborers were brought in for domestic service.

50. Coulter and Chee 1937; Glick 1980: 50–64.

51. T. Char, 1977: 107; Glick 1980: 132–33

52. Glick 1980: 69–81, 113–14; Goo 1936; W. Smith 1937: ch. 6.

53. Lind 1938: 282–83; W. Smith 1937: 108.

54. C. S. Wing was one of the first Chinese to import canned goods from the United States and grow coffee in Hawaii, although he failed in his plan to import cigarettes from the Philippines. He was very critical of the intense competition, lack of cooperation and risk taking, and outmoded managerial practices of other Chinese (Zhang 1945).

CHAPTER THREE

1. Faure and Siu 1995; H. Siu 1989a.

2. P. Siu, "Controversy of Dialects among Chinese Immigrants," EBP, box 128, file 7.

3. M. Cohen 1996; Faure and Siu 1995: 13; Leong 1997.

4. Cushman 1993; Skinner 1957: 42–45, 64; Trocki 1997.

5. Figures for 1876–98 show 1,349,705 Chinese leaving from Hong Kong, 1,042,285 from Xiamen, and 359,458 from Shantou (Skeldon 1994: 24).

6. Faure 1989; Lin 1997.

7. Leong 1997: 42; Wakeman 1966: 98.

8. Ma 1984.

9. Woon 1984a: 299–300.

10. J. Mei 1979.

11. Lin 1997: 28, 162 and Marks 1998: 280 offer different estimates of population and cultivated land in Guangdong. Lin estimates that cultivated land in Guangdong remained steady at about 32 million *mu* over the eighteenth and early nineteenth centuries, while the population boomed. From the second half of the nineteenth century to the 1930s, however, cultivated land increased to 42 million *mu,* while the population remained stable. Marks, on the other hand, argues that cultivated land increased gradually at about a million *mu* a decade from 1713 to 1853 (37 million to 53 million) and then virtually stagnated until 1953. He also

argues that population increased by more than a million per decade from 1713 to 1933, with the exception of the two decades after 1853. That is, Marks presents a picture of steadily increasing ratios of man to land, although with no special fluctuations that could suggest a cause for emigration flows. Local rather than provincial statistics are necessary to determine more precisely the relationship between man-land ratios and emigration.

12. Wakeman 1966 is the classic description of mid-nineteenth-century unrest in the Pearl River Delta area but makes few references to emigration. In fact, the local militarization, increased feuding, and banditry could have occupied potential migrants rather than pushed them out.

13. Heidhues 1992; Trocki 1979; Wang Tai Peng 1994.

14. Hu-Dehart 1993; Look Lai 1993; Rodríguez Pastor 1989a.

15. Heidhues 1996; Jackson 1968; Trocki 1990.

16. Campbell 1923: 101–4; Glick 1980: 7; Li Jinming 1996; Stewart 1951: 18.

17. Campbell 1923: 1–8; Wang Sing-wu 1978: 304; Zo 1978: 38–39.

18. Richardson 1982: 78–90.

19. Bonacich and Cheng 1984.

20. Chen Ta 1923: 142–57; Richardson 1982.

21. Light, Bachu, and Karageoris 1993 offers an excellent discussion of network theory in sociology and argues that we need a better understanding of how migration networks actively shape local economic opportunities as well as take advantage of them. See also Tilly 1990.

22. Sinn 1995a: 16.

23. Campbell 1923: 1–33; Sinn 1995b: 37–38; Wang Sing-wu 1978: 101–17; Zo 1978: 95–104.

24. Kulp 1966: 184; P. Siu 1987: 107–12.

25. See also Chan Kwok Bun 1997. The attraction of migration as a family strategy does not necessarily mean it was a happy or easy one; it often created more distress than it resolved. See M. Hsu 1996: 141–75.

26. M. Cohen 1976: 48–82. For a case study, see Liu Haiming 1992.

27. Chong 1995 and See 1995 contain excellent examples of property investments in China.

28. Chen Ta 1940: 118–45; Pei 1994; P. Siu, "Some Types of Chinese Family in America," EBP, box 137, file 2.

29. HKE 25 March 1902: 25; 4 December 1908: 96; 12 October 1917: 37a; 29 July 1918: 53/2; 30 November 1918: 70; 31 January 1934: 12; *Juventud* (September 1916): 11. By the 1930s, Mexican wives were more often found in similar situations, perhaps as a result of the expulsion of Chinese from northern Mexico in 1931.

30. Adams 1937: 147.

31. Stockard 1989; Topley 1978.

32. LCE 3 April 1909; *Boletín de Relaciones Exteriores* 32 (1909): 61–63.

33. M. Freedman 1957: 99.

34. Ching 1981: 87–89; V. Lai 1985: 149; Lum 1991: 18–19.

35. Glick 1980: 179.

36. Chen Ta 1940 is a comparison of two such villages.

37. Skinner 1976; Woon 1984b. Cole 1986 describes a county specializing in the production of officials, Mann 1974 describes Ningbo bankers, and J. Watson 1975 describes a Hong Kong village specializing in restaurants in Britain.

38. Culin 1970a: 199.

39. Siu Jang Leung 1991: 13; R. Yu 1992: 28.

40. P. Siu, 1987: 90–96.

41. CCCF 2028/68, 2028/69.

42. CCCF 332–33. The citation is a composite of interviews with the manager and the cook.

43. Herbert Wang interview, Race Relations Survey, box 22, file 24, Hoover Institute Archives.

44. Quoted in W. Smith 1937: 269.

45. M. Hsu 1996: 59–72; Liu Zuoren 1959; Sinn 1995b: 38–46; Xia 1992: 14–52.

46. INSC 52730/84, file 7, Report dated 28 February 1899: 5; Chinese Coaching Material (Densmore Investigation) 54185/138, File #21, "MEMORANDA— Confidential Information Furnished by a Chinese" National Archives, Western Region, Records of the Immigration and Naturalization Service; Situ n.d.: 76; Senate Commission on Immigration 1902: 472–88; Wu Yangcheng 1959: 80–90.

47. McKeown 1996: 77.

48. Liu Zuoren 1959; Sinn 1995b 43–45; Zo 1978: 95–104.

49. Lee 1936; Leong 1936: 61, 176–78; P. Siu, "Greater Half of the Population in Chinatown," EBP, box 136, file 8; Wu Yangcheng 1959: 24–25.

50. Armentrout-Ma 1983: 118; H. Lai 1987.

51. Crissman 1967.

52. Sinn 1999: 68 similarly argues that such associations "served as nerve centres for communication with [fellow-natives] everywhere." Altamirano 1980 and 1984 critique the dichotomous depictions of migrant associations in scholarship on regional rural-urban migration.

53. Liu Hong 1999; Sinn 1999; Xia 1992: 165–208.

54. EBP, box 128, files 6 and 7; box 137, file 5. This correspondence was translated from Chinese by Paul Siu. I have made a few minor grammatical changes where the meaning was unclear. Several of the letters are included in P. Siu 1987: 79–81, 187–92. Hsiao is the Mandarin pronunciation of Siu, and I think that the younger brother, Teh-him, was Paul Siu's father.

55. Ibid., box 128, file 6: 73.

56. Ibid., 80.

57. Ibid., 96. The kidnapping was added as a postscript and never mentioned again.

58. Ibid., 98.

59. Ibid., 120.

60. Ibid., 122.

61. Ibid., file 7: 28.

62. Ibid., box 137, file 5: 157.

63. Ibid., box 128, file 7: 47. I think this nephew was quite likely Paul Siu himself.

64. Ibid., box 137, file 5: 131–32.

65. Ibid., 153.

66. Ibid., 185.

67. Ibid., 171.

68. Ibid., 174–75.

69. Ibid., 184.

70. Ibid., box 128, file 7: 30–32.

71. Ibid., box 137, file 5: 187.

72. C. Chang 1956: 43–44; Lind 1958; Look Lai 1993: 49.

73. Lyman 1977.

74. Sinn 1999: 83 writes of interlocking "mini-diasporas."

75. Duara 1997a; Godley 1982; Huang Jianchun 1993; Ma 1990.

76. Ren 1996: 68.

77. Ma 1990: 110–11.

78. Williams 1960: 57; see also Coppel 1981 and Salmon 1996. Most of these reformers were unable to read the Chinese sources and had to depend on the anthropological work of de Groot.

79. Tan 1988: 54; see also Williams 1960: 50.

80. Bergere 1998: 90–192; Ma 1990; Rhoads 1975: 200–240.

81. Glick 1980: 310; see also B. Wong 1988.

82. Ma 1990: 47–48.

83. Duara 1997a: 55–56; Ma 1990: 85; Rhoads 1975: 47–49.

84. Duara 1997b.

85. Godley 1982; Huang Jianchun 1993: 140–48.

86. Quoted in Williams 1960: 129.

87. H. Lai 1991; Xia 1992: 249–50; R. Yu 1992: 142.

88. Chung 1999; P. Siu 1987: 224–26; Wilson 1969: 92.

89. Douw 1999: 33–34; Goodman 1995; Hamilton 1977; Murray 1993.

90. Chongzhenghui of Hawaii 1958: 68–72; Constable 1994: 32; S. Leong 1997: 87–88. Some surname associations tried to emulate this model in the 1950s.

91. Liu Hong 1998 and 1999.

92. Huang Sande 1936; Situ n.d.

93. Leong 1936: 108–11; Xie 1984: 26–29. A crude but efficient example is a University of Chicago graduate student from North China who visited the local Chinatown in the 1930s, only to have a Cantonese shopkeeper mistake him for Japanese when he could not understand his Mandarin, and throw him out of the store. As a result of this experience, the student added a paragraph to his sociology term paper criticizing the stupidity and uncivilized nature of the Cantonese (Ifu Chen, "Chinatown of Chicago," EBP, box 128, file 8: 49).

94. Dong and Hom 1980: 19–20; see also Hom 1984, 1987; Leong 1936: 183; Wu Yangcheng 1959: 28–29.

95. Mitchell 1997; Ong 1999: 74–81.

96. Skinner 1996; Tan 1988.

97. Kotkin 1992; Lever-Tracy, Ip, and Tracy 1996.

98. Chen Ta 1940 presents some of the data used here, but F. Hsu 1945 provides an interpretation of that data which is more similar to mine. See also Chong 1995: 86; Kulp 1966: 277; P. Siu 1987: 104–6.

99. M. Freedman 1957: 165–76.

CHAPTER FOUR

1. See Duara 1988a on the idea of a cultural nexus.

2. Hucker 1975: 156.

3. Marks 1998; Mazumdar 1998.

4. Freedman 1994; Goodman 1995: 107; Wakeman 1966: 56–57.

5. J. Watson 1991.

6. Fairbank 1968 describes this version of the imperial world order. Quotations are from a memorial to the emperor by an official who negotiated the first Sino-American treaty in 1844 (Arkush and Lee 1989: 15–16). In contrast, some Manchu emperors talked of the Han as just one of five peoples with equal status in the empire. The others were Manchu, Mongolian, Tibetan, and Turkic; see Millward 1998: 197–202.

7. Ng Chin-keong 1983 is a good account of the relationship between officials and overseas trade in Fujian.

8. Hevia 1996 is a good discussion of the Qing guest ritual for the reception of foreign embassies.

9. Freedman 1958 and 1966 are standard works for understanding the lineages of South China. Unfortunately many scholars built upon his work not by following the leads he laid out toward understanding other social forms in China, but by placing the lineage and kinship firmly on center stage as the core expression of Chinese culture. Both Freedman and his followers tended to consider urban and overseas Chinese social organization as decayed or secondary forms of Chinese culture. Exceptions include Watson 1982, who takes overseas and urban organizations into account in an attempt to place Freedman's classifications of lineages on a continuum ranging from segmented lineages to clans and surname groups formed around more mythical ancestors. Sangren 1984b offered a more explicit critique, writing, "Taking descent and 'kinship' as the relevant cultural principles and the Chinese lineage as their ideal expression constitutes an impoverished model of a cultural system clearly capable of generating a much greater range of creative organizational responses to changing historical and environmental circumstances" (411).

10. A. Chun 1992; Hayes 1985.

11. Chow 1994; Ebrey 1991.

12. Mazumdar 1998: 195–250.

13. Faure 1986, 1990.

14. H. Siu 1990.

15. Wakeman 1975: 4.

16. Lamley 1990.

17. On local militia, see Kuhn 1970. On delegation of commercial regulation, see Mann 1987 and Goodman 1995: ch. 4. On encouragement to settle disputes out of court, see Reed 1995. On delegation during the Republic, see Kuhn 1975.

18. Zelin 1990.

19. Watson 1975.

20. Faure 1995.

21. H. Siu 1989a, 1995.

22. Potter 1968; R. Watson 1985. Woon 1984a also points out that in the early years of overseas migration, migrant wealth often came into conflict with the established elite, but their interests increasingly coincided as the lineage commercialized.

23. Cushman 1991 describes the Khaws of Thailand, a relatively successful overseas lineage.

24. Johnson 1993: 131–32; Woon 1991.

25. M. Cohen 1993 and Fried 1966 discuss how membership as "kin" in clans in urban Taiwan is attained through contracts and shareholding, and how such groups are involved in profitable concerns like the acquisition of real estate, the sale of spots for ancestral tablets on the association altar, positioning themselves as mediators with the government, and acting as electoral constituencies in democratic politics.

26. Goodman 1995: ch. 1; K. Liu 1988; Ma 1984.

27. Kulp 1966: ch. 7.

28. Ownby 1996.

29. Culin 1970b: 4. Initiation rites continued through the 1930s and on into the 1980s in New York and Chicago. See Bresler 1980: 76; Gong and Grant 1930: 274; and President's Commission 1984: 447.

30. See Bourdieu 1991b and Gambetta 1993 for discussions of initiation rites and the value of a menacing reputation as economic and social capital.

31. Lyman, Willmott, and Ho 1977: 97–98.

32. CCCF 2028/34 (my translation).

33. Habeas Corpus case 9, District Court of Hawaii, Records of the District Court of the United States, Record Group 21, National Archives, Western Region (translation by court interpreter).

34. Wang Tai Peng 1994: 26–35 shows that the word *gongsi* was used as a title for the captain on Fujianese merchant ships financed through profit-sharing schemes.

35. Barnett 1960: 40–46; Huang, Zhang, and Wang 1981: 318–19; P. Siu 1987: 77–96, 212–21.

36. BZTZ, 47 (my translation). See also Lausent-Herrera 1997: 132–33.

37. Ma 1990: 55–56. The English-language version puts more stress on the goals of working for a strong nation.

38. Hamilton 1977. Goodman 1995 offers an analysis of Shanghai *huiguan* in this vein, and Trocki 1990 discusses Singapore.

39. Armentrout-Ma 1983.

40. Quoted in R. Smith 1990: 288.

41. M. Freedman 1957: 204–9; Kuah 1999: 148; Weller 1994: 6–19.

42. J. Watson 1985, 1988a, 1993.

43. Cohen 1988; Jordan 1972: 37.

44. Douglas 1982 highlights the importance of ritual in the modern West.

45. Feuchtwang 1992; Gates 1996; Sangren 1987; Shahar and Weller 1996; Szonyi 1997; and Weller 1987 and 1994 shape much of the following discussion.

46. Ahern 1980; A. Wolf 1978.

47. Ahern 1980 argues this most forcefully.

48. Sangren 1984a.

49. Weller 1987: 97.

50. Gates 1996: 158–62.

51. Culin 1970a: 194; see also Elliot 1955: 113–14.

52. Tobias 1977.

53. Skinner 1957, 1968.

54. Chan and Tong 1993; articles in *Southeast Asian Journal of Social Science* 23, no. 1 (1995).

55. Quoted in C. Wu 1928: 4. I have chosen to translate *gui* as "ghost" because I would like to avoid any associations with Western concepts of good and evil that the terms "devil" and "demon" might suggest.

56. P. Siu, "The Language of the Chinese Immigrant," EBP, box 128, file 7: 6. Recent Chinese immigrants in Chicago have used the term *ghost* in my presence only when referring to black people *(heigui)*.

57. A. Wolf 1978: 174.

58. Quoted in Arkush and Lee 1989: 16. See Wakeman 1966: 55–57, 76 for more about the libidinous appetites, animal demeanor, and strange foods of Westerners.

59. Weller 1987: 74–85.

60. A. Wolf 1978: 179. There is some discrepancy as to what kind of food is appropriate for ghosts. Feuchtwang 1992: 42, Thompson 1988: 78, and Wolf say unprepared snack food is most appropriate for ghosts. Jordan 1972: 35 and Weller 1987: 67 have ghosts eating fully prepared meals. This may be local variation, or it may vary with the kind of ghost being worshiped—orphaned souls getting snacks or soldiers getting a full meal.

61. Culin 1970a: 194–95.

62. Quoted in Minnick 1988: 101. Chinese laundrymen in Chicago in the 1930s gave Christmas gifts to their best customers, who often learned to bargain for better gifts. P. Siu 1987: 152–53, and "How the Laundryman Reacts for Christmas," EBP, box 128, file 7.

63. Thompson 1988 and J. Watson 1988b argue that offerings to ancestors are intended to create a state of pure, luminous maleness *(yang)* as a symbolic attempt to perpetuate descent without the impure necessity of sexual reproduction and affines brought in from outside.

64. Gates 1996: 166; Shahar and Weller 1996: 10–11.

65. Feuchtwang 1992: 41–57.

66. Harrell 1974; Jordan 1972: 164–67; Yu Kuang-hong 1990.

67. For post-imperial Taiwan, see Feuchtwang 1974; Wang Shih-ch'ing 1974; Weller 1987. On post-1970s mainland, see H. Siu 1989b and Kuah 1999.

68. Duara 1988b: 792, writes, "The bleak record of republican regimes in rural areas has a good deal to do with their inability to create a viable alternative to the Guandi myth to serve as a symbolic framework of identification and communication between state and peasant." See also Pomeranz 1991.

69. Bloch 1989: 128–33.

70. The altar at the Hakka association in Lima is still widely used today for personal divination. I know of no public temples that existed in Chicago, although at least two associational altars were open to the public in the 1920s (Fan 1926: 131–32; C. Wu 1928: 176). In Hawaii, rural temples seem to have been widespread at the turn of the century. Temples in Honolulu increased from three before the fire of 1900 to five in the 1930s, but the caretakers complained that their income was low because people worshiped at home (Sau Chun Wong 1937).

71. Fan 1926: 84–94; Glick 1980: 170–72, 181–84; Wong and Wong 1936.

72. P. Siu, "The Clan Organization of the Chinese Immigrant," EBP, box 136, file 8: 8.

73. Gates 1996: 176.

74. Goodman 1995: 90–97.

CHAPTER FIVE

1. *El Comercio,* 23 August 1909: 1.

2. BZTZ: 47, 55; De Trazegnies 1994, 1: 326–29, 389–94; and Beneficencia China to J. M. Pacheco, Oficina General Central de Matriculación de Asiáticos, 22 January 1884, in Biblioteca Nacional, Lima.

3. East Asian Library, Tom Leung Correspondence: 527.

4. BZTZ: 86, 219–29; Ho 1967: 55.

5. BZTZ: 249.

6. BZTZ: 93–94; *El Comercio,* 10 October 1921: 8; Rodríguez Pastor 1989b.

7. *Oriental* November 1934: 9, and June 1935: 15–16.

8. Bonilla 1980; De Trazegnies 1994, 1: 611; Lausent-Herrera 1997: 132–33; Rodríguez Pastor 1989a: 232, 1995: 413.

9. Lausent 1983; Lausent-Herrera 1992: 995.

10. Cotler 1978: 179. See also Camino Calderón 1945: 35–36; *El Comercio,* 2 January 1868, and 28 July 1939: 3.

11. Oliart 1995.

12. Caceres 1924: 181–82 (my translation).

13. Parker 1998: 160–61.

14. Nugent 1997.

15. Burga and Flores Galindo 1980.

16. H. Chang 1994; Rodríguez Pastor 1994: 17.

17. HKE 25 August 1903: 25; 7 September 1903: 33; 1 March 1906: special note.

18. HKE 19 August 1904: 56.

19. *El Comercio,* 20 October 1904.

20. HKE 3 February 1905: 9; 26 April 1905: 29; *El Comercio* 14 July 1910: 2.

21. HKE 9 February 1908: 7.

22. *El Comercio,* 12 June 1909, 16 June 1909, and 14 July 1910: 2.

23. HKE 7 August 1914: 70; 20 May 1915: 42, 15 April 1925: 12, and HKS 8 October 1917: 41.

24. HKE 8 August 1915: 59.

25. HKE 14 November 1919: 54.

26. HKE 2 August 1917; 37.

27. HKE 17 June 1919: confidential from Chilean consul to Peruvian consul.

28. MIP leg. 175: Julio Suarez y César Ormeño to Ministro de RREE, 5 July 1915, leg. 229: RREE, 20 February 1922; HKE 10 January 1916: 3; 3 May 1923: 10.

29. Parker 1998: 158.

30. *El Comercio,* 21 October 1904: 1.

31. Basadre 1969, 7: 3456; *El Comercio,* 27 October 1904: 3.

32. HKE 21 April 1905: 28.

33. *El Comercio,* 7 June 1905: 3; 11 June 1905: 1.

34. HKE 4 August 1907: 21.

35. HKE 9 February 1908: 2.

36. LCE 28 October 1908: 83.

37. Blanchard 1982: 34. The full text is in *La Prensa,* 16 June 1906: 2. See also Parker 1998.

38. LCE 21 November 1907.

39. Basadre 1969, 8: 3744; Rodríguez Pastor 1989b: 112.

40. *Variedades,* 24 April 1909.

41. Quoted in Ruíz Zevallos 1993: 134.

42. *El Comercio,* 4 December 1913: 2; HKE 15 December 1913: 92.

43. *El Comercio,* 6 December 1913: 2.

44. *Boletín de Relaciones Exteriores* 32 (1909): 75–79; *El Comercio,* 10 May 1909: 1; MIP leg. 125: Informe del Intendente de Policía al Prefecto, 10 May 1909.

45. Ruíz Zevallos 1993: 102–22.

46. *El Comercio,* 11 May 1909: 1.

47. *Boletín de Relaciones Exteriores* 33 (1909): 90–91.

48. Blanchard 1979.

49. *El Comercio,* 12 May 1909: 1. For descriptions of the Callejón Otaiza, see Parker 1998: 165–66; Ruíz Zevallos 1993: 111; Rodríguez Pastor 1995: 416–27.

50. *El Comercio,* 13 May 1909; *Variedades* 15 May 1909: 56.

51. Ruíz Zevallos 1993: 112.

52. LCE 8 July 1909, 23 September 1910, 20 December 1911.

53. *El Comercio,* 10 May 1909: 1.

54. MIP leg. 112: La Libertad: Circular del Ministro de Gobierno a los Prefectos.

55. de la Cadena 1998; Marcone 1995; Thurner 1995.

56. *El Comercio,* 30 April 1909.

57. MIP leg. 183: Informe de Asistencia Pública al Prefecto de Lima 12 May 1916.

58. *La Prensa,* 17 February 1918.   60. CAT 2461, 2481.

59. Gonzales Prada 1941.   61. CAT 2481.

62. LCE 27 June 1909: 25a, 9 September 1909: 37a. Municipal harassment of the pawn shops had started in 1895. See MIP leg. 126: La Libertad: "Expediente iniciado por los Prestamistas de Trujillo, Ly Ging Y Cía y Yec Chong y Cía"; leg. 133: La Libertad: "Expediente iniciado por la Junta Departamental de La Libertad sobre nulidad del remate de prendas."

63. MIP leg. 139: La Libertad: "Expediente seguido por la Inspección de Higiene."

64. BZTZ: 230–48.

65. CAT 2487.

66. MIP leg. 122: Aseng to Prefectura, 31 December 1908; leg. 125: Aseng y Cía to Prefectura 15 March 1909, Jo Lay to Prefectura, 26 March 1909; leg. 130: various letters from Aseng and others to Prefectura, Arturo Castillo et al. to Perfectura, 30 March 1909 and 29 October 1909, Jo Lay to Prefectura, 9 June 1909.

67. MIP leg. 130: Aseng y Cía to Prefectura, 10 February 1909.

68. MIP leg. 130: Aseng to Prefectura, 18 February 1909; leg. 133: La Libertad: "Expediente de Hap Lee y Co. sobre licencia" and "Expediente de Aseng y Cía pidiéndose cancele a Sen Lee y Co."

69. MIP leg. 165: Yec Li y Cía to Prefectura, 10 January 1914; leg. 173: petitions from Cho Chen and others.

70. Ten tolerance houses and eight inns, which are probably different classes of brothel, were also licensed to non-Chinese. MIP leg. 183: Memorandum to Prefectura, 20 November 1916 and report from Policía to Prefecto, 14 May 1916; leg. 188: letters from Juan Carrillos Fan Kee to Prefectura and Humberto Jo to Prefectura, 27 December 1916; leg. 189: Humberto Jo to Prefectura, 23 December 1916; leg. 201: informe sobre licensias especiales del Policía, 19 October 1918.

71. Quoted in Marcone 1995: 73.

72. For overviews of the Oncenio, see Cotler 1978: ch. 3; Nugent 1997: 176–78.

73. *El Comercio,* 11 June 1905; Morimoto 1979: 20.

74. *Wu Zhiyong* 1909: 11.

75. HKE 10 October 1919: 50.

76. Attempts to institute a system of fingerprints were successfully resisted by the Chinese legation, HKE 23 December 1919: 12.

77. Basadre 1969, 9: 4239.

78. HKE 14 November 1919: 55; 23 December 1919: 59; 5 March 1922: 25; HKS January 1922.

79. HKE 18 June 1921: 50; *Variedades,* 24 September 1921: 1428–29.

80. Basadre 1969, 8: 3933–34; Blanchard 1982: 166; *Boletín de Relaciones*

Exteriores 62 (1919): 57–58. According to Gao 1956: 22, the reparations were used by the Chinese as a scholarship fund for deserving students of any race.

81. Blanchard 1982: 109. *El Comercio,* 20 June 1922, reproduces a petition from the Anti-Asian Patriotic League to the Ministry of Foreign Relations, and the issue for 22 November 1922 reproduces one from the International Society of Businessmen to the House of Deputies.

82. LCE 7 July 1922.

83. HKE 16 September 1922: 88.

84. *Boletín de Relaciones Exteriores* 69–70 (1922): 28–35; *Diario de los Debates del Congreso* 1922: 1011–12.

85. LCE 1 December 1922, 15 May 1923.

86. HKE 7 June 1924: 28; 31 August 1924: 44; LCE 21 March 1924, 26 September 1924, 8 August 1925.

87. Basadre 1969, 9: 4219–24, 4243.

88. *El Comercio,* 25 November 1922: 2.

89. *El Tiempo,* 1 January 1923.

90. Colonia China 1924: 21.

91. Ibid., 13.

92. Ibid., 28–29. Lausent-Herrera 1997: 139 argues that the reorganization of the SBC was linked to political issues. This was probably true, although I disagree with her assertion that it was linked to the reorganization of the Guomindang, which did not take place for another three years, in 1927.

93. Ibid., 69. Despite these claims, the paper, under Aurelio Powsan Chia's influence, maintained strong ties to the Zhigongtang and firm political opposition to the *Minxingbao (Awaken the People News)* run by followers of Sun Yat-sen (BZTZ: 252).

94. Mayer de Zulen 1924: 36. Her changed attitudes toward the Chinese may have been a result of her love affair with Pedro Zulen, the half-Chinese president of the Pro-Indigenist Society.

95. Ibid., 7–8. See also *Oriental,* November 1943: 30.

96. Colonia China 1924: 23–25. See also Basadre 1969, 8: 3984; BZTZ: 57–58, 272; Gao 1956: 20–22; LCS 21 July 1926.

97. *Variedades,* 15 October 1921: 1630.

98. *West Coast Leader,* 22 December 1925: 10–11.

99. *South China Morning Post,* 25 April 1923, 8 August 1924. Clippings found in HKE 7 June 1923: 13.

100. LCE 8 August 1925, 27 August 25.

101. LCE 7 September 1925, 22 September 1925.

102. LCE 5 October 1925.

103. HKE 14 November 1926: 49; LCE 11 December 1926.

104. HKE 27 November 1930: note from ex-consul Llosa.

105. Quoted in Stern 1980: 85. Nugent 1997 describes the rise of Sánchez Cerro as the victory of popular sovereignty over aristocratic sovereignty and asserts that Leguian modernization and attacks on local powerholders had paved the way.

106. Morimoto 1979: 57.

107. Gao 1956: 16–18.

108. There is some confusion about the dates of these statues. BZTZ: 58 says they were presented for the four hundredth anniversary of Lima, but gives the date as 1925, ten years too early. Ho 1967: 13 says they were presented in honor of the founding of Lima but does not give a date. Gao 1956: 20–22 also avoids giving a clear date, just grouping them in with the 1924 fountain as part of the independence celebrations. I saw an old photograph of the llama statue in a Lima shop that was dated 1928, before the anniversary of Lima. I have stuck with the 1935 date, however, because the style of the sculptures is much more appropriate to the populist 1930s than to neoclassical Leguian Lima.

109. BZTZ: 42.

110. B. Wong 1978: 345.

CHAPTER SIX

1. *Chicago Tribune,* 7 June 1908: 4.

2. Barth 1964; S. Chan 1986; Friday 1994. The relationship of the *huiguan* to migration is a topic of debate. McClain 1990 argues against the assertion by Cloud and Galenson 1987 and 1991 that the *huiguan* imported laborers. My interpretation is that they were organizations in the service of men who independently used credit to import laborers.

3. Herbert Wang interview, Race Relations Survey, box 22, file 9, Hoover Institute Archives.

4. The following narrative is taken from Armentrout-Ma 1983; Barth 1964; H. Lai 1987; Lyman 1986: 112–220; and Ma 1991.

5. Kagawa 1983: 163–75.

6. Light 1974.

7. Gong and Grant 1930; Lyman 1977; Situ n.d.: 80–85; C. Wu 1928: ch. 11.

8. Huang Sande 1936; Leong 1936: 72; Ma 1990: 25–29, 105–7. Sun Yat-sen helped rewrite the Zhigongtang charter in 1904, giving it three branches of government.

9. Gong and Grant 1930: 210–11; Ma 1990: 151.

10. Gong and Grant 1930: 132; Winifred Rauschenbush, quoted in Thrasher 1927: 211; Xie 1984: 23.

11. Leong 1936: 29–39; Wu Jianxiong 1993: 287–91; R. Yu 1992: 18.

12. Culin 1970b.

13. Armentrout-Ma 1983: 123; Bonner 1993: 130, 142.

14. Chicago Historical Society, Newcomb and Palmer, Local Community Research Committee, v. 4, doc. 11: 11.

15. Gong and Grant 1930: 29–31, 139–41.

16. Gong and Grant 1930: 157 says the On Leong was founded in 1903. Lyman 1986: 144 suggests 1899. Situ n.d.: 57 gives two dates, 1894 and 1905, associating them with branches in Boston and New York. He claims he was a founder, although Gong and Grant do not mention him.

17. Bresler 1980: 173; Leong 1936: 81; Thrasher 1927: 210; Wu Yangcheng 1959: 90–94. An exception is Situ n.d.: 57, who conflated all his enemies into one enormous reformer/reactionary/imperialist/Hip Sing complex: "I often carried two concealed handguns, ready to fight with any enemy who might ambush me. Reactionaries all fear death. When reformers, imperialist police, dog legs, and all kinds of bad eggs saw how ferocious we were, ready to face death, they were afraid to cause trouble, and Chinatown society reaped peace."

18. The Bing Kun Tong was the competitor of the Hip Sing in the Northwest, occasionally coordinating its activities with the On Leong. Several smaller tongs continued to exist in California.

19. Gong and Grant 1930: 188, 244.

20. Quoted in Gong and Grant 1930: 10, and C. Wu 1928: 221–22.

21. Gong and Grant 1930: 270–72. P. Siu, "Greater Half of the Population in Chinatown" EBP, box 136, file 8: 10, notes that most soldiers did not join surname associations.

22. Minutes of Hip Sing Association meetings, on microfilm at the Asian American Studies Library, University of California at Berkeley.

23. Peterson 1952: 130.

24. *Chicago Record-Herald,* 2 September 1910: 5.

25. *Chicago Tribune,* 20 June 1909: 1; 28 June 1909: 3.

26. Quoted in Mumford 1997: 58.

27. Philpott 1991 gives a good panorama of Chicago reform discourse and its isolation of blacks through neglect.

28. "Where Orient and Occident Meet," *Graphic,* 17 February 1894.

29. *Chicago Tribune,* 9 April 1911: 3.

30. Asbury 1950: 130–46, 167, 243; Lindberg 1996: 108–17.

31. *Chicago Tribune,* 7 September 1926.

32. Asbury 1950: 277; Peterson 1952: 60–61; Wendt and Kogan 1943.

33. Quoted in Griffin 1977: 113.

34. Wendt and Kogan 1943: 246.

35. Landesco 1928: 32; Lindberg 1996: 126.

36. Asbury 1950: 165; Landesco 1928: 54; Lindberg 1996: 121.

37. Hostetter and Beesley 1929: 46–48; Landesco 1928: 152–56.

38. Fan 1926: 23–24.

39. Fan 1926: 23–27; C. Wu 1928: 152–54, "Where Orient and Occident Meet," *Graphic,* 17 February 1894.

40. *Chicago Tribune,* 16 April 1893: 5.

41. *Chicago Record-Herald,* 20 August 1912: 9.

42. For biographies of Wong, see Bonner 1993 and Q. Zhang 1998.

43. Quoted in Q. Zhang 1998: 55.

44. *Chicago Tribune,* 17 February 1881: 8; 18 February 1881: 8.

45. *Chinese American (Huayang Xinbao),* 14 June 1893. A copy of this and of

Wong's *Chinese News (Meihua Xinbao)*, 11 November 1896, are in the Chicago Historical Association.

46. CCCF 463, Telegram to Pembina, North Dakota, 15 January 1901. The telegram stated, "Moy Tong Te is well known to me, and I know him to be a legitimate Chinese merchant and member of the Hip Lung Company, and am satisfied he is entitled to readmission to the United States. I send this by wire because his friends are anxious for his immediate return to Chicago."

47. R. Yu 1983: 61.

48. CCCF 2/237, 2005/2770; INSC 52730/84.

49. INSC 52202/1; RCGI 1914.

50. Y. Liang 1951: 18.

51. CCCF 440; National Archives and Records Administration, Chicago Chinese Correspondence Files, 11/36; P. Siu, "A Case of Assimilation" EBP, box 136, file 7.

52. *Chicago Daily News*, 10 October 1907: 2 reports a Hip Sing member claiming his tong was founded in 1905, although Gong and Grant 1930: 238 says it was 1900. For the On Leong, see *Chicago Daily News*, 8 October 1907: 2.

53. Story told by ex-Hip Sing officer in Gong and Grant 1930: 238–39.

54. *Chicago Record-Herald*, 15 June 1908: 11; Liang Qichao 1922: 143–46.

55. McKee 1986: 179.

56. Larson 1993: 183;; Mei Binlin 1979: 115; P. Siu, "A Case of Assimilation."

57. *Chicago Tribune*, 2 November 1907: 4.

58. East Asian Library, Tom Leung Correspondence: 138 Feng Jingquan to Tan Zhangxiao, 4 September 1907; 121 Kang Youwei to Zhang Xiao, November 1907; 128 Kang Youwei to Tan Zhangxiao and Ming San, 18 August 1908; 548 a statement of receipts and expenditures dated 1908.

59. *Chicago Tribune*, 18 May 1908: 1; 7 June 1908: 4; 15 June 1908: 5.

60. *Chicago Tribune*, 7 June 1908: 4.

61. *Chicago Record-Herald*, 9 October 1907: 9; *Chicago Tribune*, 6 August 1907: 3.

62. *Chicago Tribune*, 17 October 1907: 3.

63. On the events in Boston, see Rogers 1999 and K. Wong 1996.

64. *Chicago Record-Herald*, 9 October 1907: 2; *Chicago Tribune*, 8 October 1907: 2; 10 October 1907: 2.

65. *Chicago Tribune*, 17 October 1907: 3.

66. *Chicago Record-Herald*, 25 January 1908: 9, and indictments in Cook County Circuit Court, cases 86016 and 86401, Archives of the Circuit Court of Cook County, Chicago, Illinois.

67. *Chicago Record-Herald*, 16 July 1908: 4; *Chicago Tribune*, 14 June 1908: 1; Wendt and Kogan 1943: 297.

68. Buenker 1987: 33; Morton 1990: 234.

69. *Chicago Tribune*, 19 October 1907: 7.

70. Lindberg 1996: 37, 115; *Chicago Tribune*, 7 June 1908: 4; Senate Commission on Immigration 1902: 69–72.

71. *Chicago Record-Herald,* 15 May 1908: 9; 21 May 1908: 13; 1 June 1908: 1; *Chicago Tribune,* 21 May 1908: 5.

72. *Chicago Record-Herald,* 18 June 1908: 17; 31 July 1909: 9; *Chicago Tribune,* 14 June 1908: 1; 18 July 1908: 3.

73. *Chicago Record-Herald,* 18 June 1908: 1; 24 June 1908: 2.

74. CCCF 612, 660; *Chicago Tribune,* 15 June 1908: 5. A Chinese interviewed by the *Chicago Tribune,* 20 September 1931, was perhaps recalling the Chin Wai trail when he suggested that the On Leong had nearly extinguished the Hip Sing because it had "always been able to hire the best lawyers."

75. *Chicago Record-Herald,* 21 July 1908.

76. CCCF 2008/5. Gong and Grant 1930: 165 notes that the New York Hip Sing also worked with the district attorney to harass the On Leong men with gambling raids.

77. *Chicago Record-Herald,* 12 June 1911: 1; *Chicago Tribune,* 29 January 1911: 2; 30 August 1911: 1.

78. *Chicago Record-Herald,* 10 February 1912: 3; 2 August 1912: 7.

79. Ibid., 3 July 1912: 11.   81. Ibid., 10 February 1912: 3.

80. Ibid., 18 January 1911: 1.   82. CCCF 2008/5.

83. Gong and Grant 1930: 241; Chicago Historical Society, Newcomb and Palmer, vol. 4, doc. 12: 4.

84. Asian American Studies Library, Minutes of Hip Sing Association, 1931; Chicago Historical Society, Newcomb and Palmer, vol. 4, doc. 7: 2; Soong 1931: 8; *Chicago Tribune,* 24 September 1937; C. Wu 1928: 154.

85. Chicago Historical Society, Newcomb and Palmer, vol. 4, doc. 12: 4.

86. Fan 1926: 28. C. Wu 1928: 153 also uses this explanation but locates it in 1912. The only Chinese enterprises that I know of on Twenty-second Street in 1905 were a couple of laundries and Chinese brothels that catered to whites (Asbury 1950: 265). Huang, Zhang, and Wang 1981: 318 claims there was no real Chinatown in Chicago until the First World War.

87. Xie 1984: 17.

88. Chicago Historical Society, Newcomb and Palmer, vol. 4, doc. 7: 1.

89. Ibid., doc. 11: 6.

90. Fan 1926: 97; P. Siu, "Chinese Family in Chicago" EBP, box 138, file 8: 60.

91. Drury 1932: 14.

92. *San Min Chen Bao,* 24 September 1937: 1; *Chicago Tribune,* 24 September 1937.

93. See note 74; *Chicago Tribune,* 20 September 1931.

94. P. Siu, "The Clan Organization of the Chinese Immigrant," EBP, box 136, file 8: 16–19.

95. Chicago Historical Society, Newcomb and Palmer, vol. 4, doc. 11: 9.

96. Feng Ziyou 1965, 4: 173–74; Huang Sande 1936: 17; Ma 1990: 107–8, 139–43; Mei Binlin 1979. Some accounts have dated the establishment of the Tongmenghui to Sun's much more impressive 1911 visit, such as Fan 1926: 139, which claims about one hundred original members.

97. *Chicago Record-Herald*, 26 February 1912: 3. Whatever the average Chicago migrant felt about Sun's cause, the establishment of a Chinese republic was certainly a windfall for local barbers, as hundreds of Chinese went to cut off their queues.

98. Gong and Grant 1930: 239–52; *Chicago Tribune*, 21 October 1924: 1, and several other articles in October and November. C. Wu 1928: 217–19 says "Chen" left voluntarily rather than being expelled when "May" won the presidency.

99. Gong and Grant 1930: 241–43. Chicago Historical Society, Newcomb and Palmer, vol. 4, doc. 12: 4–6 says a Chamber of Commerce was established at Clark Street in an attempt to usurp some representational functions.

100. Similarly, attorney Charles Hille, who had previously worked with the Chins against the Moys and had supported the 1912 renegades in their gambling scheme, ended up cooperating with the Moys. In the 1920s, he was working for them on retainer in Texas to try to gain permanent admission for the Chinese brought across the border by General Pershing from Mexico after having provided logistical support for his unsuccessful pursuit of Pancho Villa. See Briscoe 1959.

101. U.S. Immigration Commission 1911, 2: 198–204.

102. Fan 1926: 110–21, 126–29.   104. Landesco 1928: 205.

103. Xie 1984: 15.   105. Fan 1926: 29, 133–35.

106. Ifu Chen, "Chinatown of Chicago," EBP, box 128, file 8: 52.

107. Chicago Historical Society, Newcomb and Palmer, vol. 4, doc. 11: 9.

108. Moy 1978: 67.

109. Fan 1926: 25. Xie 1984: 18 credits Ceng Aju with opening the King Joy Lo as the first chop suey restaurant in the United States.

110. Drury 1932: 14.

111. P. Siu, "Document No. 6, P. J.'s Family," EBP, box 136, file 7: 3; "Tour Topics" in the Chicago Historical Society.

112. Moye and Chin 1935: 25–26.

113. Conroy 1978; *Chicago Daily News*, 14 February 1974, 5 July 1974; *Chicago Tribune*, 5 December 1976: Metro section.

114. Conroy 1978; President's Commission 1984: 447–59; "Close-up with John Lyou," *Chicago Tribune*, 6 March 1977.

115. Quoted in Kinkead 1992: 73–74.

CHAPTER SEVEN

1. Coulter and Chun 1937: 42–43.

2. W. J. Char 1972; Cushing 1985.

3. Dye 1997: 55–61; Glick 1980: 329–30

4. Quoted in W. J. Char 1972: 34.

5. Ching 1981: 52; V. Lai 1985: 183–85

6. Quoted in Mellen 1958: 117.

7. Dye 1997: 143–50, 171–87.

8. Daws 1968: 245; Dye 1997: 207–16; Mellen 1958: 187.

9. Kai 1974: 63, 1976: 13.

10. Daws 1968: 281; Kuykendall 1963: 174–75.

11. Merry 2000.

12. Daws 1968: 251–52, 281–82.

13. Glick 1980: 216. I have made slight changes based on the Chinese version in *Chinese of Hawaii* 1929: Chinese section 6–7.

14. Ibid., 216–25.

15. Ai 1960: 171–73; *Chinese of Hawaii* 1929: second Chinese section, 80–81; Glick 1980: 92–94, 214; Mellen 1958: 228–36.

16. Quoted in Daws 1968: 251.

17. Glick 1980: 128–31.

18. On Hongmen, see T. Char 1975: 160, 169–71; Chock 1936; J. Chun 1983: 44–46; Glick 1980: 187–98, 291–92; Mark 1975: 24–26.

19. Ganschow 1992; Ma Chaojun 1963. In 1909, a young editor of the revolutionary *Liberty News* wanted to join a Hongmen and asked Sun for advice about how to judge the validity of their competing revolutionary claims. Sun discouraged him from joining altogether (Wen 1981: 237–38).

20. *Chinese of Hawaii* 1929: second Chinese section 32–33; Feng Huolong 1956; Zheng 1963.

21. On the UCS, see Dye 1997: 187; Glick 1938: 229–41, 1980: 203–7, 212; Kuykendall 1963: 138–39.

22. Chock 1936: 23–25; Glick 1980: 239–55.

23. Glick 1980: 321.

24. *Pacific Commercial Advertiser,* 22 November 1911.

25. Ma 1990: 93.

26. Ai 1960: 301–5; Glick 1980: 274–84.

27. HCCF 1055; Ma 1990: 101–2; Wen 1981: 238–39.

28. HCCF 22: Tseng Hai to Raymond Brown, 22 June 1906.

29. HCCF 480: Exhibit "A."

30. Glick 1980: 284–86; Wen 1981: 241–44.

31. Glick 1980: 281–82.   33. *Chinese in Hawaii* 1913: preface.

32. HCCF 3087.   34. Ibid., 5.

35. *Chinese in Hawaii* 1913: 12, 17; *Chinese of Hawaii* 1929: biography section 4; *Pacific Commercial Advertiser,* 11 December 1913: 9.

36. One of the more openly brutal moments of the editorial wars occurred in June 1912, when twelve female Tongmenghui members were outraged by an editorial Ching You Hoong had written in the *Huaxingbao* and marched to his office, tore off his shirt and collar, pinned him down on the floor, and beat him with fists and umbrellas (*Pacific Commercial Advertiser,* 15 June 1912).

37. HCCF 3377: testimony, 14. These comments were made in the context of the deportation hearing of Wu Tiecheng, a revolutionary propagandist (later mayor of Shanghai) accused of fomenting anarchy.

38. Ibid., 35.

39. Ai 1960: 341.

40. T. Char 1977: 110–11; Glick 1980: 288–91.

41. Adams 1933: 17–18; Fuchs 1983: 97. Fuchs informs the following discussion.

42. Fuchs 1983: 49.

43. Habeas Corpus Cases: 17, 29 March 1902, National Archives, Western Region.

44. Hawaii Habeas Corpus: 5, 7 November 1900.

45. Arrest and Deportation Warrant cases for Hawaii, 4280/140: agent Halsey to the Secretary of Labor, 13 May 1921, National Archives, Western Region.

46. United Chinese Society 1898: 5.

47. Ching 1981: 135–38 is a description of routine opium use. Li Ling Ai 1972 frequently returns to the theme of anti-opium movements and resistance against them. See also T. Char 1975: 101–10; Glick 1980: 227–31.

48. Ai 1960: 198.

49. Reinecke 1979. Copies of petitions are in INSC 51830/199A: petition from United Chinese Society to the Administrators of the Government of the United States of America dated June 1917; 52110/1: petition to the Secretary of Commerce and Labor dated 9 August 1907; United States Congress Committee on Immigration and Naturalization 1916 and 1918.

50. *Chinese in Hawaii* 1913: 7.

51. Ibid., 8.

52. Ibid., 3.

53. INSC 51830/199: "Chinese Information Committee NEWS BUREAU," 5 August 1908.

54. *New China News,* 12 August 1911, clippings in HCCF 2426. I have adapted translations provided by bureau interpreters.

55. *Liberty News,* 21 August 1911.

56. *New China News,* 22 August 1911.

57. Ing 1929.

58. Governor of Hawaii 1933: 6.

59. Zuckerman 1978: 62.

60. *Pan Pacific* 3 (1937): 53.

61. Chock 1936: 23; Chongzhenghui of Hawaii 1958: 67; Glick 1980: 256–57, 311–12.

62. Morrison 1977: 120.

63. Glick 1980: 258–60; Morrison 1977: 134; United Chinese Society 1985.

64. T. Char 1975: 227–30; Ching and Chong 1987. Many family histories presented themselves as continuations of these genealogies, although Chong-Gossard 1992: 45 notes that contemporary additions are different in that they include women, and the biographies read like work resumes.

65. Quoted in Glick 1980: 315.

66. Quoted in Zuckerman 1978: 69.

67. Glick 1938: 430–35.

68. T. Char 1977: 174–79.

69. Morrison 1977.

70. Glick 1942: 676; see also Adams 1937: 143–59, 318–19.

71. Quoted in Burrows 1937: 55–56.

72. Porteus 1926: 26. 74. Adams 1929: 10.

73. Ibid., 100. 75. Ibid., 12.

76. Ibid.

77. K. Lai 1936: 1. The idea of racial succession is best developed in Lind 1931.

78. Goo 1936: 7.

79. Mui 1937: 45.

80. Lind 1938: 11; see also W. Smith 1937: 119.

81. Burrows 1939; Fuchs 1983: 104–5.

82. Glick 1980: 90–91; Zhang 1945: 22–23, 84. Despite criticizing these practices, Zhang still hired many family members to run his businesses.

83. Lam 1936.

84. Lind 1938: 283.

85. W. Smith 1937: 248–49.

86. Quoted in W. Smith 1927: 25–26.

CHAPTER EIGHT

1. Kingston 1980: 14–15.

2. Kingston 1989: 308.

3. From the film *Year of the Dragon* (1985).

4. Quoted in Arkush and Lee 1989: 179–81.

5. Lewis and Wigen 1997. 7. Ibid., 181.

6. Arkush and Lee 1989: 174–75. 8. Ibid., 178.

9. Bonilla 1980 uses Chinese to underline disjunctions in Peruvian society. De Trazegnies 1994 uses them to show the virtues of a liberal legal system (he is currently the Minister of Foreign Relations in Peru). Fukumoto 1993 and Rodríguez Pastor 1990, 1993 focus on the Chinese contribution to a "creole" Peru; Rodríguez Pastor 1994 emphasizes the lower-class roots of that creole identity.

10. Sahlins 1993 discusses cosmologies that construct the "other."

11. See Ong and Nonini 1997 and several essays in Chirot and Reid 1997 that compare contemporary Chinese with Jewish liberal modernity in nineteenth-century Europe.

12. Haley, Tan, and Haley 1998; Kotkin 1992; Lever-Tracy, Ip, and Tracy 1996; Redding 1990. Each of these works makes reference to the past as a basis for these recent developments.

13. Pann 1990; see also Tu 1991. Ong 1999, however, describes these assertions of cultural unity as extensions of state hegemonies.

14. Douw, Huang, and Godley 1999; Hefner 1998; Ong and Nonini 1997.

ARCHIVAL SOURCES

Archives of the Circuit Court of Cook County, Chicago, Illinois
  Circuit Court Case Files

Archives of the Ministry of Foreign Relations, Lima, Peru
  Hong Kong entradas 1900–1937
  Hong Kong salidas 1900–1937
  Legación china entradas 1900–1937
  Legación china salidas 1900–1937

Asian American Studies Library, University of California, Berkeley
  Judy Yung Collection
  Minutes of Hip Sing Association meetings (microfilm)

Chicago Historical Society, Chicago, Illinois
  Chinese American, 14 June 1883
  Chinese News, 11 November 1896
  Newcomb, Charles, and Vivien Palmer. Documents prepared by the Local
      Community Research Committee for the Chicago Historical Society
  "Tour Topics," 8–14 January, 1939

East Asian Library, University of California, Los Angeles
  Tom Leung Correspondence

Grau Regional Archives, Trujillo, Peru
  Causas Administrativas
  Causas Civiles

Hoover Institute, Stanford University
  Race Relations Survey

National Archives and Records Administration, Great Lakes Region, Chicago, Illinois
  Records of the Immigration and Naturalization Service, Record Group 85,
      Chicago Chinese Case Files
  Records of the Immigration and Naturalization Service, Record Group 85,
      Chicago Chinese Correspondence Files
  Records of the Immigration and Naturalization Service, Record Group 85,
      Minneapolis Chinese Case Files

National Archives and Records Administration, Washington, DC
  Records of the Immigration and Naturalization Service, Record Group 85,
      Subject Correspondence

National Archives and Records Administration, Western Region, San Bruno, California
  Binders labeled "Chinese Stuff"

Habeas Corpus Cases, District Court of Hawaii, Records of the District Courts of the United States, Record Group 21, Series 20

Records of the Immigration and Naturalization Service, Record Group 85, Arrest and Deportation Warrant Case Files for Hawaii

Records of the Immigration and Naturalization Service, Record Group 85, Chinese Coaching Material (Densmore Investigation)

Records of the Immigration and Naturalization Service, Record Group 85, Hawaii Chinese Case Files

National Archives of Peru, Lima
Records of Ministerio de Interior, Prefecturales
Régistros de Extranjería
Régistros de Matrimonios

National Library of Peru, Lima
Letter from Beneficencia China to J. M. Pacheco, Oficina General Central de Matriculación de Asiáticos

Regenstein Library Special Collections, University of Chicago, Illinois
Ernest W. Burgess Papers
Chen, Ifu. "Chinatown of Chicago." Box 128, file 8.
Siu, Paul. "Chinese family in Chicago." Box 136, file 8.
———. "The Clan Organization of the Chinese Immigrant." Box 136, file 8.
———. "Controversy of Dialects among Chinese Immigrants." Box 128, file 7.
———. "Greater Half of the Population in Chinatown." Box 136, file 8.
———. "The Language of the Chinese Immigrant." Box 128, file 7.
———. "Organization of a Gambling House." Box 137, file 1.
Robert E. Park Papers

NEWSPAPERS AND PERIODICALS

Annual Report of the Commissioner General of Immigration (Washington DC: United States Department of Commerce and Labor, 1903–1911, and United States Department of Labor 1911–1932)

Boletín de Relaciones Exteriores (Minesterio de Relaciones Exteriores, Lima)

Chicago Daily News

Chicago Record-Herald

Chicago Tribune

Diario de los Debates del Congreso (Lima)

El Comercio (Lima)

Graphic (Chicago)

Juventud (Lima)

Oriental 東方月刊 (Lima)

Pacific Commercial Advertiser (Honolulu)

El Peruano (Lima)

La Prensa (Lima)

Pan Pacific (Honolulu)

San Min Chen Bao 三民晨報 (Chicago)
El Tiempo (Lima)
Variedades (Lima)
West Coast Leader (Lima)

BOOKS AND ARTICLES

Adams, Romanzo. 1929. "The Meaning of Chinese Experience in Hawaii." In *Chinese of Hawaii* 1929, 10–12.

———. 1933. *The Peoples of Hawaii.* Honolulu: Institute of Pacific Relations.

———. 1937. *Interracial Marriage in Hawaii.* New York: Macmillan.

Ahern, Emily. 1980. *Chinese Ritual and Politics.* Cambridge: Cambridge University Press.

Ai, Chung-Kun. 1960. *My Seventy-Nine Years in Hawaii.* Hong Kong: The Cosmorama Pictorial Publisher.

Altamirano, Teofilo. 1980. *El campesinado y la antropología urbana.* Lima: Pontificia Universidad Católica del Perú, Departamento de Ciencias Sociales.

———. 1984. *Presencia andina en Lima metropolitana.* Lima: Pontificia Universidad Católica del Perú, Fondo Editorial.

Anderson, Kay. 1991. *Vancouver's Chinatown: Racial Discourse in Canada, 1875–1980.* Montreal: McGill-Queen's University Press.

Appadurai, Arjun. 1996. *Modernity at Large: Cultural Dimensions of Globalization.* Minneapolis: University of Minnesota Press.

Arkush, R. David, and Leo O. Lee, eds. and trans. 1989. *Land without ghosts: Chinese Impressions of America from the Mid-Nineteenth Century to the Present.* Berkeley: University of California Press.

Armentrout-Ma, Eve. 1983. "Urban Chinese at the Sinitic Frontier: Social Organizations in United States Chinatowns, 1849–1898." *Modern Asian Studies* 17: 107–36.

Asbury, Herbert. 1950. *Gem of the Prairie: An Informal History of the Chicago Underworld.* New York: Alfred A. Knopf.

Barnett, Milton. 1960. "Kinship as a Factor Affecting Cantonese Economic Adaptation in the United States." *Human Organization* 19: 40–46.

Barth, Gunther. 1964. *Bitter Strength: The Chinese in California, 1850–1880.* Cambridge: Harvard University Press.

Basadre, Jorge. 1969. *Historia de la República del Perú.* 11 vols. Lima: Ediciones Historia.

Basch, Linda, Nina Glick Schiller, and Cristina Sztanton Blanc. 1994. *Nations Unbound: Transnational Projects, Postcolonial Predicaments, and Deterritorialized Nation-States.* Amsterdam: Gordon and Breach.

Baumann, Martin. 1997. "Shangri-La in Exile: Portraying Tibetan Diaspora Studies and Reconsidering Diaspora(s)." *Diaspora* 6: 377–404.

Behdad, Ali. 1997. "Nationalism and Immigration in the United States." *Diaspora* 6: 155–78.

Benton, Lauren. 1996. "From World-Systems Perspectives to Institutional World-History: Culture and Economy in Global Theory." *Journal of World History* 7: 261–95.

Bergere, Marie-Claire. 1998. *Sun Yat-sen.* Trans. Janet Lloyd. Stanford: Stanford University Press.

Bhabha, Homi K. 1990. "Introduction." In Bhabha, ed., *Nation and Narration.* New York: Routledge.

Bilu Zhonghua Tonghui Zongju 秘魯中華通惠總局 ed. 1986. *Bilu Zhonghua Tonghui Zongju yu Bilu huaren, 1886–1986* 秘魯中華通惠總局與秘魯華人 (Sociedad Central de Beneficencia China y la colonia china en el Perú, 1886–1986). Lima: Sociedad Central de Beneficencia China, 1986.

Blanchard, Peter. 1979. "A Populist Percursor: Guillermo Billinghurst." *Journal of Latin American Studies* 9: 251–73.

———. 1982. *The Origins of the Peruvian Labor Movement, 1883–1919.* Pittsburgh: University of Pittsburgh Press.

Bloch, Maurice. 1989. "From Cognition to Ideology." In *Ritual History and Power: Selected Papers in Anthropology,* 106–36. London: Athlone Press.

Board of Health of the Territory of Hawaii, Bureau of Vital Statistics. 1930. *Report of the Registrar General, 1900–1929.*

Bodnar, John. 1985. *The Transplanted: A History of Immigrants in Urban America.* Bloomington: Indiana University Press.

Bonacich, Edna, and Lucie Cheng, eds. 1984. *Labor Immigration under Capitalism.* Berkeley: University of California Press.

Bonilla, Heraclio. 1980. "El problema nacional y colonial del Perú en el contexto de la Guerra del Pacífico." In *Un siglo a la deriva: Ensayos sobre el Perú, Bolivia, y la Guerra,* 177–225. Lima: Instituto de Estudios Peruanos.

Bonner, Arthur. 1993. "The Chinese in New York, 1800–1950." *Chinese America: History and Perspectives,* 109–50 (annual).

Bourdieu, Pierre. 1990. *The Logic of Practice.* Trans. Richard Nice. Stanford: Stanford University Press.

———. 1991a. "On Symbolic Power." In *Language and Symbolic Power,* 163–70. Cambridge: Polity Press.

———. 1991b. "Rites of Institution." In *Language and Symbolic Power,* 117–26. Cambridge: Polity Press.

Bresler, Fenton. 1980. *The Chinese Mafia.* New York: Stein and Day.

Briscoe, Edward Eugene. 1959. "Pershing's Chinese Refugees in Texas." *Southwestern Historical Quarterly* 62: 467–88.

Buenker, John. 1987. "Edward F. Dunne: The Limits of Municipal Reform." In Paul Green and Melvin Holli, eds., *The Mayors: The Chicago Political Tradition,* 35–50. Carbondale: Southern Illinois University Press.

Burga, Manuel, and Alberto Flores Galindo. 1980. *Apogeo y crisis de la república aristocrática.* Lima: Rikchay Perú.

Burrows, Edwin. 1937. *Hawaiian Americans.* Archon Books.

———. 1939. *Chinese and Japanese in Hawaii during the Sino-Japanese Conflict.* Honolulu: Institute of Pacific Relations.

Caceres, José Félix. 1924. "El problema racial en el Perú y la inmigración asiática." *Boletín de la Sociedad Geográfica de Lima:* 176–85.

Camino Calderón, Carlos. 1945. *Diccionario folklórico del Perú.* Lima: Compañía de Impresiones y Publicidad.

Campbell, Persia Crawford. 1923. *Chinese Coolie Emigration to Countries within the British Empire.* London: P. S. King & Son.

Castells, Manuel. 1996. *The Rise of Network Society.* Vol. 1 of *The Information Age.* Oxford: Basil Blackwell.

Chan, Anthony. 1981. "'Orientalism' and Image Making: The Sojourner in Canadian History." *Journal of Ethnic Studies* 9: 37–46.

Chan Kwok Bun. 1997. "A Family Affair: Migration, Dispersal, and the Emergent Identity of the Chinese Cosmopolitan." *Diaspora* 6 (1997): 195–213.

Chan Kwok Bun and Ong Jin Hui. 1995. "The Many Faces of Immigrant Entrepreneurship." In Robin Cohen, ed., *The Cambridge Survey of World Migration,* 523–31. Cambridge: Cambridge University Press.

Chan Kwok Bun and Tong Chee Kiong. 1993. "Rethinking Assimilation and Ethnicity: The Chinese in Thailand." *International Migration Review* 27: 140–68.

Chan, Sucheng. 1986. *This Bittersweet Soil: The Chinese in California Agriculture, 1860–1910.* Berkeley: University of California Press.

———. 1990. "European and Asian Immigration into the United States in Comparative Perspective, 1820s to 1920s." In Virginia Yans-McLaughlin, ed., *Immigration Reconsidered: History, Sociology, and Politics,* 37–75. New York: Oxford University Press.

———. 1991. *Asian Americans: An Interpretive History.* Boston: Twaine.

———. 1998. "Race, Ethnic Culture, and Gender in the Construction of Identities among Second-Generation Chinese Americans, 1880s to 1930s." In K. Scott Wong and Sucheng Chan, eds., *Claiming America: Constructing Chinese American Identities during the Exclusion Era,* 127–64. Philadelphia: Temple University Press.

Chang, Ching Chieh. 1956. *The Chinese in Latin America: A Preliminary Geographical Survey with Special Reference to Cuba and Jamaica.* Ph.D. diss., University of Maryland.

Chang, Hamilton. 1994. "Chinese, Chino, Chung Gwok Yan: Our Family's Journey from the Fragrant Mountain to the Gold Mountain." *Chinese America: History and Perspectives,* 61–73 (annual).

Char, Tin-Yuke, ed. 1975. *The Sandalwood Mountains: Readings and Stories of the Early Chinese in Hawaii.* Honolulu: University Press of Hawaii.

———. 1977. *The Bamboo Path: Life and Writings of a Chinese in Hawaii.* Honolulu: Hawaii Chinese History Center.

Char, Wai Jane. 1972. "Chinese Merchant-Adventurers and Sugar Masters in Hawaii, 1802–1852." *Hawaiian Journal of History* 8: 3–25.

Cheah, Pheng, and Bruce Robbins, eds. 1998. *Cosmopolitics: Thinking and Feeling beyond the Nation.* Minneapolis: University of Minnesota Press.

Chen Ta. 1923. *Chinese Migrations, with Special Reference to Labor Conditions.* Washington DC: Government Printing Office.

——. 1940. *Emigrant Communities in South China.* Ed. Bruno Lasker. New York: Institute of Pacific Relations.

Chen, Wen-hsien. 1940. *Chinese under Both Exclusion and Immigration Laws.* Ph.D. diss., University of Chicago.

Chinese Bureau of the Department of Foreign Affairs. 1896. *The Laws and Regulations Restricting Chinese Immigration to the Hawaiian Islands.* Honolulu.

Chinese in Hawaii: A Resume of the Social, Industrial, and Economic Progress of the Chinese in the Hawaiian Islands. 1913. Honolulu: Honolulu Star-Bulletin Press.

Chinese of Hawaii. 1929. Honolulu: Overseas Chinese Penman's Club.

Ching, Harold. 1981. *Grandpa: A Pioneer Rice Planter and His Times in Old Hanapepe.* Privately published.

Ching, Harold, and Douglas Chong. 1987. *The Ching Family Chronicles.* Lihue, Hawaii.

Chirot, Daniel, and Anthony Reid. 1997. *Essential Outsiders: Chinese and Jews in the Modern Transformation of Southeast Asia and Central Europe.* Seattle: University of Washington Press.

Chock Lun. 1936. "Chinese Organizations in Hawaii." *Chinese of Hawaii* 2: 22–35.

Chong, Denise. 1995. *The Concubine's Children.* New York: Viking.

Chong-Gossard, J. H. Kim On. 1992. *The Chong Family History.* Ka'a'awa: Chong Hee Books.

Chongzhenghui of Hawaii, ed. 1958. *Tanxiangshan Chongzhenghui ershiyi zhounian jinian tekan* 檀香山崇正會二十一週年紀念特刊 [Commemorative volume on the twenty-first anniversary of the Chongzhenghui of Hawaii]. Hong Kong: Kaiming Press.

Chow, Kai-wing. 1994. *The Rise of Confucian Ritualism in Late Imperial China.* Stanford: Stanford University Press.

Chun, Allen. 1992. "The Practice of Tradition in the Writing of Custom, or Chinese Marriage from *Li* to *Su*." *Late Imperial China* 13, no. 2: 82–125.

Chun, James. 1983. *The Early Chinese in Punaluu.* Hawaii: Yin Sit Sha.

Chung, Stephanie Po-Yin. 1999. "Mobilization Politics: The Case of Siyi Businessmen in Hong Kong, 1890–1928." In Leo Douw, Cen Huang, and Michael Godley, eds. *Qiaoxiang Ties: Interdisciplinary Approaches to 'Cultural Capitalism' in South China*, 45–66. London: Kegan Paul.

Clifford, James. 1994. "Diasporas." *Cultural Anthropology* 9: 302–38.

Cloud, Patricia, and David Galenson. 1987. "Chinese Immigration and Contract Labor in the Late Nineteenth Century." *Explorations in Economic History* 24: 22–42.

——. 1991. "Chinese Immigration: Reply to Charles McClain." *Explorations in Economic History* 28: 239–47.

Cohen, Myron. 1976. *House Divided, House United.* New York: Columbia University Press.

———. 1993. "Shared Beliefs: Corporations, Community, and Religion among the South Taiwan Hakka during the Ch'ing." *Late Imperial China* 14: 1–33.

———. 1996. "The Hakka or 'Guest People': Dialect as Sociocultural Variable in Southeast China." In Nicole Constable, ed. *Guest People: Hakka Identity in China and Abroad*, 36–79. Seattle: University of Washington Press.

Cohen, Robin. 1997. *Global Diasporas: An Introduction*. Seattle: University of Washington Press.

Cole, James. 1986. *Shaohsing: Competition and Cooperation in Nineteenth-Century China*. Tucson: University of Arizona Press.

Colonia China en el Perú. 1924. *La colonia china en el Perú: Instituciones y hombres representativos: Su actuación benefica en la vida nacional.* Lima: Sociedad Editorial Panamericana.

Conroy, John. 1978. "The Dark Side of Chinatown." *Chicago* 27: 112–19.

Constable, Nicole. 1994. *Christian Souls and Chinese Spirits*. Berkeley: University of California Press.

Coppel, Charles. 1981. "The Origins of Confucianism as an Organized Religion in Java, 1900–1923." *Journal of Southeast Asian Studies* 12: 179–96.

Cotler, Julio. 1978. *Clases, estado, y nación en el Perú*. Lima: Instituto de Estudios Peruanos.

Coulter, John Wesley, and Chee Kwon Chun. 1937. *Chinese Rice Farmers in Hawaii*. Honolulu: University of Hawaii.

Crissman, Lawrence. 1967. "The Segmentary Structure of Urban Overseas Chinese." *Man* 2: 185–204.

Culin, Stewart. 1970a [1887]. "Customs of Chinese in America." San Francisco: R and E Research Associates.

———. 1970b [1887]. "The I Hing, or Patriotic Rising." San Francisco: R and E Research Associates.

Cushing, Robert. 1985. "The Beginnings of Sugar Production in Hawaii." *Hawaiian Journal of History* 19: 17–34.

Cushman, Jennifer. 1991. *Family and State: The Formation of a Sino-Thai Tin-mining Dynasty.* Singapore: Oxford University Press.

———. 1993. *Fields from the Sea: Chinese Junk Trade with Siam during the Late Eighteenth and Early Nineteenth Centuries.* Ithaca, NY: Southeast Asia Program, Cornell University.

Daniels, Roger. 1983. "The Assimilation of Ethnic Groups: A Comment." *Comparative Studies in Society and History* 25: 401–4.

Daws, Gavan. 1968. *Shoal of Time: A History of the Hawaiian Islands*. New York: Macmillan.

de la Cadena, Marisol. 1998. "From Race to Class: Insurgent Intellectuals *de provincia* in Peru, 1910–1970." In Steve J. Stern, ed., *Shining and Other Paths: War and Society in Peru, 1980–1995*, 22–59. Durham, NC: Duke University Press.

De Trazegnies, Fernando. 1994. *En el país de las colinas de arena*. 2 vols. Lima: Pontificia Universidad Católica del Perú, Fondo Editorial.

Dirlik, Arif. 1996. "Asians on the Rim: Transnational Capital and Local Community in the Making of Contemporary Asian America." *Amerasia Journal* 22: 1–24.

Dong, Lorraine, and Marlon Hom. 1980. "Chinatown Chinese: The San Francisco Dialect." *Amerasia Journal* 7: 1–29.

Douglas, Mary. 1982. "The Contempt of Ritual." In *In the Active Voice,* 4–8. London: Routledge and Kegan Paul.

Douw, Leo. 1999. "The Chinese Sojourner Discourse." In Leo Douw, Cen Huang, and Michael Godley, eds. *Qiaoxiang Ties: Interdisciplinary Approaches to 'Cultural Capitalism' in South China,* 22–44. London: Kegan Paul.

Douw, Leo, Cen Huang, and Michael Godley, eds. 1999. *Qiaoxiang Ties: Interdisciplinary Approaches to 'Cultural Capitalism' in South China,* 22–44. London: Kegan Paul.

Drury, John. 1932. "A Night in Chinatown." *Chicago Visitor,* May.

Duara, Prasenjit. 1988a. *Culture, Power, and the State: Rural North China, 1900–1942.* Stanford: Stanford University Press.

———. 1988b. "Superscribing Symbols: The Myth of Guandi, Chinese God of War." *Journal of Asian Studies* 47: 778–95.

———. 1997a. "Nationalists among Transnationals: Overseas Chinese and the Idea of China, 1900–1911." In Aihwa Ong and Donald Nonini, eds., *Ungrounded Empires: The Cultural Politics of Modern Chinese Transnationalism,* 36–90. New York: Routledge.

———. 1997b. "Transnationalism and the Predicament of Sovereignty: China, 1900–1945." *American Historical Review* 102: 1030–51.

Dye, Bob. 1997. *Merchant Prince of the Sandalwood Mountains: Afong and the Chinese in Hawai'i.* Honolulu: University of Hawai'i Press.

Ebrey, Patricia. 1991. *Confucianism and Family Rituals in Imperial China.* Princeton: Princeton University Press.

Elliot, Alan J. A. 1955. *Chinese Spirit-Medium Cults in Singapore.* London: London School of Economics and Political Science.

Fairbank, John, ed. 1968. *The Chinese World Order.* Cambridge: Harvard University Press.

Fan, Ting-chiu. 1926. "Chinese Residents in Chicago." M.A. thesis, University of Chicago.

Faure, David. 1986. "The Lineage as a Cultural Invention." *Modern China* 15: 4–36.

———. 1989. *The Structure of Chinese Rural Society.* Hong Kong: Oxford University Press.

———. 1990. "What Made Foshan a Town? The Evolution of Rural-Urban Identities in Ming-Qing China," *Late Imperial China* 11, no. 2: 1–31.

———. 1995. "Lineage Socialism and Community Control: Tangang Xiang in the 1920s and 1930s." In David Faure and Helen Siu, eds., *Down to Earth: The Territorial Bond in South China,* 161–87. Stanford: Stanford University Press.

Faure, David, and Helen Siu, eds. 1995. *Down to Earth: The Territorial Bond in South China.* Stanford: Stanford University Press.

Featherstone, Mike, ed. 1990. *Global Culture: Nationalism, Globalization, and Modernity.* London: Sage.

Feng Huolong 馮或龍 (Wai Hong). 1956. "Huabao lishi ji shi" 華報曆史紀實 [Record of the history of Chinese newspapers]. In *The Chinese of Hawaii Who's Who, 1956–57* (檀山華僑), 32–33. Honolulu: Overseas Chinese Penman's Club.

Feng Ziyou 馮自由. 1965. *Geming yishi* 革命逸史 [History of the revolution]. 4 vols. Taibei: Taiwan Shangwu Yinshu Ju.

Feuchtwang, Stephan. 1974. "City Temples in Taipei Under Three Regimes." In G. William Skinner, ed., *The Chinese City Between Two Worlds,* 263–301. Stanford: Stanford University Press.

———. 1992. *The Imperial Metaphor: Popular Religion in China.* London: Routledge.

Flores Galindo, Alberto. 1990. "Bandidos de la costa." In Carlos Aguirre and Charles Walker, eds., *Bandoleros, abigeatos, y montoneros: Criminalidad y violencia en el Perú, siglos XVIII–XX,* 57–68. Lima: Instituto de Apoyo Agrario.

Foner, Nancy. 1997. "What's New about Transnationalism? Immigrants Today and at the Turn of the Century." *Diaspora* 6: 355–75.

Freedman, Edward. 1994. "Reconstructing China's National Identity: A Southern Alternative to Mao-Era Anti-Imperialist Nationalism." *Journal of Asian Studies* 53: 67–91.

Freedman, Maurice. 1957. *Chinese Family and Marriage in Singapore.* London: Her Majesty's Stationery Office.

———. 1958. *Lineage Organization in Southeastern China.* London: Athlone Press.

———. 1966. *Chinese Lineage and Society.* London: Athlone Press.

Friday, Chris. 1994. *Organizing Asian American Labor: The Pacific Coast Canned-Salmon Industry, 1870–1942.* Philadelphia: Temple University Press.

Fried, Morton. 1966. "Some Political Aspects of Clanship in a Modern Chinese City." In Marc Swartz, Victor Turner, and Arthur Tuden, eds., *Political Anthropology,* 285–300. Chicago: Aldine Publishing.

Fuchs, Lawrence. 1983. *Hawaii Pono: A Social History.* New York: Harcourt Brace Jovanovich.

Fukumoto, Mary. 1993. "Influencia asiática en las Américas: chinos y japoneses en América del Sur." *Antropológica* 11: 309–24.

Gambetta, Diego. 1993. *The Sicilian Mafia: The Business of Private Protection.* Cambridge: Harvard University Press.

Ganschow, Thomas. 1992. "Sun Yat-sen: An American Citizen." *Chinese Studies in History* 25, no. 3: 18–39.

Gao Degen 高德根. 1956. *Bilu huaqiao shihua* 秘魯華僑史話 [History of the overseas Chinese in Peru]. Taibei: Haiwai Wenku Chuban She.

Gates, Hill. 1996. *China's Motor: A Thousand Years of Petty Capitalism.* Ithaca, NY: Cornell University Press.

General Superintendent of the Census. 1897. *Report of the General Superintendent of the Census, 1896.* Honolulu: Hawaiian Star Press.

Geyer, Michael, and Charles Bright. 1995. "World History in a Global Age." *American Historical Review* 100: 1034–60.

Gilroy, Paul. 1993. *The Black Atlantic: Modernity and Double Consciousness*. Cambridge: Harvard University Press.

Glick, Clarence. 1938. *The Chinese Migrant in Hawaii: A Study in Accommodation*. Ph.D. diss., University of Chicago.

———. 1942. "The Relation Between Positions and Status in the Assimilation of Chinese in Hawaii." *American Journal of Sociology* 47: 667–79.

———. 1980. *Sojourners and Settlers: Chinese Migrants in Hawaii*. Honolulu: Hawaii Chinese History Center and the University Press of Hawaii.

Godley, Michael. 1982. *The Mandarin Capitalists from Nanyang: Overseas Chinese Enterprise in the Modernization of China, 1893–1911*. Cambridge: Cambridge University Press.

Gong, Eng Ying, and Bruce Grant. 1930. *Tong War!* New York: Nicholas L. Brown.

Gonzales, Michael. 1989. "Chinese Plantation Workers and Social Conflict in Peru in the Late Nineteenth Century." *Journal of Latin American Studies* 21: 385–424.

Gonzales Prada, Manuel. 1941. "Los chinos." In *Prosa menuda*, 207–10. Buenos Aires: Ediciones Iman.

Goo, Paul Kimm-Chow. 1936. "Chinese Economic Activities in Hawaii." In Kum Pui Lai, ed., *Chinese of Hawaii*, 5–15. Honolulu: Overseas Chinese Penman's Club.

Goodman, Bryna. 1995. *Native Place, City, and Nation: Regional Networks and Identities in Shanghai, 1853–1937*. Berkeley: University of California Press.

Governor of Hawaii. 1902–1934. *Report of the Governor of the Territory of Hawaii to the Secretary of the Interior*.

Grew, Raymond. 1993. "On the Prospect of Global History." In Bruce Mazlish and Ralph Buultjens, eds., *Conceptualizing Global History*, 227–49. Boulder: Westview Press.

Griffin, Dick. 1977. "Opium Addiction in Chicago: 'The Noblest and the Best Brought Low.'" *Chicago History* 6: 107–16.

Haley, George, Chin Tiong Tan, and Usha Haley. 1998. *New Asian Emperors: The Overseas Chinese, Their Strategies and Competitive Advantages*. Oxford: Butterworth Heinemann.

Hall, Stuart. 1994. "Cultural Identity and Diaspora." In Patrick Williams and Laura Chrisman, eds., *Colonial Discourse and Postcolonial Theory: A Reader*. New York: Columbia University Press.

Hamilton, Gary. 1977. "Ethnicity and Regionalism: Some Factors Influencing Chinese Identities in Southeast Asia." *Ethnicity*: 331–51.

———. 1996. "Overseas Chinese Capitalism." In Tu Wei-ming, ed., *Confucian Traditions in East Asian Modernity: Moral Education and Economic Culture in Japan and the Four Mini-Dragons*, 328–42. Cambridge: Harvard University Press.

Hamilton, Gary, and Tony Waters. 1997. "Ethnicity and Capitalist Development: The Changing Role of the Chinese in Thailand." In Daniel Chirot and Anthony Reid, eds., *Essential Outsiders: Chinese and Jews in the Modern*

    Transformation of Southeast Asia and Central Europe, 258–84. Seattle: University of Washington Press.

Harrell, Stevan. 1974. "When a Ghost Becomes a God." In Arthur Wolf, ed., *Religion and Ritual in Chinese Society,* 193–206. Stanford: Stanford University Press.

Harvey, David. 1989. *The Condition of Postmodernity.* Oxford: Basil Blackwell.

Hayes, James. 1985. "Specialists and Written Material in the Village World." In David Johnson, ed., *Popular Culture in Late Imperial China,* 75–110. Berkeley: University of California Press.

Hefner, Robert, ed. 1998. *Market Cultures: Society and Morality in the New Asian Capitalisms.* Boulder: Westview Press.

Heidhues, Mary Somers. 1992. *Bangka Tin and Mentok Pepper: Chinese Settlement on an Indonesian Island.* Singapore: Institute of Southeast Asian Studies.

———. 1996. "Chinese Settlements in Rural Southeast Asia." In Anthony Reid, ed., *Sojourners and Settlers: Histories of Southeast Asia and the Chinese,* 164–82. Australia: Asian Studies Association of Australia and Allen & Unwin.

Hevia, James. 1996. *Cherishing Men from Afar: Qing Guest Ritual and the Macartney Embassy of 1793.* Durham: Duke University Press.

Ho Ming Chung. 1967. *Manual de la colonia china en el Perú* (秘鲁華僑手冊). Lima.

Hom, Marlon. 1984. "A Case of Mutual Exclusion: Portrayals by Immigrant and American-Born Chinese of Each Other in Literature." *Amerasia Journal* 11: 29–45.

Hom, Marlon, ed. and trans. 1987. *Songs of Gold Mountain: Cantonese Rhymes from San Francisco Chinatown.* Berkeley: University of California Press.

Hostetter, Gordon, and Thomas Quinn Beesley. 1929. *It's a Racket!* Chicago: Les Quin Books.

Hsu, Francis. 1945. "Influence of South-Seas Emigration on Certain Chinese Provinces." *Far Eastern Quarterly* 5: 47–59.

Hsu, Madeline. 1996. *"Living Abroad and Faring Well": Migration and Transformation in Taishan County, Guangdong 1904–1939.* Ph.D. diss., Yale University.

Hsu, Ruth. 1996. "'Will the Model Minority Please Identify Itself?' American Ethnic Identity and Its Discontents." *Diaspora* 5: 37–63.

Hu, Evelyn. 1988. "Chinos comerciantes en el Perú: Breve y preliminar bosquejo histórico." In Humberto Rodríguez Pastor, ed., *Primer seminario sobre poblaciones inmigrantes,* 2: 127–35. Lima: CONCYTEC.

Hu-Dehart, Evelyn. 1993. "Chinese Coolie Labour in Cuba in the Nineteenth Century: Free Labour or Neo-Slavery?" *Slavery and Abolition* 14: 67–86.

Huang Jianchun 黃建淳. 1993. *WanQing XinMa huaqiao dui guojia rentong zhi yanjiu* 晚清新馬華僑對國家認同之研究 [A study of overseas Chinese identity problems: The Malaya Chinese and late Ch'ing government]. Taibei: The Society of Overseas Chinese Studies.

Huang Sande 黃三德. 1936. *Hongmen Geming Shi* 洪門革命史 [Revolutionary history of the Hongmen]. Los Angeles.

Huang Shun, Zhang Yongyi, and Wang Liping 黃舜，張勇毅，王力平. 1981. "Wo zai

Meiguo congshi xiyiye de jingguo" 我在美國從事洗衣業的經過 [My experience doing laundry work in America]. In *Huaqiao Shilun Wenji* 華僑史論文集 [Documents on overseas Chinese history], 15–49. Guangzhou: Jinan Daxue Huaqiao Yanjiusuo.

Hucker, Charles. 1975. *China to 1850: A Short History.* Stanford: Stanford University Press.

Ing, Ernest S. 1929. "The Legal Status of the Chinese in Hawaii." *Chinese of Hawaii* 1: 25–26.

Jackson, James C. 1968. *Planters and Speculators: Chinese and European Agricultural Enterprise in Malaya, 1786–1921.* Kuala Lumpur: University of Malaya Press.

Johnson, Graham. 1993. "Family Strategies and Economic Transformation in Rural China: Some Evidence from the Pearl River Delta." In Deborah Davis and Stevan Harrell, eds., *Chinese Families in the Post-Mao Era.* Berkeley: University of California Press.

Jordan, David. 1972. *Gods, Ghosts, and Ancestors.* Berkeley: University of California Press.

Kagawa, Lily Siu. 1983. *Gambling and the Law: A Study of the Utility of Gambling and its Prohibition in an American Chinatown.* Ph.D. diss., University of Illinois at Urbana-Champaign.

Kai, Peggy. 1974. "Chinese Settlers in the Village of Hilo before 1852." *Hawaiian Journal of History* 8: 39–75.

———. 1976. *The Story of A'lai.* Privately published.

Kim, Elaine, and Lisa Lowe, eds. 1997. *New Formations, New Questions: Asian American Studies,* special issue of *Positions* 5: 2.

King, Anthony, ed. 1997. *Culture, Globalization, and the World-System: Contemporary Conditions for the Representation of Identity.* Minneapolis: University of Minnesota Press.

Kingston, Maxine Hong. 1980. *China Men.* New York: Alfred A. Knopf.

———. 1989. *Tripmaster Monkey: His Fake Book.* New York: Alfred A. Knopf.

Kinkead, Gwen. 1992. *Chinatown: Portrait of a Closed Society.* New York: Harper Collins.

Koshy, Susan. 1996. "The Fiction of Asian American Literature." *Yale Journal of Criticism* 9: 315–46.

Kotkin, Joel. 1992. *Tribes: How Race, Religion, and Identity Determine Success in the New Global Economy.* New York: Random House.

Kuah Khun Eng. 1999. "The Singapore-Anxi Connection: Ancestor Worship as Moral-Cultural Capital." In Leo Douw, Cen Huang, and Michael Godley, eds. *Qiaoxiang Ties: Interdisciplinary Approaches to 'Cultural Capitalism' in South China,* 143–57. London: Kegan Paul.

Kuhn, Philip. 1970. *Rebellion and Its Enemies in Late Imperial China: Militarization and Social Structure, 1796–1864.* Cambridge: Harvard University Press.

———. 1975. "Local Self-Government Under the Republic: Problems of Control, Autonomy, and Mobilization." In Frederic Wakeman and Carolyn

Grant, eds., *Conflict and Control in Late Imperial China*, 257–98. Berkeley: University of California Press.

Kulp, Daniel. 1966. *Country Life in South China: The Sociology of Familism.* Taipei: Ching-Wu Publishing.

Kung, S. W. 1962. *Chinese in American Life: Some Aspects of Their History, Status, Problems, and Contributions.* Seattle: University of Washington Press.

Kuykendall, Ralph. 1963. *The Hawaiian Kingdom, 1874–1893: The Kalakaua Dynasty.* Honolulu: University of Hawaii Press.

Kwong, Alice Jo. 1958. "The Chinese in Peru." In Morton Fried, ed., *Colloquium on Overseas Chinese*, 41–48. New York: Institute of Pacific Relations.

Lai, Him Mark. 1987. "Historical Development of the CCBA/Huiguan System." *Chinese America: History and Perspectives*, 13–51.

———. 1991. "The Kuomintang in Chinese American Communities before World War II." In Sucheng Chan, ed., *Entry Denied: Exclusion and the Chinese Community in America*, 170–212. Philadelphia: Temple University Press.

Lai, Kum Pui. 1936. "Occupational and Educational Adjustments of the Chinese in Hawaii." In Kum Pui Lai, ed., *Chinese of Hawaii*, 2–4. Honolulu: Overseas Chinese Penman's Club.

Lai, Violet. 1985. *He Was a Ram: Wong Aloiau of Hawaii.* Honolulu: University of Hawaii Press.

Lam, Margaret. 1936. "Racial Myth and Family Tradition—Worship among the Part-Hawaiians." *Social Forces* 14: 405–9.

Lamley, Harry. 1990. "Lineage Feuding in Southern Fujian and Eastern Guangdong under Qing Rule." In Jonathan Lipman and Stevan Harrell, eds., *Violence in China: Essays in Culture and Counterculture*, 27–64. Albany: State University of New York Press.

Landesco, John. 1928. *Organized Crime in Chicago.* Chicago: University of Chicago Press.

Larson, Jane Leung. 1993. "New Source Materials on Kang Youwei and the Baohuanghui." *Chinese America: History and Perspectives*, 151–98.

Lausent, Isabelle. 1983. *Acos: Pequeña propiedad, poder, y economia de mercado.* Lima: Instituto de Estudios Peruanos.

Lausent-Herrera, Isabelle. 1988. "Los inmigrantes chinos en la Amazonía peruana." In Humberto Rodríguez Pastor, ed., *Primer seminario sobre poblaciones inmigrantes*, 2: 109–26. Lima: CONCYTEC.

———. 1992. "La cristianización de los chinos en el Perú: Integración, sumisión, y resistencia." *Bulletin de l'Institute Français d'Etudes Andines* 21: 977–1007.

———. 1997. "L'émergence d'une élite d'origine asiatique au Pérou." *Caravelle* 67: 127–54.

Lee, Bung Chong. 1936. "The Chinese Store as a Social Institution." *Social Process in Hawaii* 2: 35–38.

Leong Gor Yun. 1936. *Chinatown Inside Out.* New York: Barrows Mussey.

Leong, Sow-Theng. 1997. *Migration and Ethnicity in Chinese History: Hakkas, Pengmin, and Their Neighbors.* Ed. Tim Wright. Stanford: Stanford University Press.

Lever-Tracy, Constance, David Ip, and Noel Tracy. 1996. *The Chinese Diaspora and Mainland China: An Emerging Economic Synergy.* New York: St. Martin's Press.

Lévi-Strauss, Claude. 1966. *The Savage Mind.* Chicago: University of Chicago Press.

Lewis, Martin, and Kären Wigen. 1997. *The Myth of Continents: A Critique of Metageography.* Berkeley: University of California Press.

Li Jinming 李金明. 1996. Wukou tongshang hou cong Xiamen chuyang de huagong 五口通商后從廈門出洋的華工 [Laborers emigrating from Xiamen after the opening of the five treaty ports]. *Huaqiao huaren lishi yanjiu* (Spring): 74–80.

Li Ling Ai. 1972. *Life Is for a Long Time.* New York: Hastings House.

Liang Qichao 梁啟超. 1922. *Xin dalu youji* 新大陸游記 [Record of travels in the new world]. Shanghai: Shangwu Yinshuguan.

Liang, Yuan. 1951. "The Chinese Family in Chicago." M.A. thesis, University of Chicago.

Light, Ivan. 1974. "From Vice District to Tourist Attraction: The Moral Career of American Chinatowns, 1880–1920." *Pacific Historical Review* 43: 367–94.

Light, Ivan, Parminder Bachu, and Stavros Karageoris. 1993. "Migration Networks and Immigrant Entrepreneurship." In Light and Bachu, eds., *Immigration and Entrepreneurship,* 25–49. New Brunswick, NJ: Transaction Publishers.

Lin, Alfred. 1997. *The Rural Economy of Guangdong, 1870–1937: A Study of the Agrarian Crisis and Its Origins in Southernmost China.* New York: St. Martin's Press.

Lind, Andrew. 1931. *Economic Succession and Racial Invasion in Hawaii.* Ph.D. diss., University of Chicago.

———. 1938. *An Island Community: Ecological Succession in Hawaii.* Chicago: University of Chicago Press.

———. 1958. "Adjustment Patterns among the Jamaican Chinese." *Social and Economic Studies* 7: 144–64.

Lindberg, Richard. 1996. *Chicago by Gaslight: A History of Chicago's Netherworld, 1880–1920.* Chicago: Academy Chicago Publishers.

Liu Haiming. 1992. "The Trans-Pacific Family: A Case Study of Sam Chang's Family History," *Amerasia Journal* 18: 1–34.

Liu Hong. 1998. "Old Linkages, New Networks: The Globalization of Overseas Chinese Voluntary Associations and Its Implications." *China Quarterly* 155: 582–609.

———. 1999. "Bridges Across the Sea: Chinese Social Organizations in Southeast Asia and the Links with *Qiaoxiang,* 1900–49." In Leo Douw, Cen Huang, and Michael Godley, eds., *Qiaoxiang Ties: Interdisciplinary Approaches to 'Cultural Capitalism' in South China,* 87–112. London: Kegan Paul.

Liu, Kwang-ching. 1988. "Chinese Merchant Guilds: An Historical Inquiry." *Pacific Historical Review* 57: 1–23.

Liu Zuoren 劉作人. 1959. "Jinshanzhuang de Yanjiu" 金山莊的研究 [Research on Golden Mountain firms]. *Zhongguo Jingji* 101: 20–22.

Look Lai, Walton. 1993. *Indentured Labor, Caribbean Sugar: Chinese and Indian Migrants to the British West Indies, 1838–1918*. Baltimore: Johns Hopkins University Press.

Lum, Lillian Awai. 1991. *The Lum Mow Chin Family: Its Lineage and Memoirs*. Privately published.

Lydon, Edward. 1975. *The Anti-Chinese Movement in the Hawaiian Kingdom, 1852–1886*. San Francisco: R and E Research Associates.

Lyman, Stanford. 1977. "Conflict and the Web of Group Affiliation in San Francisco's Chinatown, 1850–1910." In *The Asian in North America*, 103–18. Santa Barbara: ABC Clio.

———. 1986. *Chinatown and Little Tokyo*. Milwood: Associated Faculty Press.

Lyman, Stanford, William Willmott, and Berching Ho. 1977. "Rules of a Chinese Secret Society in British Columbia." In Stanford Lyman, *The Asian in North America*, 95–101. Santa Barbara: ABC Clio.

Ma Chaojun 馬超俊. 1963. "Hongmen zongzhi yu Sanminzhuyi" 洪門宗旨與三民主義 [The purpose of the Hongmen and the Three People's Principles]. In Tanxiangshan Zhigong Zongtang ed., *Tanxiangshan Zhigong Zongtang xinlou luocheng kaimu* 檀香山致公總堂新樓落成開幕 [Opening ceremony of the new building of the Hawaii Zhigongtang], 158–61. Hong Kong.

Ma, L. Eve Armentrout. 1984. "Fellow-Regional Associations in the Ch'ing Dynasty: Organizations in Flux for Mobile People. A Preliminary Survey." *Modern Asian Studies* 18: 307–30.

———. 1990. *Revolutionaries, Monarchists and Chinatowns*. Honolulu: University of Hawaii Press.

———. 1991. "Chinatown Organizations and the Anti-Chinese Movement, 1882–1914." In Sucheng Chan, ed., *Entry Denied: Exclusion and the Chinese Community in America*, 147–69. Philadelphia: Temple University Press.

Mann, Susan. 1974. "The Ningpo *Pang* and Financial Power at Shanghai." In Mark Elvin and G. William Skinner, eds., *The Chinese City between Two Worlds*. Stanford: Stanford University Press, 1974.

———. 1987. *Local Merchants and the Chinese Bureaucracy 1750–1950*. Stanford: Stanford University Press.

Marcone, Mario. 1995. "Indígenas e inmigrantes durante la república aristocrática: Población e ideología civilista." *Histórica* 19: 73–93.

Mark, Diane Mei Lin. 1975. *The Chinese in Kula*. Honolulu: Hawaii Chinese History Center.

Marks, Robert. 1998. *Tigers, Rice, Silk, and Silt: Environment and Economy in Late Imperial South China*. Cambridge: Cambridge University Press.

Marx, Karl, and Friedrich Engels. 1992. *The Communist Manifesto*. New York: Bantam.

Mayer de Zulen, Dora. 1924. *La China elocuente y silenciosa: Homenaje de la colonia china al Perú: Con motivo de las fiestas centenarias de su independencia (28/7/21–9/12/24)*. Lima: Editorial Renovación.

Mazlish, Bruce. 1998. "Comparing Global History to World History." *Journal of Interdisciplinary History* 28: 385–95.

Mazlish, Bruce, and Ralph Buultjens, eds. 1993. *Conceptualizing Global History*. Boulder: Westview Press.

Mazumdar, Sucheta. 1998. *Sugar and Society in China: Peasants, Technology, and the World Market*. Cambridge: Harvard University Asia Center.

McClain, Charles. 1990. "Chinese Immigration: A Comment on Cloud and Galenson." *Explorations in Economic History* 27: 363–78.

———. 1994. *In Search of Equality: The Chinese Struggle against Discrimination in Nineteenth-Century America*. Berkeley: University of California Press.

McKee, Delber. 1977. *Chinese Exclusion Versus the Open Door Policy, 1900–1906*. Detroit: Wayne State University Press.

———. 1986. "The Chinese Boycott of 1905–6 Reconsidered: The Role of Chinese Americans." *Pacific Historical Review* 55: 165–91.

McKeown, Adam. 1996. "Inmigración china al Perú, 1904–1937: Exclusión y negociación." *Histórica* 20: 59–91.

———. 1997. "Chinese Migrants among Ghosts: Chicago, Peru, and Hawaii in the Early Twentieth Century." Ph.D. diss., University of Chicago.

———. 1999a. "Conceptualizing Chinese Diasporas, 1842–1949." *Journal of Asian Studies* 58: 306–37.

———. 1999b. "Transnational Chinese Families and American Exclusion, 1875–1943." *Journal of American Ethnic History* 18, no. 2, 73–110.

———. Forthcoming. "The Sojourner as Astronaut: Paul Siu in Global Perspective." In Josephine Lee, Imogene Lim, and Yuko Matsukawa, eds., *Re/collecting Early Asian America: Readings in Culture History*. Philadelphia: Temple University Press.

McNeill, William. 1998. "World History and the Rise and Fall of the West." *Journal of World History* 9: 215–36.

Mei Binlin 梅斌林. 1979. "Sun Zhongshan zai Zhijiage he Ditelü" 孫中山在芝茄哥和底特律 [Sun Yat-sen in Chicago and Detroit]. *Guangzhou wenshi ziliao* 17: 18–20.

Mei, June. 1979. "Socioeconomic Origins of Emigration: Guangdong to California, 1850–1882." *Modern China* 5: 463–501.

Mellen, Kathleen. 1958. *An Island Kingdom Passes: Hawaii Becomes American*. New York: Hastings House.

Merry, Sally Engle. 2000. *Colonizing Hawai'i: The Cultural Power of Law*. Princeton, NJ: Princeton University Press.

Millones Santagadea, Luis. 1973. *Minorias étnicas en el Perú*. Lima: Pontificia Universidad Católica del Perú.

Millward, James. 1998. *Beyond the Pass: Economy, Ethnicity, and Empire in Qing Central Asia, 1759–1864*. Stanford: Stanford University Press.

Minnick, Sylvia Sun. 1988. *Samfow, The San Joaquin Chinese Legacy*. Fresno: Panorama West.

Mitchell, Katharyne. 1997. "Transnational Citizens: Constituting the Cultural Citizen in the Era of Pacific Rim Capital." In Aihwa Ong and Donald Nonini, eds., *Ungrounded Empires: The Cultural Politics of Modern Chinese Transnationalism.* New York: Routledge.

Morimoto, Amelia. 1979. *Los Inmigrantes Japoneses en el Perú.* Lima: Universidad Nacional Agraria.

Morrison, Judith. 1977. *Being Chinese in Honolulu: A Political and Social Status or a Way of Life.* Ph.D. diss., University of Illinois at Urbana-Champaign.

Morton, Richard. 1990. "Edward F. Dunne: Illinois' Most Progressive Governor." *Illinois Historical Journal* 83: 218–34.

Mountz, Alison, and Richard Wright. 1996. "Daily Life in the Transnational Migrant Community of San Augustín, Oaxaca, and Poughkeepsie, NY." *Diaspora* 5: 403–28.

Moy, Susan Lee. 1978. "The Chinese in Chicago, The First One Hundred Years." M.A. thesis, University of Wisconsin at Madison.

Moye, Gerald, and Calvin Chin. 1935. *Ling Long Museum (The High Lights of Chinese History) and Chicago's Chinatown.* Chicago: Ling Long Museum.

Mui King-Chan. 1937. "The Chinese as Builders of Hawaii." *Pan Pacific* 1, no. 3: 43–45.

Mumford, Kevin. 1997. *Interzones: Black/White Sex Districts in Chicago and New York in the Early Twentieth Century.* New York: Columbia University Press.

Murray, Dian. 1993. *The Origin of the Tiandihui (Heaven and Earth Society).* Stanford: Stanford University Press.

Ng Chin-Keong. 1983. *Trade and Society: The Amoy Network on the China Coast, 1683–1735.* Singapore: Singapore University Press.

Nordyke, Eleanor, and Richard Lee. 1989. "The Chinese in Hawaii: A Historical and Demographic Perspective." *Hawaiian Journal of History* 23: 196–216.

Nugent, David. 1997. *Modernity at the Edge of Empire: State, Individual, and Nation in the Northern Peruvian Andes, 1885–1935.* Stanford: Stanford University Press.

Offe, Claus. 1985. *Disorganized Capitalism.* Cambridge: MIT Press.

Okihiro, Gary. 1994. *Margins and Mainstreams: Asians in American History and Culture.* Seattle: University of Washington Press.

Oliart, Patricia. 1995. "Poniendo a cada quien en su lugar: Estereotipos raciales y sexuales en la Lima del siglo XIX." In Aldo Panfichi H. and Felipe Portocarrero S., eds., *Mundos interiores: Lima 1850–1950,* 261–88. Lima: Centro de Investigación, Universidad del Pacífico.

Ong, Aihwa. 1999. *Flexible Citizenship: The Cultural Logics of Transnationality.* Durham, NC: Duke University Press.

Ong, Aihwa, and Donald Nonini. 1997. *Ungrounded Empires: The Cultural Politics of Modern Chinese Transnationalism.* New York: Routledge.

Ownby, David. 1996. *Brotherhoods and Secret Societies in Early and Mid-Qing China.* Stanford: Stanford University Press.

Ownby, David, and Mary Somers Heidhues, eds. 1993. *"Secret Societies" Reconsidered.* New York: M. E. Sharpe.

Palumbo-Liu, David. 1997. "Introduction: Unhabituated Habituses." In David Palumbo-Liu and Hans Ulrich Gumbrecht, eds., *Streams of Cultural Capital*, 1–21. Stanford: Stanford University Press, 1997.

Pann, Lynn. 1990. *Sons of the Yellow Emperor*. Boston: Little, Brown.

Park, Robert. 1914. "Racial Assimilation in Secondary Groups: With Particular Reference to the Negro." *American Journal of Sociology* 19: 606–23.

Parker, David S. 1998. "Civilizing the City of Kings: Hygiene and Housing in Lima, Peru." In Ronn Pineo and James Baer, eds., *Cities of Hope: People, Protests, and Progress in Urbanizing Latin America, 1870–1930*, 153–78. Boulder: Westview Press.

Pei Ying, 裴穎. 1994. "Huaqiao hunyin jiating xingtai chutan" 華僑婚姻家庭形態初探 [Preliminary investigations on the marriage and family patterns of overseas Chinese]. *Huaqiao Huaren Lishi Yanjiu* 2: 41–45.

Peterson, Virgil. 1952. *Barbarians in our Midst: A History of Chicago Crime and Politics*. Boston: Little, Brown.

Philpott, Thomas Lee. 1991. *The Slum and the Ghetto: Immigrants, Blacks, and Reformers in Chicago, 1880–1930*. Belmont, CA: Wadsworth.

Pomeranz, Kenneth. 1991. "Water to Iron, Widows, and Warlords: The Handan Rain Shrine." *Late Imperial China* 12, no. 1: 62–99.

Porteus, Stanley. 1926. *Temperament and Race*. Boston: Badger.

Potter, Jack. 1968. *Capitalism and the Chinese Peasant: Social and Economic Change in an Hong Kong Village*. Berkeley: University of California Press.

President's Commission on Organized Crime. 1984. *Organized Crime of Asian Origin*, Record of Hearing III. New York.

Reed, Bradley. 1995. "Money and Justice: Clerks, Runners, and the Magistrate's Court in Late Imperial Sichuan." *Modern China* 21: 345–82.

Redding, G. Gordon. 1990. *The Spirit of Chinese Capitalism*. Berlin: Walter de Gruyter.

Reinecke, John. 1979. *Feigned Necessity: Hawaii's Attempt to Obtain Chinese Contract Labor, 1921–23*. San Francisco: Chinese Materials Center.

Ren Guixiang 任貴祥. 1996. "Lun huaqiao yu Baohuanghui" 論華僑與保皇會 [Overseas Chinese and the Emperor Protection Society]. *Huaqiao huaren lishi yanjiu* 4: 68–75.

Rhoads, Edward. 1975. *China's Republican Revolution: The Case of Kwangtung, 1895–1913*. Cambridge: Harvard University Press.

Richardson, Peter. 1982. *Chinese Mine Labour in the Transvaal*. London: Macmillan.

Robertson, Roland. 1992. *Globalization: Social Theory and Global Culture*. London: Sage.

Rodríguez Pastor, Humberto. 1989a. *Hijos del Celeste Imperio en el Perú*. Lima: Instituto de Apoyo Agrario.

———. 1989b. "El inmigrante chino en el mercado laboral peruano, 1850–1930." *HISLA* 13–14: 93–147.

———. 1990. "Asiáticos y africanos en la costa peruana." *Socialismo y Participación* 51 (September): 49–61.

———. 1993. "Del kon hei fat choy al chifa peruano." In Rosario Olivas Weston, ed., *Cultura, identidad, y cocina en el Perú*, 189–238. Lima: Escuela Profesional de Turismo y Hotelería, Universidad San Martín de Porres.

———. 1994. "Asiáticos en el agro y en pueblos costeños peruanos." *Debate Agrario* 12: 11–40.

———. 1995. "La Calle del Capón, el Callejón Otaiza, y el Barrio Chino." In Aldo Panfichi H. and Felipe Portocarrero S., eds., *Mundos interiores: Lima 1850–1950*, 397–430. Lima: Centro de Investigación, Universidad del Pacífico.

Rogers, Alan. 1999. "Chinese and the Campaign to Abolish Capital Punishment in Massachusetts, 1870–1914." *Journal of American Ethnic History* 18, no. 2: 37–72.

Rouse, Roger. 1991. "Mexican Migration and the Social Space of Postmodernism." *Diaspora* 1: 8–23.

Ruíz Zevallos, Augusto. 1993. "La multitud y el mercado de trabajo: Modernización y conflicto en Lima de 1890 a 1920." M.A. thesis, Pontificia Universidad Católica del Perú.

Safran, William. 1991. "Diasporas in Modern Societies: Myths of Homeland and Return." *Diaspora* 1: 83–84.

Sahlins, Marshall. 1981. *Historical Metaphors and Mythical Realities*. Chicago: University of Chicago Press.

———. 1988. "Cosmologies of Capitalism: The Trans-Pacific Sector of the World System." *Proceedings of the British Academy for 1988*, 1–51.

———. 1993. "Goodbye to *Tristes Tropes:* Ethnography and the Context of Modern World History." In R. Borofsky, ed., *Assessing Anthropology*. New York: Macmillan.

Salmon, Claudine. 1996. "Ancestral Halls, Funeral Associations, and Attempts at Resinicization in Nineteenth-Century Netherlands India." In Anthony Reid, ed., *Sojourners and Settlers: Histories of Southeast Asia and the Chinese*, 183–214. St. Leonards, Australia: Asian Studies Association of Australia and Allen & Unwin.

Sangren, P. Stephen. 1984a. "Female Gender in Chinese Religious Symbols: Kwan Yin, Ma Tzu, and the 'Eternal Mother.'" *Signs* 9: 4–25.

———. 1984b. "Traditional Chinese Corporations: Beyond Kinship." *Journal of Asian Studies* 43: 394–411.

———. 1987. *History and Magical Power in a Chinese Community*. Stanford: Stanford University Press.

Saxton, Alexander. 1995. *The Indispensable Enemy: Labor and the Anti-Chinese Movement in California*. Berkeley: University of California Press.

Sayler, Lucy. 1995. *Laws Harsh as Tigers: Chinese Immigrants and the Shaping of Modern Immigration Law*. Chapel Hill: University of North Carolina Press.

See, Lisa. 1995. *On Gold Mountain*. New York: St. Martin's Press.

Senate Commission on Immigration. 1902. *Chinese Exclusion,* Part 2. Washington, DC: Government Printing Office.

Shahar, Meir, and Robert Weller. 1996. "Introduction: Gods and Society in China."

In Meir and Weller, eds., *Unruly Gods: Divinity and Society in China*, 1–36. Honolulu: University of Hawaii Press.

Sinn, Elizabeth. 1995a. "Emigration from Hong Kong before 1941: General Trends." In Ronald Skeldon, ed., *Emigration from Hong Kong: Tendencies and Impacts*. Hong Kong: Chinese University Press.

———. 1995b. "Emigration from Hong Kong before 1941: Organization and Impact." In Ronald Skeldon, ed., *Emigration from Hong Kong: Tendencies and Impacts*. Hong Kong: The Chinese University Press.

———. 1999. "Cohesion and Fragmentation: A County-Level Perspective on Chinese Transnationalism in the 1940s." In Leo Douw, Cen Huang, and Michael Godley, eds. *Qiaoxiang Ties: Interdisciplinary Approaches to 'Cultural Capitalism' in South China*, 67–86. London: Kegan Paul.

Situ Meitang 司徒美堂. n.d. *Wo tonghen meidiguozhuyi: Qiao Mei qishi nian shenghuo Huiyilu* 我痛恨美帝國主義：僑美七十年生活回憶錄 [I bitterly hate imperialist America: Reminiscences of a seventy-year sojourn in the United States]. Beijing: Guangming Ribao Zhongguanlichu.

Siu, Helen. 1989a. *Agents and Victims in South China*. New Haven: Yale University Press.

———. 1989b. "Recycling Ritual: Politics and Popular Culture in Contemporary Rural China." In Perry Link, Richard Madsen, and Paul Pickowicz, eds., *Unofficial China: Popular Culture and Thought in the People's Republic*, 121–37. Boulder: Westview Press.

———. 1990. "Where Were the Women? Rethinking Marriage Resistance and Regional Culture in South China." *Late Imperial China* 11, no. 2: 32–62.

———. 1995. "Subverting Lineage Power: Local Bosses and Territorial Control in the 1940s." In David Faure and Helen Siu, eds., *Down to Earth: The Territorial Bond in South China*, 188–208. Stanford: Stanford University Press.

Siu Jang Leung. 1991. "A Laundryman Sings the Blues." Trans. Marlon Hom. *Chinese America: History and Perspectives*, 3–24.

Siu, Paul. 1952. "The Sojourner." *American Journal of Sociology* 58: 34–44.

———. 1987. *The Chinese laundryman: A Study of Social Isolation*. Ed. John Kuo Wei Tchen. New York: New York University Press.

Skeldon, Ronald. 1994. "Hong Kong in an International Migration System." In Skeldon, ed., *Reluctant Exiles? Migration from Hong Kong and the New Overseas Chinese*, 21–51. Armonk, NY: M. E. Sharpe.

Skinner, G. William. 1957. *Chinese Society in Thailand: An Analytical History*. Ithaca, NY: Cornell University Press.

———. 1958. *Leadership and Power in the Chinese Community of Thailand*. Ithaca, NY: Cornell University Press.

———. 1968. "Overseas Chinese Leadership: Paradigm for a Paradox." In Gehan Wijeyewardene, ed., *Leadership and Authority*, 191–207. Singapore: University of Malaya Press.

———. 1976. "Mobility Strategies in Late Imperial China: A Regional Systems

Analysis." In Carol A. Smith, ed., *Regional Analysis,* vol. 1, *Economic Systems.* New York: Academic Press.

———. 1996. "Creolized Chinese Societies in Southeast Asia." In Anthony Reid, ed., *Sojourners and Settlers: Histories of Southeast Asia and the Chinese,* 51–93. St. Leonards, Australia: Asian Studies Association of Australia and Allen & Unwin.

Smith, Richard J. 1990. "Ritual in Ch'ing Culture." In Kwang-ching Liu, ed., *Orthodoxy in Late Imperial China,* 281–310. Berkeley: University of California Press.

Smith, William Carlson. 1927. "The Second Generation Oriental in America." Preliminary Paper Presented for the Second General Session of the Institute of Pacific Relations. Honolulu: Institute of Pacific Relations.

———. 1937. *Americans in Process: A Study of Our Citizens of Oriental Ancestry.* Ann Arbor: Edwards Brothers.

So, Alvin. 1986. *South China Silk District: Local Historical Transformation and World System Theory.* Albany: State University of New York Press.

Soong, Ruth Joan. 1931. "A Survey of the Education of Chinese Children in Chicago." M.A. thesis, University of Chicago.

Stein, Steve. 1980. *Populism in Peru: The Emergence of the Masses and the Politics of Social Control.* Madison: University of Wisconsin Press.

Stewart, Watt. 1951. *Chinese Bondage in Peru: A History of the Chinese Coolie in Peru, 1849–1874.* Durham, NC: Duke University Press.

Stockard, Janice. 1989. *Daughters of the Canton Delta: Marriage Patterns and Economic Strategies in South China, 1860–1930.* Stanford: Stanford University Press.

Stratton, Jon. 1997. "(Dis)placing the Jews: Historicizing the Idea of Diaspora." *Diaspora* 6: 301–30.

Suryadinata, Leo, ed. 1997. *Ethnic Chinese as Southeast Asians.* New York: St. Martin's Press.

Szonyi, Michael. 1997. "The Illusion of Standardizing the Gods: The Cult of the Five Emperors in Late Imperial China." *Journal of Asian Studies* 56: 113–35.

Takaki, Ronald. 1989. *Strangers from a Different Shore: A History of Asian Americans.* Boston: Little, Brown.

Tan Chee Beng. 1988. *The Baba of Melaka.* Selangor, Malaysia: Pelanduk Publications.

———. 1997. "Comments by Tan Chee Beng on Ethnic Chinese in Southeast Asia." In Leo Suryadinata, ed., *Ethnic Chinese as Southeast Asians,* 25–32. New York: St. Martin's Press.

Thistlewaite, Frank. 1964. "Migration from Europe Overseas in the Nineteenth and Twentieth Centuries." In Herbert Moller, ed., *Population Movements in Modern European History,* 73–92. New York: Macmillan.

Thomas, Nicholas. 1991. *Entangled Objects.* Cambridge: Cambridge University Press.

Thompson, Stephen. 1979. "Assimilation and Non-Assimilation of Asian-Americans and Asian-Peruvians." *Comparative Studies in Society and History* 21: 572–88.

Thompson, Stuart. 1988. "Death, Food, and Fertility." In Evelyn Rawski and James Watson, eds., *Death Ritual in Late Imperial and Modern China,* 71–108. Berkeley: University of California Press.

Thrasher, Frederic. 1927. *The Gang.* Chicago: University of Chicago Press.

Thurner, Mark. 1995. "'Republicanos' and 'la Communidad de Peruanos': Unimagined Political Communities in Postcolonial Andean Peru." *Journal of Latin American Studies* 27: 291–318.

Tilly, Charles. 1990. "Transplanted Networks." In Virginia Yans-McLaughlin, ed., *Immigration Reconsidered: History, Sociology, and Politics,* 79–95. New York: Oxford University Press.

Tobias, Stephen. 1977. "Buddhism, Belonging, and Detachment: Some Paradoxes of Chinese Ethnicity in Thailand." *Journal of Asian Studies* 36: 303–26.

Tölölyan, Kachig. 1996. "Rethinking Diaspora(s): Stateless Power in the Transnational Moment." *Diaspora* 5: 3–36.

Topley, Marjorie. 1978. "Marriage Resistance in Rural Kwangtung." In Arthur Wolf, ed., *Studies in Chinese Society,* 247–68. Stanford: Stanford University Press.

Trocki, Carl. 1979. *Prince of Pirates: The Temenggongs and the Development of Johore and Singapore, 1784–1885.* Singapore: Singapore University Press.

———. 1990. *Opium and Empire: Chinese Society in Colonial Singapore, 1800–1910.* Ithaca, NY: Cornell University Press.

———. 1997. "Boundaries and Transgressions: Chinese Enterprise in Eighteenth- and Nineteenth-Century Southeast Asia." In Aihwa Ong and Donald Nonini, eds., *Ungrounded Empires: The Cultural Politics of Modern Chinese Transnationalism.* New York: Routledge.

Tu Wei-ming, ed. 1991. *The Living Tree: The Changing Meaning of Being Chinese Today.* Stanford: Stanford University Press.

United Chinese Society. 1898. *Memorial and Accompanying Data Presented to the United States Commissioners by Chinese Residents in the Hawaiian Islands.* Honolulu.

United Chinese Society of Hawaii, ed. 1985. *Tanxiangshan Zhonghua Zonghuiguan yibai zhounian jinian tekan* 檀香山中華總會館一百週年級念特刊 [Centennial celebration of the United Chinese Society of Hawaii]. Honolulu.

United States Congress Committee on Immigration and Naturalization. 1916. "Restriction of Immigration." Washington DC: Government Printing Office.

———. 1918. "Relative to Chinese Immigration into Hawaii." Washington DC: Government Printing Office.

United States Immigration Commission. 1911. *Reports of the United States Immigration Commission,* Abstract of Reports, 2 vols. Washington, DC: Government Printing Office.

Vertovec, Steven. 1997. "Three Meanings of 'Diaspora,' Exemplified among South Asian Religions." *Diaspora* 6: 277–300.

Wakeman, Frederic. 1966. *Strangers at the Gate: Social Disorder in South China, 1839–1861.* Berkeley: University of California Press.

———. 1975. "Introduction: The Evolution of Local Control in Late Imperial China." In Frederic Wakeman and Carolyn Grant, eds., *Conflict and Control in Late Imperial China*, 1–25. Berkeley: University of California Press.

Wallerstein, Immanuel. 1947–89. *The Modern World-System*. 3 vols. New York: Academic Press.

———. 1990. "Culture as the Ideological Battleground of the Modern World-System." *Theory, Culture, and Society* 7: 31–56.

Wang Gungwu. 1981. "A Note on the Origins of *Hua-ch'iao*." In *Community and Nation: Essays on Southeast Asia and the Chinese*, 118–27. Singapore: ASAA Monographs.

———. 1994. "The Status of Overseas Chinese Studies." *Chinese America: History and Perspectives*, 1–18 (annual).

———. 1996. "Sojourning: The Chinese Experience in Southeast Asia." In Anthony Reid, ed., *Sojourners and Settlers: Histories of Southeast Asia and the Chinese*, 1–14. St. Leonards, Australia: Asian Studies Association of Australia and Allen & Unwin.

———. 1998. "Upgrading the Migrant: Neither *Huaqiao* nor *Huaren*." In Elizabeth Sinn, ed., *The Last Half Century of Chinese Overseas*, 15–34. Hong Kong: Hong Kong University Press.

Wang, L. Ling-chi. 1995. "The Structure of Dual Domination: Toward a Paradigm for the Study of the Chinese Diaspora in the United States." *Amerasia Journal* 21: 149–69.

Wang Shih-ch'ing. 1974. "Religious Organization in the History of Taiwan." In Arthur Wolf, ed., *Religion and Ritual in Chinese Society*, 71–92. Stanford: Stanford University Press.

Wang Sing-wu. 1978. *The Organization of Chinese Emigration, 1848–1888*. San Francisco: Chinese Materials Center.

Wang Tai Peng. 1994. *The Origins of the Chinese Kongsi*. Petaling Jaya, Malaysia: Pelanduk.

Watson, James L. 1975. *Emigration and the Chinese Lineage*. Berkeley: University of California Press.

———. 1982. "Chinese Kinship Reconsidered: Anthropological Perspectives on Historical Research." *China Quarterly* 92: 589–622.

———. 1985. "Standardizing the Gods: The Promotion of T'ien Hou ('Empress of Heaven') along the South China Coast, 960–1960." In David Johnson, ed., *Popular Culture in Late Imperial China*, 292–324. Berkeley: University of California Press.

———. 1988a. "The Structure of Chinese Funerary Rites." In Evelyn Rawski and James Watson, eds., *Death Ritual in Late Imperial and Modern China*, 3–19. Berkeley: University of California Press.

———. 1988b. "Funeral Specialists in Cantonese Society: Pollution, Performance, and Social Hierarchy." In Evelyn Rawski and James Watson, eds., *Death Ritual in Late Imperial and Modern China*, 109–34. Berkeley: University of California Press.

———. 1991. "Waking the Dragon: Visions of the Chinese Imperial State in Local Myth." In Hugh Baker and Stephan Feuchtwang, eds., *An Old State in New Settings: Studies in the Social Anthropology of China in Memory of Maurice Freedman,* 162–77. Oxford: JASO.

———. 1993. "Rites or Beliefs? The Construction of a Unified Culture in Late Imperial China." In Lowell Dittmer and Samuel Kim, eds., *China's Quest for National Identity,* 80–103. Ithaca, NY: Cornell University Press.

Watson, Rubie. 1985. *All Brothers Are Not Equal: Class and Kinship in South China.* Cambridge: Cambridge University Press.

Weller, Robert. 1987. *Unities and Diversities in Chinese Religion.* Seattle: University of Washington Press.

———. 1994. *Resistance, Chaos, and Control in China.* Seattle: University of Washington Press.

Wen Xiongfei 溫雄飛. 1981. "Xinhaiqian wo zai Tanxiangshan Tongmenghui he Ziyou Xinbao gongzuo de huiyi" 辛亥前我在檀香山同盟會和自由新報工作的回憶 [My reminiscences of working for the *Liberty News* and the Tongmenghui in Hawaii before the Xinhai revolution]. In *Huaqiao yu Xinhai Geming* 華僑與辛亥革命 [Overseas Chinese and the Xinhai revolution], 223–51. Beijing: Zhongguo Shehui Kexue Chubanshe.

Wendt, Lloyd, and Herman Kogan. 1943. *Bosses of Lusty Chicago.* Bloomington: Indiana University Press.

Whitehead, John. 1998. "Hawai'i: The First and Last Far West?" In Franklin Ng, ed., *Asians in America: The Peoples of East, Southeast, and South Asia in American Life and Culture,* 39–64. New York: Garland.

Williams, Lea. 1960. *Overseas Chinese Nationalism: The Genesis of the Pan-Chinese Movement in Indonesia.* Cambridge: The Center for International Studies, MIT.

Wilson, Margaret Gibbons. 1969. "Concentration and Dispersal of the Chinese Population of Chicago." M.A. thesis, University of Chicago School of Education.

Wolf, Arthur. 1978. "Ghosts, Gods, and Ancestors." In Wolf, ed., *Studies in Chinese Society,* 131–82. Stanford: Stanford University Press.

Wolf, Eric. 1956. "Aspects of Group Relations in a Complex Society: Mexico." *American Anthropologist* 58: 1065–78.

———. 1997. *Europe and the People without History.* 2d ed. Berkeley: University of California Press.

Wolfe, Patrick. 1997. "Imperialism and History: A Century of Theory, from Marx to Postcolonialism." *American Historical Review* 102: 388–420.

Wong, Bernard. 1978. "A Comparative Study of the Assimilation of the Chinese in New York City and Lima, Peru." *Comparative Studies in Society and History* 20: 335–58.

———. 1985. "On Assimilation in the Americas: A Reply." *Comparative Studies in Society and History* 27: 171–73.

———. 1988. *Patronage, Brokerage, Entrepreneurship, and the Chinese Community of New York.* New York: AMS Press.

Wong, K. Scott. 1996. "'The Eagle Seeks a Helpless Quarry': Chinatown, the Police, and the Press: The 1903 Boston Chinatown Raid Revisited." *Amerasia Journal* 22: 81–103.

Wong, K. Scott, and Sucheng Chan, eds. 1998. *Claiming America: Constructing Chinese Identities during the Exclusion Era*. Philadelphia: Temple University Press.

Wong, Marion, and Richard Wong. 1936. "Some Forms of Chinese Customs in Hawaii." *Chinese of Hawaii* 2: 18–21.

Wong, Sau Chun. 1937. "Chinese Temples in Honolulu." *Social Process in Hawaii* 3: 27–35.

Wong, Sau-ling C. 1995. "Denationalization Reconsidered: Asian American Cultural Criticism at a Theoretical Crossroads." *Amerasia Journal* 21: 1–28.

Woon, Yuen-fong. 1981. "The Voluntary Sojourner Among the Overseas Chinese: Myth or Reality?" *Journal of Ethnic Studies* 9: 673–90.

———. 1984a. "An Emigrant Community in the Ssu-yi Area, Southeastern China, 1855–1949." *Modern Asian Studies* 19: 273–308.

———. 1984b. *Social Organization in South China, 1911–1949*. Ann Arbor: Center for Chinese Studies, University of Michigan.

———. 1991. "International Links and the Socioeconomic Development of Rural China: An Emigrant Community in Guangdong." *Modern China* 16: 139–72.

Wu, Ching-chao. 1928. *Chinatowns: A Study of Symbiosis and Assimilation*. Ph.D. diss., University of Chicago.

Wu Jianxiong 吳劍雄. 1993. *Haiwai yimin yu huaren shehui* 海外移民與華人社會 [Overseas immigrants and Chinese society]. Taibei: Yunchen Wenhua Chubanshe.

Wu Yangcheng 伍揚誠. 1959. *Shenghuo zai NiuYue Tangrenjie* 生活在紐約唐人街 [Life in New York's chinatown]. Hong Kong: Jiwen Chubanshe.

Wu Zhiyong Xing Shi yu Bi zhengfu bolun keli wanglai wendu dayi gao 伍秩庸星使與秘政府駁論苛例往來文牘荟譯稿 [Transcript of the negotiations between Glorious Minister Wu Zhiyong and the Peruvian government over the harsh restrictions on migration]. 1909. Lima: Nanhai Gui Zhi Jian 南海桂填檢.

Wyman, Mark. 1993. *Round-Trip to America: The Immigrants Return to Europe, 1880–1930*. Ithaca, NY: Cornell University Press.

Xia Chenghua. 夏成華 1992. *Jindai Guangdong Sheng qiaohui yanjiu (1862–1949)—Yi Guang, Chao, Mei, Qiong diqu wei li* 近代廣東省僑匯研究 (1862–1949)—以廣，潮，梅，瓊地區為例 [Research on overseas remittances to Guangdong Province in the modern era (1862–1949)—Using the Guangzhou, Chaozhou, Meixian, and Hainan regions as examples]. Singapore: Singapore South Seas Society.

Xie Yingming 謝英明. 1984. "Lu Mei zhayi" 旅美雜憶 [Miscellaneous recollections of sojourning in America]. In *Huaqiao yuan sang lu* 華僑苑桑录 [Stories of overseas Chinese], 1–29. Guangzhou: Guangdong Renmin Chubanshe.

Yang Shan 楊山. 1995. "'Huaqiao' yu 'huaren' de chenghu shi kexue de gainian"

華僑與華人的稱呼是科學的概念 [The labels 'huaqiao' and 'huaren' are scientific concepts]. *Huaqiao Huaren Lishi Yanjiu,* 4: 9–13.

Year of the Dragon. 1985. A film produced by Dino de Laurentiis, directed by Michael Cimino, and written by Michael Cimino and Oliver Stone. Metro-Goldwyn-Mayer.

Yu Kuang-hong. 1990. "Making a Malefactor a Benefactor: Ghost Worship in Taiwan." *Bulletin of the Institute of Ethnology Academia Sinica* 70: 9–66.

Yu, Henry. 1998. "The 'Oriental Problem' in America, 1920–1960: Linking the Identities of Chinese American and Japanese American Intellectuals." In K. Scott Wong and Sucheng Chan, eds., *Claiming America: Constructing Chinese American Identities during the Exclusi on Era,* 191–214. Philadelphia: Temple University Press.

Yu, Renqiu. 1983. "Chinese American Contributions to the Educational Development of Toisan, 1920–40." *Amerasia Journal* 10: 47–72.

———. 1992. *To Save China, To Save Ourselves.* Philadelphia: Temple University Press.

Zelin, Madeline. 1990. "The Rise and Fall of the Fu-Rong Salt Yard Elite: Merchant Dominance in Late Qing China." In Joseph Esherick and Mary Backus Rankin, eds., *Chinese Local Elites and Patterns of Dominance,* 82–109. Berkeley: University of California Press.

Zhang, Qingsong. 1998. "The Origins of the Chinese Americanization Movement: Wong Chin Foo and the Chinese Equal Rights League." In K. Scott Wong and Sucheng Chan, eds., *Claiming America: Constructing Chinese American Identities during the Exclusion Era,* 41–63. Philadelphia: Temple University Press.

Zhang Shenrong 張深榮 (C. S. Wing). 1945. *Liushi zishu* 六十自述 [Autobiography at sixty].

Zheng Junlie 鄭君烈. 1963. "Zhongguo Hongmen lishi shulüe" 中國洪門歷史述略 [Brief history of the Chinese hongmen]. In Tanxiangshan Zhigong Zongtang, ed., *Tanxiangshan Zhigong Zongtang xinlou luocheng kaimu* 檀香山致公總堂新樓落成開幕 [Opening ceremony of the new building of the Hawaii Zhigongtang], 189–90. Hong Kong.

Zo, Kil Young. 1978. *Chinese Emigration into the United States, 1850–1880.* New York: Arno Press.

Zuckerman, Steven. 1978. "Pake in Paradise: A Synthetic Study of Chinese Immigration to Hawaii." *Bulletin of the Institute of Ethnology Academia Sinica* 45: 39–80.

Locators in boldface refer to figures or tables.